THE SOUL OF
A FOLKLORIST

ACTIVIST ENCOUNTERS IN FOLKLORE AND
ETHNOMUSICOLOGY
David A. McDonald, editor

THE SOUL OF A FOLKLORIST

Historical Moments, Political Representation, and the Weight of Social Responsibility

Ann K. Ferrell and Diane E. Goldstein

INDIANA UNIVERSITY PRESS

This book is a publication of

Indiana University Press
Herman B Wells Library
1320 East 10th Street
Bloomington, Indiana 47405 USA

iupress.org

First Printing 2026

Cataloging information is available from the Library of Congress.

ISBN 978-0-253-07459-1 (hardback)
ISBN 978-0-253-07460-7 (paperback)
ISBN 978-0-253-07461-4 (ebook)
ISBN 978-0-253-07462-1 (web PDF)

*This book is dedicated to all those who have pushed
our field forward recognizing the power of our subject
and the weight of social responsibility.*

*We also dedicate it to our mothers:
Rochelle Goldstein (1931–2020)
Pamela Ryals (1943–2020)*

CONTENTS

ACKNOWLEDGMENTS

THE IDIOM "IT TAKES A village" has in recent years been expanded out from its African proverbial assertion of dependence on full communities for raising children to a recognition of entire communities of people needed to support and nurture almost any undertaking. This book certainly took a village. Luckily, our field of folklore is a village, and there was never a shortage of villagers—friends, colleagues, and helpful strangers—to help us cultivate our work. Without that village, this book would not exist.

Even our research and educational institutions were part of that village. We gratefully acknowledge funding for this project from the Gerald E. and Corinne L. Parsons Fund of the American Folklife Center in the Library of Congress, the College of Arts and Sciences at Indiana University, and the former Department of Folk Studies and Anthropology and the Potter College of Arts and Letters at Western Kentucky University. Thank you to Michelle Melhouse, department manager for the IU Department of Folklore and Ethnomusicology, for administrative help processing funds. Virtually all of the archives and collections we list below provided substantial in-kind contributions, particularly of research services and duplication costs, making our work both easier and affordable.

While dozens of people assisted us in tracking down information, one group of people stands out for their continuous assistance and their gracious and patient ability to withstand our never-ending barrage of questions. These individuals are the information hubs of our field we discuss in chapter 1, always able to find information, locate a historical trail or network or person, explain rules for use and identify roadblocks, and help resolve sticky research problems. We thank in this regard former executive director of the American Folklore Society Timothy (Tim) Lloyd, head of reference services at the American Folklife Center Archive Judith Gray, retired Utah State University's Fife Folklore Archives curator and oral history specialist Randy Williams, and Indiana University collections manager and librarian for folklore Moira Marsh.

We are grateful to the hardworking and knowledgeable administration and staff of numerous archives and folklore collections. We began our search with the helpful staff and substantial resources of the Fife Folklore Archives and the American Folklore Society Manuscript Collection at Utah State University, where we were assisted by Randy Williams, Clint Pumphrey, Jen Kirk, and Joe Kinzer. We are also thankful to our colleagues and friends at Utah State University who helped us throughout and were incredible hosts during our research including Jeannie Thomas, Lynne McNeil, Terri Jordan, and Lisa Gabbert. The American Folklife Center Archives at the Library of Congress provided us with substantial resources that were central to our work. Their talented and generous administrators and staff not only withstood our in-house requests for box after box of materials but also entertained years of subsequent requests and questions. We are deeply indebted to the center's current and past army of hard workers: Jennifer Cutting, John Fenn, Judith Gray, Nancy Groce, Todd Harvey, Ann Hoog, Margaret Kruesi, Betsy Peterson, Nicole Saylor, David Taylor, and Steve Winick. Colleagues at other archives and collections around the country were also helpful. We thank Cecilia Peterson, digital projects archivist, Ralph Rinzler Folklife Archives and Collections; Betty Belanus, retired curator and education specialist, Center for Folklife and Cultural Heritage, Smithsonian Institution; Moira Marsh, librarian for anthropology, folklore, and sociology, and Carrie Schwier, archivist, for their assistance with the collections at Indiana University; Michelle Drobik, reference archivist, Special Collections and Area Studies, The Ohio State University; Aaron Smithers, special collections research and instruction librarian, Wilson Special Collections Library, University of North Carolina at Chapel Hill; and retired professor Jonathan Jeffrey, former department head for Library Special Collections and coordinator for Manuscripts & Folklife Archives, Western Kentucky University. We are also grateful to a number of individuals who shared items from their private collections including CeCe Conway, Carl Fleischhauer, Jerrold Hirsch, Michael Owen Jones, Micah Ling, Tim Lloyd, Rusty Marshall, Evangeline Mee, Neil Rosenberg, Marilyn White, and Henry (Hank) Willett. We are grateful to colleagues and friends who discussed these issues with us and helped point us in the right direction including Marie Ellen Brown, Erika Brady, Peggy Bulger, Larry Danielson, Eric Garcia, Henry Glassie, Barbara Lloyd, Solimar Otero, Jim Leary, Marsha McDowell, Elliott Oring, Jeanmarie Rouhier-Willoughby, Pravina Shukla, Kay Turner, Sydney Varajon, and Michael Ann Williams.

We were humbled by the generosity of so many members of our field who agreed to talk to us and who, to a person, were remarkably candid and thoughtful in their responses. We owe a great debt to those who agreed to be interviewed for this project or who preferred not to be interviewed but communicated with us off the record by email, phone, or Zoom or in person. Those individuals we interviewed or spoke with on the record are listed on pages 409–410. We also thank Kazuko (Kaz) and Miiko Toelken, who assisted us in interviewing Barre Toelken, and Karen Jabbour and Margaret (Peggy) Parsons, who helped us reconstruct events involving their family members.

We are indebted to the staff of the American Folklore Society who supplied information, shared photographs and documents, and repeatedly pointed us in the right direction. We especially thank Jessica Turner, executive director; Lorraine Cashman, former associate director; Meredith McGriff, former director of membership and information systems; and Cassie Rosita Patterson, special projects consultant.

Numerous student assistants helped us process and prepare the materials for this book. We thank them for their hard work, care, and passion for our project. They include Allison Cate, Tazwar Choudhury, Cara Forke, Brielle Freeman, Susanna Pyatt, and Jennifer Roberts from Western Kentucky University; and Ben Bridges, Jesse Fivecoate, and Holly Mathews from Indiana University.

Several people associated with Indiana University Press were involved with this project. We thank Allison Chaplin, acquisitions editor; Gary Dunham, director; Janice Frisch, former acquisitions editor; Sophia Hebert, assistant acquisitions editor; and David McDonald, series editor for Activist Encounters in Folklore and Ethnomusicology. We also thank our anonymous reviewers who made our volume stronger with their comments.

Last but not least, we thank our inner village—the family and friends who supported us through the long process of writing and publishing this volume. We thank Scott, Russell, Matthew, and Mia Goldstein; Lori Fritz; Tom Mills; Brent Bjorkman; and Josie, Elsie, and Claudie Ferrell-Bjorkman for their love and support.

THE SOUL OF
A FOLKLORIST

ONE

INTRODUCTION: THE SOUL OF A FOLKLORIST

"There Are Years That Ask Questions and Years That Answer"

PERIODICALLY, WHEN WE ARE TALKING to someone about a prospective student or a scholar from another field, a folklore colleague will comment that they "have *the soul of a folklorist.*" What we mean by the phrase is ill defined, but the content and context of this statement suggest that we know it when we see it. In fact, the sentiment is so pervasive that Betty Belanus has written, concerning public folklore, "a true public sector folklorist is 'born, not made'" (1994, 210). The soul is sometimes understood as that which moves us, the essence and totality of who we are at a core level, our true nature. When we say that someone has the soul of a folklorist, we mean that we perceive that in their heart, at their very essence, they feel or understand that amorphous thing that characterizes our discipline's passion. While we could surmise that this characteristic is a love of the skills and knowledge that form our disciplinary toolbox—fieldwork, ethnography, documentation, transcription, and so much more—there is a larger philosophical and ideological stance that propels that toolbox toward its work. Folklorists value vernacular culture, pluralism, and artistic expression, but at the crux of our disciplinary philosophy is a willingness to take seriously and centrally the perspectives and importance of regular people, more than the dominant elite, more than institutions, and focused more often than not on the subaltern, the marginal. That is not to say that we don't study elite cultural institutions, but when we do it is with an eye toward their makeup of or impact on the vernacular. The soul of a folklorist, as we understand it, is at its core about being on the side of the less powerful, about focusing on the importance of voice and agency. As Amy Shuman and Charles Briggs note, "Championing the folk is built into the discipline, and it may not even be possible to avoid advocacy" (1993, 130). The potential student or colleague we identify as having the *soul of a folklorist* seems fundamentally to be moved by that very same vernacular-first political ideal.

Honing that political perspective, however, has not been always easy or straightforward or evenly shared by folklorists. Like other fields, folklore studies became increasingly cognizant of representational politics in the 1960s, '70s, and '80s, following on the civil rights movement, the antiwar movement, the women's movement, the gay rights movement, and the environmental justice movement—in part because many folklorists were themselves involved in these movements.[1] This was also a time in which, in the United States, the field had only recently come to see itself as an independent discipline, no longer a subset of anthropology or English (see Zumwalt 1988), which means that much of what we discuss here involves the first generations of those who were trained as, and fully embraced a professional identity as, *folklorists*.

This volume chronicles the growing pains folklorists felt as the field engaged in new or different ways of thinking about expressive culture, inequality, and political representation. Using a series of case studies from the 1970s and '80s, we examine particular discussions that arose during the period as some folklorists explored progressive social change initiatives as part of their professional work as folklorists while others questioned the scholarly appropriateness of applied or political engagement or, in various ways, challenged professional engagement in the political issues of the day. Moving into the latter part of this period, the field's engagement progressed outward as folklorists recognized a need to educate lawmakers and others about expressive culture, diversity, communities, and political representation. Like other fields of study, particularly but not only in the humanities and social sciences, folklorists faced a series of questions about the inequities that existed within the field and the potential for resulting adverse effects on what and whom was studied, the repercussions of simultaneous engagement with both scholarly and public-facing work, the existence and location of a line between research and advocacy, the wisdom of crossing that line, and the nature of our responsibilities, as individual folklorists and as a field, to those with whom we study and to the communities in which we live and work. As folklorists moved toward a perspective that increasingly explored the responsibility of presentation and representation of gender, race, class, and other areas of inequities, the discipline gradually came to understand both the power of its own subject and structures of subordination within the field.

This study is not intended as a history of public or applied folklore. Other volumes have done this well (see, e.g., Feintuch 1988a, Baron and Spitzer [1992] 2007, Jones 1994c, and others). Instead, this could be described as a history of uncertainty, a snapshot of disciplinary identity struggles and the search for representational adequacy and social accountability. In this study, we explore the battles that ensued as academics and those in the growing sectors of public and applied folklore grappled with who we are, who we represent, and where our social responsibilities lie in relation to the communities with which we work.

While folklore studies is our focus in this volume, folklore was not the only field trying to get its representational legs underneath it during this period. By the end of the 1960s, those in anthropology, sociology, history, and other fields in the humanities, social sciences, and beyond were also questioning their colonialist legacies, their relationship to the politics of the moment, and other aspects of the social responsibilities of their respective disciplines. Engaged folkloristics arose out of similar concerns combined with growing practical interests.[2] By the early 1970s, as Barbara Kirshenblatt-Gimblett noted, the folk song revival was creating an appetite for folklore training just as the academy was becoming saturated with "more professionals than it could absorb" (1988, 140). Applied and public folklore presented possible places for the expansion of employment opportunities as well as places for engagement but not without debates about the nature of the field and its ideological interests. This volume is about some of those debates.

We did not begin our study with the period discussed here. Initially, we conceived of this book as a study of folklore and activism in the United States from, as Ann would joke, "the time of Christ to the present." Our intended scope was, we came to realize, ridiculously large. More importantly perhaps, as we began to pursue our work through a variety of venues, it became clear that the extant documentation was sorely lacking for some periods and overwhelmingly rich for others. As we explored available primary sources, contemporaneous documents from archival collections, and widely scattered research on our activist history, our scope narrowed. The American Folklore Society (AFS) records at Utah State University in Logan helped shape a more focused approach. Initially disappointed by the lack of substantive materials in the archives from the '30s, '40s, and '50s, which we hoped would contain primary source material on folklorists and wartime issues, the Works Progress Administration (WPA), the early civil rights movement, and the labor movement, we took stock instead of the vast quantity of interesting materials from the 1970s and '80s. Our hopes of locating material for a volume that took stock of folklore's pull toward and simultaneous discomfort with social engagement were more than satisfied as we recognized the richness of the debates from this period and the insights these debates provided. The primary source materials displayed less a cogent history of activism and more a history of the field's struggle as it matured and attempted to understand its own ideological positions. These decades saw fulsome debates about the responsibilities of the field, the nature of representation, political alignments, what it means to be political, and the role of folklore in social change. While we may have started with a mistaken image of a somewhat confident field, ever focused on a politics we understood, our survey took us to places where the discipline was still exploring whom we are and whom we need to be. And that is how it should be. Who we represent and how and why was not entirely clear to a field both born in and historically steeped in romanticism and, like all academy-based fields, white male privilege. It was at these moments that folklore gradually came to understand how the discipline could facilitate greater representation, equity, and social responsibility—a learning curve that the field still pursues with greater and lesser success.

In our research and writing, we worked to be mindful of not imposing the understandings of today on the historical activities described here. While we have had sometimes quite passionate individual and joint opinions on the politics surrounding the case studies and issues discussed here, our focus is on exploring the pedagogical processes at work in the debates encountered here. Even in those cases where we found a position or a particular rhetorical construction disturbing, we often also found ourselves sympathetic to the processes involved, all of which ultimately led to the slow growth of representational awareness. We acknowledge that this is recent history, and we know—in part through those we interviewed—that for some of those involved the issues are still raw even decades later. We also acknowledge that in regard to both the individual debates and the larger questions they raise, there is, in many cases, still no shared ideological stance in the field, and perhaps there shouldn't be. While some readers may wish that we had taken clear stands on all of these issues, we instead look to

Zora Neale Hurston, who famously wrote, "There are years that ask questions and years that answer" ([1937] 1996, 20). Despite the years that have elapsed, we are still asking some of these very same questions.

That said, in some cases the politics were clear to everyone, and there was even some level of ideological agreement, but the extent and nature of the field's involvement was at issue. This was true, for example, in the case of the Tennessee-Tombigbee Waterway project discussed in chapter 4, in which all sides agreed that the waterway project itself was a disaster for both the people and the environment of the region. But they did not agree on whether and how folklorists should be involved. These were, after all, times when folklore was beginning to find a foothold in the academy and in public practice, and some members of the field worried about the possible chilling effect of political advocacy or intervention on our disciplinary reputation. The explicit use of folklore by the Third Reich had provided a grave caution for the mixing of folklore and politics/government, not only in Europe but in the United States as well, and this was still felt by some in this period.[3] Others were still keenly traumatized by the fallout from the McCarthy hearings, particularly since McCarthy had blacklisted so many participants in the folk song revival.[4] For others, many of whom were brought into the discipline through the protest music of the labor movement or the music of social change associated with much of the folk song revival, politics were a clear and central part of the discipline (Reuss and Reuss 2000), and scholars were thought to have a role in criticizing or advocating for social policy. Bringing these disparate positions together was complex for the players, as well as for us, as we tried to understand historical motives. Each of these case studies involves particular folklorists, and we work to contextualize the central players throughout. However, we were for the most part interested in an analysis of the broader implications underlying these events and debates rather than analyzing individual actors. Importantly, these same disputes about the field's responsibility toward political action has played itself out over and over not only throughout our history but in recent years. No agreed-on algorithm for folklore and political advocacy existed then, and although we have continued to grapple with these questions in the intervening years, none exists today.

The research for this volume is grounded in primary sources, including contemporaneous documents from archival collections (most particularly the AFS records in Logan, Utah; the American Folklife Center [AFC] collections at the Library of Congress; and the archives at Indiana University, The Ohio State University, and Western Kentucky University); diaries, letters, and personal reflections from the private holdings of numerous folklorists that were shared with the authors; newsletters of the AFS and its interest sections; interviews with members of the field conducted for this project; recorded or transcribed interviews initiated for other purposes by earlier fieldworkers; recordings of actual events and debates; and secondary historical sources published in a variety of academic and public venues. In many cases, conversations with one individual led to a trail of others, sometimes unveiling the existence of a tape of the actual debates in question or an earlier interview someone before us had conducted with individuals who were no longer accessible.[5] Throughout this volume, we have included extensive quotations, purposefully allowing, where possible, the interlocutors of the time to tell the story. In fact, in many cases the quoted material comes from documents or recordings not previously published or even widely seen. We have found it important to make space for such primary material.

In too many cases, we missed the opportunity to speak to important participants in these events and debates. Indeed, folklorist Archie Green warned Sandra Jill Gross Bressler, who in her dissertation documented the long fight by Green and others to pass what became the American Folklife Preservation Act (AFPA): "In a few years, literally, we will be gone and no one will be able to reconstruct the story from documents, because too many of these things were never written down" (Gross Bressler 1995, 6). While Gross Bressler and others have done an admirable job of chronicling and analyzing some of these events and debates, others have gone undiscussed, and many of the participants are now deceased or otherwise unable to engage on these matters. Recent years in particular have taken a toll on the health and lives of those central to this era of the discipline. While we mourned the loss of our colleagues, we also observed how close we came to being able to talk directly to those whose positions we were working to reconstruct. A few years earlier, we might have been able to engage directly on these topics with Alan Jabbour, Roger Abrahams, Judy McCulloh, Joe Goodwin, William (Bert) Wilson, Polly Stewart, and others. If only we had started earlier and worked faster! Of course, we say this cognizant of the likelihood that at any point there would always be a similar list of missed colleagues and missed opportunities. We were able to engage others, such as Barre Toelken, only very briefly, piecing together, with the help of his family, brief answers and nods, ever mindful of the energy required to think that far back and respond. Throughout this project, however, we were fortunate to have access to a number of information leaders in our field—people like Timothy (Tim) Lloyd, former executive director of the AFS; Judith Gray, folklife specialist, Reference Services at the American Folklife Center Archive; Randy Williams, retired curator and oral history specialist at Utah State University's Fife Folklore Archives; Moira Marsh, Indiana University collections manager and librarian for folklore; and others who seemed to always be able to deconstruct information trails or historical networks that helped us fill in the holes.

HISTORICAL MOMENTS: GROWING
PAINS OF THE 1970S AND '80S

This volume is divided into a series of five case studies, each focused on a different debate that rose to the fore within folklore in the 1970s and '80s. Some of these debates will be more familiar to a folklore audience than others, and while readers outside of folklore studies may not be familiar with these debates, we think they will resonate because adjacent fields have faced parallel questions. The Point Park discussions in chapter 2 or the Tenn-Tom debates in chapter 4, for instance, have been referenced within the discipline repeatedly in recent years, but those references, while descriptive, have largely lacked the extent of historical content and dialogue contained here. In other cases—such as the occupational/organizational folklore controversy, some of the feminist debates, or the square dance bills—the discussions are now barely remembered, or they flew under the radar in their own time as multiple simultaneous events overtook the field's attention. We have chosen these case studies for two reasons: because they were seriously and extensively debated at the time and because they highlight representational issues that garnered significant concern not only in that moment but also over time. Both the later part of this introduction and the final chapter, which we call our coda, frame the case studies through identification of larger themes that run through the multiple debates.

Chapter 1: Introduction: The Soul of a Folklorist: "There Are Years That Ask Questions and Years That Answer"

In this first chapter, we introduce our volume and our case studies, placing them within the context of the representational crisis in folklore and other social science and humanities fields. In order to contextualize the chapters that follow, we first briefly describe the institutions that were the sites, literally or figuratively, of these events and debates and then describe contexts that frame this period, including the turn to contextualism in folklore studies, the growing recognition of a representational crisis in cultural fields of study, and the growth of public folklore. Because the founding and early years of the American Folklife Center are so central to our cases studies, we provide an overview of the center as part of the context of the growth of public folklore in the 1970s. Finally, we examine key threads running through the case studies: the power of our subject, concerns about unintended consequences, professionalization, tradition and modernity, and attitudes and actions related to pluralism, diversity, and inequities. This chapter chronicles the content and context of ideological factors and debates, within the field and beyond, that eventually led to the events considered in the volume and makes a case for the consideration of disciplinary history, not only as seen through the accomplishments of a field but also as revealed through debates that may not have resulted in disciplinary action or even reached resolution.

Chapter 2: "Some of My Best Friends Are Applied Folklorists":
Disciplinary Identity and the Point Park Debates

Chapter 2 traces the attempt to create a Center for Applied Folklore. In 1969, the AFS created a standing Committee on Applied Folklore, modeled in large part on applied anthropology and applied linguistics. On the suggestion of the committee, in the spring of 1971 the Middle Atlantic Conference on Folk Culture, together with the AFS, held a conference at Point Park College in Pittsburgh on the topic of applied folklore, at which a proposal for an Applied Folklore Center was presented. The proposal ultimately failed, but not before it became the impetus for important debates about the responsibility of folklorists to the communities with which we work. Though this case study is centered in the

AFS, the energy for the Applied Folklore Center shifted over to the efforts to create the AFC, connecting these two institutions.

Chapter 3: "Who Are We?": Feminist Folklorists and the Study of Women's Cultures

Although the early years of the AFS saw more women in leadership positions than in many other learned societies of the time, by the mid-twentieth century women scholars were noticeably underrepresented, particularly in leadership positions. Chapter 3 considers the movement to address gendered inequities affecting both women folklorists and the documentation of women's folklore through linked representative examples in which male power was both exerted and challenged. This chapter examines the AFS Committee on the Status of Women in the Profession (active in 1972–73), followed by the establishment of an AFS Women's Caucus (later the Women's Section); the difficulties involved in the publication of two special issues of the *Journal of American Folklore* (*JAF*) on women's folklore, the first in the 1970s and the second in the 1980s; and the debates surrounding the 1978 AFS Annual Meeting in Salt Lake City over the state of Utah's refusal to ratify the Equal Rights Amendment (ERA).

Chapter 4: "Righteous Morality": The Rise and Fall of the Tennessee-Tombigbee Waterway Folklife Project

Chapter 4 takes up a controversy faced by the AFC just after its founding: plans laid in 1977–79 to conduct a folklife survey in the region of the Tennessee-Tombigbee Waterway, one of the largest projects in the history of the Army Corps of Engineers and one widely described as a "boondoggle" and "pork barrel" project. Federal legislation passed in this period changed the federal government's approach to cultural resource management dramatically, opening the door for broadening mitigation efforts to include folklife documentation. The project was hotly debated by members of the field, with opposition coming from those who argued that any participation in a project funded by the Army Corps of Engineers would permanently stain the reputation of both the AFC and the field. Others argued that the project was both an opportunity to ensure that the folk culture of the region was documented and an opening to future involvement by folklorists in federal impact statements. Ultimately, the AFC opted to back out of the project.

Chapter 5: "Corporate Culture" versus "The Shop Floor": The Organizational and Occupational Folklore "Controversy" in Retrospect

Chapter 5 looks beyond what might have appeared to be a dispute between two individual folklorists to the underlying issues that were at stake. In the early 1980s, a group of folklorists entered into the interdisciplinary study of the culture of organizations. Set off by a one-page section on "Folklore and Organizational Life" in the AFS Centennial Publication *Folklore/Folklife* (Jackson, McCulloh, and Weigle 1984, 14), responses to this new focus decried such actions as "misrepresent[ing] virtually the entire subfield of occupational folklore," which had historically approached work from the perspective of "the shop floor" (McCarl 1984, 2). This chapter examines this controversy and how it highlighted perspectives within the field about the roles of folklorists as researchers, activists, and advocates as they grappled with core questions including "who are the folk?"

Chapter 6: One Step Back and Two Steps Forward: The Controversy over the Bills to Designate the Square Dance the American National Folk Dance

Chapter 6 is less about controversies within the field but rather tells the story of the successful efforts of folklorists and our allies in diverse communities to defeat multiple attempts to declare the square dance the national dance. Testifying in congressional hearings, folklorists took this moment to educate lawmakers and the public on the nature of expressive culture, diversity, and tradition bearers, fighting against melting pot ideologies and amalgam-based notions of community. This involved both the AFS as a major supporter and the AFC (staff member Gerald Parsons was officially enlisted by Congress to assist in the preparations for the hearings) as well as the leadership of related government agencies and other folklore organizations including the Smithsonian, the National Council for the Traditional Arts, and others. In this chapter, we trace both folklore's involvement in the hearings and the construction of their challenge to the square dance bills.

Chapter 7: Codas, Complexities, and Ongoing Conversations:
The Continuing Weight of Social Responsibility

Like the coda in William Labov's model of narrative analysis, we use our conclusion, the book's coda, to bridge the gap between our story and the current moment. In this chapter, we revisit some of the themes undertaken in the earlier chapters and bring them forward to the representational debates of recent years within the field. We explore our changed contexts: new approaches to politics and policy; growth in approaches to diversity, equity, and inclusion; the handling of political barriers in annual meeting locations; and the growing preference for advocacy over applied folklore. We center our overview of recent events and debates primarily on the AFS as the organization that brings the largest number of our colleagues in the US together virtually, in real time at meetings, and through journals, newsletters, and events.

FOLKLORE AND ITS INSTITUTIONS

Although regional and group-centered folklore societies (e.g., the Texas Folklore Society [founded in 1909], the Kentucky Folklore Society [1912], the Tennessee Folklore Society [1934], and the Hoosier Folklore Society [1938]) have played important roles in the field, a small number of larger national organizations became the centralized spaces where these debates about the nature of the field and its participants, activities, goals, ideology, theories, and methods took place.

We've very purposefully chosen to keep a small number of national institutions as our focus because in this period folklorists were gradually coalescing around, and in some cases building, these organizations and institutions as the field overtly imagined itself into being. The American Folklore Society, the American Folklife Center, the Smithsonian Institution, and the National Endowment for the Arts (NEA) represent major shared spaces in which those who had only recently begun to claim membership in an independent discipline called *folklore* were engaging with one another. Though these institutions have all been well chronicled and well analyzed elsewhere, some brief background is warranted here, beginning with the American Folklore Society.

The American Folklore Society

The AFS is the largest professional organization for folklorists in the United States, with members based both in the US and throughout the world. From the time of its founding, the society has published the *Journal of American Folklore* (followed later by a newsletter), produced an annual meeting providing opportunities for professional exchange, supported the work of interest groups within the society (which became sections in 1976[6]), and taken a leading role in national and international folklore projects. Established in 1888, and founded on the model of the Folklore Society of Great Britan organized a decade earlier, the AFS sought to bring together those with an interest in the collection of particular genres of expressive culture then understood to be *folklore* from particular groups then understood to be *folk*.[7] As Rosemary Zumwalt (1988) thoroughly demonstrates, founders William Wells Newell and Franz Boas, in particular, quickly moved to enact a vision of the AFS as a professional society with an agenda to promote the scientific collection and study of folklore. However, as Zumwalt discusses, and as we return to later in this chapter, they grappled with the inclusion and exclusion of "amateurs," a topic that plagued numerous fledgling scholarly societies during the period and into the future.

The leadership structure of the AFS—which becomes an important backstory to some of our case studies—evolved over the years. For decades, the executive board and officers did the unpaid work of running the society and organized the annual meetings with the substantial labor of folklorists in the regions in which the meetings, which rotate each year, were held. The secretary-treasurer became the primary person who did this work, though there remained committees of members who assisted with the conference program and local arrangements. Even after folklore came to see itself as an independent field, connections with anthropology remained. Beginning in 1978, the American Anthropological Association (AAA) was contracted to handle the annual meeting logistics and other aspects of AFS administration. The AAA's involvement ended following the creation of the position of executive director in 2000, when Timothy (Tim) Lloyd, who had served as secretary-treasurer (1986–91), was hired as the first in the position (2001–18).

The AFS Business Meeting, held during the annual conference each year, truly was a place where the business of the society was conducted and discussed, and the meetings were often venues for battle. Both of us recall moments in the business meeting that were thrilling to us as graduate student witnesses, though in different periods. For instance, Diane recalls that the organizational/occupational folklore controversy (chap. 5) was "like watching a fast-moving game of tennis," and she recalls that in the late 1980s / early 1990s there was heated discussion about the exclusion of reviews of museum exhibit catalogs by *JAF* reviews editor Dan Ben-Amos. We both remember angry debates about AFS responses to the Iraq War in 2003, mentioned in chapter 7. Three of our five case studies were major items of discussion and debate at the annual AFS Business Meetings. The debates also played out in the pages of the newsletter of the society and within its interest sections. That said, it has been pointed out to us multiple times that not all folklorists of the times had or expressed passionate feelings about these debates. Tim Lloyd commented that he wasn't sure "how widespread the strong feelings about some of these issues were among the membership [of the AFS]."[8] Elliott Oring indicated that he didn't recall any issue "that actually *really* ever divided the Society"; rather, "you're talking about smaller groups, who often try to convince you that what they're doing is reflective of what's going on in the Society as a whole."[9] Both Lloyd and Oring (and others) suggested, however, that while for the most part these case studies involved passionate debate among only a few, the wider AFS membership were certainly interested and watching from the sidelines. Even though individuals, and individual personalities, were central to each of these cases, each can be viewed as proxy for larger issues, and the small number of central characters does not diminish the import of the debates and the ways in which each reflects the struggle to develop a disciplinary identity in this period. In fact, it is likely that in some cases it may have been precisely *because* the issues appeared in the moment to be disagreements between individuals that more members did not take a public stand. This book looks back from the distance of forty to fifty years to see that there was more at stake.

The American Folklife Center

The AFC was established by an act of Congress in 1976 to "preserve and present American folklife" through programs of research, documentation, archival preservation, reference service, live performance, exhibitions, publications, and training. Lobbying for the center was a long and laborious process but serves as one of the greatest professional accomplishments of American folklore. The bulk of the lobbying that led to the eventual passage of the American Folklife Preservation Act (AFPA), which created the AFC, was carried out by Archie Green, who had spent much of his life as a shipwright and carpenter before becoming a folklorist. Described by biographer Sean Burns as a "worker-intellectual" (2011, 108), Green coined the term "laborlore" (107) and devoted himself to documenting working-class culture and music. Within the discipline this is a well-known story, but what may be less known is that this complicated story began with an attempt to create a third endowment (in addition to the National Endowments for the Arts [NEA] and the National Endowment for the Humanities [NEH]). For this reason, and because the AFC is central to three of our case statues, we address this history in some depth below.

While the AFS and AFC can be seen as central spaces in which American folklorists came together in the period covered in this volume, the Smithsonian Center for Folklife and Cultural Heritage (CFCH) and the Folk and Traditional Arts program of the NEA figure less prominently, but both are nevertheless important in the stories to come.

The Smithsonian Center for Folklife and Cultural Heritage

The Smithsonian Folklife Festival began in 1967, founded by Ralph Rinzler,[10] a musician with a great deal of festival experience and a member of the New York City bluegrass band the Greenbriar Boys. Folklorist Robert Baron (2016, 11) has described Rinzler's motivation and timing: "Dissatisfied with decontextualized festivals of the 'folk music revival,' committed to presenting material culture alongside music and dance and developing strategies to safeguard folk traditions no longer widely practiced, Rinzler connected with Smithsonian secretary S. Dillon Ripley at just the right time." The festival became an enactment of Ripley's "vision" "for pivoting America's national museum complex to more directly engage with the public" (Cadaval, Kim, and N'Diaye 2016, 20), and the timing of its birth was no accident.

The early years of the Festival coincided with a time in American
history when many mainstream institutions were transform-
ing in response to the civil rights activism of the late 1960s
and early 1970s. Universities were establishing the first ethnic
studies classes and departments. Community-based cultural
programs and institutions were mobilized entirely through
grassroots efforts. Similarly, the Festival advocated a populist
vision of culture—one in which the traditional expressions and
knowledge based in communities were foregrounded. Artists
and culture bearers were to "speak in their own voice," and the
diversity of contemporary traditional culture in the United States
was celebrated. (Cadaval, Kim, and N'Diaye 2016, 20)

Rinzler intended the festival both to celebrate traditional art forms
in America and to educate the public. Considering itself "an international exposition of living cultural heritage,"[11] the festival, which
continues to be produced annually on the National Mall, has featured participants from fifty states, the District of Columbia, the
US Virgin Islands, and over one hundred countries. The festival
and Rinzler himself played important roles in both the creation of
the AFC and the attempt to block the square dance bills (chap. 6).

What is now the Smithsonian Center for Folklife and Cultural
Heritage (CFCH) was established as the Smithsonian Office of
Folklife Programs to produce the festival, with Ralph Rinzler as
its head (Cadaval, Kim, and N'Diaye 2016, 25–26). More recently,
the CFCH has become a research and educational unit of the
Smithsonian Institution. In addition to curating the Smithsonian
Folklife Festival, the CFCH houses the Smithsonian Folkways
Recordings and the Ralph Rinzler Folklife Archives and Collec-
tions and produces exhibits, research, videos and films, symposia,
publications, and educational materials.

National Endowment for the Arts

The NEA was established by Congress in 1965 as an independent
federal agency that is the largest funder of arts and arts education
in the country. The NEA primarily funds grants to nonprofit arts

organizations, public agencies, tribal communities, and creative writers and translators. The NEA also funds research and is itself a leader in research on the arts. In the early years, the NEA provided little support or funding for folk arts. However, the push to create a folklife center that would fund folk and traditional arts (the effort that led to the creation of the AFC, discussed below) propelled the NEA to create an office of Folk and Traditional Arts in 1974 (cf. Gross-Bressler 1995, 121-26). The office became a crucial source of funding and support for the folk and traditional arts in the years that followed.[12] NEA seed money was largely responsible for the creation of the network of state and local public folklorists employed across the country and continues to be an important source of public folk arts funding at the state and local levels. First directed by Alan Jabbour and then by Bess Lomax Hawes from 1977 to 1992 (Hawes 2007, 67), the program seeks "in part to help perpetuate traditional art forms, skills, and knowledge" (Jones 1994a, 8). It has granted funds in various ways over the years to support master and apprentice programs, festivals, media projects, and other folk and traditional arts projects and programming. Through the folk and traditional arts program, the NEA recognizes traditional artists through the annual bestowal of National Heritage Fellowships.

This program also provided the first years of funding for folk arts coordinator positions in state arts councils, with Bess Lomax Hawes famously advocating for the growth of state folklore positions. These folklorists, along with some in humanities councils and nonprofits, were responsible for preserving and presenting folk and traditional arts throughout their states. Between 1976 and 1979, numerous states as well as several cities had "hired people with training in folklore or ethnomusicology to coordinate the documentation and presentation of traditional arts, performers, and craftsmen" (Jones 1994a, 8).

While national organizations play central roles in the debates we describe in this book, it is important to note that they follow on a history of folklore institutions that debated or initiated representational and social change agendas but who had structural impediments to moving the field forward in those areas nationally. Histories of American folklore studies point to the need to broaden our understanding of "the field" beyond the primarily white and primarily male institutions that our historiography has long centered (cf. Moody 2006; Moody-Turner 2013; May-Machunda 2022). There were other organizations doing folklore work outside of the AFS in the late nineteenth and early decades of the twentieth century, though in some cases with interactions with and even support from the AFS—including, for example, the Hampton Folklore Society, established in 1893 by Black Americans collecting Black American folklore (see Moody-Turner 2013), and the "fotched on women" (an insider term for the women who came in from elsewhere) who applied the urban settlement house model to the creation of settlement schools in Appalachia (see Whisnant 1983).

These institutions, and others like them, often worked with political agendas. Shirley Moody-Turner demonstrates that the Hampton folklorists saw their agenda as overtly political, particularly Anna Julia Cooper, who spoke in 1894 of "interrogating, or 'de-naturalizing,' the assumptions underlying the discourses of civilization, while also working to expose the biases encoded in the prevailing epistemologies employed to study and analyze black 'folk' and black folklore. Cooper thus challenged the notion that the 'folk' stand on the opposite end of a temporal and spatial divide" (Moody-Turner 2013, 89).[13] "For Cooper," Moody-Turner writes, "The politics of cultural representation were intricately linked to issues of equality, social injustice, and democracy" (89). In Appalachia, the settlement-school women sought to fight poverty through cultural interventions that had lasting impact, though they were not always positive (see Whisnant 1983). Even the early regional folklore societies mentioned above, and others, debated and fought for social change. The four national folklore institutions mentioned here, however, were positioned to provide the venues and structures (and sometimes funds) to consolidate debates and pursue representational change.

THE HISTORICAL MOMENT AND THE BECKONING CALL OF CONTEXT, REPRESENTATION, AND EXPANSION

The period that we call attention to in this volume could be characterized by our advancements in three major areas of growth. First, during this time, folklore changed its definition and scope by adopting contextualism as the defining focus of both theory and method. Tied to contextualism and its partner ethnography was a revaluation of issues of representation and a kind of alternative epistemology that sought to understand our biases in how we gather information, how we understand it, and how we represent it. Finally, as both our understanding of context and representation changed, so, too, did the infrastructure for fieldwork, interpretation, and presentation as the field expanded into the public sector.

The Turn to Contextualism and the "Crisis of Representation"

Folklore's intellectual development has often run parallel with other fields of study in the humanities and social sciences, particularly with our sister field of anthropology. After all, many of our departments arose out of anthropology; the AFS and *JAF* were founded and developed in part by Franz Boas and his students (Zumwalt 1988); from the late 1970s through the early 2000s, the AAA administered our meetings; and we share many members and field leaders. The two disciplines (along with sociology, linguistics, and others) often experienced the same institutional and intellectual struggles in close temporal proximity. The first decade of the period we discuss in this volume saw a concern among scholars in our sister field about the continued relevance of the discipline, as anthropology went through a revision of its tenets and practices, including its understandings of political representation. By the second half of the twentieth century the ethnographic focus of anthropologists had significantly changed. The movements for civil rights in the 1960s and '70s, along with reactions to the Vietnam War, anti-colonialism, and anti-capitalism, all created far-ranging changes in the discipline. Pushed by these movements and related intellectual developments in the 1970s such as postcolonial studies, advocacy studies, and feminist theory, "new" communities became the focus of anthropological research, including women, ethnic minorities, and subcultures closer to home. And as anthropology changed politically, analytically, and epistemologically, so, too, did folklore.

The period that we discuss here falls just before and during what in anthropology is sometimes referred to as the "crisis of representation" (Marcus and Fischer 1986), a watershed moment that captured uncertainty about the ethical and political dimensions of representation, epistemological and ideological assumptions about objectivity, claims about the "other," unchecked biases, and the need for reflexivity. The crisis of representation transformed anthropology, along with other social and historical sciences from the early 1980s forward, calling into question the political representation of marginalized groups and claims to representation (Vargas-Cetina 2013).

Like anthropology, folklore struggled to get its footing during this period, but this was also an exciting time for the field. As anthropology moved beyond an emphasis on hunter-gatherer and colonialized societies, folklore was moving beyond Redfield-like peasant communities (Redfield 1989) and isolated text-based notions of verbal genres. The late 1960s heralded what folklorist Richard M. Dorson termed in his 1972 discussion of "Current Theories of Folklore" the "contextual approach to folklore" (Dorson 1972, 45–47).[14] Contextualists, according to Dorson, shared doctoral training in folklore at Indiana and Pennsylvania in the 1960s as well as "a leaning toward the social sciences, particularly anthropology, linguistics, and the cultural aspects of psychology and sociology; a strong preoccupation with the environment in which the folklore text is embedded; and an emphasis on theory" (45). "They object strenuously," wrote Dorson, "to the text being extrapolated from its context in language, behavior, communication, expression, and performance" (45). From the late 1960s through to the 1980s, American folklore embraced ethnography and developed notions of communication in context, moving beyond item-based conceptions of oral tradition to recast texts in performance. In 1967, Dan Ben-Amos proposed a new definition for folklore on an AFS panel about "Oral and Written Literatures" (Ben-Amos 2014). His definition moved the ball from earlier definitions of and definitional statements about folklore, such as "literature orally transmitted" (Utley 1961), to "artistic communication in small groups" (Ben-Amos 1971), replacing notions of folklore *the thing* with ideas of folklore *the process* and simultaneously casting light beyond the text to performance. Folklorists' discontent leading up to this time was focused on the static nature of text-based study and the indefiniteness of disciplinary definitions (Bronner 2016). Contextual folklore studies required more than a text and instead looked to field research, ethnography, and the research and documentation promoted by sociolinguistics in the form of Dell Hymes's and Richard Bauman's work on the ethnography of communication. The paradigm shift that occurred in the theory and methods of folklore studies eventually fostered greater awareness of the class, gender, ethnicity, race, and national bias embedded in older concepts of folklore. Now cast in ethnography, contextualism, and performance, the same reflexive impulses that triggered anthropology to look at political representation, exclusionary practices, and othering infiltrated folklore.

The period we pursue here saw the development of numerous paradigms that called into question the field's understandings of political representation. In 1976 Dan Ben-Amos edited *Folklore*

Genres, a collection of eleven essays by contributors from folklore, anthropology, literary criticism, and linguistics, originally published in three issues of the journal *Genre* between 1969 and 1971 (Ben-Amos 1976b). These essays provide an early example of the ethnographic influence on folklore and its impact on concepts of political representation even within conceptualizations of oral tradition. Ben-Amos's own piece introduced the concept of "ethnic genres," signaling a paradigm shift within the study of oral tradition away from predefined Eurocentric notions of the categories of folkloric expression to native taxonomies, which he argued constitute a "cultural affirmation of the communication rules which govern the expression of complex messages within cultural context" (Ben-Amos 1976a, 285). The concept of ethnic genres, more often referred to as emic genres, recognized that folkloric notions of the forms of oral literature were largely Western, white, male, and academic. They thus sought to replace those notions with a view of folk expression generated by the communities themselves and attempted to redefine folklore categories as they were understood within their cultural contexts. Numerous publications developed this new understanding of genre including Gary Gossen's "Chamula Genres of Verbal Behavior" (1971), Barre Toelken's "The 'Pretty Languages' of Yellowman: Genre, Mode, and Texture in Navaho Coyote Narratives" (1976), E. Ojo Arewa and Alan Dundes's "Proverbs and the Ethnography of Speaking Folklore" (1964), and Henry Glassie's "Silence, Speech, Story, Song" in *Passing the Time in Ballymenone* (1982). During this period Dell Hymes pushed for an ethnography of communication that moved beyond traditional genres to an understanding of the "genres of everyday life," including conversational genres, in context (1975, 351). The move to emic or ethnic genres signaled a concern with the inherent bias of earlier folklore studies and a reformulation based on the understanding of and rules for performance of folklore in context, focused on the perspectives of communities especially insofar as they differ from the perspectives of scholars.

This period was highly interdisciplinary, arising out of folklore's kinship with anthropology, sociology, literary criticism, and linguistics through collaboration with scholars such as Erving Goffman, Kenneth Burke, Ward Goodenough, Keith Basso, and William Labov. The "crisis of representation," a term coined by George Marcus and Michael Fischer (1986), referred specifically to the uncertainty within the human sciences about how to design adequate means of describing social reality. The crisis arose from the realization that no interpretive account can ever directly or completely capture lived experience and that "reflexivity" is necessary because there can be no position that is fully objective.[15] This was reflected in another volume published in the same year as Marcus and Fischer's volume, a collection of essays edited by anthropologists James Clifford and George E. Marcus focused "on text making and rhetoric" in order "to highlight the constructed, artificial nature of cultural accounts" (Clifford 1986, 2). For folklorists, the period of new genre paradigms, contextualism, ethnography of communication, and performance placed the emphasis on communities and individuals themselves as they created, performed, and interpreted meaning in culturally specific and variable ways. Even the import of verbal artistry or performance itself was not assumed to be the same from culture to culture or person to person (Hymes 1964). Out of this period came two important anthologies, both of which shifted focus from text to context and concentrated on primary ethnographic observation rather than universalistic notions of folklore performances and events: *Toward New Perspectives in Folklore*, edited by Américo Paredes and Richard Bauman (1972), and *Folklore: Performance and Communication*, edited by Dan Ben-Amos and Kenneth S. Goldstein (1975). Both volumes arose out of AFS panels from the late 1960s.[16]

The contextual and performance approaches had an impact on concepts of fieldwork, ethnographic methodologies, and even transcription (Tedlock 1983), calling into question research and collection methodologies that did not engage with community notions of who could say what to whom and under what circumstances. As a result, folklorists gradually became more aware of researcher interventions in the field and the ways performers interacted with fieldworkers. Notions of who "the folk" were and therefore who was worthy of being collected from and by whom were reexamined, and critiques of lingering romanticism and evolutionary theory within the discipline were taken up. The construction of an elite/folk hierarchy—which, for example, encouraged stereotypical notions of Afro-American "folkness"[17] as well as folklore as "survivals" (merely remnants from earlier periods) in the face of geographic isolation, poverty, and lack of education in Appalachia and elsewhere—began to be questioned. As awareness of missing perspectives of field research grew, so, too, did writings on women's folklore typically missed by male fieldworkers, such as Susan Kalčik's notion of the "kernel narrative" (1975a) and differences in women's and men's performance habits and traditions including assertions about choices of public and private venues or events (Kodish 1983). Transcription methods also became the focus of a reflexive lens as proponents of ethnopoetics highlighted the problematic practices of transcribing Native American performances, for instance, by organizing recorded texts according to non-native (white, Western) patterns, paragraphs, and sequences of lines. Defining the field, selecting collaborators and informants, establishing rapport, and recording and transcribing texts all were examined for their role in disciplinary ethnocentrism. Theory and method of this period questioned the ethical and political dimensions that were considered in constructing representations of culture. Just as in anthropology, the reflexive movement in folklore recognized that no interpretive account could ever directly or completely capture lived experience and that no single perspective would ever be complete or without bias.

Expanding Outward: Public Folklore

At the same time that academic folklore was blossoming with the development of contextualism and performance studies, forcing a more refined reflexivity and a greater understanding of political representation, the field was also expanding into new sectors outside of academia. Although there was important growth in this period, public sector engagement with folklore certainly did not come out of nowhere. Public agencies in the United States had long engaged with folklore, particularly folklore collection, from the Bureau of American Ethnology, founded in 1879 to document the vanishing cultures of Native Americans (cf. Brady 1988, 1999) to the first national center for the study of folk song, the Archive of American Folk Song, established by Robert Winslow Gordon in 1928 in the Library of Congress (cf. Kodish 1986; now the Archive of Folk Culture within the AFC), to the Works Progress Administration (WPA)'s Federal Project Number One, which operated between 1935 and 1939 (Hirsch 1988, 2003).

The WPA was the largest of the federal government agencies created as part of Franklin D. Roosevelt's 1933 New Deal, agencies developed to combat the Great Depression in the United States and put Americans back to work. The WPA employed millions of men and women to carry out public works projects. While most of the jobs were in construction, the government also created Federal Project Number One to employ musicians, artists, writers, actors, and directors. Federal Project Number One included the Federal Writers Project, the Historical Records Survey, the Federal Theatre Project, the Federal Music Project, and the Federal Art Project. A number of folklorists worked for various divisions, including John Lomax, Benjamin Botkin, Charles Seeger, Zora Neale Hurston, and Herbert Halpert. WPA fieldworkers collected and documented local traditions, and these collections were archived and were disseminated through published anthologies and radio broadcasts. Both John A. Lomax and Benjamin Botkin served as national folklore editors of the Federal Writers Project.[18]

In the period considered in this book, the work of Botkin—known (by some) as the "father of public folklore"—and others was markedly expanded, and two areas of public folklore that have remained vital in the field were born, due in large part to the work of Bess Lomax Hawes and Archie Green.[19] Hawes, the youngest child of American folklorist John A. Lomax, led the establishment of state folklife programs throughout the US, while Green lobbied for the creation of what became the American Folklife Center in the Library of Congress. In 1975, Hawes moved to Washington, DC, to take the position of Smithsonian deputy director for presentation, running the summerlong 1976 Bicentennial Festival of American Folklife (Sheehy 2011). The bicentennial festival, which was, according to folklorist Charles Camp, "imagined to be the penultimate folklife festival [with] the biggest staff, the biggest cast of tradition bearers,"[20] played a pivotal role in the creation of a network of folklorists from around the nation interested in the representation of grassroots culture, many of whom became public sector folklorists. In 1977, Hawes joined the NEA as director of its Folk Arts Program, where she was able to substantially raise the profile of the folk arts. Through her advocacy, folk arts funding was raised from a hundred thousand dollars to over $4 million, which enabled the funding of numerous state-based folk arts programs, many of which employed state folklorists (Schofield 2010). Hawes's goal was a "state folklorist in every state."[21] "Her efforts to create state-based folk arts programs were successful in fifty of the fifty-six states and territories" (Sheehy 2011, 87).

Among that pioneering generation of state folklorists made possible by the leadership of Hawes was Henry (Hank) Willett, who started the folk arts program in the Alabama State

Council on the Arts in 1977. According to Willett, "Folklorists employed in the public sector in the late 70s were being hired by government agencies, chiefly state arts agencies. At the time, government was not generally viewed as a consistently effective agent for positive social action, and government arts agencies were, more often than not, instruments of elitism and classicism. When meeting with other public sector folklorists, we often referred to ourselves as cultural guerrillas, waging a clandestine battle against the forces of cultural elitism" (1996, 4). The political nature of public folklore mentioned by Willett was also emphasized by Deborah Kodish, founder of the Philadelphia Folklore Project in 1987, who described public folklore as "cultivating folk arts and social change" (2013, 434).

Public folklorists, who not only work in government, as described by Willett, but also work for arts agencies and nonprofits; as educators, museum specialists, and directors of local historical societies; and in other public roles, collaborate with communities to document, promote, and conserve their traditions. While documenting the culture of a community, a region, an occupation, or a skill, public folklorists work with communities to negotiate their preferred forms of representation. In so doing, they find ways to document groups and traditions that might otherwise be lost from the historical or cultural record. Many public programs also assist community members in conducting their own fieldwork, including through community scholar training programs (see Belanus 2021). In communities with contested profiles, public folklorists assist members in creating agreed-on frames of presentation and in facilitating communication. In some communities, where relationships between groups are strained, public folklorists have worked to mediate, often through the identification of shared or similar traditions.[22] Public folklorists Robert Baron and Nick Spitzer, who together edited one of the first major collections of work on public folklore, characterize it as "by nature collaborative and dialogical, involving folklore applied and/or presented in new contexts, within and beyond the communities where it originates" ([1992] 2007, viii).

In the period leading up to the development of state folk arts programs, the advocacy for another major federal office took place, as Archie Green began to lobby for what was to become the AFC. Because it is central to multiple case studies in this book, and because, as Peggy Bulger described in her AFS presidential address, "the struggle to enact the legislation that created a national Folklife Center ironically pitted folklorists against folklorist" (2003, 379–80), we provide here an overview of the work that led to its establishment in 1976.[23] Chapter 2 will add to this discussion, linking these efforts to the attempt to create an Applied Folklore Center.

The act that established the AFC within the Library of Congress, the AFPA, was described by Sandra Gross Bressler in her thorough dissertation on this effort as "the only piece of Congressional legislation that signifies a national commitment to cultural diversity and the advocacy of myriad forms of cultural expression" (1995, 1). The work that led to the passage of the AFPA was difficult and complex but resulted in what is arguably among folklore's greatest achievements.

The creation of what eventually became the AFC was in part inspired by the Festival of American Folklife, first presented by the Smithsonian Institution in 1967, as noted above, and initially led by Ralph Rinzler (Bulger 2003, 379). Numerous people, including Rinzler, worked hard for the passage of the AFPA, but none harder than Archie Green,[24] who dedicated himself to lobbying Congress—and inspiring others to do so—from 1969 to 1976 as the effort went through multiple revisions and congresses. In our research in the archives listed above, we found a trail of evidence from different periods of his lobbying effort—his notes, some scribbled on bits of paper, some typed out, with a growing list of names of senators and representatives who had agreed to sign on to the bill or whom he was lobbying; others pleaded

CITIZENS COMMITTEE FOR AN AMERICAN FOLKLIFE CENTER

209 National Press Building
Washington, D.C. 20004

Aug 14, 73

Roger — We are finding many friends on the Hill. When you return to your office please send thank you letters to abourezk + the Texas co-sponsors.

        Permit me in this letter to report that the Citizens Committee for an American Folklife Center is active again, and that folklife legislation is now under consideration in Congress. Some weeks ago Senator James Abourezk introduced SB 1844. A copy is enclosed as well as a current list of co-sponsors. Several House companion bills have also been introduced. The full list of House co-sponsors is included. The breadth of Congressional support to this legislation is impressive.

        We wish to secure additional co-sponsors in the Senate and the House. We need personal letters of thanks to those Congressional members who have already signed the bills as well as letters to other members explaining our aims. Please send copies of your letters to the CCAFC office.

        I shall appreciate a note from you after you have had a chance to write and receive a few replies. Only by exchanging views with each other as well as with members of Congress can we reach beyond our present limited circle. I close with warm thanks for your past assistance to the CCAFC, and in the belief that we shall all contribute to the understanding of folk culture.

                Cordially,

                Archie Green

Enclosures

NOTE: Write to Senators c/o Senate Office Building, Washington, D.C. 20510; to Representatives c/o House Office Building, Washington, D.C. 20515.

Rog What can we do to get more Texas support??

Figure 1.1 Open Letter from Archie Green Reporting on the Status of the Citizen's Committee for an American Folklife Center August 14, 1973, with handwritten notes to Roger Abrahams reporting on and requesting strategies for enhancing support from Texas senators and representatives. Courtesy of the American Folklore Society Collection, Utah State University Special Collections & Archives.

with AFS presidents, secretary treasurers, and other colleagues to speak to their representatives. Issues of *AFS Newsletters* in the period frequently included pleas to AFS members to also contact their congressional representatives. It took more than seven years, and numerous folklorists helped in the fight: writing letters, testifying to Congress, and lobbying.

These efforts began in the late 1960s, as folklorists began to advocate for legislation to create an American Folklife Foundation, originally conceived of as "a third endowment," to join the NEA and NEH but dedicated to funding folk culture and housed in the Smithsonian (Gross Bressler 1995; Bulger 2003). As years passed and opposition reared, the efforts evolved and changed as advocates worked to make the proposed legislation palatable to folklorists who "attack[ed] the bill on scholarly grounds" (Bulger 2003, 381) and to those working in federal cultural institutions who feared that the foundation would compete with their own agencies for limited arts funding.

The first bill, the American Folklife Foundation Act, introduced into Congress in 1969, failed in large part due to opposition voiced during the congressional hearing by Secretary of the Smithsonian S. Dillon Ripley, who opposed it mainly due to the granting functions of the proposed foundation (as did the NEA for the same reason [cf. Gross Bressler 1995, 115]). Since the foundation would be placed under his stewardship, Ripley's support was crucial. Ripley was followed by "panels of folklorists who offered [supporting] testimony, often impassioned" (Gross Bressler 1995, 52) and others in favor of the act, including Alan Lomax, Vada Butcher, Roger Abrahams, L. Quincy Mumford (librarian of Congress), Theodore Bikel, Katherine Redcorn, Reverend Frederick Douglas Kirkpatrick, Jimmy Driftwood, Henry Glassie, Archie Green, and Don Yoder (Bulger 2003, 380; see also Gross Bressler 1995). The last speaker, Richard Dorson from the Folklore Department at Indiana University, warned against the bill, invoking his

Dear Friend:

Senator Fred Harris (D-Okla) and Representative Frank Thompson (D-NJ) have introduced in Congress a landmark proposal to create an American Folklife Foundation.

The people listed on this letterhead think that the Harris-Thompson bill represents a long-needed national commitment to the study, preservation and presentation of American folklife, so they have constituted themselves as a Citizens' Committee to press for passage of the bill. It is our hope that you and others who are involved with American folklife will help us in this legislative effort.

Enclosed are materials relating to this bill. If you are willing to work for its passage, a good first step is to write a personal note to your Representative and to your two Senators, urging them to give their active support to the bill. Write to Senators c/o Senate Office Building, Washington, DC, 20510. Write to Representatives c/o House Office Building, Washington, DC, 20515. In addition, please encourage your colleagues, friends and organizations to go to work for this proposal.

Like any citizens' effort, this one is dependent financially on private contributions. If you share our enthusiasm for this legislation, please contribute $10 or so to help bear the necessary costs. This is a no-frill operation, so you can be assured that your contribution will go directly and entirely into legislative work. Because we definitely seek to influence public policy, contributions to our effort are not tax deductible.

We need your involvement---political and financial--- if we are to have any hope of success. We hope that you will be with us for an American Folklife Foundation.

Sincerely yours,

Jim Hightower

Figure 1.2 A 1971 letter about the proposed American Folklife Foundation legislation from Jim Hightower, legislative aide to US senator Ralph Yarborough, Texas Republican. The Citizens' Committee for an American Folklife Foundation stationery demonstrates the number of folk song tradition bearers and revivalists brought into the effort. Courtesy of The Ohio State University Archives.

characteristic concerns about scholarly merit and the misap-
propriation of folk culture by Nazi Germany and the Soviet
Union and in Eastern Europe.

> You may say that is a large step from our endeavoring to retrain
> the American people in their own folk roots, but it is not such
> a large step when you begin to use Federal agencies as instru-
> ments of national policy. So I am opposed to this concept of the
> revival and promotion of folklore through the staging of popular
> festivals. I am completely in support of the language of the bill
> as I read it to promote research and scholarship in folk studies.
> [Quoted in Gross Bressler 1995, 62; see also Bulger 2003, 380–81;
> for a discussion of these topics raised by Dorson in the context of
> the Applied Folklore Center debates, see chap. 2.]

The first attempt to secure a bill was the first of several failures,
but nevertheless, the effort continued. In 1970–71, to stimulate
interest, Senator Fred Harris (D. Oklahoma) and Representative Frank Thompson (D. New Jersey) organized two hearings
outside of Congress, one at the Festival of American Folklife
in Washington, DC, and the second at the Grand Ole Opry in
Nashville (see Gross Bressler 1995). Green described Harris and
Thompson as among the principal sponsors in the Senate and
House, respectively. Regarding Thompson, Green noted, "Curious about Frank Thompson's determined loyalty to our cause, I
once asked him why he had worked so diligently for the bill. His
reply, almost brusque, was, 'Because I listen to people'" (Green
[1976] 1988, 269–70). According to Gross Bressler, "Senator Harris explained that this was a 'people's hearing' on a 'people's bill.'
It was designed to hear from the men and women 'who can speak
most eloquently about the need to preserve and promote the
cultural heritage of America . . . the people who themselves have
created that heritage'" (1995, 90). Testimonials were made by
numerous musicians, including Bill Monroe and Roy Acuff, and
others such as Jim Hightower, aide to Senator Ralph Yarborough

(D. Texas),[25] and folklorists Ralph Rinzler and Bill Ivey (93). Ivey recalled,

> The hearings were a combination of performers testifying and then people like me coming in. All I remember about my testimony is that [it was just] one month into my new job as director of the Country Music Foundation. I was just a 27 or 28-year-old, new character. I know I was interested from the beginning in how to preserve historical American music that had been captured on record, and I think I just was saying, "This shouldn't be left to the commercial recording industry and their commercial archives, but it should be public responsibility." And that the Smithsonian would be a great place to locate such a thing.[26]

The second attempt failed. A new version of the bill was introduced in the Senate and the House in 1971, and it was this version that first included a proposal that the foundation be housed in the Library of Congress. Up to this time, Green had been "in and out of Washington quite a bit," but beginning in 1972, he largely stayed in Washington, DC, dedicated to serious lobbying efforts (Gross Bressler 1995, 99). Archie Green was nobody's fool. He saw the many simmering and difficult political issues that shaped opposition (most particularly perceptions of potential threats to the NEA and NEH, perceptions of folklore as being too esoteric in relation to recession concerns, and regional jealousies) (Clark 1976, 47). Green noted in his report following the passage of the final bill, "A View from the Lobby":

> At the surface we called only for a small national center, in a library setting, to preserve and present folklife. Below this proposed structural entity, however, lies a congeries of forces, some with explosive potential. Many polarities divide the American people: native/foreign origins, melting pot/pluralistic commitments, commercial/community endeavors, cultivated/popular esthetics. We are still a restless nation, ambivalent about the past, apprehensive about the future. Although no one expects a

> library center, with a small staff and modest budget, to resolve
> long-standing stress in national life, there is no way folklorists
> can escape large issues. Folkloric work involves commentary
> on artistic and symbolic forms which, in turn, derive from and
> speak to identity, ethnicity, and community. (Green [1976]
> 1988, 270)

Green lobbied in earnest from 1972 to 1976, helped by folklorists Wayland Hand, Judy McCulloh, Roger Abrahams, Richard Bauman, Kenny Goldstein, Bess Lomax Hawes, and others (Gross Bressler 1995, 98). According to Gross Bressler, "By Washington standards, the lobbying effort for the folklife legislation was an idiosyncratic enterprise. [According to Green,] 'Normally you have a paid staff and young, bright people who can write, do position papers . . . and who work from their offices. . . .' In this case, the lobbying was a purely volunteer effort" (98).

Trying to enlist as much congressional support as he could for the legislation, Green secured the cosponsorship of Mark Hatfield (R. Oregon). Green hit it off with one of the six legislative assistants to Senator Hatfield, Janet Anderson, and she became crucial to the effort. She helped "nurse the bill through the Senate" (Gross Bressler 1995, 105), providing knowledge on process, assisting with contacts, and helping to get Green past the office doors of senators.[27] In 1973, the bill was revised from the Folklife Foundation Act into the American Folklife Preservation Act, with a focus on preservation—"a change from creating a folklife foundation to creating a folklife center, and a reigning in of funding power" (Bulger 2003, 382). Shaking off the financial threat of creating a new foundation gave the effort a new life.

The AFPA was introduced in the Senate (S. 1844) on May 17, 1973, and in the House (H.R. 8770) on June 18, 1973, with hearings held in the Senate on May 8, 1974 followed by two days of hearings in the House. Those testifying from the world of folklore and folk music included Dell Hymes (president of the AFS at the time), Glenn Ohrlin (musician), Elizabeth Cotten (musician),

Ellen Stekert (folklorist and a member of the AFS Executive Board at the time), and Archie Green.[28]

There were multiple panels of witnesses in the House. The first included Librarian of Congress Quincy Mumford; Joe Hickerson, acting head of the Archive of American Folk Song; Robert Brooks and Ralph Rinzler from the Smithsonian; Alan Jabbour, who had just joined the staff at the NEA; and folklorists Wayland Hand, Richard Bauman, and Américo Paredes. They were followed by a diverse panel that included Richard Kolm, president of the National Ethnic Studies Assembly; African American folklorist William Wiggins; and Colonel Casimer Lenard, executive director of the Polish American Congress. This group was followed by Walter Davis, director of the Department of Education for the American Federation of Labor; folklorist Barbara Kirshenblatt-Gimblett; Eliot Wiggington and a group of high school students from the Foxfire project; folklorist David Whisnant; and dance anthropologist Sharon Leigh Clark.[29]

Revisions of the bill continued, and the final version was introduced to both houses of the Ninety-Fourth Congress. "On May 1, 1975, James Abourezk [(D. South Dakota)], Hugh Scott (D., Pennsylvania) and Mark Hatfield [(R., Oregon)] introduced the Senate version of this legislation (S. 1618). In their remarks, they stressed several points: the bill focused on preservation; it would coordinate programs rather than compete with them; and it was a center of committed scholars, not a multi-million dollar endowment" (Gross Bressler 1995, 193). The bill passed the House on September 8, with 272 yeas, 117 nays, and 44 members not voting. According to Green, "The actual House vote on the bill . . . not only gained the needed majority, it exceeded the two thirds [*sic*] margin as well" (quoted in Gross Bressler 1995, 202). As it moved to the Senate, two-thirds of the membership had signed on as cosponsors; the bill passed the Senate on December 19, 1975. Despite what must have seemed an endless process, "the American Folklife Preservation Act passed in record time with a remarkably broad and deep level of Congressional support" (Gross Bressler 1995, v). In fact, the effort was successful in a way that surprised those who were most engaged in the effort but who were also painfully aware of the steep learning curve involved in what Archie Green called "our lobby-in-a-hat-box" (Green [1976] 1988, 274). Throughout the effort, numerous people testified eloquently to the importance of the initiative; among the most pointed and resonant statements was David Whisnant, who testified:

> As a citizen of the United States . . . it embarrasses me to have to say that folk culture has survived in the Appalachian region, not because of national policy, but in spite of it. . . . For generations, other nations have recognized folk culture for what it is: not a nonessential frill, but a vital and priceless resource. . . . Contrary to popular belief, the eradication of folk culture is neither inevitable nor the result of mysterious, uncontrollable forces. It is the result of conscious choices among alternatives. . . . The question, after all, is not whether we shall have a (cultural) policy. As in so many other areas of our national life, the very absence of policy is itself policy.[30]

While Green credited many folklorists with the success of the bill, he gave equal or perhaps greater credit to five senators and representatives: Senator Yarborough[31] of Texas (D), Senator Harris of Oklahoma (D), Senator Abourezk of South Dakota (D), Representative Nedzi of Michigan (D), and Representative Thompson of New Jersey (D) (Green [1976] 1988, 269).

The passage of the AFPA, which was signed into law by President Gerald Ford on January 2, 1976, elevated the importance of the documentation of folklife in the United States, creating a budget and venue for research, preservation, publication, and training related to cultural expression. Despite not having created a third endowment as many had hoped, the AFPA created the AFC at the Library of Congress and demonstrated the importance of folk culture in the context of governmental agencies that were seen to favor elite artistic endeavors.

Public Law 94–201
94th Congress

An Act

To provide for the establishment of an American Folklife Center in the Library of Congress, and for other purposes.

Jan. 2, 1976
[H.R. 6673]

Be it enacted by the Senate and House of Representatives of the United States of America in Congress assembled, That this Act may be cited as the "American Folklife Preservation Act".

American Folklife Preservation Act. 20 USC 2101 note. 20 USC 2101.

DECLARATION OF FINDINGS AND PURPOSE

SEC. 2. (a) The Congress hereby finds and declares—

(1) that the diversity inherent in American folklife has contributed greatly to the cultural richness of the Nation and has fostered a sense of individuality and identity among the American people;

(2) that the history of the United States effectively demonstrates that building a strong nation does not require the sacrifice of cultural differences;

(3) that American folklife has a fundamental influence on the desires, beliefs, values, and character of the American people;

(4) that it is appropriate and necessary for the Federal Government to support research and scholarship in American folklife in order to contribute to an understanding of the complex problems of the basic desires, beliefs, and values of the American people in both rural and urban areas;

(5) that the encouragement and support of American folklife, while primarily a matter for private and local initiative, is also an appropriate matter of concern to the Federal Government; and

(6) that it is in the interest of the general welfare of the Nation to preserve, support, revitalize, and disseminate American folklife traditions and arts.

(b) It is therefore the purpose of this Act to establish in the Library of Congress an American Folklife Center to preserve and present American folklife.

DEFINITIONS

SEC. 3. As used in this Act—

20 USC 2102.

(1) the term "American folklife" means the traditional expressive culture shared within the various groups in the United States: familial, ethnic, occupational, religious, regional; expressive culture includes a wide range of creative and symbolic forms such as custom, belief, technical skill, language, literature, art, architecture, music, play, dance, drama, ritual, pageantry, handicraft; these expressions are mainly learned orally, by imitation, or in performance, and are generally maintained without benefit of formal instruction or institutional direction;

(2) the term "Board" means the Board of Trustees of the Center;

(3) the term "Center" means the American Folklife Center established under this Act;

Figure 1.3 Signed into law by President Gerald Ford on January 2, 1976, Public Law 94–201, the American Folklife Preservation Act, marked the success of a long fight by Archie Green and others to create the American Folklife Center in the Library of Congress.

As outlined in the AFPA, "The Center receives policy direction from a Board of Trustees that is made up of representatives from departments and agencies of the federal government concerned with some aspect of American folklife traditions and the arts; the heads of four of the major federal institutions concerned with culture and the arts; persons from private life who are able to provide regional balance; and the director of the Center."[32] The presidents of the AFS and the Society for Ethnomusicology are ex officio members of the board. The board "meets several times a year, in Washington, D.C., or in other locations around the country, to review the operations of the Center, engage in long-range planning and policy formulation, and share information on matters of cultural programming."[33] The AFC has, over the years, created and supported numerous projects focused on grassroots community traditions, heritage, traditional arts, and multiculturalism, and it has provided the field with inspiration and guidance promoting American cultural traditions and provided assistance when the field has decided to try to navigate legislative pathways. The center also conducts two large oral history initiatives authorized by Congress: the Veterans History Project, established in 2000, and the Civil Rights History Project, established in 2009, and it houses the archive of the popular collection project StoryCorps.[34]

ECHOES: REVERBERATIONS AND RECURRING ISSUES

Perhaps surprisingly, we did not find significant examples of those involved in these case studies explicitly referencing the others, but we have to assume that those involved saw some connections between them. In the case studies that follow there is a recurrence of themes that ground, both positively and negatively, the efforts to expand and improve the field's approach to social change and political representation. These are not the themes we have chosen to determine this volume's scope and content but instead a pattern of concerns, perceptions, and sensitivities that emerge from the case studies and crisscross through the debates. These themes, which it appears now (with the benefit of hindsight) go sometimes too far and other times not far enough, provide conceptual insight into the thinking of the historical players. They include the power of our subject, concerns about unintended consequences, professionalization, tradition and modernity, and attitudes and actions related to pluralism, diversity, and inequity.

The Power of Our Subject

One common theme in the chapters that follow is the power of our subject, the way folklore itself engages audiences and has the potential to affect change through its familiarity, its accessibility, and often—but not always—its beauty. Folklore also often promotes a sense of shared experience, the comfort of continuity, a sense of egalitarianism, and the recognizable authority of convention. As we describe in more detail in chapter 2, Archie Green knew that local traditions would do half the job he needed to do to convince lawmakers to vote for his bills, and Ralph Rinzler recognized the potential political impact of exposing bureaucrats to the tradition bearers featured in the Smithsonian Folklife Festival and those invited to speak at the congressional hearing at the Grand Ole Opry. Participants, both lawmakers and folklorists, commented on the moving nature of the performers and performances brought before Congress. Green consistently researched the regions of the lawmakers he visited and was prepared to drop a reference to a local tradition or a beloved legendary figure. He recognized that it wasn't just folklorists but folklore itself that could facilitate change.

The strategy used by Rinzler and Green, to invite speakers and performers to speak on behalf of folklorists' attempts at legislation, was borrowed once again when folklorists and others mounted opposition against legislative efforts to make the square dance the national folk dance. In both 1984 and 1988, folklorists testified against the square dance bills, primarily on the basis of what they perceived to be a total lack of understanding of American cultural diversity (see chap. 6). Once again, the Folklife Festival served as a resource as it coincided with the hearings, and folklorists invited tradition bearers to testify, demonstrating that the square dance was not recognized as a central tradition to a majority of Americans. African American and Native American dancers and dance teachers spoke to Congress about their own dance traditions and total lack of connection with the Western square dance tradition. As was so often noted in relation to the AFPA, the tradition bearers that spoke against the square dance bills brought a powerful and engaging sense of community richness and cultural diversity and a denial of melting pot homogeneity seemingly not otherwise fully recognized by some of the legislators.

Many of the case studies share a joint sense that our subject, folklore, is powerful in its focus on cultural distinctiveness, the pull of the local, its connection to and reflection of experience, and, most of all, what we might call, following Dorothy Noyes, "humbleness"[35] or "near to the groundness" (2008, 37; 2016).[36] It is that humbleness, our field's interest in and connection to what Archie Green liked to call "regular folks" (Burns 2011), that Rinzler and Green recognized as having the power to move legislators. It is also our field's connectedness to that "humbleness" that provides the center of some of the debates here. Chapter 2, for example, on the Applied Folklore Center, explores debates about folklore's role and responsibilities in advocacy and intervention for the often poor and oppressed communities with whom we engage. Chapter 4 on the Tennessee-Tombigbee Waterway folklife project debates addresses the question of whom folklorists serve and perceptions of how sources of funding might affect ethical research and responsibilities to communities. The debates about occupational and organizational folklore discussed in chapter 5 were in part about the fears, for those who saw themselves as advocates for the "working man," that the study of organizations might elevate those invested in the oppression of those who labor. In each of these cases it is our connection to "humbleness" that simultaneously signals the power of our subject and forces us to consider the consequences of our work.

Unintended Consequences

Running through these case studies is an awareness that our actions always have unanticipated effects on the communities with whom we work. As disciplinary reflexivity has grown, it has become increasingly clear that there are gaps in our critical knowledge of potential impacts of our work. We do not always know, for example, as some of those involved in the applied folklore debates (see chap. 2) asserted, what will become of the materials we collect or how our collection will impact the traditions or tradition bearers we promote. Writing in 1972 about the attempt to create an Applied Folklore Center (see chap. 2), Dell Hymes pointed out that we don't always know what will become of the materials we collect: "One of the weaknesses of the conception of 'applied' is that it suggests application by established agencies, authorities, governments etc. to communities with the professional scholar serving the purposes of those in power, but not necessarily the needs of those in the communities. . . . Future research is going to confront the question of 'what use will be made of it' before it can even begin."[37] Numerous studies of the political uses and misuses of folklore (such as in Nazi Germany or, more recently, in the creation of UNESCO masterpiece nominations [see Foster 2015b]) point to the reasonableness of concerns about unintended consequences.[38]

As we work to raise traditions up, making them more visible, we recognize that while visibility can enhance political footing, it can also be dangerous in expanded contexts. As Goldstein and Shuman argue, "the 'public flaunting' of cultural practices, whether by a group itself or by others who appropriate and recontextualize practices, creates hypervisibility in contrast but always connected to invisibility" (2016, 9). In a report responding to the idea of creating an Applied Folklore Center, Richard Dorson, Robert Georges, and Dell Hymes asserted, "As long as libraries and archives are open to the public, anyone of a mind to 'use' folklore for any purpose whatever is free to do so, and there is nothing the AFS or the professional folklorist can do about it, except possibly, get out there and use it himself to greater advantage."[39] Folklorists on both sides of the debate about the AFC's planned Tennessee-Tombigbee Waterway folklife project (chap. 4) had concerns about unintended consequences. On one side there were fears about the consequences for the field of accepting funds originating with the Army Corps of Engineers, and on the other side there were fears of the consequences of not documenting the communities in the path of the waterway project. The debates about occupational and organizational folklore (chap. 5) echo both of these examples in some ways, with concerns expressed about funding sources and the loss of control over the results of research on one side and missed opportunities for the field and for organizations on the other.

Folklorists' concerns about unintended consequences come not only from our reflections on Nazi and other nationalistic and state-based misuses of folklore but also from memories of the ensnarement of anthropologists, including some who collected and studied folklore, in problematic WWII government initiatives. In 1942, the AAA passed a resolution placing "itself and its resources and the specialized skills and knowledge of its members at the disposal of the country for the successful prosecution of the war" (Price 2002, 16). In 1947, it was estimated that half of all professional anthropologists worked full time in some war-related governmental capacity and a further one-quarter worked part time for the war (Price 1998, 379),[40] and as Gregory Bateson noted at the time, working for the war meant that social scientists had little control over the scope of research or what was done with the fruits of their labor (Price 1998, 380).

In 1942, people of Japanese ancestry on the Pacific Coast of the United States were evacuated from their homes by army order. The War Relocation Authority (WRA) was created to assume responsibility for the displaced population, which included 110,000 people in ten relocation centers scattered around the western United States (Spicer 1946, 16). After a number of strikes and riots at some of the camps, the WRA decided to send a social scientist to each of the relocation centers. Twenty-one anthropologists were hired to study camp life and advise administrators, including, among others, Conrad Arensberg, Weston La Barre, Margaret Lantis, Robert Redfield, Edward H. Spicer, and Rosalie H. Wax (Starn 1986, 717n1).[41]

Anthropologists hired by the WRA at least initially understood their job responsibilities as easing the relocation process for Japanese Americans and improving quality of life in the camps. But in some cases, largely as articulated retrospectively, the ethnographers were accomplices of the government in maintaining what were essentially concentration camps. Rosalie Wax (1953) was especially critical of anthropological involvement in the camps while Edward Spicer referred to the internment as "America's worst war-time mistake" but still argued that as anthropologists committed to the welfare of Japanese Americans, ethnographers had a duty to assist the WRA and to help reintegrate the evacuees into normal American life (Spicer 1979, 220). For many of the anthropologists who worked on the WRA, relocation was a mistake, but they felt they were helping to at least make sure it was carried out in as humane a way as could be negotiated. But, as Orin Starn writes, "The anthropologists began from the contradictory position of trying to aid Japanese Americans while at the same time directly serving the administrative machinery of the WRA. Ultimately, their unquestioning adoption of contemporary anthropological interpretive strategies and their unwillingness to take a public stand against internment metamorphized the aim of advocacy into legitimation of domination" (1986, 716). In any case, the work of the WRA anthropologists had a number of unintended consequences including legitimation of the relocation and assimilationist views of the government as well as the promotion of racial stereotypes about the Japanese. This work by applied anthropologists suggested a nascent tradition of alignment with administrative authority and the vision of the ethnographer as a social engineer.

And yet, while we worry about unintended consequences of our actions, in her AFS presidential address Michael Ann Williams reminds us that "unintended consequences result from what we don't do, as well as from the action we take" (2017a, 138). Referencing the unintended consequences of the AFC's cancellation of the Tennessee-Tombigbee Waterway folklife project, she continues, "There are people we could have acted as advocates for and didn't" (138; see chap. 4). Bulger emphasizes this as well, saying in her AFS presidential address, "Despite well-meant impulses, folklorists missed an opportunity to be central to the work of cultural conservation and the environmental survey work that is still going on today" (2003, 387). Such critiques from former AFS presidents demonstrate that unintended consequences are understood in more complicated ways today.

Professionalization

American folklore studies has concerned itself with professionalization since at least the founding of the AFS in 1888. Although the most active founding leaders of the AFS, William Wells Newell and Franz Boas, did not identify as folklorists and did not wish to see folklore as an independent discipline—that professional identity would come decades later—Zumwalt recounts their attempts to act as gatekeepers of the collection and study of folklore in the United States, keeping it in the hands of "professionals" rather than "amateurs." They were not successful, despite an explicit editorial policy (Zumwalt 1988, 28–29, 43). As Zumwalt notes, professionalism was, in the period in which the AFS formed, "equated with" science, and therefore Newell and Boas insisted that research published in *JAF* be grounded in science (Zumwalt 1988, 3).[42] Efforts to "professionalize" folklore studies in the US, though ever present, have been raised in different ways and intensities in different periods. This includes the period leading up to and in which our case studies took place.

Perhaps the conflict most well known to students of folklore is that between Richard M. Dorson and Benjamin Botkin. Dorson taught at Indiana University beginning in 1957 and "was devoted to establishing folklore as an autonomous department and elevating it to the ranks of other disciplines" (Harrah-Johnson 2020, 79). Dorson's aspirations did not just concern IU. Rather, he saw his responsibility as rescuing the AFS and all of folklore studies from what he famously characterized, in 1948, as its status as "a tiny barnacle clinging to the American Anthropological Association" (Brunvand 1982, 349). Benjamin Botkin, discussed elsewhere in this and other chapters, provided a sharp contrast to Dorson in every way. Jerrold Hirsch and Lawrence Rodgers describe him succinctly as working "to broaden the subject matter of American folklore and the role of the American folklorist. He always insisted on approaches to folklore that did not separate the lore from the folk who created it" (2010, 2). Among his many endeavors in support of this approach, some discussed elsewhere in this volume, was his series Treasuries of American Folklore, written for a nonacademic audience.

While it is widely understood that Dorson objected to Botkin and others as "popularizers" (Botkin couldn't be an "amateur" since he had a PhD, but the implication was the same), his objections were grounded in his efforts to professionalize, as he understood the term, the field. "Nothing less than the future security of folklore study in America consumed Dorson's diligent efforts. By ensuring its rigor and purity, his goal was to professionalize the discipline, thereby justifying permanent financial and academic support for its continuation. Botkin's treasuries formed the eye of a turbulent storm that relentlessly pitted these contrasting views against one another for decades" (Widner [Sharp] 2010, 42).

John Alexander Williams, interested in folklore as just one example of the wider context of the movement toward "academic professionalism," demonstrates that Dorson's ongoing conflict with Botkin was thoroughly linked with his attempts to separate the AFS—and, through it, folklore studies—from left-wing politics to achieve the goal of "remak[ing] this old but traditionally heterogeneous and undisciplined body into a professional organization capable of acting as the [in MacEdward Leach's words] 'custodian of folklore and folklore studies in the United States'" (Williams 1975, 224). Williams describes the attempts of Dorson, along with Stith Thompson (IU), MacEdward Leach (UPenn), Wayland Hand (UCLA), and others in the 1950s to professionalize the AFS through efforts ranging from limitations on what was reviewed in *JAF* to the formation of a small executive board and the creation of the Fellows of the American Folklore Society in 1960. "The antiradicalism of the professionalizers was thus one aspect of a drive for academic respectability that manifested itself chiefly as a search for money and status" (225).[43]

In the period we examine here, professionalism continues as a thread in more and less overt ways but is nevertheless ever present. In chapter 3, we describe the creation of the AFS State of the Profession Committee, which was established as a standing committee of the executive board with the creation of a new AFS constitution, implemented in 1976 as one result of the short-lived Committee on the Status of Women in the Profession. The issues addressed by the State of the Profession Committee were many over the years, but initially, as we discuss, included the creation of a directory of professional folklorists, which never happened, and the development of a code of ethics, which took ten years.[44] Beyond this period, as we discuss in chapter 7, our coda, this committee was charged in 1992 with "developing recommendations for 'enhancing minority participation' in the field of folklore" (Roberts et al. 1994, 9), which began an important period of professionalization through addressing barriers to minority participation in the field.

Professionalization is in the background of the other chapters, often directly linked to Dorson himself. For instance, chapter 2 describes his arguments against the creation of a center for applied folklore, and in this chapter and in chapter 2, we describe his similar arguments in opposition to the AFC in his testimony to Congress. While his objections were overtly about the government's role in folklore, they were also grounded in his overriding interest in the professionalization of the field, which for him meant a strict agenda of scholarship and *not* appeals to a lay audience, whether through publications or festivals. Both the debates over the AFC's involvement in the region of the Tennessee-Tombigbee Waterway project (chap. 4) and organizational and occupational folklore (chap. 5) were, broadly speaking, also debates about the form that professionalism of the field should take. The national square dance bills, while employing the testimony of many nonfolklorists, still created a purposeful tension between folklore professionals and enthusiasts. Again, like other fields of study, folklorists have long had disagreements over what it means to be a professional, including how professionalism overlaps with or does not overlap with advocacy and political involvement.

Tradition and Modernity

The late 1970s through the mid-1980s was a period of critical discourse concerning tradition and modernity, particularly as postmodernism became fashionable in the arts, literature, philosophy, and the social sciences (Anttonen 2005, 17). In 1967, Dan Ben-Amos deliberately left "tradition" out of his definition of folklore as "artistic communication in small groups"

(1971). Dell Hymes just as deliberately included "tradition" in his "five key notions" of folklore in his presidential address to the AFS soon after, but he emphasized his take on "tradition" as a process, to *traditionalize* (1975). Central to the case studies we discuss here are, on the one hand, challenges to positivistic universalism, consumerism, totalizing discourses, marginalization, "othering," and master narratives, all characteristic of the concerns of postmodernism, and resistance to these efforts at change, particularly by those who saw in both modernity and postmodernity a disintegration of values. Dorothy Noyes discusses three main orientations of our notions of tradition—as a communicative transaction, as a temporal ideology, and as communal property (2009), and all three are reflected in the representational debates of the 1970s and '80s. As Simon Bronner notes, "Tradition is wrapped up in talk of technological and social change and the search for solutions to various political problems facing groups and nations cognizant of the force of tradition in the connectedness of citizens or members" (2011, 2–3). It is not surprising that a field with roots in "saved from the fire" metaphors of modernity would have an uneasy relationship with postmodernity. The coexistence of traditional folklore with industrialization, consumerism, and bureaucratic control was tested and debated in the efforts to address representation, particularly harkening back to questions of "who are the folk?" (Dundes 1977), as discussed in chapter 5.

All of our case studies reflect on, although not always transparently, concepts of tradition and modernity, and we are reminded throughout that "there is no such thing as tradition without the individuals who enact it" (Cashman, Mould and Shukla 2011b, 2). "Tradition," Henry Glassie tells us, "is the means for deriving the future from the past" (1995, 409), and so it is no wonder that tradition must be interwoven with debates about the past and the future of the field, both in terms of our understandings of the wider universe of tradition and with disciplinary traditions themselves. For example, the debates about applied folklore explore the potential for political misuses of tradition, bemoan appropriation, and question consumerism. In chapter 3, about debates that arose as women demanded their place in the field, we see women and some men critiquing normative male behavior at the same time that they brought attention to gendered traditions that counter long-standing notions of coherent homogenous local tradition. The debates concerning the study of corporate folklore in the context of more typical disciplinary privileging of the traditional worker were at their core questions about our subject ("who are the folk?"), which in turn raise questions about tradition and modernity. Our fifth case study demonstrates the resistance of tradition bearers, folklorists, and others to state-imposed assimilation through modernity's universalizing of expressive forms such as dance. It is no surprise that each case study is linked to tradition, modernity, and postmodernity, nor should it be a surprise that each is concerned with what some argue is the core of the field, even as approaches and definitions differed over time: pluralism, diversity, and inequity.

Pluralism, Diversity, and Inequity

From its earliest foundations, the AFS understood pluralism and diversity, although not necessarily equity, as intrinsic to its mission. As we discuss in chapter 5, AFS cofounder and first editor of *JAF* William Wells Newell identified four areas of collection crucial to the newly established society's attention. These included "a. Relics of Old English Folklore . . . b. Lore of Negros in the Southern States of the Union, c. Lore of the Indian Tribes of North America . . . d. Lore of French Canada, Mexico, etc." (Newell 1888, 3). Roger Abrahams wrote of this focus by Newell and his founder colleagues, Franz Boas and Francis James Child, as radical and progressive.

> This list not only indicates a pluralistic vision of the American cultures worthy of study, it sets an agenda for folklore study in North America that has been followed ever since. But in the 1880s, cultural pluralism was not regarded as a viable model *of* or *for* describing American society. This social pluralistic impulse within the American Folklore Society echoed radical fringe abolitionists, such as Wendell Philips, who argued "an idea of American Civilization," which was "not a rendering of Protestant, middle class uniformity" as the historian George Frederickson pointed out, not the "new England writ-large" that it was to most of Philips' abolitionist contemporaries, but rather a nation made up of peoples of "all races, all customs, all religions, all literature, and all ideas" under the rule of laws "noble, just, and equal." Wittingly or unwittingly, the group coming together to form the American Folklore Society resuscitated this older, radical vision of America that had become extremely unfashionable, even among the inheritors of the abolitionist spirit. (Abrahams 1989, 614–15)

In some ways, Newell stayed true to the commitment to cultural pluralism for which Abrahams praised him. For instance, as editor of *JAF* he published over one hundred articles and notes on Black folklore in the first twenty-five issues of the journal (Wiggins 1988, 29). However, even as he and Franz Boas have been credited with working against the ethnocentric theory of cultural evolution that dominated nineteenth-century thinking (see Zumwalt 1988), that very theory was embedded in Newell's list of priorities for *JAF*, as for him these regions and groups provided "the fast-vanishing remains" that were "soon to be absorbed and lost in the uniformity of the modern world" (1888, 3). Cultural evolutionary theory, while positing that all cultures pass through the same stages from savagery to barbarism to civilization, also assumed that certain cultures lagged behind in part due to lack of education and geographic isolation. Newell was not unusual in holding these perspectives, but it is clear that while he promoted the importance of cultural pluralism he also held fast to the belief that these cultures were pre-modern and backward. Shirley Moody-Turner provides particular examples of how although Newell, along with Boas, was working against the theory of cultural evolution, he was far from free of it. "In the report on the third annual meeting of AFS, for instance, Newell explained that systems of knowledge could be partitioned into three categories, noting that even among the 'lowest' or 'most savage' there had been 'attempts at such understanding,' asserting that in general, a peoples' 'system of explanation' could be correlated with these stages of development, consisting of 'savagery,' 'barbarism,' and civilization" (Moody-Turner 2013, 25). If we fast forward nearly a hundred years to the period considered in this volume, the vestiges of evolutionary theory still can be seen to affect the field's continuing commitment to pluralism, including in how "the folk" has been understood.[45]

In the early 1990s John W. Roberts addressed what he referred to as a discourse of "folkness" in folklore studies, "a discourse that renders virtually impossible a recognition of the influence of diversity not only on culturally specific creative traditions but also between diverse cultural traditions" (1993, 158). Folkness, according to Roberts, "can be conceptualized as a mode of ideation based on a perceived ontological and epistemological distinction between 'folk' and 'nonfolk' which has served traditionally as the basis for folkloristic theorizing" (158). Roberts (2000) argues that by the late nineteenth century this discourse of folkness was distinguishing between those individuals who were perceived as participating in processes of vernacular creativity (the folk) and the nonfolk who participated in other modes of cultural production. The concept of folkness was heavily influenced by paradigms of romanticism, rationalism, and cultural evolutionary theory reinforcing the elite/folk hierarchy. Moody-Turner demonstrates that even as Newell was quite supportive of the work of the Hampton Folklore Society, the concept of "folkness" described by Roberts was clearly evident in his thinking.

For instance, she cites an 1894 speech to the Hampton Folklore Society in which he "defines 'folk' as synonymous with race" (Moody-Turner, 2013, 27). Belief in cultural evolutionary theory persisted well into the twentieth century, and, despite having been discarded in the later half to third of the century, its residue in the discourse of folkness remains.

Writings such as Patrick B. Mullen's "Belief and the American Folk" (2000) and Mary Hufford's "Interrupting the Monologue: Folklore, Ethnography, and Critical Regionalism" (2002) illustrate and critique the traces of cultural evolution and romantic regionalism ingrained in the discipline, as folklorists describe those cultures (isolated, undereducated) in which folklore flourished. As the 1994 Report of the State of the Profession Committee of the American Folklore Society on Minority Participation in the Field of Folklore noted, this discourse of folkness stereotyped minority communities as backward, hardly a stance that would lead members of minority groups to embrace folklore as either an academic discipline or a profession (Roberts et al. 1994). And indeed, the 1994 report was prompted by a dearth of minority participation within the field.

Phyllis May-Machunda writes in *Recentering the Periphery, Coloring the Discourses, and Expanding the Frames: A Guide to the Notable Folklorists of Color Exhibitions*, sponsored by the AFS, that "folklore studies was not alone" in perpetuating racial stereotypes and supporting the colonialism of people of color in scholarship, "and in fact was a field more progressive than some in even recognizing the cultures of BIPOC [Black, Indigenous, People of Color] communities as worthy of study" (May-Machunda 2022, 28). May-Machunda also notes, however,

> From its beginning, folklore studies as a field also didn't question
> or challenge the assumptions and conditions under which BIPOC
> communities lived—the dispossession of indigenous lands,
> segregation of BIPOC peoples, the exploitation of people's labor
> and deprivation of economic opportunities and citizenship rights,

> and the precarity and violence used to disrupt or manage BIPOC communities, assigning these groups to a variety of biologically, culturally and economically inferior statuses, worthy of "exotic"[46] and sometimes exploitative study, but not full equity. (28)

Proving May-Machunda's point, the debates from the period discussed in this volume largely lack the reflexive comprehension of race and minority communities noted by her, though some kernels of higher levels of reflection concerning assumptions and conditions under which minority communities lived can be found in the debates and initiatives from the period, particularly in the case studies most strongly focused on perceptions of pluralism, diversity, and inequity. This is not to say that those involved in these case studies did not inadvertently reinforce or replicate the dynamics of inequality so often present in research. But as we underscore here, these case studies illustrate the beginnings of representational reckoning, the growing pains folklorists experienced as calls for social change from within the discipline and the work of folklore increased.

For example, in the debates concerning the creation of an Applied Folklore Center, folklorists pointed out the nature and consequences of systemic racism. Overall discussions concerning applied folklore addressed big issues such as the relationship between scholarly objectivity and advocacy, the perception held by some folklorists that political activism was a threat to the reputation of the discipline, the role of reciprocity and accountability in the work of folklorists, and the end goal and potential utility of engagement with communities. Within those debates, some of the individuals who participated in the discussions spoke more directly than others of the role of folklorists in challenging racial disparities and the ways power structures propagate racism. Roger Abrahams, for example, argued, "All I know is that I could not square it with my own conscience if, after working with Blacks for the last 15 years, I didn't somehow recognize the ways in which the power structure was impinging constantly and degrading constantly the very culture which I see them maintaining in spite of this kind of impingement."[47] Abrahams, along with Archie Green, Kenneth Goldstein, and Ray Browne, spent much of the discussion exploring the possible real impacts of applied folklore, the potential intermingling of advocacy and imperialism, and the nature of what Gerald Davis later referred to as the "the thoughtless trumpeting of our proud heritage of liberal progressive postures" (1996, 115).

The topic of chapter 4 is the Tennessee-Tombigbee Waterway project and the cancellation in 1979 of the AFC's planned folklife survey in the region. The cancellation is most often recalled by folklorists who remember it as a missed opportunity for the beginnings of folklorist involvement in cultural impact statements on federal projects; however, the cancellation also meant missed opportunities for those living in the region, many of whom were Black and poor. The archival record reflects attention to this in different ways as well as some level of support for the project from Black leaders. For instance, notes regarding the planning of the project show that the AFC intended to recruit and train Black fieldworkers, including individuals from the region. AFC director Alan Jabbour's notes about responses to his call to folklorists for comments on the project in early 1979, when the project came under fire, include that folklorist and SNCC leader Worth Long visited to express his support for the project.[48] Based on meetings and discussions with Jabbour and others, the Minority Peoples Council on the Tennessee-Tombigbee Waterway (MPC)—formed in 1974 in order to investigate the potential effects of the waterway project, good and bad, on the people of the region—was cautiously supportive of the AFC project. This included Black artist, professor, and activist Jane Sapp, who was the lone voice from the region—and nearly the only Black voice—at the debate at the AFC in February 1979 that preceded the cancellation of the project. Sapp argued passionately for what she saw as both the cultural and economic benefits of documenting the lives and traditions of Black people in the region, and we quote from her extensively in chapter 4 precisely because she was the lone voice in that room.[49]

Chapter 6, which explores the 1984 and 1988 bills to designate the square dance as the American national dance, focuses on the problems of homogenizing discourses concerning vernacular culture but also on the assimilationist treatment of Native Americans and communities of color. The 1984 bill's sponsor in Congress, Leon Panetta (D. California), said of the square dance, "It truly represents an amalgam of what our country is all about."[50] In addition to debates about the origin and types of square dance, testimonies by folklorists in opposition focused on the problematic nature of melting pot views of immigration, diversity, and pluralism, the importance of cultural distinctiveness, and a concern with holding one dance tradition as superior over the vernacular traditions of the majority of Americans who come from a variety of ethnic backgrounds. Most significantly, folklorists argued that the square dance was used to assimilate immigrants and create conformity in Native American residential schools where the square dance was used to replace the Native American traditional dances forbidden within the educational system. Panels of opponents to the bill organized by the AFS featured African American, Latin American, and Native American experts, each testifying on their own community's relationship, or lack thereof, to the square dance. The effort underscored philosophical problems with assimilationist views, the structural racism built into governmental and educational approaches to expressive culture, and the role of community members as cultural experts.

Shirley Moody-Turner notes that part of the stereotyping of African American folklore arose from a disciplinary historical record that tended to focus on African American folklore but not on African American folklorists, writing, "By presenting African Americans as always the folk, but never the folklorists, both traditional and revisionist histories of folklore studies continue to perpetuate the idea, as Melvin Wade[51] states, that blacks are considered 'peripheral participants in the evolution of their own intellectual history, fully involved in the performing of folklore, but rarely reflective about their involvement'" (Moody 2006, 33).

Indeed, there are few minority scholars from the period discussed in this volume visible in our case studies, due in part to the lack of diversity of the institutions involved, including the AFS and the newly created AFC. Women scholars from this period, who were present in the AFS in large numbers and, as can be seen in chapter 3, were beginning to organize, are less present in some of these debates than one might expect—or less than we expected—at least as documented in the historical record. For instance, the extant recording of the Point Park conference debates on the Applied Folklore Center contains very few women's voices despite our knowledge that there were women on the relevant committees. A closer look does illuminate important contributions by BIPOC scholars. Gladys-Marie Fry, the first African American scholar to earn a PhD in folklore in 1967 (Wiggins 1988, 32), was referred to in AFS Business Meeting minutes as having inspired the earliest mention of the potential for applied folklore[52] at an AFS meeting, but we found no further information on her contributions. Cherokee folklorist and former AFS president Rayna Green was active in several of the case studies, and the opposition to the square dance bills included testimony and letters to Congress not just from Green but from a number of Native American scholars including Paul Tiolono from the King Island Eskimo Group of Alaska. Katherine Redcorn of the Osage tribe testified at the American Folklife Preservation Act hearings. Charles "Honi" Coles—actor, past president of the Negro Actors Guild, manager of the Apollo Theater, singer, tap dancer, and teacher—joined Rayna Green on a panel testifying to Congress, as did LaVaughn Robinson, tap dancer from Philadelphia and instructor at the Philadelphia

College of the Performing Arts, and singer, activist, and scholar of African American culture Bernice Johnson Reagon.

However, we do know there were African American folklorists engaged in the community of folklorists in the period in question. According to William (Bill) Wiggins (2001), a group of twenty-five African American professors, graduate students, museum staff members, and community-based researchers founded the Association of African and African American Folklorists (AAAAF) at a gathering on the campus of Howard University in 1974. Wiggins served as president, Gladys-Marie Fry as vice president, and Gerald Davis as secretary treasurer, and Stephen E. Henderson, Bernice Johnson Reagon, Roland Freeman, and James Early formed the executive board (Wiggins 2001, 62). Folklorist and former AFS president Marilyn White told us that the first conference held by the AAAAF, which she attended, took place at Howard in 1975.[53] Opening remarks were given by Stephen E. Henderson, director, Institute for the Arts and the Humanities,[54] followed by panels that included a host of well-known Black scholars: Kathryn Morgan, James Early, Jane Sapp, Worth Long, Bernice Johnson Reagon, Gladys-Marie Frye, Gerald Davis, Larry Neal, Lance A. Williams, and others. The keynote address, entitled "The Decolonization of Folklore," was given by Leon G. Damas.

The association held subsequent meetings at Indiana University and the University of Maryland at College Park. The proceedings of the third annual meeting of the AAAAF, which examined the state of Afro-American folklore scholarship, were published in 1979 as *The Role of Afro-American Folklore in the Teaching of the Arts and the Humanities*, edited by Adrienne Lanier Seward, and Lance Williams produced an hour-long video documentary in 1977 of the conference entitled *What Time Is De Meetin'?* In 1979, the AAAAF began meeting during the annual AFS conference. White explained that members decided it was a lot to ask people to attend a separate meeting, with the associated expenses, in addition to the AFS Annual Meeting and meetings of other professional societies. "We wound up deciding to meet at AFS, but to meet separately. And that's why we've been having, for example, our dinners," which are brought together through word of mouth. White stressed that while the AAAAF has a relationship with the AFS, the organization has never been officially affiliated as an interest section of the AFS.

> Because as you know, for AFS sections, anybody can be a member of any of the sections. . . . We had, amongst ourselves, a really long discussion about what we were going to call ourselves and why. And we wound up calling ourselves the Association *of* African and African American Folklorists. We wanted to indicate basically, who we were, who we were encompassing. What was included in the "African" was certainly the diaspora. We did not want to be thought of as being "hyphens" and that's why there is no hyphen in our name. And we specifically said "of," because this is kind of like a "FUBU," for us by us.[55]

As White described to us, the group is "still meeting," and the issues that prompted the formation of the group "are still relevant." Separately, the African American Folklore Section of the AFS was formed in 2019, open to anyone.

Latinx folklorists have historically been somewhat better represented in the AFS, and "the [American Folklore] Society, has benefitted from a sizable Latino presence and participation" (Agozzino 2012, 45). Norma Cantú and Olga Nájera-Ramirez outline numerous *pioneras* writing and working in the field from the 1920s and '30s onward, including the decades covered by this volume (2002b, 3–7).[56] Latinx members have served as officers in virtually all AFS executive roles, on important committees, and as editor of the society's journal, beginning with the election of Aurelio Macedonio Espinosa to the AFS presidency (1923–24). Mexican American folklorist Américo Paredes served as editor of *JAF* (1969–73) and was involved in case studies discussed in this volume. Referred to by José R. López Morín as a voice for Chicano consciousness in the late 1960s and thereafter

(Morín 2006), Paredes was both an early participant in the applied folklore initiative and someone whose applied work became a part of the subsequent debates. Paredes, along with African American folklorist William Wiggins, testified in the congressional hearings on the AFPA. The AFS also has two sizable Latinx interest sections created in the decade following the period examined here: the Folklore Latino, Latinamericano, y Caribeno Section (established in 1992) and the Chicano and Chicana Folklore Section (established in 1998).

Other minority communities are poorly documented in this period of folklore studies. Juwen Zhang (2015) notes that the influx of Asians to the US in the 1960s and '70s did not result in recognition of Asian folklore and that, despite public folklore's focus on Hmong and other Asian refugee lore, academic folkloristics in the 1980s took no account of Asian American folklore. It was not until 2005 that the first Asian interest section of the AFS, the East Asia Folklore Section, renamed in 2014 the Transnational Asia/Pacific Section, was established.

William Clements's edited volume, *100 Years of American Folklore Studies: A Conceptual History* (1988), makes an effort to document African Americans, Native Americans, and women in the discipline, but more often than not the authors focus on male scholars writing about women or white authors writing about people of color. As Susan Kalčik (1988) noted in that volume, by the 1970s academic disciplines were informed by feminist theory, but it took a while before writings about women were not dominated by men. Despite the lack of documentation of minority communities during this era, pluralism, diversity, and concerns about inequities run through all of the case studied but most overtly are central to chapters 2, 3, 4, and 6.

WHY IT MATTERS: HISTORICIZING
UNFINISHED QUESTIONS

Folklore is fortunate, particularly as a small field, that there have been a host of excellent disciplinary histories and historically useful anthologies, and it is important to call out many of them by name, including Simon Bronner's *American Folklore Studies: An Intellectual History* (1986); Rosemary Lévy Zumwalt's *American Folklore Scholarship: A Dialogue of Dissent* (1988); William Clements's *100 Years of Folklore Studies: A Conceptual History* (1988); Robert Baron and Nick Spitzer's *Public Folklore* ([1992] 2007); Michael Owen Jones's *Putting Folklore to Use* (1994c); Regina Bendix's *In Search of Authenticity: The Formation of Folklore Studies* (1997); Jerrold Hirsch's *Portrait of America: A Cultural History of the Federal Writers' Project* (2003); Patrick B. Mullen's *The Man Who Adores the Negro: Race and American Folklore* (2008); Shirley Moody-Turner's *Black Folklore and the Politics of Racial Representation* (2013); Olivia Cadaval, Sojin Kim, and Diana Baird N'Diaye's *Curatorial Conversations: Cultural Representation and the Smithsonian Folklife Festival* (2016); Bill Ivey's *Rebuilding an Enlightened World: Folklorizing America* (2017); Patricia Sawin and Rosemary Lévy Zumwalt's *Folklore in the United States and Canada: An Institutional History* (2020); Solimar Otero and Mintzi Auanda Martínez-Rivera's *Theorizing Folklore from the Margins: Critical and Ethical Approaches* (2021); Rosemary Lévy Zumwalt's *Franz Boas: Shaping Anthropology and Fostering Social Justice* (2022); and others. Of course, it helps that these disciplinary histories arise out of a field that understands history as dynamic, never comprehensive or complete, as much about forgetting as remembering, about the present as much as the past, and about silencing as much as voicing.

This volume arises out of these same things, and it is about the messy bits, the often-unfinished thoughts of our discipline's history. For us, in this research, the discipline's attempts to get "there" is as interesting as, perhaps more interesting than, the ultimate "there" to which our discipline has gotten or not gotten. And in fact, half of what we discuss here (such as the Tenn-Tom folklife project, the Applied Folklore Center, the ERA) never came to be. Yet, as our final chapter, which tries to follow some of these issues into the present, shows, we are still reliving, re-thinking, reviving, regenerating, and rearranging some of these very same issues but without the benefit of remembering our fragmented past. For many of these cases, we have known *that* it happened but not *how* it happened. We aim to fix that.

George Santayana is credited with the aphorism "Those who cannot remember the past are condemned to repeat it" (1905, 284). And so we do. As we've explored here, members of AFS have again and again debated appropriate ways to respond when the politics of the places we meet to hold our annual meeting let us down. Over and over members of our field have wondered whether funding sources with questionable ethics can be or should be exploited to fund potentially really good work. We don't repeat history only due to what we forget. The issues discussed here never fully go away, in part because political representation is not a thing that ever arrives at an end. It propels us forward (and perhaps also back) as we strive to understand new or different ways of thinking about equity, inclusion, advocacy, and change. As a field, we are always searching to find better means of addressing our disciplinary responsibilities and the means that will allow us to better understand the modalities of intellectual and political growth we hope will be reflected in the soul of a folklorist.

NOTES

1. Henry Glassie is one example. See Cashman, Mould, and Shukla 2011a.

2. These were not entirely new issues and questions, but this was a new context. See Williams 1975.

3. Cf. Kamenetsky 1972, 1977; Ortiz 1999; Williams 1975; James 1948.

4. Pete Seeger, Woody Guthrie, and others were blacklisted during that period while others avoided social commentary in order to fly under the radar (see "Folk Singers, Social Reform, and the Red Scare," Library of Congress, accessed May 7, 2025, https://www.loc.gov/item /ihas.200197399.

See Dorson 1962, "Folklore and the National Defense Education Act" in *JAF*, in which he includes his letter to the chair of the Senate Education subcommittee arguing that fellowship funding is needed for folklore in order to fight communism. He wrote, "Trained folklorists can expose the Communist use of folklore behind the Iron Curtain and within the labor unions in the democracies" (163).

As Rosemary Zumwalt wrote, quoting Clifford Geertz in "From the Native's Point of View," "'The trick is to figure out what the devil they think they are up to.' The same can be said of historical research" (Zumwalt 1988, xiii).

5. We made every effort to interview all of the major living players involved in these case studies. In most cases we were successful in doing so. In very few cases, those who were no longer active in the field did not respond to our requests. In a few other cases, individuals chose not to be interviewed due to time constraints, memory concerns, or lingering sensitivities over the issues. In all of those cases, they instead offered off-the-record insights or personal notes to assist in our efforts to fill in the historical record.

6. As discussed in chapter 3, sections were formalized with a new AFS constitution, implemented in 1976.

7. For thorough histories of the AFS, including critical histories, see Zumwalt 1988; Clements 1988; Roberts 2008.

8. Timothy Lloyd, interview with authors, March 18, 2022. Zoom.

9. Elliott Oring, interview with authors, March 15, 2022. Zoom.

10. Originally the Smithsonian Festival of American Folklife.

11. "Mission and History," Smithsonian Folklife Festival, accessed May 7, 2025, https://festival.si.edu/about-us/mission-and-history/smithsonian.

12. The creation of the Folk and Traditional Arts program within the NEA was an attempt to subvert the need for a third endowment focused on folk and traditional arts. As a result of the NEA's resistance, the AFC does not have grant-making authority. They do fund small fellowships, whose recipients have made valuable contributions to research in the field.

13. Moody-Turner provides an important history of the Hampton Folklore Society, which was established in 1893 at the Hampton Institute, a school for Blacks established by whites in 1868 with an assimilationist mission. Despite this, the Hampton Folklore Society was devoted to the "collection and preservation" of Black folklore (2013, 64) by Black students, alumni, and others. Black intellectuals and educators such as Anna Julia Cooper, W. E. B. DuBois, Paul Lawrence Dunbar, and many others were involved with the Hampton Folklore Society (74). The society was closely

connected with Newell and the AFS as well, as Newell spoke at Hampton meetings and Hampton members spoke at AFS meetings (cf. 79).

14. Published initially in *Current Anthropology* in 1963, the article was revised, including the addition of the "contextual approach," for inclusion in the introduction to his 1972 introductory collection *Folklore and Folklife*.

15. See Myerhoff and Ruby 1982.

16. *Toward New Perspectives* was originally published as a special issue of *JAF* (1971). There were later critiques of the volume for lingering colonial, ethnocentric, and male-centric positions. See Briggs and Shuman 1993.

17. See John Roberts on "folk" as a racialized category (1993, 2000).

18. For more on the Federal Writers Project, see Hirsch 2003; on Benjamin Botkin, see Rodgers and Hirsch 2010. As national folklore editor, Benjamin Botkin also edited and indexed the interviews that became *Born in Slavery: Slave Narratives from the Federal Writers' Project, 1936 to 1938*, "consisting of more than 2,300 first-person accounts of slavery and 500 black-and-white photographs of former slaves . . . collected in the 1930s as part of the Federal Writers' Project (FWP) of the Works Progress Administration, later renamed Work Projects Administration (WPA)." See https://www.loc.gov/collections/slave-narratives-from-the-federal-writers -project-1936-to-1938/about-this-collection, accessed May 7, 2025. These narratives of formerly enslaved people changed the narrative of enslavement in the US, as they "revealed the brutality" of enslavement as well as the cultural life that enslaved peoples were able to create (Broussard 2011, 187).

19. This was also a period when terminal master's programs in folklore that focused on public aspects of folklore work began, including MA programs in American folk culture and history museum studies at Cooperstown, New York, in 1964 and the folk studies MA program at Western Kentucky University in 1972. Cooperstown included training in museum studies along with more standard folklore training; the program closed in 1979. The WKU MA program was long known for training students in public folklore and offered specialities in historic preservation and museum studies along with all areas of folklore; the last MA students finished at WKU in 2024, following the suspension of the program. See Sawin and Zumwalt (2020) for histories of North American folklore studies programs.

20. Charles Camp, interview with authors, October 16, 2019, Baltimore, MD.

21. See the film "US Public Folklore: The Watershed Years" (2008) produced by the Public Programs Section of the American Folklore Society

for an overview of the development of public folklore in those years, and the role of Hawes as well as Archie Green and others. Available at https://www.folkstreams.net/films/united-states-public-folklore-the-watershed-years, accessed May 7, 2025.

22. See, for example, the Eldridge Street Synagogue Festival "Egg Rolls, Egg Creams and Empanadas" bringing together Jewish, Chinese, and Puerto Rican traditions on the Lower East Side of New York, https://www.eldridgestreet.org/eee-festival, accessed May 7, 2025.

23. For detailed accounts, see Green's 1976 report (Green [1976] 1988, 269–79); Gross Bressler 1995; and Bulger 2003.

24. For more on Green, see Burns 2011.

25. Gross Bressler writes, "The beginning of the legislative history can be traced to 1968, when Jim Hightower arrived in Washington to work as a legislative aide to Senator Ralph Yarborough, a powerful Democrat from Texas" who was so enamored by the Festival of American Folklife that he suggested they create a foundation (1995, 38–39). Senator Yarborough lost reelection after the first attempt, and Hightower moved on to other things, but he did provide advice to Green, who took over at the point of the second attempt (see Gross Bressler 1995, 79).

26. Bill Ivey, interview with authors, October 17, 2018, Buffalo, NY.

27. Archie Green describes Janet Anderson as knowing "from the beginning the strengths and weaknesses of the various players and how to move the whole thing" (Gross Bressler 1995, 15) Anderson subsequently sat for many years on the board of trustees of the AFC (see chap. 4) and married Roger Abrahams, who had also worked on the effort.

28. At the House hearing, Lucien Nedzi (D. Michigan) presided, and representatives present included Frank Thompson (D. New Jersey), John Brademus (D. Indiana), Tom Gettys (D. South Carolina), and Bill Frenzel (R. Minnesota).

29. Gross Bressler describes these panels in detail in chapter 6 (1995, 136–86).

30. *American Folklife Preservation Act: Hearings on H.R. 8770, Before Subcommittee on Library and Memorials, Second Session*, 93rd Cong. (May 9–10, 1974), 82–85.

31. Yarborough was an active supporter of civil rights and a leader of the progressive wing of the Democratic Party.

32. "Board of Trustees," The American Folklife Center, Library of Congress, accessed May 7, 2025, https://web.archive.org/web/2023063001 4249/https://www.loc.gov/folklife/board/index.html.

33. "Board of Trustees."

34. See "VHP History and Timeline," Library of Congress, accessed May 7, 2025, https://web.archive.org/web/20230530021900/https://www .loc.gov/programs/veterans-history-project/about-this-program /vhp-history-timeline/; "About This Collection," Civil Rights History Project, Library of Congress, accessed May 7, 2025, https://web.archive.org /web/20250413223255/https://www.loc.gov/collections/civil-rights-history -project/about-this-collection/; and "The StoryCorps Archive," accessed May 7, 2025, https://archive.storycorps.org/.

35. Noyes notes, if we are proud of anything (as folklorists) "it is of being near to the ground" (2008, 37).

36. Margaret Mills reminds us that this "'vernacularization' is sometimes thought of pejoratively as 'vulgarization'" (2016, 56).

37. Letter from Dell Hymes to Robert Byington, August 11, 1972. American Folklore Society records, 1890–2011. (COLL MSS 206). Utah State University. Special Collections and Archives Department.

38. See, for example, Kamenetsky's "Folklore as a Political Tool in Nazi Germany" (1972) or Ortiz's "The Uses of Folklore by the Franco Regime" (1999).

39. Report of the Applied Folklore Committee to the Review Committee, August 1, 1972. American Folklore Society records, 1890–2011. (COLL MSS 206). Utah State University. Special Collections and Archives Department.

40. Best known in this regard is Ruth Benedict's *The Chrysanthemum and the Sword: Patterns of Japanese Culture,* published in 1946 and compiled for the office of war information. The book was an example of distance ethnography, created from literature, popular and traditional culture, and interviews without ever going to the location.

41. Also included were Gordon Armbruster, G. Gordon Brown, Elizabeth Colson, John de Young, John Embree, David H. French, Asael T. Hansen, E. Adamson Hoebel, Solon T. Kimball, Marvin K. Opler, Morris E. Opler, John Provinse, Rachel R. Sady, Elmer R. Smith, Laura Thompson.

42. The push for a science of folklore is also a thread that runs through the disciplinary history, though it is not a thread we will pick up here in detail. For a recent example, see Oring 2019.

43. In 1970, Williams sent Dorson a copy of an earlier version of this paper, which he was preparing to read at an upcoming meeting of the American Historical Society, and invited him to attend and publicly comment on his paper. Edited versions of both Williams's paper and Dorson's response were later published in the *Journal of the Folklore Institute,* which was published at Dorson's home university, Indiana University (Dorson 1975). Also

see Baron [1992] 2007 on public folklore and the professionalization of the field of folklore.

44. See the "AFS Statement on Ethics: Principles of Professional Responsibility," accessed May 7, 2025, https://americanfolkloresociety.org/our-work/position-statement-ethics.

45. For more on William Wells Newell, see Bell 1973, 1979.

46. This is beautifully illustrated by Patrick B. Mullen's 2008 book, *The Man Who Adores the Negro*, which explores how folklorists such as John Lomax, Newbell Niles Puckett, Alan Lomax, and Roger Abrahams helped to create the popular concept of African Americans as "folk."

47. Transcription of Point Park third session discussion, May 22, 1971. Transcribed from digitized reel-to-reel recordings of the Point Park sessions in the Lynwood Montell collection in the Manuscripts & Folklife Archives, Special Collections Library, Western Kentucky University.

48. Handwritten notes titled "Comments on Tenn-Tom rec'd since letter mailed out." Tennessee-Tombigbee Waterway Folklife Project collection (AFC 1985/035), Archive of Folk Culture, American Folklife Center, Library of Congress, Washington, DC.

49. Recording of the public portion of the February 1979 Meeting of the American Folklife Center Board of Trustees, transcribed by the authors. Tennessee Waterway Folklife Project collection (AFC 1983/002), Archive of Folk Culture, American Folklife Center, Library of Congress, Washington, DC.

50. *A Bill to Designate the Square Dance as the National Folk Dance of the United States: Hearings on H.R. 1706, Before the Subcommittee on Census and Population, Committee on the Post Office and Civil Service*, 98th Cong. (1984). Retrieved from Square Dance Legislation collection (AFC 1984/024), Archive of Folk Culture, American Folklife Center, Library of Congress, Washington, DC.

51. Moody cites the source as, Melvin Wade, "The Intellectual and Historical Origins of Folklore Scholarship By Black Americans: A Study of the Response to the Propaganda of Racial Superiority at Hampton (Virginia) Institute 1893–1939," Hampton University Archives, unpublished manuscript, June 14, 1982.

52. AFS Annual Meeting: Business Meeting Minutes, November 13, 1971. American Folklore Society records, 1890–2011. (COLL MSS 206). Utah State University. Special Collections and Archives Department.

53. Marilyn White, interview with authors, March 16, 2023. Zoom.

54. It is unclear whether Henderson, a literary scholar, was involved in folklore studies or whether his involvement was prompted by someone else at Howard University.

55. Marilyn White, interview with authors, March 16, 2023. Zoom.

56. Cf. Cantú and Nájera-Ramírez (2002b) for an overview of contributions by *las folkloristsas*.

"SOME OF MY BEST FRIENDS ARE APPLIED FOLKLORISTS"

Disciplinary Identity and the Point Park Debates

IN 1971, FOLKLORISTS HELD A conference at Point Park College in Pittsburgh in part to debate the creation of an Applied Folklore Center. Expected initially by the organizers to be fairly uncontroversial, the discussion flared, growing in intensity until anger took over and norms of collegiality were cast aside. Robert (Bob) Byington, in his own inimitable way, characterized those debates in his applied folklore entry to the volume *Time & Temperature* by recalling a raucous discussion in which Richard Dorson called Don Américo Paredes a professional Chicano, Archie Green called Richard (Dick) Dorson a liar, and Byrd Granger got so incensed that she fell off the stage (1989, 77). Dick Sweterlitsch, editor of a collection of some of the papers from the conference in *Folklore Forum*, also noted the surprising strength of the debate. He wrote, "The general plan of the conference suggested that there is little opposition to applied folklore. . . . Yet, a charged discussion on the propriety of applied folklore occurred" (1971, 15).

The drama of the angry quips cited by Byington, while perhaps amusing all these years later in their outrageousness, should not, however, call our attention away from the very real expression of concerns about our individual and collective disciplinary identities debated in Point Park regarding the challenges presented by applied work, activism, advocacy, and social engagement. Discussions were quite polarized, as they addressed big issues such as the relationship between scholarly objectivity and advocacy, the threat of political activism to the reputation of the discipline, the role of reciprocity and accountability in the work of folklorists, and the goal and potential utility of our engagements. Sifting through the concerns of our colleagues back in 1971, it is clear that several main themes pervaded the Point Park discussions: definitions of applied folklore, the values of our field and the potential for applied projects to go bad, our disciplinary place in the academy, and the role politics should play in folklore. The proposal for an Applied Folklore Center ultimately failed but not before it became the impetus for important discussions about the responsibility of folklorists to the communities in which we work. This chapter will explore those concerns as articulated around the Applied Folklore Center discussions, consider Point Park's role in folklore's identity construction, and contrast the failure of the Applied Folklore Center initiative with the success of the American Folklife Preservation Act.

While some of the Point Park history is generally known and parts of the conference were published in *Folklore Forum* (1971) and discussed in a special issue of the *Journal of Folklore Research* (*JFR*), dedicated to "Point Park Revisited" (1998), on the twenty-fifth anniversary of the conference, there has not been an effort to really explore what happened at Point Park or with the Committee on Applied Folklore[1] of the American Folklore Society (AFS) or to really penetrate the core of the concerns about applied folklore. Here, we begin with a chronological accounting of what happened in Point Park and with the applied folklore efforts of the time, and then we continue by pulling on threads of the discussion, isolating the various concerns of the applied folklore debates as they took place both at the conference and in related documentation dedicated to the topic. As is the case throughout this volume, we focus on the debates themselves, giving primacy to the voices of those who engaged in those discussions.

This chapter is based on recordings[2] of the Point Park debates that we were able to locate, digitize, and transcribe combined with numerous never-before-published letters, votes, questionnaires, and reports concerning the Applied Folklore Center held in the AFS archives at Utah State University, as well as interviews with some of the main participants in the debates. The Applied Folklore Committee included Richard (Dick) Bauman, Henry Glassie, Rayna Green, Patrick Mullen, Kenneth (Kenny) Goldstein, David Hufford, and Harry Oster and was initially chaired by Dick Bauman and then Bob Byington. The ad hoc committee commissioned to explore membership responses to the proposal included Richard Dorson, Robert (Bob) Georges, Dell Hymes, and the president of AFS at the time of the Point Park debates, D. K. Wilgus.

THE CONTEXT FOR POINT PARK

In 1969, Kenneth (Kenny) Goldstein, then secretary-treasurer of AFS, created a standing committee on the topic of applied folklore, modeled in large part on applied anthropology and applied linguistics. The committee, chaired by Richard Bauman, held lengthy discussions about definitions of applied work, ultimately agreeing to define applied folklore as "the utilization of the theoretical concepts, factual knowledge, and research methodologies of folklorists in activities or programs meant to ameliorate contemporary social, economic, and technological problems."[3] The definition was an outgrowth of a characterization of applied anthropology coined by George Foster: "When anthropologists utilize their theoretical concepts, factual knowledge, and research methodologies in programs meant to ameliorate contemporary social, economic, and technological problems, they are engaging in applied anthropology" (1969, vii).

On the suggestion of the committee, in May 1971[4] the Middle Atlantic Conference on Folk Culture together with AFS held a conference at Point Park College in Pittsburgh focused entirely on the topic of applied folklore. According to Byington, "All folklorists known to be interested in applied folklore had been invited to the conference," and "the letter of invitation contained the definition of applied folklore upon which the Committee had finally agreed" (1989, 78). The conference included extensive consideration of the definition of applied folklore, its implications for the field, and a proposal for the establishment of an Applied Folklore Center. Applied folklore was originally conceived of as an instrument for social reform; proponents asserted the role folklore could play in medicine, historic preservation, law, drug abuse, and numerous other areas. Papers presented at the conference included some topics oriented toward social reform as well as many others that appeared to be regular folklore fare, such as updates on plans for the forthcoming bicentennial[5] (Sweterlitsch 1971, 17).

Sweterlitsch describes the papers by saying, "The majority of the papers clearly showed what practical applications folklore has, and that it is not impossible to apply folkloric material in solving problems." Applications of folklore illustrated by the papers included, among others, the durability of folk architecture and its potential lessons for professional builders and architects, applications of folklore to modern medicine, the use of folklore to break down social barriers, historic preservation and the role folklore could play in creating and changing zoning ordinances, and folklore's potential in teacher education.

The third session, chaired by Richard Bauman, involved a panel of participants including Kenny Goldstein, Roger Abrahams, Ray Browne, and Richard Dorson. Bauman began with remarks that led to his proposal for the creation of an Applied Folklore Center. In his remarks, he anticipated some potential objections to the idea. He noted, "It may be that we are being forced to realize that society can no longer afford the luxury of 'pure' disinterested scholarship without reference to its practical applications; it may also be that we are coming to recognize that theory and method—the central concerns of the scholarly folklorist—may be advanced as well by applied folklore, insofar as the latter affords opportunities to test methods and hypotheses and draws attention to new problems for investigation; it may be that it is finally penetrating our consciousness that even to study folklore is to change things" (Bauman 1971, 2). Bauman referenced the spin-off of the Society for Applied Anthropology from the American Anthropological Association, a separation that, he noted, "might seem to reaffirm and validate the essential separateness of applied and 'pure' anthropology" (3). The proposal of setting up a center suggested both separation and connection, a way of turning toward the applied and institutionalizing an extension in the range of what folklorists do while rejecting the separation model.

In an interview with us, Bauman recalled the choice of creating a center:

> Well . . . this is edging toward the period when some of that explosive growth of the mid to late '60s was going on. There was still a kind of impulse toward institutionalization of various things. R1 universities were setting up centers for this, and programs in that. And new departments in some other thing, and it seemed that one of the best ways of solidifying an enterprise whatever it was, intellectual or research or otherwise, was to institutionalize it. So, alright, let's set up a Center. And that would become a focus for clearinghouse activities, publication, the organization of sessions, and things of that kind. That's what motivated the proposal.[6]

Bauman's proposal suggested five activities that the center could undertake, serving as an agency of AFS and administered by committee. Finances for the endeavor would be underwritten by AFS combined with other institutional support from a college or university to provide office space and clerical assistance (possibly from Point Park) along with the potential for subscription or dues for membership in the center helping to defray costs. The activities to be undertaken by the center included the establishment of a central registry of resources and personnel in applied folklore, the publication of materials for the use of folklorists and their clients, the publication of a newsletter, the development and coordination of liaisons with allied disciplines, and the coordination of applied folklore regular sessions at the AFS Annual Meeting (Bauman 1971, 3–4).

Bauman noted that his proposal followed on a similar proposal suggested by Benjamin Botkin ten years earlier. He indicated that he had not known about Botkin's proposal before he began his own. Nevertheless, in his introductory comments, he acknowledged Botkin's effort, indicating that it was "apparently ahead of its time" (Bauman 1971, 1). Botkin was an early devotee of applied folklore, publishing an article in 1953 entitled "Applied Folklore: Creating Understanding through Folklore." Jerrold Hirsch notes that by 1971, Botkin had been living "the life of an 'impure' 'interdisciplinary' and 'applied' folklorist for over forty years" (1998, 279) and that as early as 1938, Botkin wrote "folklore is not for folklorists alone" (288). According to Bruce Jackson, Botkin traced his first annunciation of his "applied folklore concept" to 1939, which he characterized as "folklore for understanding and creating understanding" (Jackson 1976, 3).

Botkin's (1961) proposal, published in *New York Folklore Quarterly* in 1961, was similar to the activities outlined for an Applied Folklore Center. His plan included a repository for related materials; a clearinghouse and service bureau for the collection, documentation, preservation, and dissemination of materials; and an information center for the development and utilization of materials (153). His focus was on the importance of not only collection and analysis but also utilization,[7]

Figure 2.1 Benjamin Botkin, at the American Folklore Society Annual Meeting in Los Angels in 1970. Author of the first proposal for an Applied Folklore Center published in *New York Folklore Quarterly* in 1961. Photo by Michael Owen Jones, courtesy of the American Folklore Society Collection, Utah State University Special Collections & Archives.

diversity, and human relationships. He explained the genesis of the idea.

> The idea germinated in a conversation between Yiddish folk singer and folk song authority Ruth Rubin, Rachael Davis Dubois, founder and for twenty years director of the Workshop for Cultural democracy, and myself. Like most conversations of the kind (and I have been through more of them than I care to remember), this initial session grew out of our mingled frustration and inspiration. We were frustrated by the lack of communication and coordination among the various disciplines and fields concerned with intercultural and human relations—sociology, psychology, education, community, Church, and foreign-language organizations, communications, the arts, labor, creative maturing and folklore. . . .
>
> As folklorists, Ruth Rubin and I were particularly frustrated by the gap (which seems to be widening rather than narrowing)

between collection and utilization, as the accumulation of folklore data continues to outstrip the application. (Botkin 1961, 151)

Botkin included a list of more specific activities including (among others) the development and improvement of techniques for the interpretation and presentation of folklore in schools, settlement houses, community centers, adult education programs, clubs, and camps; the training of community leaders; supplying public libraries and schools of social work with materials and sources; guiding social workers in the use of folklore materials in group work; and in-service courses in folklore for teachers.

Botkin was more specific than Bauman in articulating the political aspirations behind the effort. He addressed the importance of cultural understanding through a lens of encouraging tolerance and mutual respect and condemned, as he so often did, the problematic forces of conformity. He wrote of the center's aims,

> Our aim is not to eliminate or play down group differences but to enable groups to become better acquainted with one another's differences, to develop a positive, creative attitude toward these differences, and to exchange cultural gifts so that all may enjoy them. The rediscovery of our group heritages for mutual appreciation and acceptance is threatened not only by group conflict but also by the growing pressure toward standardization and conformity. Conformity is a detriment to society in so far as it results in the loss of cultural diversity. Under the impact of the dominant American culture recessive or minority groups, especially their young people, lose not only their cultural identity but also their incentive to preserve it. To combat both cultural conflict and cultural uniformity we propose to establish an applied folklore center. (Botkin 1961, 152)

Botkin's call for an Applied Folklore Center was clearly put forward with ambitions of using folklore to make a difference in larger political ways and with international implications. Bauman's proposal was not as obviously political as Botkin's, but it nevertheless garnered intense response. Botkin's call and Bauman's contrast the left-wing popular front of the '30s with the 1970s generation of folklorists and their call for a pluralistic and egalitarian view of American culture.[8] Botkin's proposal never came to fruition,[9] and neither did Bauman's Point Park[10] proposal for an Applied Folklore Center. But the Point Park initiative brought AFS debates to a whole new level. Byington wrote of the debates, "The polarization which had occurred in Pittsburgh now spread to the AFS, forming roughly along Penn-Texas/Indiana-UCLA axes, and the ensuing dialogue was as 'lively' as any that had occurred in living memory" (1989, 78).

BEYOND POINT PARK

While the debates about applied folklore were heated in the final sessions at Point Park, they continued months later. On November 13, 1971, at the meeting of AFS in Washington, DC, the "Proposal for the establishment of a Center of Applied Folklore" was presented at the AFS Business Meeting, where the proposal was eventually tabled and a detailed exposition of both the committee's conception of applied folklore and the idea for a center to facilitate activities in applied folklore were requested. Prior to the decision to table the proposal, several people argued against AFS's involvement with applied folklore.

Richard Dorson responded to the motion to approve the center at the AFS Business Meeting by clearly stating his opposition. He said, "Well, some of you know that we had a discussion along these lines at Pittsburgh in the Spring, on the whole concept of applied folklore. Most of the people there were in favor of it. A couple were negative, principally Dan Ben-Amos and myself. And I would be ready to speak quite strongly against this motion. . . . I would ask that we not commit ourselves to this motion until there has been quite thorough discussion of the membership and they have had a chance to think about it."[11] Dorson was followed by Thelma James (who, we should remember, was an early user of the term *applied* and chair of the AFS Utilization Committee), who responded,

> Mr. Chairman, in the history of this Society when Dick Dorson and I agree so wholeheartedly it should be noted in the minutes, I think. I was not at Pittsburgh; I will support Dick wholeheartedly in making a motion that this be tabled, a committee appointed. I belong to two other organizations at the moment; I'm leaving the board of each because perfectly innocent beginnings of this kind have now become political organizations. I am distrustful of the phrase, Mr. Chairman, "to ameliorate." This leaves a very wide door through which many queer animals may come and go. This, I think, is a clear statement of my concern that we have been hitherto not an activist Society and I have watched the struggle in MLA, and this was not the organization I was referring to, they are local organizations[12].

It appears James, who had been clearly in favor of the term *applied* and the concept of utilization years earlier, was now not in favor of the political potential of applied work.

The motion to table the proposal was seconded by Frank Hoffman, and since a motion to table is nondebatable, the motion moved to a vote. Forty-five attendees voted to table the proposal; thirty-eight were opposed. The motion to table carried. Following the vote, John West requested that a session at the following AFS meeting be devoted to applied folklore to provide more background on the topic.[13]

Shortly after the DC meeting, AFS president D. K. Wilgus created an ad hoc Review Committee on Applied Folklore, consisting of Richard Dorson, Robert Georges, and Dell Hymes. The Review Committee, as created, was mandated to "examine and criticize" the report submitted by the Applied Folklore Committee "and submit a report to both the executive board and members of the applied folklore committee."[14] The Review Committee was understood by the Applied Folklore Committee, based on their comments and visible votes at the AFS Business

Meeting, as unsupportive of the initiative. Further, D. K. Wilgus announced the appointment of the Review Committee to the original Applied Folklore Committee with a statement of his own misgivings on the center proposal. In a letter to Byington, Bauman, Glassie, Green, and Oster (of the Applied Folklore Committee) and Hymes, Dorson, and Georges (of the Review Committee) Wilgus wrote,

> I am on one hand opposed as anyone else to the Society's taking any sort of political stance, or even engaging in any activity which would give that impression. I am on the other hand becoming even more deeply aware of the moral debt we owe to "the folk"—specifically our informants. As human beings we have an obligation, but as folklorists we have a special imperative to return at least something to those groups and members of those groups whom we have studied and whose lore has enabled us to build our works and thereby our reputations and our academic positions. To take a blatant example, no one of us would advocate the continuation of chain-gang labor because of the rugged beauty of the songs produced. Should we be content to study and analyze the material produced, or should we also use this material and this analysis to eliminate conditions which most of us find abhorrent?[15]

Wilgus continued, "To take another tack, I find a problem in the definition of 'applied folklore' set forth by the Applied Folklore Committee. I do not question the fact that 'applied folklore' exists. Rather I note that 'applied folklore' is a continuing process practiced by many persons, groups, and agencies, but seldom by folklorists. In other words, 'applied folklore' is not always used to 'ameliorate contemporary social, economic, and technological problems'; it may be, and has been, used to perpetuate (what to me are) injustices in our society."[16]

Letters from each member of the Review Committee prior to the release of their report highlight their individual issues with the proposal. The longest, most detailed of the letters was from Robert Georges. Most of Georges's comments were focused on details of how the center would be set up, how it would function, and how its activities might differ from the work of AFS in general. As the letter moved to conclusion, he summarized his objections.

> In my overall judgement, then, the report of the Committee on Applied Folklore does <u>not</u> present a very convincing case for the establishment of a Center. Lacking are specific objectives, functions, details of actual organization, a scheme of the ways in which responsibilities are to be delegated, a discussion of the ways in which the Center would complement and supplement what the Society is already doing through its multiple publications and functions, and—last—and most importantly—a set of specific criteria for defining what is meant by "applied folklore" and for distinguishing "applied folkloristic research/work" from what the committee members apparently conceive to be "non-applied folkloristic research/work."[17]

Georges avoided the political issues brought up by Wilgus, focusing for the most part on infrastructure concerns. Dell Hymes focused on the contrast between applied and other folklorists but concluded with his concerns about whose needs would be served by applied work. He wrote in his individual response, prior to the committee report,

> The principal thought that occurs to me now is that the problems confronting folklore in this regard are much the same as those facing anthropologists and linguists. Insofar as the issue of responsibility to those from whom one obtains information is inevitably looming larger and larger, some aspects of applied folklore merge with the general practice of folklore research.
>
> If this is so, then it seems to me that applied is not the happiest term or concept (as you appear to sense). Perhaps we are faced with the general question of the use of folklore material—a question that comprises our own habitual uses of it in publication and teaching as well as uses of it by governments, agencies, etc. not by any means to exclude use of it by communities themselves. I face this question directly now, as do others whose work is with American Indian communities.[18]

Hymes continued,

> So while I quite agree with the stress on the misuses already
> being made of folklore (and such a Center might well monitor
> those), I should like to see more stress on responsibilities to
> those communities and persons of whom the material is the
> folklore. One of the weaknesses of the conception of "applied" is
> that it suggests application by established agencies, authorities,
> governments, etc. to communities, with the professional scholar
> serving the purpose of those in power, but not necessarily the
> needs of those in the communities. . . . "Applied" is unfortunately
> associated with an unconsciously rather "colonial" relationship
> between scholar and community, whatever the goodwill and
> understanding actually present.[19]

Richard Dorson's response to the report was shorter than the
others and was submitted last. Having indicated his reservations
vocally at the conference, Dorson was brief in his letter. His primary concern expressed in the letter was the competing need for
funding for students and fieldwork, but as was the case with his
conference comments, his underlying concern was folklorists
straying outside the academy.

> The crux of the matter is, what will your center do? Bob Georges
> has gone into detail on the areas of ambiguity in your report on
> this score. It looks to me as if you will be operating some kind of
> goodwill service station for folklorists and fakelorists. What we
> desperately need in this country is support for fieldwork. Our IU
> students run off to Canada every summer because the National
> Museum of Man has grants for them—and jobs too, although
> the pressure is now on the museum to hire only Canadian
> citizens. We also urgently need to increase academic offerings in
> folklore. These are our two great needs. The Center for Applied
> Folklore will, as far as I can see, provide a clearing house for
> nothing very meaningful. You have no central resource of a
> major archives or literary collection to draw upon, and no plans
> for such a resource other than to find out what so-and-so may be
> doing.[20]

On March 27, 1972, Bob Byington wrote a letter to Kenny Goldstein candidly describing his own feelings on the reactions to the proposal and to the establishment of the Review Committee. He began,

> Here is a rough draft of a letter cum questionnaire from our committee to the AFS membership, purpose of which is to reduce anxieties, allay fears, and jus' generally inform people to such an extent that they won't turn down our proposal for a Center of Applied Folklore next time around as well as elicit information from them that may be helpful when we are writing the report that has to be submitted to that hostile ol' Review Committee.
>
> You will note in this new definition-apologia-counterattack... the elimination of such words as "amelioration" and "change," not because they ain't appropriate but because they scare people; but I don't want to misrepresent what we are about neither, so if you think I have, say so.[21]

Subsequently the Applied Folklore Committee drew up a letter to the AFS membership along with a brief questionnaire eliciting the views of the membership. Of the 609 mailed questionnaires, 74 were returned, with 62 expressing approval of applied folklore and a center and 12 expressing opposition to one or both.[22] The Applied Folklore Committee's efforts nevertheless failed in part due to lack of funds, no clear venue for the center, and no clear motivated champion, but not before it became the impetus for important discussions and debates about the responsibility of folklorists to the communities in which we live and work.

Bauman suggested in his conversation with us that much of the pushback on applied folklore was generational. He said, "Even at that, at that meeting, when ... [Kenny] sort of announced the formation of this, there were mutterings around you know, 'there's very much a generational divide.' The generation of scholars who were, you know, 'You, want to be politically engaged, you take off your scholarly hat you put on your activist hat, but your scholarship and your work in the world need to be kept separate, and you need to be objective.'"[23] Bauman noted that those opposed were vocal about their objections; among the most vocal were Richard Dorson, Alan Dundes, D. K. Wilgus, and Horace Beck. In terms of generational responses, Bob Byington reported that student respondents were unanimously in favor of the center.[24] And in a letter to D. K. Wilgus, Archie Green[25] noted, "I am aware that a number of people in the society are hostile to Dick's [Bauman] committee. I do hope that this hostility does not turn off the many marvelous young people who are emerging. In this connection the recent Pittsburgh [Point Park] meeting was splendid . . . a model for clarity and constructive interaction."[26]

Both Botkin's and Bauman's center proposals raised the specter of the socially and politically engaged and activist folklorist, but at Point Park, discussions became quite polarized as they addressed big issues about who we are and who we wish to be. The discussions were so heated that on April 10, 1972, in the Applied Folklore Committee letter to the membership, the committee noted that "applied folklore" had been "expounded, discussed and debated with such resulting emotionalism, confusion, polarity and schismatic tension that its proponents (who look[ed] upon it as wholly benign) can only conclude that Applied Folklore has been misnamed, ill-defined or inadequately explained to such an extent that resistance and heat have been generated where only conductivity and light had been expected."[27]

Returning to the Point Park debates as well as comments made during the AFS meeting helps to isolate the crux of the disputes and provides insight into contemporaneous attitudes toward politics, representation, and attitudes concerning the responsibility of folklorists. While much of the dispute is hidden behind differences in definitions of applied folklore, the real debates focus on the values of our field, folklore's place in the academy, and the role politics should play in folklore. As Barbara Kirshenblatt-Gimblett has argued, the definitional dichotomy between pure and applied folklore obscured the field's basic "ideology, national political interests, and economic concerns" (1988, 142). The definitional debates certainly caused a lot of "noise" in Point Park and later at AFS, but it is clear that disputes over definition were intricately tied to ideology.

"RESISTANCE AND HEAT": DEFINING APPLIED FOLKLORE

The term *applied* had been used by folklorists, although not frequently, for some time before Point Park, with various definitions and connotations. The definition of the term ranged from public entertainment to political intervention or, as Botkin used it, "utilization" (Hirsch 1998, 289). It is clear, however, that uses of the associated terms did not have the same meanings for everyone. In 1947, Thelma James published a report of an AFS Committee on the "Utilization of Folklore," which she defined as "the uses to which folklore materials are put" (1947, 173). James's committee report, however, was oriented toward the publication of bibliographies on the academic fields that use folklore and did not discuss the type of political or advocacy meanings more clearly associated with Botkin's use.[28] Thelma James again, in 1948, used entertainment, education-based, and more community-centered notions when writing, "In America today, there are many ways of earning a living from 'applied' folklore: as professional and semiprofessional entertainers in song, music, dance, and storytelling; as craftsmen in carving, weaving, metal working, ceramics, and cookery; as writers, play producers, radio and film script writers, artists, and musicians using folk materials; as librarians, teachers, collectors, museum directors, archivists; as scholars and pseudo scholars producing monographs, anthologies, and other books of varying value" (1948, 311). This time, James covered more ground, but her use of the term still avoided advocacy and political connotations, and in fact James saw parallels between folklore use by fascists and the use of folklore by contemporary activists (James 1948, 311). Her questions related to utilization for the most part focused on sources and authenticity (James 1947, 173). For Bauman, the definition fell in line with that used by applied linguists and anthropologists, suggesting problem-solving and representation of community interests. For Byington, advocacy was the key.

Much of the original pushback on the Applied Folklore Center proposal concerned definitions of *applied*. Definitions pointed to connotations, both positive and negative, that could include or exclude, on one hand, the skillful builders of vernacular housing or, on the other hand, Nazism and popularizers. Byington wrote that "the model the founders of [the] applied folklore [committee] had in mind was, of course, applied anthropology; and, like the applied anthropologists, they spent a great deal of their early energy on definition, which process was not satisfactorily completed until the spring of 1971" (1989, 77). For some, as Bob Byington joked, *applied* meant "simply letting someone else use your archive."[29] For others, it conjured up etic pairing of the term *folklore* with the word *applied*, resulting in discussion of the way folklore was "applied" to justify political ideologies such as Nazism. David Hufford noted the connection of applied folklore to endeavors that he argued damaged the respectability of the term—what he referred to as "silly and misguided attempts to apply so called folklore," which he characterized by describing largely the work of enthusiasts.[30] Hufford's comments were not intended to degrade applied endeavors but rather to distinguish between the applications of the knowledge and skills of the discipline versus the uses of popular notions of folklore engaged in by those lacking training. Definitional discussions typically focused on concerns about dividing the field up into applied and not applied, useful and not useful, pure and not so pure.

As the Applied Folklore Committee wrote, "The term applied itself may be a misnomer to the extent that it suggests a distinction between applied folklore and other kinds of folklore analogous to the common misconception of that between 'pure' and 'applied' science."[31] Dell Hymes wrote, "I am unhappy about the dichotomy that the history of the term applied implies, between kinds of folklore and kinds of folklorists. While many of us would not think of ourselves as applied, most of us, I would think, must recognize our involvement with materials having to do with the uses of folklore."[32] Later that year, in their rejoinder to the Review Committee, Byington's group wrote, "We have been cognizant for some time of the power to aggravate that the term applied folklore (however it is defined) seems to have, and we agree with our critics that another term might be preferable. But what should that term be? 'Used folklore' will hardly do and Applied folklore (whatever the cluster of negative images it evokes) has at least the advantage of a comparable and well known precedent in linguistics and the sciences."[33] Nevertheless, as Byington indicated to Kenny Goldstein in that same letter concerning the "hostile" Review Committee, the Applied Folklore Committee had perceived the desirability of modifying its definition in the interest of receiving AFS approval.[34] According to Byington, writing in retrospect, "the hard advocacy implicit in the original definition was softened—in fact, eliminated. Applied folklore became 'an expansion of the folklorists' customary activities (research, fieldwork, publication and teaching), particularly teaching, into areas beyond the walls of the academy'" (1989, 78). The change in definition combined with a forced denial of the charge that the committee had a political platform and were "dissidents" or "revolutionaries" led Byington to assert, "Thus, the heart of the original idea stopped beating; and 'applied folklore' became sufficiently broad a category to include what appears to be an almost limitless range of possibilities" (79). The new definition set aside the political agenda central to the original definition, calmed the fears of those who felt it suggested a "not useful" folklore in contrast with the suggested "usefulness" of applied work, and broadened the mandate to one that ultimately would fit well with the work of the emerging field of public folklore. But for Byington, the political advocacy element, which he saw as the heart of the concept, was lost.

IVORY TOWERS, POPULARIZERS, QUALITY,
AND THE MERITS OF APPLIED WORK

Discussions at Point Park, the AFS Business Meeting, and the AFS Annual Meeting and in letters and reports demonstrated that conversations concerning definition invariably drifted to discussions of quality, questioning the merits of work done under the mantle of *applied*. Richard Dorson had made his feelings about popularization known repeatedly over the years, turning his wrath for such issues most strongly on Ben Botkin. In "A Theory for American Folklore," Dorson wrote,

> The one group in the United States who profess most concern
> with American traditions have least interest in its study ... the
> popularizers, whose organ is the *New York Folklore Quarterly* ...
> [and] whose leading figure is Benjamin A. Botkin, the treasury
> manufacturer.... Folklore did not become big business until the
> 1940s, when Botkin began issuing his treasuries, Alan Lomax
> took to the air, and Burl Ives hit the nightclubs. The cavernous
> maw of the mass media gobbled up endless chunks of folksiness
> and a new rationale appeared to the folklorist: his mission is
> to polish up, overhaul, rearrange and distribute folklore to the
> American people. (Dorson 1959, 202)

In his comments at Point Park, Dorson once again turned to his concerns about popularization, fakelore, and the danger to the field if scholars strayed beyond the academy. He spoke with particular disdain about scholars as "social reformers."

> Now any scholar can have his separate public and civic role, and if
> he wants to be an activist, that's one role, that's fine, but if he's gonna
> mix these two, I think that he's gonna be the lesser scholar, and if
> that makes one out to be an ivory-tower, detached scholar, well so
> be it. Alan [Dundes] used the phrase that "social scientists will cease

to be cool witnesses of human events," which is a moving phrase. None of us want to be cool, detached, objective witnesses of human events, but I think that we will accomplish more in our role as folklore scholars observing the rules of our game than attempting to be social reformers at the same time.[35]

Numerous participants in Point Park disagreed with the notion that participating in social reform was somehow antithetical to quality scholarship. Archie Green responded to a swipe from Dorson at Américo Paredes in which Dorson said, "I see that Américo Paredes has stopped being a folklore scholar; he's become a professional Chicano." Green responded, "When Paredes writes a book or writes an article, he's not writing a tract, and he writes a scholarly book or he does not, but that's a judgment that, you know, you all make as you read his books. He doesn't become unscholarly; he doesn't move away from his discipline because he chooses at a particular time in his life to become involved in a struggle that is important to him."[36]

Bruce Jackson wrote of Dorson's attitudes toward popularization and politics, "Dorson's mission was to make the discipline of folklore legitimate and honorable in the university. He attacked anything and anyone he thought stood in the way of that goal" (1986, 24). For Dorson, the rise of folklore as a discipline relied on drawing sharp contrasts between folklore and what he called "fakelore" (Baron [1992] 2007). Numerous scholars have noted that Dorson's dismissive attitude toward Paredes, Botkin, and many others he saw as "reformers," popularizers, or promoters of "fakelore"[37] ignored their demonstrated concern for maintaining the integrity of both folkloric materials and the scholarly standards of the discipline (Baron 1995, 17), and indeed Paredes and others Dorson called popularizers were involved in efforts through AFS to professionalize the discipline (Williams 1975, 224). Robert Baron argued that Botkin's "popular writings incorporated a great variety of sources, utilized within works designed to appeal to mass audiences. . . . Botkin sought to make folklore accessible to a mass public while maintaining personal standards of professional responsibility and accountability" (17). Years later the dichotomy of applied or public folklore and professional scholarly work would be critiqued as false and unnecessary by several scholars including Barbara Kirshenblatt-Gimblett in her article "Mistaken Dichotomies" (1988) and by David Shuldiner in his piece "The Politics of Discourse: An Applied Folklore Perspective," in which he argued that the rigor of applied work suggests a "discourse of cultural praxis that avoids false distinctions" (Shuldiner 1998, 199)

At Point Park, Dorson returned to issues of popularization and fakelore (see Hirsch 1998), referring to the testimonies in the early efforts to establish what became the American Folklife Center (we should remember here that Dorson spoke against the American Folklife Preservation Act in his testimony to Congress). In Point Park, he argued,

> Alan Lomax testified that the festival being held by the Smithsonian Institution on the Mall had brought together the American people in a new, joyous spirit of exhilaration, and that the glassy light in their eyes, which had become torpid through staring at the TV tube, was now being lit up with the new spirit of common humanity. Well, maybe in the festival it's a good thing, and maybe there's nights when people will get together and sing songs that may or may not be folk songs and do dances that may or may not be folk dances, I don't really quite see that it matters as to the purity of the revived so-called folklore; I just don't think that that is the business of the folklore scholar.[38]

While most at Point Park and among the membership did not voice the strong concerns about disciplinary trivialization voiced by Dorson, responses by the committee replied to what they noted was "an assumption that the scholar who ventures outside the Academy runs grave risks."[39]

The Review Committee noted concerns of some of the membership related to misuse of folklore by enthusiasts and others, perhaps telegraphing Dorson's well-known dislike for both politics and popularists, by arguing, "A historical survey of application in Europe reveals that folklore can be misused and become a dangerous tool in the hands of enthusiasts, dictators of the left and right, nostalgic antiquarians, etc."[40] The Applied Folklore Committee replied, "This objection to applied folklore, however well-intentioned appears to overlook the fact that as long as libraries and archives are open to the public, anyone of a mind to 'use' folklore for any purpose whatever is free to do so, and there is nothing the AFS or the professional folklorist can do about it, except possibly, get out there and use it himself to greater advantage."[41]

David Hufford, who has considered himself primarily an applied folklorist for the past fifty years,[42] agreed with Dorson that quality could be an issue, but Hufford's concern was not the work of folklorists; rather, it was the work of folklore enthusiasts. He argued, however, that the sometimes-problematic work of enthusiasts[43] would not be made better by folklorists restricting their work to the academy. He told the conference audience at Point Park, "Applications through revival movements, which have frequently been based on poor and skewed understandings of psychological and social operation and function, and incomplete grasp of the material used, and failure to analyze and define the goals of the movements have helped to further define the term. Coupled with this have been, frequently, silly and misguided attempts to apply so-called folklore to education, through songbooks, over-organized teaching of folk dance, and so forth, and these have damaged the respectability of the term also."[44] It is important to note here, however, that Dorson's response to the Smithsonian Festival and Hufford's response to folk dance teachers and others, while sounding similar, are not based on the same argument. Hufford's comments refer to his concerns about the untrained enthusiast, while Dorson was concerned about the work and scholarly profile of folklore scholars. Hufford continued, "Non-folklorists and amateurs will almost certainly continue to apply folklore, often badly. Refusal of trained scholars to have a try will not prevent misapplications.... If there are ways in which our special and unique training and experience can make it possible for us to contribute something to a solution, it strikes me that we have a moral obligation to do what we can."[45]

The Applied Folklore Committee addressed the quality of work critique in their April 10, 1972, letter to the AFS membership on the Proposal to Create an Applied Folklore Center. They wrote,

> Another objection to applied folklore (hence to a Center or anything else having to do with it, we guess) rests on the contention, vigorously, if vaguely expressed, that applied folklore somehow subverts scholarship in the process of extending its results to those who can use it. This contention is hard to come to grips with since, so far at any rate, it has lacked demonstration and consists mostly of hypothesis and suggestion. As we understand it however, it assumes that the scholar who ventures outside the academy runs grave risks, qua scholar. The stresses of extra-academic activity such that either one's capacities for accurate observation, lucid thought and dispassionate judgment are seriously impaired, or one becomes _so_ involved that he has no time for the research and publication he presumably would have engaged in otherwise. In either case scholarship suffers; _ergo_ scholars interested in applied folklore should receive no official encouragement.
>
> How can we respond to this assertion except to state that _saying_ applied folklore and the interests of scholarship are antithetical does not make them so, and to date we have seen no evidence. On the contrary, our experience indicates that the relationship between scholarship and applied folklore is a healthy reciprocity, a mutual dependence, in which one feeds the other and vice versa. For one thing, the application of scholarship imposes upon the scholar a higher degree of accountability for its soundness than circulation among his peers, and this would tend to enhance, not subvert, its integrity.[46]

Hufford continually argued that applied work could be the very test of folklore theory that the discipline needed. This assertion remained an important part of his understanding of applied folklore throughout his career. In fact, in 1985, he repeated his assertions from Point Park. "I see applied folklore standing in the same relation to basic folklore research as engineering does to the basic natural sciences. Such an application of academic folklore knowledge to practical problems provides an excellent setting for the empirical testing of folklore hypotheses and generates by necessity a rich interdisciplinary approach. Applied folklore, therefore, should be as productive for the academic folklore enterprise as vice versa, and this reciprocal advantage is best realized by folklorists with both basic and applied training and interests" (Hufford 1985, 23). Barbara Kirshenblatt-Gimblett appears to have agreed with Hufford's essential stance when she critiqued folklore programs for trivializing applied work by treating it as a "largely practical, rather than intellectual undertaking" (1988, 141).

The Applied Folklore Committee also underlined the interdependent relationship between applied work and theory in their later report. Agreeing with Hufford, they wrote, "The relationship between the development of theory and method in folklore and their application to the solution of practical problems should be one of mutual interdependence. Applied folklore can only be as good as the theory and method by which it is guided; theory and method may be advanced by applied folklore insofar as the latter affords opportunities to test methods and hypotheses and draws attention to new problems for investigation."[47]

For a field intent on establishing its independence and importance, the maintenance of standards of excellence was bound to rise to the fore, and yet for Hufford and others, taking the field outside of the ivory tower was the only way to test and demonstrate the tenets of the discipline. The center of the quality debate, however, as David Shuldiner articulated so well, was based on the notion that "scholarly rigor and professionalism are the sole province of academic folklore practice" (Shuldiner 1998, 199), the core of a critique that still occasionally surfaces leveled against public folklore. For Henry and Betty Joe Glassie, as articulated in their Point Park paper, pure and applied work can't be separated. They wrote, "One may aspire to a pure research model and have no intentions beyond truth's pursuit, but the research itself and particularly, the open presentation of the results of research, will have consequences beyond scholarship" (Glassie and Glassie 1971, 31).

"THE DEVIL OF BEAUTY": VALUES AND ETHNOCENTRISM

The debates concerning applied folklore necessarily led the participants to discussion of cultural values, exploring concerns about the imposition of scholarly values on communities and community values that might lead to problematic solutions. Hufford concluded his comments in Point Park by noting, "We have the information to quite nicely devastate the ethnocentric assumption that this or that group value is essentially superior to an alternative one embraced with equal fervor by another group." He continued,

> This rather basic position can be—can make many problems magically disappear, especially in a situation of intergroup conflict. Suppose that public education officials pose the problem of how to make people from rural Pennsylvania Dutch country stop talking like people from rural Pennsylvania Dutch country and start speaking like the people on television. This is a matter they currently consider a problem requiring solution. The folklorist working on applications in that region need not accept the problem and desired solution as posed. He might instead suggest some of the positive values of fitting well into a regional group. He could point out that the student who intends to remain in his community and not become like—need not become like people in another community, because one has been arbitrarily selected as normal, and that one does a disservice by making a youngster

consider his speech—his parents' speech patterns to be backward, and setting up rather serious conflicts for him between those he loves and those he's taught to consider respectable. It can be added that sufficient skill to avoid practical communications problems with outsiders will be more easily achieved if approached with sympathy. It would no doubt be difficult to persuade the authorities of this position, but success with this problem would probably be substantially more rewarding than it would be if achieved with the problem as originally stated.[48]

Hufford was careful, however, to note that the matter of values would get complicated if the folklorist felt that community members' choices were not in their own best interests. He continued,

> If the group involved agrees with our hypothetical applied folklorist that such-and-such should or should not happen, the folklorist may have a major role to play in explaining to the government, business, or whoever has authority in the case, what the sound reasons are for the people feeling this way. Unfortunately, however, there are bound to be many times when a folklorist examining these issues comes to the conclusion that people are making decisions that are not in their own best interests. These will obviously be the most dangerous situations. At these points, it would be wrong to go to authorities and attempt to thwart what appears to be a misguided action, whatever the chances might be of success. The only possible solution that I can see is to attempt to persuade and educate the people involved into an understanding of the folklorist's point of view. This should not require that they all pack up and go to school for a couple of years. It appears to me that folklorists have the information and experience necessary to be able to talk to people about their own culture in terms which they can understand. At least if we can't, then no one can. It should certainly be worth the effort.[49]

For Hufford, the issue of values was also a response to Dorson's professed desire for dispassionate research. He said,

> Value judgments have been strictly forbidden to us, for good reason, for a long time now. Objectivity is essential to pure research,

and ethnocentrism is a devastating problem. Explicitly evaluative positions therefore have the [stamp?] of the nineteenth century, romanticism, imperialism, and prejudice. As I have said, this is all essential in the context of pure research, but applied folklore requires evaluation, and any approach to practical problems which attempts to refuse to consider values simply puts the authority for such judgments in the hands of others. I would suggest this is what has generally happened to folklore misapplications in the past. I would further urge that folklore and the social sciences in general have very significant contributions to make to discussions of values in their cultural context.[50]

The Glassies, however, noted that values are tied to exposure, experience, and education. Writing of the urban planner, they argued that the planner defines "areas like Boston's West End as slums when they are not slums but only areas he has been unable to appreciate as artistic and social entities" (Glassie and Glassie 1971, 35).

Hufford's discussion of values at the conference led to debate about whose ethics, whose aesthetics, and whose values hold sway when our disciplinary values compete with those of communities. Warren Roberts asserted during the paper sessions the applied potential of vernacular architecture based on the strong and sound condition of unpainted but brilliantly built vernacular houses in New Harmony, Indiana. He described the condition of the houses, quoting in part from a community member with knowledge of the buildings:

> "Visitors to Harmony reported that many of the frame houses were not painted, and the silver gray of the unpainted wood was outstanding. One of the houses that was razed in 1945"—that is, a hundred and thirty years after it was built—"one of these houses had never had a coat of paint. The weatherboarding and the exposed members of the frame were in such good condition that they were used in rebuilding other houses. The houses were designed so that the rain ran off before the boards were water-soaked and damaged." Well, it seems to me in this area

that contemporary builders, contemporary architects could learn a great deal from studying, observing the functional, practical features of folk architecture. Unfortunately, as many of us who live in houses that have been built in recent times can testify, the builders have ignored many of these old traditional practices, and, as a result, the houses do not last anywhere near as well as those built in New Harmony lasted and can't be expected anywhere near that long.[51]

Roger Abrahams, playing devil's advocate, addressed the perhaps ethnocentric notion that a building lasting was a universal goal.

I think we need to protect ourselves as folklorists. This is in the sense of against a certain kind of [pastoral] ethnocentrism. In other words, what I'm trying to get at is that, in the—in your studies of folk architecture, you make the assumption, as obviously the folk architects did, that it was best to build for lasting. Yet, if one studies other architectural traditions, it becomes clear that this is not necessarily characteristic of all architectures, and that perhaps we're involved in a different aesthetic and a different ethic with the building of houses that are not built to last. I think specifically of West African housing, not of all West African groups, but of many—of many that are built in order to *not* last. The Yoruba have a saying, in fact, that the devil of beauty burns down palaces by which they mean that the decay of buildings and the actual destruction of buildings is just as important as the erection of buildings, that they're not into the monumental tradition, and perhaps we're ignoring something in the building that we ought to be taking into consideration. And perhaps we're ignoring it because of an ethnocentric bias.[52]

The resolution to the problem of ethnocentrism of values for many of the applied oriented scholars was to ideally intervene only in those problems that have themselves been identified by the communities in question and where intervention is shaped through dialogue. Further, Hufford and others asserted that the imposition of outside scholarly values can be avoided by recognizing that emic constructions of any problem targeted for intervention must be given priority. As Sandy Rikoon, William Heffernan, and Judith Heffernan later argued, "Because our subjects are the 'true cultural specialists,' it behooves us to take our cues from how they analyze their own struggles, what their strategies, needs, and hopes are" (1994, 192).

"ONCE WE CEASE TO BE COOL":[53] APPLIED FOLKLORE AND POLITICS

The discussion of values at the conference overlapped with the real core of the debates: differences in opinion concerning the wisdom of folklorists' involvement in politics and the extent of overlap between politics and applied endeavors. It is important to remember the historical context for these initiatives. Several of the Point Park participants commented on the role played by the political moment in their attitudes toward applied work, particularly in relation to their understanding of the importance of intercultural work. Bruce Jackson, for example, noted "being tear gassed on the Pentagon porch in October 1967 as a personal turning point."[54] The applied folklore debates occurred within the larger backdrop of the war in Vietnam, civil rights protests and violent racial clashes connected with school desegregation, the Ohio National Guard's killing of four and wounding of nine unarmed college students at Kent State protesting the expansion of the Vietnam War into Cambodia, and the publication of the Pentagon Papers in the *New York Times*, demonstrating that the Johnson administration had lied to Congress and the public about the scope of incursions into Vietnam—all of which took place in 1970 and 1971. The 1970s were, in general, also a continuation of the concerns of the 1960s, including women's rights, African American and Native American rights, and the continued fight for all types of equity. The Black Power movement and the Women's Liberation movement were still in full swing. It was a period of intense antiwar protest, division, distrust, and a "New Right" mobilized in defense of political conservatism.

The strongest voices opposing political involvement came from Richard Dorson and Dan Ben-Amos. In his paper for the conference, Dorson famously wrote, "I contend that it is no business of the folklorist to engage in social reform, that he is unequipped to reshape institutions, and that he will become the poorer scholar and folklorist if he turns activist" (1971, 40). In the conference discussion, Dorson delivered the following argument:

> DORSON: Archie Green gets very emotional when he's caught up in these problems, and when he was testifying before Senator Yarborough [regarding what would later become the American Folklife Center], he brought Vietnam and Cambodia into the matter—
> GREEN: [Because that's where it's at?]
> DORSON: —and I don't think that we can combine our social and political and emotional feelings with an objective and scholarly study. I don't think that we can combine our social and political and emotional feelings with an objective and scholarly study. Now I think you could do something about Vietnam as a folklorist if you went to Saigon and did some collecting, and, you know, people from the countryside have all come into the city and be able really to present the information that we just don't have about the Vietnamese people and that might make this whole business more meaningful to us. I think that's the kind of task that the folklorist could fulfill. But once we cease to be cool, calm, detached, imperturbable scholars, and get carried away, then we get in trouble. Thank you.[55]

Green responded by indicating that the dichotomy between scholarship and one's political positions is an illusion.

> I'll comment on Professor Dorson's comment on my emotions. Of course I'm emotional, but I will add something of substance. I see no contradiction between being passionately against President Nixon's policy in Vietnam and Cambodia and being a scholar in folklore. In terms of scholarship, the books, or the book that I have coming out, the articles I've written, the records

I've edited, they'll have to be judged by my peers. That's all that I can say for scholarship. Scholars traditionally in Western Europe have been liberals, conservatives, radicals, Catholics, Protestants, Jews, atheists, agnostics, even in the Soviet Union today there are scholars who are not Marxist and who struggle to find expression within that very repressive intellectual system, but it's simply— it's what Dick [Dorson] says is false, false, false! He's lived all of his life in terms of a false dichotomy. One does not lose objectivity by taking political positions if he understands his positions, if he states them clearly, if he checks his biases as he goes, if he defines his positions, because the best you do is do what you can and then the judgment is made initially by your peers and eventually by posterity.[56]

Dorson had deep concerns about folklorists getting politically involved in the name of the discipline. He said, "Now any scholar can have his separate public and civic role, and if he wants to be an activist, that's one role, but if he's gonna mix these two, I think he's gonna be the lesser scholar, and if that makes one out to be an ivory tower, detached scholar, well so be it."[57]

While Dorson tied political involvement to popularization and trivialization in contrast to scholarly detachment, his thoughts on the matter of politics were also integrated with his feelings about the Cold War and the leftover impact of the political repression of McCarthyism. He was concerned about the bearing on folklore's disciplinary standing if folklorists became too political. Dan Ben-Amos took a similar approach in the Point Park discussion, arguing, "It seems to me that scholarly activity should be free of political argumentations in the sense that it should be a place for discourse and dialogue which relates to theories and ideas which are pertaining to the problems we have apparent in terms of scholarship rather than the external problems which are politically oriented or politically initiated."[58]

Ben-Amos was particularly concerned with folklorists working on behalf of politicians and political parties. He said,

If the Republic[an] or Democratic Party comes to a folklorist and tells him, "Look, we have a certain problem we'd like to defeat the other party. You are a folklorist, you know how to deal with these problems, tell us how to do it." Now, in this particular case, a folklorist, as far as I'm concerned, can take upon himself the role of an advertisement man or an applied person and he can do the work, but at that particular time he does not do and it should not be a pretense under any circumstances that he does scholarship, and I think this is a process that actually should be excluded from a scholarly society. He can do it; I don't care what people do, but it is not a scholarly activity, and it seems to me that the scholarly activity should be free of political argumentations in the sense that it should be a place for discourse and dialogue which relates to theories and ideas which are pertaining to the problems that we have apparent in terms of scholarship rather than the external problems which are politically oriented or politically initiated. Now, some of my good critics actually with whom I argued this say to me, "Well, you are—" and this is also something that we talked about from the very beginning, actually, that everybody has his own bias and his own predispositions, premises upon which he works.[59]

Ben-Amos's perspective on this aspect of applied folklore has not changed in the years since Point Park. In 2022, he voiced the same concerns about government support[60] and the potential political manipulation of folklore and folklorists.

Politics are dependent on politicians. And politicians may recruit folklore to their own needs. The worst example of that was in Nazi Germany. That *volkskunde* and the Volkish movement, basically, was utilized to uphold and support Nazism, anti-Semitism, and anti-anything that is human. Now, obviously, in Russia, and under Stalin, folklore was used for political purposes to uphold the communist regime.[61] . . . But I don't like folklore being ruled by a political entity. And therefore, I think the academy is a much better place to conduct folklore research, because in the academy, at least we have academic freedom. . . . So folklore is not restricted by rules. When politicians try to restrict it, I object to it. And in government, that's can you imagine, say probably the Folklife Center in Washington had its own defense mechanisms against Trump, but you can imagine if this man would have tried to manage and to manipulate what is there?[62]

At Point Park, others argued passionately that folklore was not and could not possibly be apolitical. Kenny Goldstein argued,

> One of the things that stands out in all of this is—to me, is that there is a concern here with the potential politicization of folklore. That is that folklore will be made political somehow, that it will be manipulated and utilized in the way, say, the Nazis or the Russians or the Red Chinese or other people whom we are supposed to have—whom we are supposed to dislike utilize it, forgetting also that folklore has been used by the United States, in some cases by people whom we liked ourselves, in exactly the same way. Folklore is political. There is no way of separating the political nature of folklore from any of its other ways of being described. The very fact that the NIMH, the NIH,[63] and other governmental institutions give money to support students, to support research involving folklore, research where they recognize it as folklore, not where it is disguised with terms like anthropology or in some cases verbal arts or other excuses given to disguise what it actually is, folklore itself is political. We are continually playing with the lives of people when we deal with their dreams, their frustrations, their wishes, their every means of—and their best means of expression. We know what they are saying, we proceed to do nothing with them, and that is a political act, to do nothing in reaction to hearing what they have to say, what they have to feel, and what they have to think is also a political act, and a negative political act is as strong in its directions as a positive political act should be on our part to counter exactly that.[64]

Abrahams argued, like Goldstein, that the folklorist's engagement in fieldwork made avoiding politics impossible. His work in East Texas schools during desegregation was reflected in his comments.

I think that the switch which has occurred, and which has made applied folklorists more and more of us all is that we feel identified more and more with our informants, and for this reason we look at life, and especially we look at the power structure which diddles around with their lives all the time, and we say we can't sit back and allow this to happen anymore! And whether this is simply a new brand of cultural imperialism or not, I don't know. I have no way of knowing because I don't know how effective the applied folklore movement could be, but all I know is that I could not square it with my own conscience if, after working with Blacks for the last 15 years, I didn't somehow recognize the ways in which the power structure was impinging constantly and degrading constantly the very culture which I see them maintaining in spite of this kind of impingement, and if I didn't at that point at least offer myself up in some advocacy role. I'm not convinced that advocacy ever works. I agree that there's a very good chance that I'm spending a lot of badly used time in cracking heads in East Texas and trying to do something about the schooling situation there.[65] One or two instances of breakthroughs that we've been able to make in certain small-town environments encourage me that perhaps change can be brought about. Some other movements which are coinciding with what we're trying to do that are actually originating within the Black community and coinciding, as I say, with what we're trying to do, the whole Black culture movement, it seems to me will make it possible.[66]

Ray Browne agreed with Goldstein and Abrahams, asserting that political involvement was an obligation for responsible citizens and responsible scholars.

I can quite understand Dick Dorson, whose scholarship I admire, whom I admire personally, being somewhat frightened by the notion of getting politicized. I wonder, first of all, if his fear is not a little bit overly apprehensive. I also wonder if there's not a great deal of potential evil or irresponsibility in the other. It seems to me that if in fact we are anything, it ought to be that we are rather responsible citizens, and I guess I really am a little bit tired of the responsible citizen—the self-proclaimed responsible citizen—not getting out and being responsible. I sort of feel that that is our obligation. It would seem to me, the danger lies in not doing it rather than—than in doing it. Of course it lies in—there is a certain amount of political danger in overdoing it. I guess—but minimal. I guess the thing that really surprises me is, Richard [Bauman], that you would propose this before the AFS and ask for their approval. You know, if I'da been you I'd have just gone ahead and done it, and told 'em two years later that I had.[67]

Browne's comments highlight the fear of unintended consequences discussed above. Like many who have responded to the issue of unintended consequences in folklore over the years (see chap. 1 for comments by Michael Ann Williams and Peggy Bulger, and Roger Abrahams above) the concern often ends up questioning what was missed or caused by the choice not to act.

Like Goldstein and Browne, Archie Green addressed the way politics are integrated in matters of scholarly engagement and culture. Likely referencing the campaign for dedicated funding for folk culture and the early efforts to establish the American Folklife Center, Archie Green argued,

I generally try to make my contributions in terms of substance, but you know, you judge my scholarship; don't let Dick [Dorson] judge it. Okay. [laughter] Now. On the matter of substance, one of the realities of the 1970s is the fact that the government of the United States is deeply into the support of culture at all levels to the tune of 50 or 60 million dollars a year. Regardless of where you stand on the spectrum, you know, President Nixon spends more on culture than did President Johnson. It's not, you know—Nixon's personal idea of culture is the score out of a musical comedy or a rally at a football game, but he's deeply committed to spending money on culture because he *has* to be in terms of technology today, in terms of the tax structure, in terms of the decline in private philanthropy. When private philanthropists could support the New York Philharmonic, that's how it was handled, and it was at that time that certain well-to-do New England spinsters made it down to Appalachia to set up little red schoolhouses—there was a whole complex that made folklore complement high culture and the [finance?]

of high culture at a time. That's ended. Private symphony orchestras turned to governmental support and foundation support. The government recognizes that it needs to support culture to help bind society together, again regardless of the values of any man in the White House.[68]

Green's argument continued, reflecting his initial efforts leading up to the American Folklife Preservation Act to create a foundation for the support of folklife, mirroring the National Endowment for the Arts and its funding of what Green considered elite arts. His concern was with who would be the decision-makers concerning money spent on culture.

> Now what's happening in Washington through the Arts Foundation, through the Humanities, is that gradually a political constituency is being built of people who make a living at culture or make a living transmitting it or interpreting it, and these people work for arts councils, they work for publicly supported foundations or quasi-public foundations, and these people collectively are in the process, they have been for the last two or three years of forming lobbies comparable to the lobbies of farmers, of trade unionists, of truckers, of metallurgists; lobbyists to develop a relationship with Congress on the appropriation of money. Now, it doesn't really matter what our Society does or what this committee does; the money is going to be appropriated and spent. A complex technological society in the 1970s can't exist without spending public money on culture. Our particular problem is, is any of that dough going to be spent on folk culture, and is it going to be spent by people who have a feeling for tradition or people who want to turn folk culture towards pop ends or towards political ends? All of us—you know, this really isn't a matter of whether we're left, right, center, scholarly, or unscholarly—all of us are going to be involved in that problem. Is the folk foundation people, Smithsonian people, Henry [Glassie] alluded to curators who are taking care of homes, you know, everyone in this room, whether he likes it or not, is going to be involved in the next decade in the expenditure of tax money for culture, and that's going to at some level involve folk culture, folk society, modify

it, destroy it, enhance it, and this—this session today, you know, gives us an opportunity to prepare to cope with this new state in the politics of culture.[69]

The problem of political involvement had built into it a sort of catch-22. Several of the participants in Point Park continually asserted that all of our work is by definition political, applied or not, in that all expressive culture is tied to equity, need, social welfare, and justice and that our real problem is that we don't own up to our work as socially situated and inherently political. Our problem, in other words, is not in being political, which cannot be avoided; it is in not articulating the ideological nature of our work. Yet for Dorson, Ben-Amos, and others who feared politicization, it was the public articulation and demonstration of political ideology that might jeopardize the field's position in the academy.

APPLIED WORK AND THE LESSONS
OF OTHER DISCIPLINES

In addition to these themes voiced as concerns at Point Park and in the reports, minutes, and letters of leaders in AFS, several AFS members referenced obliquely the problematic history of applied research in linguistics, anthropology, and literature. Thelma James (above) noted the problematic nature of applied work in the Modern Language Association (MLA); Hymes referred to concerns about a divide between the Linguistics Society of America and the Independent Center for Applied Linguistics,[70] and numerous scholars made reference to problems caused by applied work within the American Anthropological Association. While none of these comments articulate the precise nature of the concerning divisions caused by applied work in other disciplines, three common critiques of applied scholarship held sway in the 1970s and provide a likely backdrop for folklore's response: attitudes concerning "pure" versus applied research, concerns about colonialism and the applied enterprise, and historical reflections on the unintended consequences of applied work.

The debates about pure versus applied or engaged research echo some of Richard Dorson's concerns about fakelore, popularization, and politics. Pure research in the 1970s was research conducted without a specific goal, with the aim of simply advancing knowledge, whereas applied research was conducted with the goal of solving specific social problems (see Bauman 1971). For some, "pure" was the tacit ideal state of professional being (Greenwood 2008, 324). Like the ivory tower and professionalism debates (Williams 1975; Baron [1992] 2007) in folklore, theoretical/applied dualism is found throughout the social sciences, with theorists arguing for pure or "basic" research in which knowledge is acquired for the sake of knowledge and applied researchers who argue that scholars must "make a difference" in the world.

The 1970s were a time when the assumptions of every field came into question. Linguistics, anthropology, and literature were all beginning to call into question ongoing colonialization in research, as did Hymes (above) when he noted "applied" is "unfortunately associated with an unconsciously rather 'colonial' relationship between scholar and community, whatever the goodwill and understanding actually present."[71] For Hymes and others who asserted postcolonial concerns in applied debates, colonial privilege still held unequal power relations that exerted control over research and reinscribed the power of the academic elite in the production of native representation and the lack of native perspectives in research.

By far, however, the most haunting and concerning issue observed from our sister disciplines as they undertook applied work was the potential for unintended consequences. Hymes wrote in his letter to Byington, "Future research is going to confront the question of what use will be made of it before it can even begin, answering that question will be a condition of even doing the research. (It is so increasingly with American Indian communities.)"[72] Folklorists at Point Park would have known about social scientists who were employed in a number of applied projects that went bad, but few were so disturbing as anthropology's involvement in the War Relocation Authority (WRA). As noted in the introduction to this volume, in 1942, anthropologists were hired by the American government WRA to work as ethnographers in the Japanese internment camps. Their intention was to improve conditions in the camps and defuse anti-Japanese public opinion. The WRA hired twenty-one anthropologists—including Robert Redfield, Edward Spicer, Weston La Barre, Conrad Arensberg, and Margaret Lantis—but their work had a number of unintended consequences including legitimization of the relocation and assimilationist views of the government as well as the promotion of racial stereotypes about the Japanese (Starn 1986). While many of the researchers involved downplayed the ethical issues involved in their participation, social scientists in general were deeply uncomfortable with the project, feeling that ethnographers had become accomplices of the government in relocation.

THE HEART THAT STOPPED BEATING

Other things had happened too. The Applied Folklore Center was destined to go to Point Park College and was dependent on an offer of funding from the college to subsidize the center. In 1972, the offer of funding was retracted due to college financial concerns. Following the Point Park college withdrawal, there was interest expressed by folklorists at University of Kentucky that also did not come to fruition. Ralph Rinzler at the Smithsonian Institution offered to try to bring the center to the Smithsonian, but shortly after his offer a confluence of activity at the Smithsonian, the creation of the National Endowment for the Arts Folk Arts Program in 1973, and ultimately the creation of the American Folklife Center at the Library of Congress in 1976, superseded the Applied Folklore Center. In 1974, Robert Byington stepped down as chairman of the Applied Folklore Committee, writing in his report to AFS to explain the committee's inactivity,

> One important reason for this has been the near total absorption of the chairman's energies by a new job; and since that derelict chairman sees no light at the end of his tunnel, it is possible that the Committee will remain inert until a new chairman, a new mission, or both, appear to reinvigorate it. Both paths should be explored. And, by way of clearing an entrance to the first, I hereby submit my resignation as chairman of the Committee in the hope that the torch of applied folklore, thus relinquished, will not gutter for long in a puddle of AFS indifference. (AFS 1975, 18)

By this time, however, as Byington said, "the hard advocacy implicit in the original definition was softened, in fact, eliminated" and "applied folklore became sufficiently broad a category to include what appears to be an almost limitless range of possibilities" (1989, 79). He wrote, "Applied folklore was originally conceived as an instrument for social reform which necessarily involves the folklorist as an agent in the process. It implied a melioristic stance which amounted at times to hard advocacy and tough negotiation. . . . In brief, applied folklore could, and should rattle a lot of cages" (78).

But this was not to be the case. The excitement over Archie Green's lobbying efforts for what eventually became the American Folklife Center took over. Bauman recalled, "It very quickly morphed into what emerged as public sector stuff. And the notion of applied folklore faded from the scene."[73]

THE POWER OF OUR SUBJECT: A DIFFERENT TAKE ON THE POLITICAL POWER OF FOLKLORE

If we briefly shift our lens from the failure of the Applied Folklore Center proposal to the subsequent lobbying effort for the American Folklife Preservation Act, as did Byington and Bauman in their comments, a few things come into focus. First and most clearly, the initiative's success or failure was tied to an external not an internal lobbying effort—and surprisingly it seems it was easier to convince those in government of the wisdom of folklore's applications than it was to convince the field. Second, Archie Green's commitment and tireless lobbying (although he had help from other committed folklorists such as Ralph Rinzler) were missing from the Applied Folklore Center effort, especially as the definition widened and supporters like Byington, who missed the community problem-solving and political connotation, lost heart. Third, Green's lobbying efforts for the American Folklife Center *were* exciting, in large part because Green was able to convince so many politicians of the political power of folklore, even as in Point Park some of his colleagues shied away from that idea.

Over time, Green developed a system and a style for lobbying that responded to potential threats to legislators and their constituencies that he understood could be posed by the effort. In the process of lobbying for the American Folklife Preservation Act (see chap. 1), Archie Green became aware of two major problems that placed those involved in the endowments, and also numerous other politicians, in an awkward position related to the effort. He outlined these:

> (A) if money is diverted to 'low' folk expression, the 'high'
> subsidized forms (for example, humanities lectures, opera, ballet)
> will suffer; [and]
> (B) the egalitarian partisans of folklife (rurality, ethnicity,
> artisanship) are more numerous in Congress than their elite
> peers; hence a folk center will dilute the political support needed
> by other cultural institutions.[74]

In other words, while folklife provided a threat to elite institutions in its appeal, it was ultimately more widespread, egalitarian, accessible, and popular than those institutions, especially in difficult economic times. He observed that in the face of the recession mentality of the ninety-fourth Congress, "folkloric conscious-ness seemed to make sense in hard times—folk artifacts and projects carried modest price tags" and "more importantly, every Representative and Senator could identify quilt makers and bal-lad singers or wood carvers and yarn swappers back home, but not every district or region supported an opera company" (see Green in Feintuch 1988a, 269–79).

It is hard to know if Archie Green absorbed the potential po-litical impact of this information early or late in the lobbying process, but it is clear that he knew from early in his congressional work that the folklore of family life, region, cultural background, community, and occupation had the power to move votes.

Jim Hightower, aide to Senator Ralph Yarborough, Democrat of Texas who helped support the early efforts to create a founda-tion, said of Archie Green's approach, "It was the raw populism; the recognition that we have all these cultures we're celebrating and that we ought to celebrate our own—both folk art as well as fine art. And that approach was very compelling to a number of members of Congress.... This was not just another arts program to spend your money on, but one that common folks are tied into.... And bringing that to the fore—the music of the people, the artistic expression of the people—that was very popular" (Gross Bressler 1995, 109).

Indeed, intent on garnering the support of as many represen-tatives as possible, Green walked the halls of Congress, getting into as many offices as he could and talking about the traditions of each individual's region or ethnicity. Gross Bressler notes ex-amples of this strategy as Green himself described them:

> "Senator Abourezk was Lebanese.... I think he grew up in a
> poor immigrant family in the Dakotas. His father had an Indian
> trading post in or near a reservation. So from his youth he was
> well acquainted with Native Americans...." Senator Sam Irvin,
> (the chief prosecutor) "of Watergate fame ... had heard lots of
> fiddling and mountain singing as a youngster." His aide, Rufus

> Edmonston, "was an admirer of Doc Watson. . . . The moment
> Rufus told (Senator Irvin) 'this bill is OK,' it was just—Irvin
> didn't need an intimate knowledge of the bill. And I had *carte
> blanche* to that office." Senator Mark Hatfield "was married to a
> woman from Yugoslavia . . . (who) knew about ethnic dancing"
> and he was also an ardent proponent of Indian rights in Oregon.
> (Gross Bressler 1995, 111)

Described by many who encountered him during his lobbying
efforts as different from the norm in the halls of Congress, Green
described himself as kind of "folksy," and he was described by
Janet Anderson as casual, wearing tennis shoes and carrying a
Hecht bag out of which he would pull piles of 4×6 cards (Gross
Bressler 1995, 104). Richard Bauman described him to us as "just
plain folks. Just Archie. He's just got his green bookbag and he
wanders the halls of Congress."[75]

For Green, the goal was to work with "a Congressman's in-
tuitive, natural, understanding of folklore, folklife, and folk processes" (Gross Bressler 1995, 82). In an interview conducted by
Kieran W. Taylor with Green twenty years later, he said, "So I had
to prove my affection for the material, for living lore. And I had
to know a lot about the lore in the whole country."[76] The strategy was so successful that difficult but necessary relationships
on the Hill were altered by Green's enthusiasm and persuasion
(see Gross Bressler 1995 for a discussion of those relationships).
Cosponsors of the bill also found the approach compelling and
adapted Green's strategy. Senator Harris, for example, used a similar approach when he introduced the bill in Congress. He said,

> The legislation proposed here today is an effort to invest in the
> culture of America's common man. It says that the country fid-
> dler need not feel uncultured simply because his fiddle does not
> produce a concert tone; it says that the pottery of Jugtown, N.C.,
> and the sandpainting of the Southwestern Indians are artistic
> treasures in the same sense as those from the dynasties of China;
> it says that the black bluesmen along the Brazos Valley in Texas

are recognized as pure artists and welcome as a national treasure; it says that the American Indian philosopher has something urgently important for America today and that this society wants to hear him as well as the ancient Greeks; it says that the total lifestyles of Swedish-Americans in Milwaukee, of Polish Americans in Chicago, and of Italian-Americans in Boston have brought a perspective and a contribution to this country that has ennobled us as a society; and it says that the bluegrass band has developed a music with a complexity and a richness that will grow and that will endure always as a living monument to American musical genius. In short, the bill I am proposing says that there is a vast cultural treasure in America's common man, and that our society will be a better one if we focus on that treasure and build on it.[77]

The two hearings held outside of Congress—at the Smithsonian Folklife Festival on the National Mall in Washington, DC, and at the Grand Ole Opry in Nashville—both made use of this strategy and included performances interspersed with testimony from participants. Of course, public performances had been a mainstay of public folklore even before there was consciously a field of public folklore, but these performances were different, targeted at affecting public policy. Ralph Rinzler had for a long time understood the incredible political impact of bringing folk artists to the National Mall.[78] Working closely with Green in the early efforts, he assisted with the festival hearing on the mall, which included festival participants such as Blues and Cajun musicians, performers from the featured state of Ohio, and representatives from the American Indian and Working American sections. The hearings tied these participants to the argued need to invest in the quality, range, and talent of a diversity of Americans.

The hearing at the Grand Ole Opry was suggested by singer-songwriter John Hartford with the same idea of integrating tradition bearers with academics and policymakers, and it was broadcast on WSM Radio as part of the weekly broadcast of the Opry. Performances and testimonies were provided by Tommy Simmons and Jimmy Driftwood, Mac Wiseman, Kirk and Sam

Figure 2.2 Elizabeth Cotten. 1984 NEA Heritage Fellow, performer/speaker at the 1988 American Folklife Preservation Act Hearings. Photo by Diana Jo Davies, courtesy of Ralph Rinzler Folklife Archives and Collections, Center for Folklife and Cultural Heritage, Smithsonian Institution.

McGee, Jimmy Newman, Bill Monroe and the Blue Grass Boys, Roy Acuff, Dave Akeman ("Stringbean"), and Jean Shepard (Gross Bressler 1995, 90). For Rinzler and later for Green, the sheer power of the diversity that was represented, the talent of the performers, and the familiarity of the songs and stories had a significant positive impact on the policymakers who would be the deciding voices.

The panels that were ultimately mounted for the congressional hearings borrowed from these integrated performances and testimony by tradition bearers to bring that same power to Congress. Janet Anderson recalled that when eighty-one-year-old Elizabeth Cotten, a North Carolinian African American singer and guitarist, played for Congress, "people were lined up in the halls, peering in to see what was going on. It was very, very moving—people had tears in their eyes. It was a sense that 'here is something valuable and deep and important'" (Gross Bressler 1995, 146).

In addition to the performances, representatives and senators reached back into their own memories, reciting or citing songs, poems, and rhymes. Congressman Henry Gonzales, Democrat of San Antonio, concluded his remarks by saying,

> Higgledy, piggledy, my little white hen,
> She lays eggs only for gentlemen,
> I cannot persuade her with pistol or lariat,
> To come across for the proletariat.[79]

The success of the American Folklife Preservation Act effort, based on the near universal response to the familiar and the local, for the most part shifted the folklorists' gaze from the somewhat fraught discussion of applications to community problem-solving and politics to the moving power of cultural performances.

APPLIED FOLKLORE AND DISCIPLINARY IDENTITY

Applied folklore certainly had sputters of organized revitalization over the years. In 1977, the AFS announced the establishment of an Applied Folklore Section, and that same year, an applied folklore forum and workshop was on the program. Some years later, the section ceased to meet. This is not to say, however, that there are not a number of folklorists who continue to do the work the Applied Folklore Center envisioned. There are many applied folklorists in the field, especially working in areas of medicine, gerontology, social work, and geographical planning. In 1998, David Shuldiner, Jessica Payne, Mary Ellen Brown, and Inta Gale Carpenter noted, as editors of the Point Park Revisited special issue of *JFR*, that "today, applied folklore remains without an organizational 'center,'" yet "despite Byington's rather pessimistic conclusion that the hard questions raised by application may not render the effort worthwhile, increasing numbers of folklorists are renewing calls for applied folklore and are deeply immersed in applied folklore work" (Shuldiner et al. 1998, 186).

The battles at the Point Park conference, however, had a lasting effect on our disciplinary identity and on the potential for a concentrated focus on applied folklore. For nearly fifty years, that effort has been held back by the same five issues: definitions of applied folklore, the values of our field, the potential for applied projects to go bad, our disciplinary place in the academy, and the role politics should play in folklore. Fifty years later, the carving off of applied folklore as a distinct part of the field is plagued by the same concerns—that such a distinction might suggest that all folklore is not useful and that a dedicated part of the field that focuses on the amelioration of social problems might suggest that "not applied" is not helpful, not useful, without social merit. In fact, in 1992, in the introduction to their book *Public Folklore*, Robert Baron and Nick Spitzer wrote, "We eschewed the term 'applied folklore' with its associations of folklorists determining objectives, agendas and interpretive frameworks, whether for beneficent ends of social amelioration or malevolent purposes well documented in studies of the manipulation of folklore by extremist regimes. We were also concerned that that in contrast, academic practitioners not be labeled 'unapplied'" (Baron and Spitzer [1992] 2007, x).

Fifty years later, we struggle with whose values we serve and where we should stand if the values of our field themselves stand in contrast to those we study. We still worry about the unintended consequences of our involvements, arguing about the choices made by those who pulled out of the Tennessee-Tombigbee folklife project in the late '70s or whether we should engage with this or that because of such concerns. We still monitor our engagements out of genuine concern for further trivializing a field all too often associated with, as Elliott Oring (2012) and Fivecoate, Downs, and McGriff (2021) note, the trivial, the uncertain, the silly. And fifty years later, we still are exploring the role political activism should and does play in our field and in our work, despite our growing understanding of the power of our subject. Point Park was pivotal for many things, not the least of which was highlighting concerns about our disciplinary identity—concerns that remain, even these many years later.

NOTES

The quote used in the chapter title comes from one of Richard Dorson's comments during the Point Park debate.

1. Referred to throughout the chapter and notes as simply the Applied Folklore Committee.

2. We were lucky enough to discover a note in the AFS files that indicated that Lynwood Montell had recorded the sessions. Those reel-to-reel recordings had been archived in Montell's collections at Manuscripts & Folklife Archives, Special Collections Library, Western Kentucky University and were made accessible to us for listening and transcription. A letter from Kenneth Clarke to Kenny Goldstein concerning *Folklore Forum*'s publication of transcripts suggests that the recording had been made by Lynwood Montell and Kenneth Clarke for Ellen Stekert, who had requested that the sessions be recorded since she was unable to attend (Letter from Kenneth Clarke to Kenneth Goldstein, July 6, 1971). WKU Folk Studies MA student Susanna Pyatt took on the difficult task of transcribing these tapes for us once they were digitized. Due to the sound quality, occasional words are indecipherable and are noted as such through bracketing and a question mark. Unless otherwise noted, all references to AFS-related minutes and letters in this chapter are from AFS records, 1890–2011. (COLL MSS 206). Utah State University. Special Collections and Archives Department.

3. Transcription of Point Park first session discussion, May 21, 1971. Transcribed from digitized reel-to-reel recordings of the Point Park sessions in the Lynwood Montell collection in the Manuscripts & Folklife Archives, Special Collections Library, Western Kentucky University. (hereafter cited as Point Park: First Session).

4. May 22, 23.

5. The papers included David H. Hufford, "Some Approaches to the Application of Folklore Studies"; Bruce Jackson, "Folklore as a Behavioral Science"; Warren Roberts, "Function in Folk Architecture"; W. F. H.

Nicolaisen, "The Mapping of Folk Culture as Applied Folklore"; William R. Ferris, "Documentary Film and Applied Folklore"; Henry Glassie and Betty Joe, "Folklore and Municipal Zoning"; Roger D. Abrahams, "Folklore and Community Action: Housing and Educational Systems"; Byrd H. Granger, "Folklore as a Key to Cultural Awareness" and "The Future of Folk Museums in the United States"; Richard Bauman, "Proposal for a Center of Applied Folklore"; S. K. Stevens, "The Bicentennial Plan to Date: An Overview"; Don Yoder, "'Preliminary Proposals' for Folklore in the Bicentennial Celebration"; and James Deetz, "The Feasibility of an Urban Open Air Ethnic Museum" (Sweterlitsch 1971, 17).

6. Richard Bauman and Beverly Stoeltje, interview with authors, August 1, 2021, Bloomington, IN.

7. Jerrold Hirsch notes that what Botkin called utilization in the 1930s, he began to call "applied folklore" in the 1950s (Hirsch 1998, 289).

8. We are grateful to our book reviewer for IU Press for this observation.

9. Richard Bauman told us, concerning Botkin's presence in Point Park, "Well, you know, his position was so fraught. Sometimes he came, sometimes he didn't. He was already getting up in years. But I don't remember him being there—it's more like being an honored elder" (Interview with authors, August 1, 2021, Bloomington, IN). Nevertheless, Botkin appears to have been at session one of the Point Park conference. The moderator twice calls on "Ben" from the audience for comments, but in both cases, the speaker (who we suspect was Ben Botkin) was too far from the microphone, and his comments are inaudible on the only known recording of the conference.

10. The proposal was Bauman's own contribution, not that of the committee.

11. AFS Annual Meeting: Business Meeting Minutes, November 13, 1971. The executive board meeting and business meeting minutes were largely verbatim until the late 1970s.

12. AFS Annual Meeting: Business Meeting Minutes, November 13, 1971.

13. This did take place. On November 16–19, 1972, in Austin, Texas, there were three paper sessions on applied folklore and two on folklore and politics. The applied sessions were chaired by Bauman, Byington, and Goldstein, and both politics sessions were chaired by Goldstein ("Program for the Annual Meeting of the American Folklore Society," American Folklore Society, Austin, TX, 1972).

14. Letter from D. K. Wilgus to Members of the Applied Folklore Committee and the Review Committee, November 22, 1971.

15. Letter from D. K. Wilgus to Members of the Applied Folklore Committee and the Review Committee, November 22, 1971.

16. Letter from D. K. Wilgus to Members of the Applied Folklore Committee and the Review Committee, November 22, 1971.

17. Letter from Robert Georges to Robert Byington, August 23, 1972.

18. Letter from Dell Hymes to Robert Byington, August 11, 1972.

19. Letter from Dell Hymes to Robert Byington, August 11, 1972.

20. Letter from Richard Dorson to Robert Byington, September 5, 1972.

21. Letter from Robert Byington to Kenneth Goldstein, March 27, 1972.

22. Report of the Applied Folklore Committee to the Review Committee, August 1, 1972.

23. Richard Bauman and Beverly Stoeltje, interview with authors, August 1, 2021, Bloomington, IN.

24. Letter from Robert Byington to Richard Bauman, July 11, 1972.

25. Interestingly, David Shuldiner notes that Dorson continually castigated Archie Green for being motivated by a progressive social agenda and attacked him as an "applied folklorist." Shuldiner indicates that when he approached Green about contributing remarks to the inaugural issue of the *Journal of Applied Folklore*, he refused to do so unless the term *applied* was removed from the title. He did, however, ultimately consent to do an interview, which was included in the issue (Shuldiner 1998, 190).

26. Letter from Archie Green to D. K. Wilgus, June 2, 1971.

27. Letter from the Applied Folklore Committee to the AFS Membership, April 10, 1972.

28. It is unclear who was on the utilization committee. What we do know was that Thelma James was the chair and that she specifically mentioned Charles Seegar in her report.

29. Transcription of Point Park third session discussion, May 22, 1971 (hereafter cited as Point Park: Third Session).

30. Point Park: Third Session.

31. Letter from the Applied Folklore Committee to the AFS Membership, April 10, 1972.

32. Letter from Dell Hymes to Robert Byington, August 11, 1972.

33. Letter from the Applied Folklore Committee to the Review Committee, October 1, 1972.

34. Letter from Robert Byington to Kenneth Goldstein, March 27, 1972.

35. Point Park: Third Session.

36. Point Park: Third Session.

37. The term *fakelore* was coined in 1950 by Richard Dorson in his article "Folklore and Fake Lore," published in *The American Mercury*. Dorson wrote of fakelore in a critique of the work of James Stevens, who had written about Paul Bunyan as well as critiqued Botkin. He called both of them purveyors of fakelore, indicating that they were creating a synthetic product claiming to be an authentic oral tradition but which was actually tailored for mass edification.

38. Point Park: Third Session.

39. Letter from the Applied Folklore Committee to the AFS Membership, April 10, 1972.

40. Report of the Applied Folklore Committee to the Review Committee, August 1, 1972.

41. Report of the Applied Folklore Committee to the Review Committee, August 1, 1972.

42. Hufford noted,

> In 1968 I had decided to devote my career to the use of folklore method and content to medical practice and education, which is obviously why I entitled my dissertation "Folklore Studies and Health: An Approach to Applied Folklore." . . . I believe all fields should have a serious applied side, like applied physics, applied linguistics, applied psychology, etc. and that applied and "pure" academic fields should both respect and provide useful knowledge to each other. I am especially focused on the mutual benefits (practical problems solved by folklore and folklore knowledge and methods advanced in the process) between pure and applied. [David Hufford, personal communication with the authors, November 3, 2022.]

43. *Enthusiast* is used here for a person who is absorbed with amateur interest in folklore versus a specialist. It should be noted that this distinction was even more messy fifty years ago than it is today, since specialists were rarely trained in folklore.

44. Point Park: Third Session.

45. Point Park: Third Session.

46. Letter from the Applied Folklore Committee to the AFS Membership, April 10, 1972.

47. Report of the Applied Folklore Committee to the Review Committee, August 1, 1972.

48. Point Park: Third Session.

49. Point Park: Third Session.

50. Point Park: First Session.

51. Point Park: First Session.

52. Point Park: First Session.

53. Quoted from Richard Dorson. The full statement is, "Once we cease to be cool, calm, detached, imperturbable scholars, and get carried away, then we get in trouble" (Point Park: First Session).

54. Point Park: Third Session.

55. Point Park: Third Session.

56. Point Park: Third Session.

57. Point Park: Third Session.

58. Point Park: Third Session.

59. Point Park: Third Session.

60. It should be noted here that indeed, there are arts agencies that employ folklorists as well as folklore divisions of governmental institutions that have political appointees on their boards. For instance, the American Folklife Center was created by the US Congress in 1976 through Public Law 94–201, the American Folklife Preservation Act (see Introduction, this volume). "According to the law, the Center receives direction from a Board of Trustees that is made up of representatives from departments and agencies of the federal government concerned with some aspect of American folklife traditions and the arts; the heads of four of the major federal institutions concerned with culture and the arts (see below); persons from private life who are able to provide regional balance; and the director of the Center." See "Board of Trustees," accessed May 7, 2025, https://web.archive.org /web/20230630014249/https://www.loc.gov/folklife/board/index.html.

61. Numerous books and articles have been written on the political uses and misuses of folklore. See, for example, Christa Kamenetsky, "Folklore as a Political Tool in Nazi Germany" (1972) and *Children's Literature in Hitler's Germany: The Cultural Policy of National Socialism* (2019); Felix J. Oinas, "Folklore and Politics in the Soviet Union" (1973) and "The Political Uses and Themes of Folklore in the Soviet Union" (1975); or Carmen Ortiz, "The Uses of Folklore by the Franco Regime" (1999).

62. Dan Ben-Amos, interview with authors, March 16, 2022. Zoom.

63. National Institute of Mental Health and National Institutes of Health.

64. Point Park: Third Session.

65. This is a reference to Abrahams's paper presented at the conference "Folklore and Community Action," accessed May 22, 2025, https://web .archive.org/web/20170810012333/https://scholarworks.iu.edu/dspace /bitstream/handle/2022/2637/BSS%208%2022-25.pdf?sequence=1.

66. Point Park: Third Session.

67. Point Park: Third Session.

68. Point Park: Third Session.

69. Point Park: Third Session.

70. Letter from Dell Hymes to Robert Byington, August 11, 1972.

71. Letter from Dell Hymes to Robert Byington, August 11, 1972.

72. Letter from Dell Hymes to Robert Byington, August 11, 1972.

73. Richard Bauman and Beverly Stoeltje, interview with authors, August 1, 2021, Bloomington, IN.

74. See Green in Feintuch 1988a, 269–79.

75. Richard Bauman and Beverly Stoeltje, interview with authors, August 1, 2021, Bloomington, IN. Green was a shipwright and a carpenter by trade before studying folklore. He remained deeply devoted to the union movement. Interviewed for Green's obituary, Roger Abrahams described Green's time lobbying Congress by saying that he was dressed in a T-shirt and sneakers. "He looked like a hobo, and carried everything around in a paper bag," Abrahams said. "He would just sit in the corridors of Congress and wait until people let him in to talk" (Grimes 2009). For more on Archie Green, see Burns 2011.

76. Interview by Kieran W. Taylor with Archie Green, San Francisco, July 27, 2005. Archie Green Collection UNC July 27–28, 2005.

77. *American Folklife Foundation Act: Hearings on S. 1930, First Session*, 92nd Cong. (May 24, 1971), 16584.

78. In fact, the mission and history statement of the Smithsonian Center for Folklife and Cultural Heritage demonstrates a strong consciousness of their role in public policy: "Our philosophy is to join high-quality scholarship with strong community participation and engaging educational outreach. This has led to activities that have affected cultural heritage policies and practices at local, national, and international levels" ("Mission and History," Smithsonian Folklife Festival, last modified April 20, 2021, https://festival.si.edu/about-us/mission-and-history/smithsonian).

79. Reported in Green (1976) 1988; reprinted in Feintuch 1988a, 269–79.

"WHO ARE WE?"

Feminist Folklorists and the Study of Women's Cultures

IN 1974, THE EDITORS OF the fourth issue of the newsletter *Folklore Feminists Communication* (*FFC*) asked, "Who are we?": "Who are the women in the American Folklore Society? We are only beginning to find out." They went on to list then-current efforts to highlight women's roles in the American Folklore Society (AFS) and the field of folklore studies, past and present, and they introduced themselves, and it is important to name them here: Rosan Jordan de Caro, Susan Kalčik, Lorre Weidlich, FA [Frank] de Caro, and Kay F. Stone. They wrote, "We at FFC would like to emphasize, moreover, that FFC exists for the express purpose of promoting communication among folklorists interested in the study of women's folklore and culture" (de Caro et al. 1974, 2).

The 1970s were, of course, the peak of what came to be called second-wave feminism in the West, as women were demanding equality in their personal and professional lives.[1] In the academic world in the US, this was the era of serious and increased attention to women's history research and the birth of women's studies programs with the National Women's Studies Association founded in 1977,[2] leading in turn to calls for the examination of women's contributions and perspectives in a full range of academic fields. Much of the early work was corrective, bringing attention to the unrecognized accomplishments of women and calling for additional study of women by women, but feminists also developed their own bodies of theory.

In folklore studies this meant calling attention to women scholars, reassessing past work written about women primarily by men but also by women and published in the *Journal of American Folklore* (*JAF*) and elsewhere, and "examining both the images of women and the genres through which women's creativity has been viewed . . . suggesting genres and approaches not previously recognized" (Farrer [1975] 1986, xii). The history of participation by and leadership of women in folklore studies in the US is mixed. In the early years of the discipline in the US, there were more women members and leaders than there were in many other disciplines, particularly the sciences. According to folklorist Susan Kalčik, writing in *100 Years of American Folklore Studies: A Conceptual History*, 10 percent of the founding members of AFS in 1888 were women (1988, 44). AFS elected its first woman president, Alice Fletcher, in 1905, and AFS was "one of only 3 national scientific societies to elect a woman president before 1940" (44). Franz Boas—known as the "father" of American anthropology, who was important to the early collection of folklore and a leader of the AFS from its founding to his death in 1942—is often lauded as in part responsible for bringing women into the study of folklore in the early twentieth century, and women whom he had some role in training attained leadership roles in the AFS. For instance, Elsie Clews Parsons was the second woman president of AFS (1919–20), and Ruth Benedict was the first woman editor of the AFS flagship journal, *JAF* (1925–39). Benedict was also the second longest serving editor, after Boas himself (1908–24).[3]

We describe these out-of-the-ordinary data in folklore studies because by 1950 this had changed, and the events we describe in this chapter evidence that change. The decline of women in leadership positions has been attributed at least in part to Boas's death and the shift in AFS leadership away from anthropology, as described thoroughly by Rosemary Lévy Zumwalt in her disciplinary history (1988). Of course, there were other factors both at the level of American society (e.g., the post-WWII push for the return of women to the home) as well as within folklore studies, as men like Stith Thompson and Richard Dorson of Indiana University worked to establish folklore studies as an independent field. In her 1987 essay "Autobiography of a Woman Folklorist," Ellen Stekert described Richard Dorson's approach to women students as not conducive to keeping women at IU, much less in the field. While Boas has been praised for bringing women into the field, and perhaps part of the reason that women's participation dropped off was the loss of Boas, the reverse also needs consideration. Another factor may have been that those who replaced Boas as the de facto leaders of the emerging field were not encouraging nor even perhaps welcoming to women.

The resulting differences between the first and second half of the twentieth century are striking. Although there had been eight women presidents of AFS between 1905 (when Alice Fletcher became the first) and 1950, there was no woman president from 1951 to 1977, when Ellen Stekert was elected after running by petition,[4] and no woman edited *JAF* between 1954 (there had been four prior to 1954) and 2001, when Elaine J. Lawless became editor. The Fellows of the American Folklore Society, an honorary body, was founded in 1960; by 1973, seven of the fifty-seven fellows were women (Reuss 1974, 32); by the centennial of the AFS in 1988 not much had changed: there were thirteen women out of eighty-two fellows.[5] While women were largely absent from AFS leadership for a long period, Debora Kodish's point in regard to folklore fieldwork applies more broadly: "gender is never absent" (1993, 48).

The 1975 special issue of *JAF* "Women and Folklore: Images and Genres," discussed in this chapter, was an important turning point of approaching women's folklore with new perspectives. Editor Claire Farrer and the authors within challenged previous methods and assumptions about the collection and categorization of folklore, arguing that male collectors believed women's expressive behaviors fell only into very particular categories such as charms, quaint customs and beliefs, home remedies, some folktales, marriage customs, and birth practices. Some genres that women tended toward were not acknowledged in the genre-based approach to folklore grounded in male-dominated expressive culture. For instance, while men told "tall tales," women exaggerated; while men told stories or even "lies," denoting an admired storyteller, women "gossiped," which was not recognized as a genre (Farrer [1975] 1986, xiii–xiv). Women have been defined in terms of men, roles described in terms of male attitudes and perspectives, and attention paid to women only when they fit the appropriate image of *woman*. Men have assumed that because women didn't perform in their presence, they didn't perform (ix–x).

By the 1970s, folklorists were working to call attention to women's folklore but also to the role of male power in women's careers. Beverly Stoeltje—whose folklore training took place at the University of Texas at Austin, which, as discussed in this chapter, was a center of early feminist folkloristics—said in an interview that as a field, and she likely meant society more generally as well, "we really need to pay attention to power as well as sexual harassment," and she gave examples of her experiences and observations of "male power getting in the way of" women's careers.[6] Stoeltje's point contextualizes this chapter, as this book has been largely researched and written—and Stoeltje's interview took place—in the time of the #MeToo movement.[7] Sexual harassment was of concern to 1970s feminist folklorists, but the term was not yet in use, and the raising of the issue, as we will see, was met with ridicule. Sexual assault surely was of concern as well, but it wasn't yet discussed in the public forums examined here, at least according to the archival record. As Stoeltje reminded us, other exertions of male power were of primary concern, though, of course, neither she nor we are suggesting that such concerns have been resolved any more than those of #MeToo have.

While the other chapters in this book center on a particular debate, this chapter examines separate but related moments in the history of the folklore studies of this period in which male power was "getting in the way" of women's attempts at a fuller representation of women's folklore and women's cultures, as well as of women's careers. Within the context of the larger women's movement of the 1970s, women as well as men within the field of folklore studies became active in attempts to spur change as it pertained to both the recognition and agency of women folklorists and the intertwined study of women's folklore and women's cultures. It was clear to many who led these efforts that the lack of representation of women in the disciplinary leadership was intrinsically tied to a lopsided orientation in the field to male-centered performances and genres. Ellen Stekert wrote in 1974, while a member of the AFS Executive Board, "If anyone wonders whether or not the leading professional society in the United States addressing itself to the study of tradition is free of the traditional pattern of male dominance shown in society at large, the answer is clearly 'no'" (1974, 6). This chapter considers feminist folklorists and the study of women's cultures in the 1970s and '80s, particularly early attempts to make feminist change within the American Folklore Society and in relation to its practices, publications, and meeting sites. Although some of the underlying issues of the events described in this chapter are particular to folklore studies, and other fields of study have their own histories, the struggle for women to gain footing in academic contexts is universal.

The chapter begins with the Committee on the Status of Women in the Profession, a short-lived effort in the early 1970s that reflects connections with efforts at various levels of government and within professions, as we will describe. Though little-known today, it was significant in that it was a formalized attempt by members, both women and men, to document and redress grievances. Internal disagreements apparently led to the inability of the committee of three to come to collective agreement on issues or solutions, seemingly suggesting that the committee achieved little. However, we argue that there were less direct outcomes that did contribute to changes in the AFS and to the study of women's folklore. The chapter goes on to further examples that demonstrate the types of grievances raised by members of the committee, including two instances in which male editors exerted their power over the publication of feminist work aimed at the representation of women's folklife from a feminist perspective and to debates over meeting in Utah, one of the states that did not ratify the attempt by American women to attain the guarantee of equal representation and treatment under the law—the Equal Rights Amendment. Together these case studies demonstrate a growing sense that questions of representation embedded in the question "Who are we?" pertained to both women folklorists and women's folklore.

"WOMEN STILL HAVE TO BE JACKIE ROBINSON TO ADVANCE": THE AFS COMMITTEE ON THE STATUS OF WOMEN IN THE PROFESSION

The AFS Committee on the Status of Women in the Profession (CSWP) was a short-lived standing committee of the AFS Executive Board formed in 1971. This committee represented the first organized attempt "to take some action to clarify the status of women within the discipline of folklore" (de Caro 1975b, 4). This effort was part of a larger international movement of the time to establish committees and commissions charged with examining the status of women as a step toward working for change in institutions as well as in society more generally. In 1946, the newly formed United Nations established the Commission on the Status of Women, "dedicated to ensuring women's equality and to promoting women's rights" (see UN Women 2019). According to the National Association for Commissions on Women, the US movement to create such commissions began with President John F. Kennedy's establishment of the President's Commission on the Status of Women in December 1961.[8] Chaired by Eleanor Roosevelt, the president's commission issued a report in 1963 that included a call for every state to establish such a commission; by 1967 all states had. Throughout the 1970s and '80s, commissions on women were established at all levels of government as well as by professional societies and associations. For instance, in 1969, the Modern Language Association established the Commission on the Place of Women in the Profession (changed to the Commission on the Status of Women in the Profession in 1970)[9] and the Committee on the Status of Women in Anthropology was established in 1970 "to monitor the status of women in the American Anthropological Association (AAA) and in the discipline at large" (Brondo et al. 2009, 5). The model of the work of such commissions and committees was to collect data regarding inequalities as experienced by women in a particular constituent group and make recommendations for change.

The three members of the AFS Committee on the Status of Women in the Profession were appointed by the AFS president, D. K. Wilgus of UCLA, in 1971: Eleanor Long ("chairman"), a ballad scholar who had been a student of Wilgus and later married him; Rayna Green, a specialist in folklore and culture of American Indians; and Frank A. Hoffmann, founding editor of *Keystone Folklore Quarterly*. When later asked about the origins of the committee at the first official Women's Caucus meeting, Ellen Stekert explained that the committee originated in a suggestion from the floor of the 1971 AFS Business Meeting from Frank de Caro "that the status of women in the discipline of folklore be investigated."[10] Wilgus agreed to create a committee of the executive board; he later set up the committee "after being reminded of his declaration of intention by Ms. Stekert herself."[11] His letter of invitation to the three members of the committee, dated December 1, 1971, was short, and in it he requested a report by the following October though he did not charge the committee with goals or outcomes: "I have no particular charge to present to the Committee, except the normal one which came up in connection with the Committee on Applied Folklore: that an AFS Committee operates as a data-gathering organization and takes only those actions in the name of the Society that are granted by the membership or the Executive Board."[12]

Reading through the archival record of the CSWP from the vantage point of fifty years hence, the committee members' recommendations for change may seem minimal, and their deferential tone is striking, as is how seemingly willing they were to walk back their proposals when they were challenged. However, it is vital to remember the US historical context as it relates to the issues with which they grappled. The CSWP was established prior to Title IX of the Educational Amendments, which prohibited discrimination based on sex at all levels of publicly funded education (1972); prior to bans on sex-segregated "help wanted" advertising (1973); prior to the Supreme Court decisions that established the rights to access to birth control (1972) and abortion (1973);[13] prior to the coining of the term "sexual harassment" (1975) or the recognition of a "hostile or abusive work environment" as a basis for "discrimination based on sex" (1986); and on and on.[14] As one introductory women's studies text published following this period noted in regard to women scholars generally, "In the late 1970s, careful women did not profess an interest in feminist scholarship until they had received tenure, and ambitious women avoided the field altogether" (Ruth 1990, x). As we will demonstrate through representative examples from these discussions, while the proposers often appeared to acquiesce to the significant challenges to their proposals, they opened up vital discussions about the status of women in folklore studies; the issues raised by committee members pertained to women's careers as teachers and scholars and ultimately their abilities to collect and interpret women's folklore. We note that although it is beyond the scope of this work, such discussions were being held across academic disciplines, and discipline-specific retrospectives of the period have since been published (see, for example, Brondo et al. [2009] on anthropology and Monk [2006] on geography).

The CSWP reported to the executive board twice, in 1972 and 1973, and the complexities of such a committee were apparent in part through their inability to provide a report representing all three members either time. While we are fortunate to have a detailed account through the AFS Business Meeting minutes, which were in narrative form and partially transcribed verbatim in this period, as well as the AFS annual reports, we were not able to obtain any firsthand recollections of the committee, as two of the three members are deceased.[15]

The committee first reported to the AFS at the business meeting in 1972 in separate oral reports given by each member, and the minutes note that no written report was "available at the time the agenda was printed."[16] Though unstated, this suggests that the committee could not come to agreement, and in fact in a retrospective panel on feminism and folklore in 2016, Susan Kalčik—a leader in the development of the Women's Caucus—remarked that "there were three reports because they could not agree on it."[17] They had sent out two surveys: one to 225 women members of AFS, to which they received 84 responses, and a second to universities with folklore programs and courses, to which they received 114 out of 160 responses. They each registered complaints that the membership mailing list given to them by the AFS was incomplete and not up to date; Frank Hoffmann noted that "a stack about a foot high [were] returned 'no address.'"[18]

Eleanor Long gave what she called the "Chairman's minority report" and began by stating that the survey responses suggested good news, in part that employment statistics for women folklorists were similar to folklorists as a whole[19] and that women folklorists "are just a small bit ahead of other professions regarding women."[20] "In other words," Long contended, "it is something of an advantage to a woman in the academic world to be a folklorist."[21] Of those surveyed, 64 percent either "had no complaints" or were "particularly satisfied" "about their work in folklore"; "10% said they felt they were discriminated against as women."[22] Long provided brief recommendations to women and to the AFS, including that women "pick up that English degree somewhere along the line,"[23] as English departments were more likely to hire women, and that graduate students look at positions in high schools and community colleges. "The potential for trained women in folklore exists in these schools as well as in positions such as secretarial work in programs of folklore" and in folklore libraries.[24] Long noted that "women still have to be Jackie Robinson to advance" and then went on to say, "I believe it might be the same for men, too these days."[25] While this pair of statements appears nonsensical, according to Long, "our responses indicate that most of the women who are involved with folklore, academically or otherwise express themselves as being happy with their work in folklore and happy with their choice. I would say to women, stick with folklore—it is still the more rewarding thing to do."[26] Long recommended that AFS, via the CSWP, look more carefully at the situation of women graduate students, as they appeared to be the category of women most aggrieved.[27] Although the committee did not officially gather data on this, they planned to if they were able to continue. At this point Wilgus noted, "This is a continuing, not an ad hoc committee."[28]

In his brief report Hoffmann also began by noting the problems with the mailing. He then listed the six questions from the questionnaire, which included questions about professional training, present employment and income, AFS membership, and feelings about their "present status as a folklorist."[29] He then listed five grievances in order of importance: "discrimination in graduate school" and in hiring, "nepotism rules" "applied against wives of male faculty," the need for women to exert a "greater effort than men in order to advance themselves," and "the poor record of the American Folklore Society in electing and appointing women to positions of responsibility."[30]

Rayna Green focused the first portion of her report on the survey sent to universities, which suggested that a large number of folklore courses were being taught by women without academic rank. She then turned to other concerns, noting that "some of the concerns I am presenting to you right now are not by any means restricted to women."[31] The first concern she noted was that while affirmative action initiatives were resulting in "men being discriminated against because of us. . . . That does not mean the imbalances are being redressed. Most of the major folklore programs do not hire women faculty or minority faculty even in proportion to the population of folklorists available." Like Hoffmann, she pointed out the role of nepotism in limiting women's careers, and then she urged folklore programs to better utilize women: "There are many ways in which we all can attempt to overcome the built-in patterns of action and attitude toward women to which we have been unconsciously socialized. Why do people feel it necessary to write, when recommending a woman for a position, that she dressed well when they hardly ever mention the dress habits of men?"[32]

She then turned to the AFS: "President Wilgus has mentioned that the most certain manner in which to get on a committee is to disagree. That is probably why I am on this committee since I have irritated him for some time."[33] She noted that "women and other minority groups" need to be more aggressive in order to be appointed to positions of leadership, but she then made her rhetorical strategy clear: "We must also remind the Society that our aggressiveness is not hostile, but a necessity and we can go about it in the most tactful way possible that will achieve results." She ended by recommending the establishment of an affirmative action plan for the AFS, although she didn't suggest specifics of such a plan.[34] Following the three reports, Wilgus asked for questions or comments; perhaps surprisingly, according to the minutes there were none. Wilgus then thanked the committee and, according to the minutes, "The reports were passed and placed on file 'with the appropriate admonitions to the new Executive Board.'"[35] The second report would not be met with such silence.

The membership of the committee remained in place, and the second report, in two parts, was delivered the following year, 1973. At this time the AFS president was Dell Hymes, professor of anthropology at the University of Pennsylvania.[36] Although a formal written report was submitted and included in the meeting agenda and was presented by chair Eleanor Long, it once again did not represent the full committee.[37] Although Long did not provide details, she suggested a disagreement: "It became clear early, and those of you who were at the meeting last year know, that the Committee itself had three persons and three very different concepts of what this Committee was to do," and it was therefore "not really a committee report because I do not feel it is fair to call it that."[38]

During her preface to the proposals, a member spoke up and "pointed out that at the present time there were a number of memberships of the AFS held jointly by husband and wife [and] . . . they are sent only one ballot in elections." Secretary-Treasurer Richard Bauman responded that the situation was being rectified. Part one of the report begins quite similarly to the previous report, with Long again presenting results of a survey, this time of ninety-five women folklorists, sent to an "outdated mailing list"[39] and repeating that women folklorists appeared to be doing slightly better than women in other disciplines. "Clearly," she said, however, "it behooves members of the American Folklore Society to refrain from simply resting on their laurels in regard to these problems."[40]

Figure 3.1 Photograph of Eleanor Long, appointed chair in 1971 of the AFS Committee on the Status of Women in the Profession. Photo taken at the American Folklore Society Annual Meeting in Los Angeles in 1970. Photo by Michael Owen Jones, courtesy of the American Folklore Society Collection, Utah State University Special Collections & Archives.

Once again, Long spent some time on what women folklorists could be doing, including diversifying their academic training beyond folklore and looking for nonteaching jobs, such as writing children's books and learning computer programming. In terms of academic training, she seems to suggest that the development of degrees in folklore, which was in progress at the time, might be a factor that was narrowing women's opportunities.[41] She vaguely described "more subtle forms of discrimination against women" identified through the survey, followed by what she pronounced "an interesting historical pattern" displayed by the American Folklore Society "regarding its female membership."[42] Here, she briefly described the early high level of involvement by women in the early days of the field in the US as contrasted with later periods and went on to what was really her most specific and severe criticism in either report, particularly if one reads between the lines. "The contrast," she said, "is sharpened by the observation that while prior to 1950 a woman might reasonably expect to be elected to any office in the Society's power to bestow, for the last twenty years women have consistently held only the offices of First Vice-President or member of the five-person Executive Board."[43] She continued,

> Together with the fact that since 1963 it has been necessary to go beyond the borders of the United States to find women of sufficiently distinguished reputation to be nominated as Fellows of the Society, this pattern suggests that highly-qualified women ceased to be attracted to Folklore as a discipline during the 1950's and 1960's—unless one is prepared to believe that a systematic form of discrimination involving, among other things, the "tokenization" of the office of First Vice-President as the "women's slot," has developed within the Society in direct correlation to the expansion of Folklore as an academic discipline. Whichever interpretation one is inclined to accept, the record of the American Folklore Society is wholly consistent with the "generation gap" noted above: in 1973 the status of women in Folklore is far from being that of a pioneering group seeking admission in the face of traditional mores, but is rather a deteriorating one, in which women as women are experiencing a distinct and progressive loss of the status available to them in an earlier period.[44]

She then listed five proposals, which we discuss below.

The focus of part two of the report was primarily discrepancies between the survey data from 140 universities and from 95 women respondents. This was followed by three points of discussion, two of which included a specific proposal, as well as tables of survey data. The gist of part two was a call for the AFS to actively advocate for affirmative action in the hiring of women within university folklore programs.

The membership voted unanimously to accept the report, and Hymes requested that Long read each of the five proposals. As the proposals for change generated discussion, we summarize them all in brief here:

I. "That the AFS go on record as disapproving in principle the following practices in University employment":[45] preferential hiring, salary and tenure differentials, and the effects of nepotism rules, followed by an implementation note that AFS members "seek actively to abolish such practices . . . in their home institutions";[46]

II. That assistance be provided for women with MA degrees in folklore in getting additional training or PhDs in other disciplines or in folklore, followed by an implementation note that AFS members associated with such programs "make every effort to ensure" the resources are available;[47]

III. That AFS create a central repository of information about jobs, degree programs, fellowships, and so forth, followed by a note that this be implemented by the "newly established Applied Folklore Center,"[48] but as noted in the minutes by then-president Dell Hymes, it had become clear by this point that such a center was unlikely;[49]

IV. That the AFS "move to censure that behavior on the part of its members . . . which exploits and belittles the woman folklorist: flirtation as a substitute for recognition of individual achievement . . . [etc.]";[50] this was to address observations noted by Long based on the survey that AFS needed to address "more subtle forms of discrimination"[51] and members needed to "behave accordingly";[52] and

V. "That the membership of the American Folklore Society take due notice of the apparent discrepancy between past and present patterns of governance of the Society in terms of the presence of women in positions of honor and responsibility."[53]

Based on the minutes, which summarize and at times directly quote the comments made by the members in attendance, a lively debate ensued.

Proposal I was met with a lengthy discussion about the means through which the AFS would actually disseminate its stance on university policies, if the proposal were passed. Richard Dorson voiced his opposition to the proposal on the grounds that everybody knows "that there is the need to hire women and representatives of minorities. The American Folklore Society coming in on the tail end of this certainly does not make any sense to me."[54] This was followed with more discussion of the efficacy of such declarations as well as the survey data that supported the need for it. Eventually Hymes suggested that the vote be held, and the minutes report that a "request that a letter be sent as part of the 'Implementation' section would be taken up when all the Proposals of the Committee had been voted upon. [Based on the minutes, this did not happen.] The question was called. The membership voted, with one 'no' vote, to accept Proposal I."[55]

The discussion of the second proposal, regarding assistance to women with an MA degree, revolved around questions of "how the situation of women folklore MAs differed from that of men folklore MAs," and the motion to approve the proposal was tabled. Perhaps it was for this reason that Long prefaced the third proposal with a reminder to "the membership that the mandate of the committee was to survey only women. . . . She said that she would prefer it if the suggestions in the Proposals she was putting forth also applied to men. 'Most of the things that we can propose for the betterment of women in academics in general and in folklore in particular, certainly apply precisely as well to men, and should be extended to men; we just happen to be the ones who are doing the protesting right now, that's all.'"[56]

Regarding the third proposal, the creation of a central portal for opportunities in the field, the discussion in part revolved around whether the role of the AFS, as a scholarly society, should be to "set itself up as an employment agency" or, as one member is quoted as saying, "a place for people to go on the slave block and be hired."[57] As summarized in the minutes, Dorson argued that recruitment should happen at the AFS meeting, but it "will happen naturally," and he wondered "what the Proposal sought to accomplish."[58] "Happening naturally" is, of course, what women and people of color know has long worked well for white heterosexual men to the exclusion of others. Long noted that she shared the fears expressed, yet she "hoped that such a 'center' would allow information to be disseminated or sought by folklorists more democratically than had been the case in the past."[59] A common theme throughout both Long's report and the discussions—voiced by women and men alike—was that in regard to many of the issues raised, "men were in as difficult a position as women."[60] It is very possible that Long's strategy may have been to agree with arguments against her proposals and then slip in her disagreement as an alternative view, cloaked in that agreement, but we will never know. Amid this discussion, the suggestion was made that the AFS board "implement a report on the status of the profession" as a whole,[61] a point we return to. This third proposal passed with one vote in opposition.

In the discussion regarding the fourth recommendation, that the AFS "move to censure that behavior on the part of its members . . . which exploits and belittles the woman folklorist," the use of the term *censure* was questioned. "It was asked what type of 'censure' . . . would be implemented. President Hymes pointed out that the word 'censure' often carried a technical meaning. The word 'deplore' was suggested and substituted for 'censure.'"[62] A male member was quoted as saying that this "seemed to be asking men and women to be giving up their sexual identity,"[63] to which Long replied, "We do not want to give up our femininity; we will flirt with you all you like after hours and in addition to—but please when our professional identities are at stake—do not put us off with telling us what nice women we are."[64] A female member spoke against the proposal on the grounds that she found it "tendentious and shrill," according to the minutes; she said that everybody should respect each other regardless of gender and the proposal should be deleted.[65] Long "responded that she felt the discussion had brought the matter to the attention of the membership, and consequently could support [the] suggestion to delete it." According to the minutes, the discussion of the fourth proposal ended with President Hymes noting that the sense seemed to be that problems exist but there wasn't agreement on how to word the proposal. The proposal was "noted and withdrawn."[66]

Proposal V addressed women's declining numbers in "positions of honor and responsibility."[67] The focus of this tense discussion came to be the argument that, as "Rayna Green pointed out the finding in chart #5 of the report: 'since 1963, no US citizen who is a woman has been elected a Fellow of the American Folklore Society.'"[68] This led to what reads as a tense conversation between Dorson and Long, as Long objected to what Dorson seemed to hear as an attack on Linda Dégh, a Hungarian-born folklorist he had recruited to Indiana University, who had been elected to the Fellows in 1971.

According to the minutes, with agreement from Long, "President Hymes announced to the membership that no vote was necessary here since the intention was for the Society to take note of the situation" based on the wording of the proposal.[69] The minutes also show that the two agreed that Part 2 of the report was "meant to be noted and not voted upon."[70] There being no further discussion, "President Hymes thanked Ms. Long for her report,"[71] and they moved on to a report from Archie Green on the status of the American Folklife Preservation Act.

In summary, then, proposals I and III were each passed with one "no" vote, proposal II was tabled, proposal IV was withdrawn, and no vote was held on proposal V. Although the CSWP continued and was in fact expanded the following year, this appears to be the last report presented by any member of the committee. In late summer and early fall 1974, there was correspondence between Hymes and both Eleanor Long and Virginia Briscoe (chair of the Women's Caucus Steering Committee, discussed below) about the continuation of the committee with additional members. In late July, Hymes wrote to Secretary-Treasurer Richard Bauman about several matters including the CSWP.[72] Hymes told Bauman that Briscoe had contacted him requesting that he enlarge the committee and providing a list of nominees chosen by the Women's Caucus.[73] In a letter dated August 20, Long tells Hymes that she heard from Briscoe as well, and they'd both like an update.[74] The next correspondence in the files is not until September 10, when Hymes wrote separate letters to Long and Briscoe apologizing for not acting in regard to the committee, but he "thought he was waiting to hear from others before being in a position to act."[75] He asked them each to let him know what they wanted to do, and he then mentioned the growing push since the discussion at the 1973 meeting for establishing a "committee on the general status of the profession, regarding employment especially; if the board feels it should act in this regard, then some relationship between such a committee and the women's committee would need to be established. But at this point the essential thing is to know what the people concerned with the women's committee would wish to do. This is a subject on which I don't want to be unilateral, more even than on others."[76]

It is unclear what other information he wanted from them, but the CSWP did not meet at the 1974 meeting. According to a report in the *FFC*, at the 1974 Women's Caucus meeting Eleanor Long reported on the history of the CSWP and Virginia Briscoe then reported that Karen Baldwin, Camilla Collins, Frank de Caro, Janet Langlois, and Janice Owen were added to the committee (de Caro 1975a). Though the committee didn't meet during the annual meeting, it appears that some of them either met or corresponded at some point, as Eleanor Long, Rayna Green, Frank Hoffman, Frank de Caro, and Camilla Collins sent a letter to the AFS Executive Board in January 1975. The letter was printed in the *FFC*, and in it they briefly followed up on four issues of ongoing concern, with a mix of praise for AFS's actions and further suggestions (Long et al. 1975). The CSWP was mentioned again in the summary of the 1975 Women's Caucus meeting, but there is no indication that they had met or were working (Bromberg-Ross 1976, 17). Mention of the CSWP faded, and it appears that its business moved in two directions within the AFS: the Women's Caucus, which would later become the present-day Women's Section of the AFS, and the State of the Profession Committee.

The Women's Caucus of the AFS was formed the very same day as the 1973 business meeting at which Long presented her report.[77] The connection between the two was made explicit by Rosan Jordan de Caro in the second issue of *Folklore Feminists Communication*:

> That the AFS is still unable to come to terms with the needs of women in the Society, however, became apparent at the annual business meeting. The reaction to a set of rather innocuous proposals presented by the chairman of the Society's Committee on the Status of Women was, to say the least, disheartening. In effect, the Society failed to take any meaningful stand on issues or to involve itself in any kind of affirmative action. Also disturbing, however, was the way in which the Society revealed its lack of supportiveness for its female constituents; at several points, in fact, women's very real problems were simply made into a subject for ridicule. The session was a clear demonstration of the need for the formation of the Women's Caucus. (de Caro Jordan 1974, 2)

The Women's Caucus resulted from discussions among women and men interested in both political and scholarly attention to women's folklore and women folklorists, and many of these discussions began at the University of Texas at Austin. The Center for Intercultural Studies in Folklore and Oral History was established at UT in 1967 (Bauman 2020, 131), followed by the creation of a graduate program that welcomed its first class of students in 1971. In these years, there were a great number of women students at UT, and Frank de Caro and Rosan Jordan spent a year there when de Caro was a visiting faculty member. According to Jordan, being at Texas that year led to meeting the students there, and "we all got involved in working together."[78] Former AFS president Kay Turner, who began her folklore training at UT in 1977—after Jordan and de Caro had returned to LSU, where they both spent their careers—echoed Jordan's sentiment: "I look back on that time and I realize that even though, of course, we didn't know each other [prior to graduate school], we were immediately engaged in this kind of formative feminist work." This continued for over a decade; according to Turner, until about "[19]86, Texas was definitely pushing the forefront of feminist folklore."[79] In 2016, Turner described the almost exclusively male faculty at UT of the time and said, "These men—they loved our feminist folklore. I never got any flak from any of those guys. They were like 'Go for it, Kay. This sounds really interesting. This sounds really, really good.' And I think it's important to bring that forward. Because those guys were young at the time too."[80]

The 1972 AFS Annual Meeting, held in Austin, provided "the impetus for beginning [the] publication" (de Caro Jordan, Farrer, and Kalčik 1973, 2) of the *Folklore Feminists Communication* (*FFC*) newsletter following a panel on "Folklore and Women"[81] as well as "informal meetings of women."[82] The first issue of the *FFC* was edited by Rosan Jordan, Claire Farrer, and Susan Kalčik, out of the Folklore Center at UT Austin, and the "primary aim [was] to serve as a medium of communication among those folklorists interested in the field of women's lore" (de Caro Jordan, Farrer, and Kalčik 1973, 2).[83] In the first and subsequent issues, the *FFC* provided a space for announcements, reports and queries on research in progress, bibliographies of works on women's folklore, biographies of women folklorists, and reports on the Women's Caucus and on the issues facing women as they took place within the AFS. Today, it is an extraordinary record of the times.[84]

Although the impetus grew out of the 1972 meeting, plans for both the *FFC* and the Women's Caucus were hatched at the home of Rosan Jordan and Frank de Caro in Austin in the summer of 1973, and the formal meeting to form the Women's Caucus took place at the annual meeting in Nashville that fall.[85] According to a report of the meeting in the *Folklore Feminists Communication*, there were about 80 people present at the meeting (de Caro 1974), demonstrating a strong interest in women's folklore and in change for women in the Society. Rosan Jordan said in 2016, "our first impetus was political more than theory."[86] According to de Caro writing in the *FFC*, at that meeting "It was generally agreed that the initiation of political action within the Society was desirable, although it was felt that a caucus might also help to promote women's studies in folklore" (de Caro 1974). The *FFC* was declared the official communication of the Caucus. The minutes reflect complicated discussions about the purpose, role, and structure of the caucus, as well as discussion of an issue that would come up again later, whether "the use of the term feminist might be inappropriate if the Caucus is to have nonpolitical functions."[87] A sentiment voiced by many at the business meeting in response to the CSWP report was present at the Women's Caucus meeting as well, but with a slight twist: "The point was made that the problems of women in folklore are not necessarily the problems of folklorists as a whole. Someone else agreed, but said that women can lead the way in seeing that power and responsibility within AFS are equitably distributed. Younger men within the Society may have similar problems, but experience indicates that women can force recognition first."[88]

The minutes of that first Caucus meeting and subsequent discussion in the *FFC* reflect strong feelings about the need for attention to the issues raised by the CSWP, as well as anger about the responses of some members to the report. There was brief discussion of Long's proposal regarding behaviors toward women members. Rosan Jordan expressed anger about the reaction of members to the proposal, noting that "the proposal represented real pain that women feel, yet this had been laughed at" (as summarized).[89]

According to the meeting minutes, "Rayna Green and Frank Hoffman[n] announced that they would resign as members of the AFS Committee on the Status of Women, so that this committee could get a fresh start," and attendees voted to put names forward to the AFS president (the names put forward included Green and Hoffmann, as well as Long).[90] The minutes do not list all attendees, and there is no mention of Eleanor Long's presence, but the first suggestion of a list of areas of concern was "Revision of the motions made in regard to the Long report."[91] While there had clearly been disagreement between the members that was shared among those in the newly formed Caucus, Long's report was not merely thrown out.

The steering committee met the following day, and Virginia Briscoe was elected chairperson,[92] leading to her attempts to work with Hymes to see that the CSWP continued and was enlarged, as described above. In the fall 1974 issue of the *FFC*, Briscoe provided a "progress report" on the Women's Caucus in which she discussed the primary issues of concern to the caucus in preparation for the AFS meeting in Portland. The issues included the status of the committee as well as some of those raised by Long, including women's leadership in the field and the "unease" of women graduate students. Kenneth Goldstein, in his role as secretary of the Fellows, was "asked to cooperate with the Women's Caucus. He agreed, and subsequently sent out with his request for nominations" a letter from the Steering Committee asking not for the election of more women to the Fellows, but to make "special efforts" to support women's access to the opportunities that would be necessary for them to meet the criteria for election to the Fellows (Briscoe 1974, 7; the letter to Goldstein is included in the issue).

Briscoe wrote, "With President Hymes' help the proposal to enlarge that Committee to include wider representation is in the process of being implemented. Unfortunately, this was not done early enough for the Committee to perform any active role during the year, but it should certainly be able to meet together in Portland and to proceed effectively from then on. . . . People who attend the Women's Caucus meeting in Portland should be prepared to state and defend" goals appropriate to the committee (1974, 8). As described above, while such discussions were held, the CSWP released no further reports—together or separately. By 1976, the committee appears to have dissolved with no formal announcement.

A second development within the AFS resulting at least in part from the CSWP was the establishment of the State of the Profession Committee. There are several links between the former Committee on the Status of Women and the State of the Profession Committee (SPC). The SPC was established as a standing committee of the executive board with the creation of a new AFS constitution, implemented in 1976, around the same time that the CSWP appears to have dissolved. The Women's Caucus was proactive in the constitution process, having established their own Task Force on the Reorganization of AFS, chaired by Susan Kalčik, who also served on the Committee on the Reorganization of the American Folklore Society. According to Kalčik, the committee was tasked with rewriting "the AFS Constitution to make the Society more efficient and democratic and to clarify confusions and vagueness in the Constitution and the Society's procedure [sic]" (1975b, 11), changes that would "affect the participation of women in the Society mainly by broadening the power base of AFS and thus offer[ing] more opportunities for input from women" (14).

The establishment of the SPC was part of this movement to "democratize" the AFS through the inclusion of more members in society business and decision-making. However, its formation was almost certainly stimulated if not prompted by the rhetoric of those involved in the CSWP and particularly the responses to Long's report in 1973: the challenges faced by women in folklore were also faced by men. The charges to and the work of the SPC link back, broadly speaking, to the issues raised by the CSWP, particularly to access to and qualifications for folklore jobs in both academic and public sectors and to the notion of a formal body to which AFS members could bring ideas and grievances. In a familiar scenario, when a group that had historically lacked power called attention to its position, they were told "everyone faces challenges," followed by a call for more generalized efforts for improvement.

The State of the Profession Committee was appointed by Ellen Stekert at the end of her term as AFS president, and it first met at the 1977 annual meeting in Detroit. Stekert provided a comprehensive charge to the committee in her president's report, based on the functions assigned to it in the new constitution, which were to make "suggestions to the Executive Board regarding constructive ideas and procedures relating to the state of folklore" and to act as "a monitor and a forum for grievances and concerns relating to the state of folklore, making specific recommendations to the Executive Board."[93] At their first meeting, Lynwood Montell of Western Kentucky University was elected chair, and the committee discussed many issues stemming from Stekert's charge. "The Committee members are anxious to help expedite solutions to problems which surface within the Society, and which vitally affect us all as folklorists. We do not want to be viewed solely as a grievance committee, but as a committee concerned with ethics, professional development and positive image projection in the public sector as well as academic."[94] This statement in the minutes is indicative of the major issues with which the new committee would concern itself, particularly two that were debated for years: the creation of a directory of professional folklorists, which entailed the difficult first step of defining the criteria for *professional folklorist*, and the development of a code of ethics.[95] In addition, the SPC also grappled with "the question of the American Folklore Society as a learned society or as a professional association." This question is particularly interesting as the underlying question it poses is in fact, "Who are we?" at a time at which folklore studies was still developing as an independent field, an increasing number of folklorists were creating jobs in the public sector, and issues of representation were increasingly being raised.

It is no surprise that as members of the field continued to ask "who are we?" within the context of the social and political climate of the 1970s, the three members of the Committee on the Status of Women in the Profession were not in agreement about how best to represent women in the profession and, by extension, the study of women's folklore. At a 2016 Feminism and Folklore Retrospective session, Susan Kalčik briefly described attending the AFS Annual Meeting for the first time and said, "That was the year that Rayna wrote her Report on the Status of Women in Folklore. [They had] three people on the Committee, and there were three reports because they could not agree on it. And you can imagine whose report we agreed with, and that was of course Rayna Green's. It was shocking and upsetting. There was a lot of energy and a lot of positive motion, but there was a lot of negative energy too."[96]

Eleanor Long was interviewed by folklorist Luisa Del Giudice in 1986, and Del Giudice asked Long whether she was aware of "women's networks within folklore groups." Long responded that while she was sure they existed, she'd not been involved: "Heavens, no. I was their worst enemy." Del Giudice asked her why, and she explained, "Well, D. K. [Wilgus] innocently appointed me to chair a commission to inquire into the status of women in folklore," and there had been difficulties with the "women's network" and with the response to her report from men and women. "I was between the fires of those who just think everything is lovely and those who would do anything just to have a fight." According to Long, the other members of the commission did not participate because the women's network "was apparently already working to sabotage the whole thing," and she sent out the questionnaire and "painfully" worked to create a report from the responses on her own. She expressed surprise at the "vehement responses about specific harassment of females by males," explaining that she was "familiar with that in other disciplines . . . [but] I've never had that kind of an experience with folklorists."[97]

Despite some apparent internal tensions and a lack of agreement on how best to represent women folklorists as well as their work with women's expressive cultures, women and men made strong calls for women's representation through the Committee on the Status of Women. Although immediate and satisfactory changes were certainly not made, there were indirect results. Both the Women's Caucus, which became the Women's Section in 1977,[98] and the CSWP opened discussions about women folklorists and by extension women's folklore. The State of the Profession Committee provided a means through which grievances and issues could be brought to the AFS, and among the first of such grievances was a call for a resolution against the AFS meeting in states that had not ratified the Equal Rights Amendment. We discuss this issue later in this chapter; first however, we turn back yet again to the 1973 AFS meeting. On the very same day that Eleanor Long reported her perspective on the status of women in folklore and the Women's Caucus was organized, feminist folklorists were also presenting their research on women's folklore, demonstrating that feminist folklorists were both engaged in the political questions of the day and working toward increased attention to researching women's expressive cultures.

"WORLD VIEW FROM THE MOP BUCKET": WOMEN'S FOLKLORE AND MALE EDITORIAL POWER

November 3, 1973, was a busy day for those involved in women's folklore, as in addition to the CSWP report and the Women's Caucus organization, two preorganized panels on folklore and women took place, entitled "Women in Groups: The Organization of Expressive Culture Among Women." Chaired by Claire Farrer, then a graduate student at the University of Texas—Austin, the panels included papers on Disney, folklorist Zora Neale Hurston, Native American costume, Mexican girls' play, women's consciousness raising groups, and other topics.[99] "Women in Groups" was, of course, a play on and critique of Lionel Tiger's 1969 *Men in Groups* in which, in Claire Farrer's words, "men were credited with establishing social life through their bonding" ([1975] 1986, vii). Farrer later wrote that she had originally wanted to entitle the panels "World View from the Mop Bucket." She explained, "Most of us, even while full time graduate students, were holding down jobs, raising our children alone (but with ample help from each other) and doing all the usual mommy things—including coping with the mop bucket and diaper pail on one hand and holding a book with the other hand while trying to learn to become scholars. The mop bucket was still very much part of our lives" (viii). "[Professors Richard] Bauman and [Roger] Abrahams, however, insisted that, if we wished to be taken seriously by a scholarly community, our inside jokes would have to be forgone in favor of a title that would suggest respectability" (viii).

Farrer also later noted that the sessions were "gratifyingly packed despite our being scheduled opposite some of the most productive and well-known male scholars in our discipline" ([1975] 1986, ix). Indeed, a check of the program demonstrates this, as two concurrent panels featured important topics of the day by heavyweights of the period: "Poetics and Folklore" included Richard Bauman, Dan Ben-Amos, Dell Hymes, William Labov, and others; "Black American Material Culture" featured John Burrison, Gerald L. Davis, William R. Ferris, Gladys-Marie Fry, and John M. Vlach.[100] This was 1973, and folklorists were busy challenging old perspectives on folklore in a myriad of ways.

JAF editor Barre Toelken immediately laid out plans to publish a special issue based on the Women in Groups panels, and it became the first of two twentieth-century issues of *JAF* dedicated to feminist folklore; both would turn out to be cases in which male editorial power got "in the way of" women's publications. As Margaret Mills described it in 1993, as she attempted to "re-hear" "the last twenty years of folklore theory and feminist theory as a dialogue," both special issues "were editorially contested" (Mills 1993, 175). "The feminist assemblers of these collections were second-guessed in each case by the male general editors of the journal, perhaps claiming paternity, or at least godfatherhood, of the ideas being delivered" (175).

Like other case studies in this book, some may dismiss these difficult situations as simply about personalities and interpersonal conflict, but we—like Mills—argue that such simplifications mask more significant issues in not only folklore but academics more widely, in this case gendered power over rights of representation. Not only were these exertions of power troubling at the time, but the second case in particular continues to deeply trouble the women scholars involved. In both cases, the male editors espoused their dedication to publishing work on women's folklore, but at the same time, they each undermined the efforts of the women involved to maintain control over their work. Further, in both cases, they enlisted other women in challenging the work, even as they published it.

The issue, entitled "Women and Folklore: Images and Genres," ended up with both some of the papers from the original panels and additional papers that Claire Farrer solicited. Farrer did ensure that the issue was published in book form and that it was reissued in 1986. In the reissue, she provided "A Personal, Retrospective Introduction" in which she expressed gratitude to Barre Toelken for being "willing to risk publishing" the issue (Farrer, [1975] 1986, ix). However, she also described editorial changes that she was not informed of, such as a reordering of the articles, which she had organized based on the title ("images" and "genres"), and the cutting of entire portions of articles (ix).[101]

JOURNAL OF
AMERICAN
FOLKLORE

Figure 3.2 *Journal of American Folklore* 88, no. 347 (1975) was the first issue of the journal devoted to women's folklore. The issue resulted from two pre-organized panels on folklore and women at the 1973 Annual Meeting of the American Folklore Society entitled "Women in Groups: The Organization of Expressive Culture Among Women," chaired by Claire Farrer. Courtesy of the American Folklore Society.

Rosan Jordan described some of the difficulties of the 1975 special issue of *JAF* based on the 1973 panels in an editorial in the *FFC* in 1976: "First there was the long delay in the publication of the issue; and then there was the decision not to bring out *Women and Folklore* in a hardback edition as has been done for previous special issues of JAF. Finally, there was the snafu involving an out of date mailing list and the switchover of responsibilities from the University of Texas Press to the American Anthropological Association; as a result many subscribers failed to receive the issue" (1976, 4). Then, as she went on to describe, there was the shock of receiving the issue and seeing the inclusion of a response that was highly critical, discussed below.

Toelken began his short foreword with praise for the ways in which the field has in fact seen the participation of more women than many fields, naming prominent women in the disciplinary history as well as the history of the AFS. "Why, then, are we now told in this collection of essays that we have not done all right? The answers to that will be many, and I will not presume to give more than one possible exoteric comment on the matter: the women listed above have had to operate in a field that for the most part has been conceived of by men" (Toelken 1975, iii). He went on to say that the "existence of women in the field" did not automatically equate with sufficient attention to "the topic of folklore among women" (iii). He then suggested that the authors ignored exceptions to this and that due to the lack of "an extensive foundation of previous scholarship which might otherwise have provided some terminology and theory," the authors had "sense[d] the topics must be approached by intuition and experience and by analogy to other fields of inquiry" (iv). As Jordan described it, "What he really seems to be saying is that the writers involved in this issue have simply not done their homework in searching for a solid theoretical basis for their arguments" (1976, 5). This will remind readers of the infamous statement by James Clifford, in his introduction to *Writing Culture: The Poetics and Politics of Ethnography* a decade later, that "Feminists had not contributed much to the theoretical analysis of ethnographies as texts" (1986, 20), sparking, among other things, the publication of the collection *Women Writing Culture* (Behar and Gordon 1996).[102]

"A Response to the Symposium" by Polly Stewart Deemer was solicited by Toelken "so that," he wrote, "there could be an actual sense in this issue of a scholarly discussion generated but not supplied by the participants themselves" (Toelken 1975, iv). Jordan argued that Toelken's choice to solicit Deemer's response was based in his "doubts about the academic respectability of the articles" (1976,4), and she critiqued Deemer's response for her focus on "flaws in the methodology of the researchers."[103]

Deemer spent the first two pages discussing women's socialization "to be 'pleasing'" and "not to argue" and said that "the difficulty is compounded when I—a feminist—am asked to respond critically to papers written by women, some of whom are also feminists and with whom I am seeking certain political goals for the Women's Movement" (Deemer 1975, 102). She called for a separation of folklore scholarship from politics, characterizing such moves "tiresome at best, and at worst . . . fascistic. While I am happy to report that none of the articles in this symposium approaches anywhere near fascistic, it does seem that some of them verge on the tiresome" (102). She went on to critique the individual articles for, among other things, being too political, "pointing out the obvious," and demonstrating bias.

Although Farrer critiqued neither Toelken's foreword nor Deemer's response in her later introduction, the fact that neither was included in the reissue suggests that like Jordan she was unhappy with both. Clearly, at least some of those involved in this experience felt that the issue had been taken out of their hands in ways that exemplified what women were fighting for in this period. The implication seems to have been that the control over the scholarly attention to women's folklore was still controlled by men.

A decade later, feminist folklorists once again experienced the exertion of power by a male editor of *JAF* over their attempts to publish their work. In 1986, a committee of feminist folklorists at the University of Texas at Austin—Linda Pershing, Patricia Sawin, Suzanne Seriff, Beverly Stoeltje, Kay Turner, and M. Jane Young—organized a feminist symposium held within the annual meeting of the AFS: "A Feminist Retrospective on Folklore and Folkloristics." As will become important in this brief look at what followed, most were students at the time; Stoeltje and Young were early career faculty. The symposium was an all-day event on Friday, October 24, with multiple panels (papers and forums) held concurrently with the regular paper sessions, as well as a morning plenary and luncheon session. The planning committee described the purpose of the symposium in the *AFS Newsletter* as "a concentrated effort toward the further delineation of feminist theory as applied to women's folklore." They continued, "Folklorists have a significant contribution to make to the growing body of feminist theory and feminist theory in turn can advance our understanding of folklore" (Pershing et al. 1985, 1).

Linda Pershing, Suzanne Seriff, Beverly Stoeltje, and Kay Turner all said in interviews that the organizers intended for the symposium papers to be published. *JAF* editor Bruce Jackson began making plans to publish a special issue even before the symposium took place, and as evidence from the AFS archives make clear, he also had a book version in mind long before the publication of the issue. For instance, in a letter to AFS Secretary Treasurer Timothy Lloyd dated October 25, 1986—the day after the symposium—he asked how royalties would work if the special issue became a book.[104] A postcard to Judith McCulloh of the University of Illinois Press dated January 10, 1987, proclaimed, "Folklore & feminism book is yours," suggesting that he and McCulloh were already in discussions about UIP publishing the book, months before the *JAF* issue was published the following fall.[105]

Kay Turner told us she had phone conversations with Jackson in the spring of 1987 in which she repeatedly told him that his plans for the book were not acceptable. Yet, in a July 1987 letter to the contributors, he informed them that he was planning to reprint the issue with no opportunities for revision; the only addition would be an introduction by a yet to be determined "feminist scholar," and he would provide a "different editor's foreword."[106] In other words, he planned to remain the editor and maintain full control. According to Turner, "Our pushback was simply that we never, ever gave him an inch about the fact that this book was

The American Folklore Society Newsletter

Women's Folklore News

Women's Section To Meet

The AFS Women's Section will be convened this year by Susan Kalčik and Polly Stewart. (See the preliminary program in this newsletter for the time and date of the session.) To obviate difficulties encountered in the past, we're making some changes. For one, we will not commit ourselves to a cash bar, believing there must be less financially onerous ways to have a drink or two. Second, Frank de Caro has generously agreed to render himself momentarily *hors de combat* by serving as recording secretary. Finally, sensing that newer members of the Women's Section are puzzled and even frustrated at oldtimers' references to events of ancient times (eg, 1972), we are initiating what we hope will become a tradition—a brief oral history of the Women's Section, including the reasons we formed at the outset and the changes we have since undergone. Accordingly, we have tentatively set the following agenda:

Call to Order (Polly)
History (Susan)
Old Business (Susan): AFS Centennial preparations
New Business (Polly):
    Memorial for Barbara Myerhoff (Barbara Kirshenblatt-Gimblett)
    Other
Adjournment

Inside . . .

Preliminary Program for the 1985 Annual Meeting

See pages 3-8

If you would like to add items to the agenda, please notify Susan (202/357-4008) or Polly (301/546-3860).

Polly Stewart

"Feminism and Folklore" Sessions Planned For '86

Women folklorists of the University of Texas propose the organization of a special program "Feminism and Folklore: Women's Analytical Perspectives" to be convened during one full day of the AFS Annual Meetings in Baltimore, Maryland in 1986. Within the past 10 or 15 years, folklore *of* and *about* women has become an area of increasing interest within the discipline of folklore. Although a great deal of data has been collected, much of it has not been analyzed from a theoretical perspective, largely because there has been a need for the formulation of new theories and new terminology to apply to these data. For this reason, the purpose of the day is to exert a concentrated effort toward the further delineation of feminist theory as applied to women's folklore. Folklorists have a significant contribution to make to the growing body of feminist theory and feminist theory in turn can advance our understanding of folklore.

The program will run concurrently with other regularly scheduled AFS panels, but will have its own internal coherency in terms of a preplanned format, consistent location within the hotel, and so on. The day is planned to include an opening plenary session, several panels and workshops throughout the morning and afternoon, organized lunch gatherings devoted to specific concerns of women in the profession, and an evening women's section meeting followed by a party.

Panel themes and individual papers should be analytically based. They should demonstrate the relationship between contemporary feminist theory and folklore scholarship. A range of themes is encouraged; some possibilities include: "A Feminist Reconsideration of the Folklore of Domesticity," "Feminism, Totem and Taboo," "The Folklore of Birth/Reproduction and Social Reproduction," "Tradition: A Feminist Perspective," "Feminists Revamp the Folklore Canon," "Feminist Interpretations of Myths, Legends and Tales," "Women's Words of Power: Speech Acts and Social Strategies," and "Ritual and Performance: A Feminist View."

Workshops will offer the opportunity for women to meet in small groups in order to informally discuss their own research with respect to feminist theory. For those who want to participate in either the panels or workshops, there will be special boxes to check on the regular abstract forms for the Baltimore meeting. Discussion of details is invited at a meeting in Cincinnati; time and place will be announced at the women's section meeting.

Linda Pershing
Suzy Seriff
Beverly Stoeltje
Kay Turner
M. Jane Young

Job Bulletin

Recruitment has either begun or will begin during the coming summer for 11 new full-time positions for public sector folklorists. In these unusual circumstances, the NEA Folk Arts Program has volunteered to act as a temporary clearinghouse, passing along information as it comes in to interested candidates at 202/682-5449.

Figure 3.3 Feminist folklorists at the University of Texas planned the 1986 symposium "A Feminist Retrospective on Folklore and Folkloristics." An overview of the early planning was published in *The American Folklore Society Newsletter* (14 [4]: 1 [1985]). Courtesy of the American Folklore Society.

going to be edited by women. It was a women's project about feminism and no, he couldn't take the candy home and eat it himself. It was not gonna happen."[107]

While the many letters written by Jackson to various people connected in some way to the publication of the special issue leave no doubt that this was a brutal exertion of male power, conversations with Pershing, Seriff, Stoeltje, and Turner made it clear that of course the archival record does not fully represent the experiences of the women involved. While our space here is limited, it must be noted that all of those we interviewed described Jackson's behavior as abusive, and they stressed that all involved were particularly vulnerable because they were students and early career women. Turner told us that Jackson repeatedly threatened her over the phone, saying at one point that he could ruin her. Most of them stressed that, in Linda Pershing's words, "The only way this could have happened is when senior members of the Society, including senior women, remained silent."[108] Pershing also stressed that the women involved weren't all in agreement about how best to handle the situation—for instance, she had favored speaking out more publicly and loudly about Jackson's actions—but they maintained their personal and professional relationships.

In July 1987, Jackson canceled the plans with UIP for the book. The special issue, "Folklore and Feminism," was published as the centennial issue in the fall of 1987. While its place as "the final issue in the *Journal*'s first century of continuous publication" (Jackson 1987, 387) suggests a major emphasis on feminist folklore studies in the field, the backstory suggests a different story. Turner told us, "I think the whole idea of folklore and feminism could have been easily crushed at that moment in history." She continued, "[The discipline of] folklore was conservative around sex and gender. It just was. The history shows it."[109]

In his introduction to the special issue, Jackson described the situation as he apparently saw it; he noted that a book had been his intention, "But a curious and unfortunate sequence of events, none the fault of the university press, the AFS Executive Board, or the staff of JAF, prevented publication of that inexpensive and timely paperback" (1987, 388). His introduction is a glowing review of the symposium itself as well as the range of topics included in the sixteen essays in the issue. In a repeat of the 1970s, however, Jackson published a response that was a complete surprise to the authors, though this time it appeared in the issue that followed. Written by Diane Christian, who was married to Jackson, the response was a scathing essay entitled "Not One New Truth and All the Old Falsehoods" focused entirely on the article by Turner and Seriff (Christian 1988). After its publication, Turner and Seriff wrote a detailed letter to the AFS Executive Board, arguing that this was a vindictive and retaliatory act resulting from Turner's adamant refusal to allow Jackson to have editorial control of a book. Among their points, they noted that Christian had been thanked by Jackson in his introduction to the special issue "for her essential help throughout this project—ranging from an insightful critical reading of the final papers and galley sheets to discovery of the Hudson Talbott painting we used for the cover" (Jackson 1987, 389). In their letter, Turner and Seriff pointed out that the response by Christian raised a number of ethical questions, including the fact that Jackson had written in the introduction that she'd provided a "critical reading" prior to publication.

> It seems odd to us that we never received the benefits of
> Christian's criticism <u>before</u> our article was published. . . .
> In fact, we received a letter of acceptance from Jackson (see
> attached) stating simply 'Your article is terrific.' He required
> no substantive revisions from us, regarding either theory or
> the content of our paper. Christian's commentary opens with a
> casual and innocent air ' . . . I turned with interest to the article
> in the Folklore and Feminism issue of JAF on women's role
> in a St. Joseph's Day celebration,' as if she had never before
> seen the manuscript until she opened her published copy of
> JAF 398.[110]

The publication of the response in the issue that followed certainly opened the space for an assumption that the response was formulated after the issue was in print. Turner and Seriff go on to note that they "were never given the opportunity to prepare a rebuttal that would appear in the same issue as Christian's criticisms," as is common editorial practice, indicating to them that

"Jackson consciously thwarted scholarly discussion on this subject in order to gain retribution."

The matter of this special issue was not discussed only among the symposium planners and the contributors; it was also taken up in several venues by those directly involved as well as some who were not. For instance, according to the minutes of the Executive Board Question and Answer Session in October 1988, University of Houston folklorist Carl Lindahl raised concerns about the circumstances of Christian's response. This was followed by a discussion involving several AFS members, including defenders of Jackson, though the minutes note that none of those directly concerned were present.[111] In October 1988, the board discussed "the recent history and controversies surrounding current *Journal* editor Bruce Jackson," and "members expressed both support for Jackson's editorship and criticism of it." The board then voted to reappoint Jackson as editor without considering other candidates.[112] According to Linda Pershing, reflecting on this fact, "There were so many people in positions of authority who were willing to either stay silent or to condone what he was doing, and that tells you a lot about the Society. . . . You can be a bully, and not only can you get away with it, people will pat you on the back and give you another term to edit the journal."[113]

The women involved succeeded in seeing two collections of feminist folklore scholarship through to publication in 1993, each including papers that had been part of the symposium and special issue, along with other papers. *Feminist Theory and the Study of Folklore,* edited by Susan Tower Hollis, Linda Pershing, and M. Jane Young, was a direct result of the symposium and special issue while *Feminist Messages: Coding in Women's Folklore,* edited by Joan Newlon Radner, developed from interest in the concept of "feminist coding" following presentations by Radner and Lanser during the symposium.[114] Both of these collections remain benchmarks of feminist folklore study and continue to be read and assigned in folklore courses. Although Turner described these publications as a sign that they had ultimately "won" because Jackson didn't get to edit the books, Pershing—with a different perspective as a coeditor of *Feminist Theory and the Study of Folklore*—stressed to us that she had not felt that they had control of the publication process due to what she described as "residue" from the fact that Judith McCulloh had worked so closely with and supported Jackson. As Mills wrote that same year, "The two books now emerging from the 1987 collective effort (Radner 1993; Hollis, Pershing, and Young 1993) to sum up our theoretical labors, have also gotten long and intense editing, in part because the foregrounding of theory has taken some extra effort. Certainly all collected-paper 'concept' volumes are hard to edit for similar reasons, but it seems to me gender theory in folklore offers a particularly intense case" (Mills 1993, 175).

The publication of both *JAF* issues devoted to feminist folklore are important milestones that suggest editorial support, and perhaps support from the field more widely, for serious scholarly attention to women's folklore from a feminist perspective. However, in both cases male authority was wielded behind the scenes by male editors with the support of the AFS and other folklorists. The women involved in each issue were simultaneously fighting to control the publication of work that represented women's expressive culture grounded in feminist theory and fighting for their rights to control that representation as women scholars. Meanwhile, one of the most hotly debated issues within the AFS involved how best to respond, as a society, to the national debate over women's rights to equality and representation under the law. Like our other examples, the debates related to the ERA are important reminders of the ties between folklore studies and other academic disciplines as well as the broader US feminist movement.

THE EQUAL RIGHTS AMENDMENT AND THE 1978 AFS ANNUAL MEETING IN SALT LAKE CITY, UTAH

The 1978 annual meeting of the AFS was held at the Hotel Utah in Salt Lake City, Utah, on October 12–15. The year leading up to the meeting was a tumultuous one for the AFS Executive Board and at least a portion of the membership, as well as for the newly created Women's Section and State of the Profession Committee. As reflected in executive board and business meeting minutes and in correspondence, the decision to meet in Utah, and particularly at the Hotel Utah, created a perfect storm of controversy that exemplified a central issue of the times but also one that has still not been resolved, either for the AFS or for other professional societies: whether to make meeting site decisions based on "politics." It was far more complicated, of course, as the debates encompassed questions of not only politics but also gendered power, religion, legends and rumors, personal attacks, and the unfortunate timing of the shift of the AFS Annual Meeting logistics planning to the American Anthropological Association (AAA). While this example is about the debate within the AFS, it represents difficult discussions that continue within academic societies across disciplines today. As the sites of professional meetings and conferences become contested, such debates represent deeper questions about relationships between academia, politics, and activism.

Utah was among the fifteen states that had not ratified the Equal Rights Amendment, section one of which states, "Equality of rights under the law shall not be denied or abridged by the United States or by any state on account of sex." The ERA had passed Congress in 1972, and three-quarters of the states had to ratify it by March 1979 for it to amend the US Constitution. In 1977, only three more states were needed for ratification. As we know, even though Congress extended the date to 1982 it was never fully ratified (and Utah never ratified it), and therefore the

US Constitution has yet to be amended to guarantee equal rights to women.

In this period, the AFS Executive Board met on the days immediately prior to and following the annual meeting. This is relevant because in 1977 the board voted prior to the annual meeting *not* to meet in Salt Lake City, Utah, the following year and then reversed its decision four days later and continued with plans to meet in Utah. The archival record tells some of what happened in that time. At their November 2 meeting, the AFS Executive Board considered a motion to "accept the invitation from [Utah folklorist and AFS member] Jan Brunvand for the 1978 AFS meeting to be held in Salt Lake City." This led to "extensive discussion" "regarding the issue of meeting in a place which had not ratified and was actively campaigning against the Equal Rights Amendment; the issue of whether Board decisions should be made on political grounds; and whether it was possible for such decisions not to be political." The motion to accept Brunvand's invitation to meet in Salt Lake City then failed, having resulted in a tie vote. Two additional motions were then made, seconded, and carried: that the meeting be held in another city and that the American Anthropological Association—purely coincidentally for the first time—"be instructed to handle local arrangements for the 1978 meeting according to its standard protocol, including hotel negotiations."[115] Unfortunately for the historic record, it is at this time that the minutes shifted from a detailed narrative summary that included partial transcription of discussion to a record only of actions taken.[116]

Two days later, AFS President Barre Toelken had second thoughts. For reasons not clear, Toelken had to leave the AFS meeting suddenly on Saturday, November 5, prior to both the business meeting and the second executive board meeting. He wrote a letter to David Hufford, Secretary Treasurer of the AFS, at three a.m. on the fifth, scrawling at the top of this handwritten letter, "Feel free to read any or all of this to Board or Business mtng if germane." Toelken briefly mentions other matters of business and then focuses on his regrets about the vote not to meet in Utah: "A bothersome matter: on further reflection, and after discussion with Brunvand/Wilson/Cannon, I feel we really botched ourselves up on the vote to cancel Utah. I hope someone will reintroduce it for vote," and he lists four reasons, including the effects on those who have started the planning and on Utah folklorists as well as the lost opportunity to meet in such a "folkloristically interesting place." Most germane here:

> It meddles in the politics of the State of Utah, and in a partisan way; and connected to this—since many people there are guided in this instance by religious conviction—it forms the precedent for the AFS to appear aligned against people for their political[117] application of religious beliefs (what will this do for credibility of those folklorists working with other[118] religious groups, or those working in areas which are politically sensitive?)[119]

We quote from this letter at length not only because it frames much of how the debates about meeting in Utah would play out but because the perspective he articulates is one that continues to be articulated today, and not just within AFS.

> I am concerned (maybe "horrified" is a better term) that if we let this action stand, we will have made a large policy decision which we cannot possibly live with: behind the move is the general dictum "The AFS shall bestow its presence on[120] (or withdraw it from) those places where the membership by so doing can show disapproval of political stances not to their liking." I would anticipate that any reasonable person—and I shall be among them—will want to ensure that we not meet in states which have not outlawed the KKK, where abortion is illegal, where Indians starve to death, where Mexican-Americans are systematically mistreated, where Chinese are imprisoned in sweat-shops, where large corporations supply war material or other aid to South Africa, where all citizens do not have access to a regular education. Do I hear any nominations for next year's meeting within the continental US?
>
> More disturbing in some ways is the fact that by meeting in Utah we could have demonstrated the many central ways in

which women function in our profession. What do we demonstrate by <u>not</u> going? Nothing but narrow-mindedness.

I would like the Exec. Board (and the membership) to take a look at the question of whether they envision a professional organization <u>such as ours</u>—with the delicate relationships we often claim to have with folks in the street—putting political action (that is passé anyhow, since Utah will not likely revote the issue—especially not on our account) <u>over</u> the professional welfare of our colleagues in folklore.

If the AFS is moving in that direction, I would like to suggest that they may want to reexamine the credentials of their leaders. I, at any rate, do not feel adequate to the task of political action on ERA or any other such issue, leading the troops angrily out of town. I would feel better leading the friendly troops into town to show people what we do and what it has to do with their real lives. I am interested in supporting and nurturing folklorists in such places as Utah and I don't think that argues against the ERA at all. If these matters <u>are</u> in conflict with each other, I am serving under false pretenses.[121]

The following day the business meeting was held, and the rules were suspended "in order to allow immediate discussion of new business concerning the 1978 annual meeting."[122]

Although the Women's Section requested that a resolution be placed on the agenda, a representative asked that it be removed; in the next issue of the *Folklore Women's Communication*, the section Steering Committee provided a complicated explanation for withdrawing the resolution due to a lack of time for reaching agreement by members of the section.[123] The resolution, which was printed in the *FWC* along with a ballot for voting by the section membership, included a call for AFS support of the ERA and for the AFS to hold annual meetings only in ratified states. It also included an amendment calling on the State of the Profession Committee to develop "a code of ethics which would include a statement on the rights and responsibilities of its members with regard to human rights, especially of those persons who are elderly, female, homosexual or handicapped and those who belong to an ethnic or cultural minority. That moreover, the Committee should instruct the membership in drawing up a policy of equal opportunity within the Society itself, to apply to all persons regardless of age, national origin, gender, sexual preference, race or physical disability."[124] This call points to the connections between the SPC and the push for women's representation in ways discussed earlier in this chapter. It also represents how the ERA issue had come to be framed as a human rights issue, broadening it beyond the immediate call for support of women's rights.

During the business meeting, two motions regarding the Utah meeting were made and carried—each by paper ballot, suggesting discomfort with a public voice vote—by the membership in attendance: to ask the board to reconsider not meeting in Utah and to instruct the board to select Utah as the meeting site. The minutes do not report the vote count. Later in the meeting, a motion carried "To instruct the Executive Board to separate the issue of whether or not to meet in Salt Lake City from the issue of support for the Equal Rights Amendment."[125] The following day, November 6, the board voted to meet in Salt Lake City in 1978 and to ask Jan Brunvand and William (Bert) Wilson to serve as cochairs of the Local Arrangements Committee, noting the motion approved at the November 2 meeting that the AAA handle the logistics, including hotel negotiations. Through this, AAA director Edward J. Lehman became a central actor in the decisions to come. A motion was also made and carried "That Board decisions are not to be construed as politically motivated."[126]

Of course, the board's decision was seen by some as politically motivated, and this fueled rather than ended the controversy. It was in fact reignited when, in January 1978, the Hotel Utah was chosen as the conference hotel. This resulted in letters back and forth between board members regarding just what the discussion had been at the November 6 meeting regarding the choosing of a hotel—namely, whether they had decided not to choose a hotel owned by the Mormon Church *and* whether the Hotel Utah was actually owned by the Mormon Church. Hufford attempted to quell the situation in March with a letter to the board describing his "understanding of the Board decision":

> At the Sunday Board meeting I asked the board to instruct me to tell Ed Lehman not to select the Hotel Utah because I had gained the impression that there was a lot of concern that this would increase whatever controversy the Salt Lake meeting selection might ultimately cause. However, the Board responded with the point that a decision had been made not to make business decisions for the Society on such political grounds, and that this should apply to the hotel too. In other words, we should let AAA select whatever hotel could provide the best deal and meeting facilities. This is therefore what I instructed Ed Lehman. He did just that, and that is how the Hotel Utah was selected.[127]

Barre Toelken followed this up with a letter to the board three days later, reiterating that the board decided to leave the matter of choosing the hotel to Lehman to get the best terms and accommodations (although he was not in attendance). He then went on to discuss the ownership of the Hotel Utah in terms especially appropriate to folklorists: "Someone should write a book about modern legends about all the corporations and business enterprises owned by the Mormon Church. One hears that the Mormon Church owns Western Airlines, Coca Cola, US Steel, and many other large businesses. If the American Folklore Society does indeed wish to stagger the Mormon Church by boycotting all those businesses which in legend are owned and operated by the Church, where would we begin?" He went on to say that the church owns very little, though members are on boards and give proceeds to the church, and that the hotel is owned by a real estate corporation and that "many of the directors of this corporation are in fact leaders of the Mormon Church."[128]

This raises an issue that does not show up in the sparse minutes of the business meeting the previous fall, but it is referenced in the archival record and remembered by some who were present: one or more of those arguing for the AFS to meet someplace other than Utah couched their argument in terms that others heard as anti-Mormon. This is the basis of a March 1978 letter from Toelken, a letter of "formal apology" to Bert Wilson, a prominent folklorist and a Mormon, "for the attack upon the Mormon Church which was allowed to occur at the Annual Business Meeting in Detroit—unchallenged by officers and uninterrupted by the Chair." He did not quite say, though it seems implied, that he was not present at the meeting; in his absence, the meeting was chaired by past president Ellen Stekert. He described the "attack," which he suggested was made by one speaker in particular though he names no one, as "extend[ing] political passions into the odious arena of religion-baiting. Indeed, it has been axiomatic among folklorists in recent years to insist that sensitivity to the beliefs and worldviews of other groups is a basic ingredient of the right to work among them and discuss their traditions."[129]

Hufford wrote to the board again in April, framing the controversy in terms of rumors—"The Board, Ed Lehman, the Society, and some members of the Society are currently the victim of a set of erroneous rumors, the potential consequences of which are very serious"—and offered a point-by-point rebuttal to a three-part set of rumors regarding the choosing of the Hotel Utah: That the board agreed not to choose that hotel, that Ed Lehman did so anyway due to pressure from Brunvand, and that Lehman then refused to continue the planning due to Brunvand's pressure. Hufford's tone seems one of panic. He feared it was about to grow worse, as the FWC was preparing "to publish some materials from various individuals on precisely the topics of these rumors," though editor Marta Weigle had agreed to wait for a statement to be approved by the board before doing so.[130] His draft statement on behalf of the board was approved at the June 1978 board meeting.[131] The board also unanimously signed off on the "Board Statement of Chronology," a nineteen-point list beginning with the initial invitations for the 1978 meeting site, through Lehman's request that "the Local Arrangements Committee handle the remaining tasks of hotel liaison" in order to "avoid confusion" while the AAA would continue to handle "registration services, etc."[132]

Over the course of the spring and summer, AFS members who opposed the meeting in Utah, including those who favored a boycott of the annual meeting, made their voices heard in various ways. The FWC provides a valuable accounting of the opposition. In the spring 1978 issue, the Women's Section Steering Committee provided an update, including that they were investigating the organization of an alternative conference and that they created a questionnaire, included in the issue, regarding interest in boycotting the meeting.[133] The issue also includes a nearly six-page piece by Rayna Green, entitled "On AFS, Human Rights, and the Salt Lake City Meeting: Thoughts and Strategies" (R. Green 1978).

Green's piece exemplifies the perspective that a line cannot be drawn between academics and politics—in any field, but certainly not folklore studies, due to our subject. She began by stressing that her initial "instinct was to convince everyone to go [to the Utah meeting] and raise hell. Still trapped by a nice vision of working within the system, I reasoned the AFS was too tiny to make any economic impact in the organized boycott" (R. Green 1978, 4).[134] However, "The choice of the Hotel Utah once again proves that individuals who are part of the structure run things, and individuals have the power. New rules don't change old boys, and the old boys' rules seem to be running both AFS and the women they allow into the system." "Executive Board resolutions to the contrary, that choice was a political action" (4).

She laid out seven steps that could be taken by those in opposition to the meeting site, including resigning from the AFS, boycotting the meeting or portions of it, and "raising hell" at the meeting (R. Green 1978, 7–8). "Raising hell" might include various forms of speaking out (she recommends stopping short of being jailed). "But ask yourself if we would still be in Vietnam if everyone had kept silent. Ask yourself if the Hotel Utah would let Blacks sleep there now if someone hadn't protested Marian Anderson's exclusion there years ago. Ask yourself if even the few female tokens in the Fellows or on the Executive Board would be there if protest had not been heard. Ask yourself if you want your reputation to depend on keeping your mouth shut" (9).

She framed the issue in terms of the Mormon Church in this way:

> Nevertheless, is it wrong of AFS to be political when the issues are out of our appropriate sphere of action—folklore? What defines that sphere? Are issues of race and sex extraneous to our true and professional concerns? Should we say that we are only interested in the "cultures" of our "informants," and not in those political and economic factors which share and form their lives and cultures? Some colleagues have charged that to oppose the actions of the Church is to oppose their "folk culture." In the name of non-interference in the folk cultural practices of our informants, must we abrogate our responsibilities to ourselves, our discipline, and to society as a whole? And do we not reduce them and ourselves to the colonizer and colonized roles in acts of simpleminded and patronizing withdrawal from ethical judgment about what we, and not they, do? (R. Green 1978, 5–6)

In a "postscript," she wrote, "The President of AFS, Barre Toelken, has apologized to a Mormon member of AFS for the offense to his religion that occurred on the floor of the business meeting last year. He has specifically apologized for the remarks I made and for Past President Ellen Stekert's failure to stop those remarks," pointing out that he was not present at the meeting (R. Green 1978, 9).

Her statement highlights differences between her framing of the issues and the framing by Toelken and others, including those who today recall that opposition to the meeting in Utah was framed at least in part by arguments couched in religious bias. Green may well have made comments at the business meeting that were heard and felt as anti-Mormon; however, by this time, the business meeting minutes, like the executive board minutes, included only actions and no details of discussion, so her comments are not part of the record. In this statement, however, she is writing specifically about the formal efforts of the church in "actively attempting to influence legislation" (R. Green 1978, 7). Indeed, the Mormon Church took an official position of opposition to the ERA in 1976 and actively encouraged members to act against it. The church's position was reiterated in an October 1978 letter to its brethren that also urged "our people to join actively with other citizens who share our concerns and who are engaged in working to reject this measure on the basis of its threat to the moral climate of the future."[135] This points to a larger key thread that runs throughout this book: those on both sides of the issue argued that the other was being political. In this case, it is certainly possible to argue that the Mormon Church made it "political" when they formally opposed the amendment and asked members to work to defeat it.

The following issue of the FWC, fall 1978, included "official letters and statements" from Jan Harold Brunvand, David J. Hufford, Edward J. Lehman, Ellen Stekert, and Barre Toelken. Generally, these letters repeat points made in earlier letters. Brunvand argued that "it is not literally true" that the Hotel Utah is a Mormon Hotel; Hufford made a point-by-point rebuttal to rumors, similar to his earlier letter to the board; and Lehman briefly recounted his role, which was to choose a hotel based "solely on facilities, convenience, concessions and the interest demonstrated by the hotels' responses to me," which he did (Women's Section 1978, 5). Ellen Stekert, whose statement was transcribed from a tape she sent to FWC editor Marta Weigle, provided a lengthy summary of her perspective on how the decision was made to meet in Utah, including the role of the formalization of the site selection process in the midst of planning for the meeting. As a result, Brunvand and others had already begun the planning before the board had voted to meet in Utah. Stekert noted,

> It left the Executive Board having to vote not on the issue before it but really on several issues of a very complex nature which had never been raised in this historic way, namely: the fact that people in Utah had already begun to move even though they had no sanction to do so, but to move in a way that had been traditional with the AFS. Consequently, our changing tactics midstream looked malevolent to them perhaps. It certainly looked unfair to them, and the issue became personalized, politicized, and very, very ugly—I think because of our being in a transition year. (Women's Section 1978, 6–7)

Stekert stated that she consistently voted against meeting in Utah (Women's Section 1978, 5), though she would attend the meeting (9). She said, "I do agree with Rayna and with what Dell Hymes said at the business meeting: There is no way to avoid the fact that anything we do as a public society is essentially a political action" (7). She expressed her objections to Toelken's letter of apology to Bert Wilson, and she defended both herself and Green: no one objected to Green's comments at the time, giving her no reason to stop her, and Green's comments contained nothing "that could be construed as a slur on the Mormon Church itself or on Utah as a class of people" (8).

In the final statement (the letters and statements were intentionally printed in alphabetical order), Barre Toelken noted that he replaced his longer statement with a shorter one dictated to Weigle over the phone in which he primarily rebutted statements made by Rayna Green about how decisions were made regarding the meeting site. He ended by addressing his letter to Wilson:

> In point of fact, what I did was to send a letter of formal apology to a prominent member of our Society who felt that remarks made on the floor put Mormon members in the untenable position of arguing for their church rather than the issues on the floor of a business meeting of a professional society. The anti-Mormon remarks by some speakers, and the feelings generated among those present, were felt to be out of order and unjust by a number of AFS members. Since I did not hear the event myself, I named no one in my letter, but apologized for what I consider a technical faux pas by our Society. (Women's Section 1978, 11)

In addition to the Women's Section and the FWC, other constituencies within and allied with the AFS weighed in on this debate through resolutions, some narrowly focused on the issue of the ERA and some broader. For instance, in May 1978, students from the University of Pennsylvania sent notice, signed by twenty-six students, that they would be boycotting the meeting, stating in part that "the AFS decision to meet in a state which has not ratified the ERA must be interpreted as a move in support of those who oppose such ratification. Furthermore, we feel it is inconsiderate of the AFS to ask us as members to violate our political convictions in order to participate in scholarly activities. In addition the desire of the membership not to meet in a Mormon hotel has been disregarded."[136] Also in May, the Middle Atlantic Folklife Association passed a resolution that they would not meet in states that hadn't ratified the ERA, and "suggest[ed] and encourage[d] the larger organizations of professional folklorists to do the same."[137]

There were also calls for defining politics and "social issues" in preparation for dealing with not only the ERA but future issues. For instance, the Indiana University Folklore Student Association passed a resolution that the AFS "create a mechanism whereby issues of fundamental social import can be discussed in a forum that allows for conscientious and orderly self-expression" as well as a means for members to vote on such matters.[138] Correspondence between the students and David Hufford / the AFS Executive Board and the State of the Profession Committee ensued, and in a May 4, 1978, memo to the executive board and the SPC, the Student Association wrote, "Perhaps there should not be an *a priori* definition of fundamental social issues because, as evidenced at the last AFS meeting, opinions differ widely and strongly. It therefore appears that the definition of an issue as fundamental should occur as a result of a process of consideration."[139] By May, the board was already planning to create a forum during the meeting in Utah for open discussion, perhaps but not necessarily in response to the students' request, and a motion to do so was formally carried at the June executive board meeting.[140]

The minutes of the SPC meeting held during the Utah annual meeting include sparse details of a discussion of the resolution sent to them from the Women's Section of the AFS and the "problems raised by the decision to hold the 1978 AFS Annual Meeting in a state which has not passed the Equal Rights Amendment." Although they'd been sent the resolutions from the IU students and MAFA, these were not mentioned in the minutes. The committee voted to recommend to the executive board "that a mail ballot be sent to the membership to determine whether they do or do not wish the Society to endorse the ERA." They also approved the Amendment to the Women's Section resolution described above, regarding a code of ethics, with minimal edits.[141]

It is difficult to ascertain exactly what impact the ERA debates had on the 1978 meeting in Salt Lake City, Utah. In a letter to Ellen Stekert in February 1979, David Hufford wrote, "I especially wanted to tell you that I thought you were superb at the meeting. It was such a delicate time and there were so many opportunities for arguments that I was amazed at how smoothly and pleasantly everything went."[142] It is also difficult to know how many ended up boycotting the meeting. Meeting registration numbers that year compared with the years prior to and following it demonstrate a significant drop, though we can't be sure that this is all due to the boycott. The totals of combined pre- and on-site registration were New Orleans 1975, 475; Philadelphia 1976, 637; Detroit 1977, 435; Salt Lake City 1978, 332; and Los Angeles 1979, 461.[143] Following the 1978 meeting, Lynwood Montell wrote to folklorist Charles Perdue regarding business of the SPC: "We missed you at AFS, but we also missed about two hundred others since the meetings were far less attended than usual."[144] The low turnout clearly did not go unnoticed, although, again, a direct connection to the boycott cannot be made with any certainty. Apparently, some found other means of boycotting. Elliott Oring said in an interview that although he did not think many boycotted the meeting, "ultimately, at the Utah meeting, a lot of the women came but would not stay at the Hotel Utah, they stayed elsewhere, at another hotel. So, for some of them, that became a solution not to support a church hotel, which essentially stood against the ERA. So that was the ultimate resolution, as I recall."[145]

The 1978 meeting at the Hotel Utah did not end discussions of the ERA for the AFS. The board voted during the Utah meeting "to distribute a mail ballot to the membership to determine the position of the membership on the possibility of avoiding as future meeting sites states which have not ratified the ERA" in the future.[146] Those in favor prevailed, with 301 votes to 189 (AFS 1979, 1). On the surface it may seem surprising that this vote turned out differently from the 1977 vote at the business meeting regarding meeting in Utah. This was likely due to both who voted and the stakes as they were understood in each context. In 1977, those present probably considered the costs of moving the meeting so late in the planning; this second vote was regarding a location in the abstract. We also don't know how close the vote was, as the count was not included in the minutes. It is also conceivable that when the membership was polled in 1979, those with strong feelings in favor of the boycott were more likely to vote, outnumbering not only those with strong feelings against it but, perhaps more importantly, those who were indifferent to the issue in the more abstract. As we were reminded several times by our interviewees in preparation for this book, the issues we describe were all most hotly debated among a limited number of folklorists; others remained on the sidelines at least in part because they did not necessarily have strong feelings.

The *AFS Newsletter* included a brief summary of the comments made on the returned ballots—for instance, "The greatest number (about 30 [of comments by those in favor of boycotting non-ERA states]) rejected the notion that learned or academic groups (or individuals) could or should be separated from political stands, ethical issues, or 'real life'" (AFS 1979, 1), while over half of those opposed to boycotting who made comments "said in one way or another that they did not want to involve a scholarly group in what they saw as a political issue" (2). The following year the board passed a resolution confirming the results of the poll (see AFS 1983, 1).

On June 30, 1982, the ratification period ended without passage of the Equal Rights Amendment. The AFS boycott remained in place throughout this period. In 1983, the executive board discussed and sought member comment on whether to continue the boycott (AFS 1983, 1). According to the minutes of the October 1983 executive board meeting, a motion to not meet in states that had not ratified the ERA "was debated at length, and it was agreed that the motion be tabled until May 1984, by which time the Amendment is expected to have been passed by Congress and submitted to the states."[147] In May, the issue was deferred "until such time as the Amendment is passed by Congress and presented to the states for ratification."[148] This, of course, never happened as, although the ERA was reintroduced numerous times, it never again made it out of Congress and back to the states for ratification.[149]

"WHAT SEXISM INFECTS IS DIFFICULT TO DISINFECT"

Although it is no surprise that we can look to the discussions and actions within a learned society, its journal, and its other publications and see social movements of the time playing out, the specifics are instructive—not just for folklore studies but for what they suggest about the negotiation of scholarship, politics, and activism then and now. Over the course of the 1970s, American women moved from more hesitant requests for a seat at the table to strong demands for inalienable equal rights under the law, and folklorists joined their colleagues in other academic disciplines and occupational categories in these calls. Women folklorists were fighting for increased equality for themselves and, by extension, the increased valuing of women's folklore.

It was 2017 before the AFS instituted a "Policy Statement on Appropriate Annual Meeting Behavior" due to experiences reported by students and others at the 2016 meeting. This policy states that the AFS will "not tolerate any discrimination or harassment on the basis of age, body size, class, disability, ethnicity, gender, gender identity and expression, physical appearance, political perspective, race, religion, sexual orientation, or any other legally protected characteristic." It goes on to detail the meaning of "harassment" and provides procedures for reporting inappropriate behavior. Although this was an important step, it is rather astounding that it took over four decades to institute this policy from the point at which feminist folklorists began raising such issues.[150]

Feminist folklorists have also made important strides in the publication of research on women's expressive culture. Following on the foundational works of the 1970s and '80s that established a place within folklore study for the study of women performers, women's genres, and women's experiences from a feminist perspective (Farrer [1975] 1986; Jordan and Kalčik 1985) and the efforts of the early 1990s to ask "why and how the analysis of women's lore changes the study of all folklore, why studying any folklore with a feminist eye makes a difference, and how folklorists can contribute to the growing body of feminist scholarship that is developing in many disciplines" (Hollis, Pershing, and Young 1993, ix–x; see also Radner 1993), feminist folklorists have continued to expand the canon. Earlier work admittedly sorely lacked the cultural expressions of women of color, LGBTQIA+ communities, and women with disabilities, and strides have been made to remedy this as well (cf. Cantú and Nájera- Ramírez 2002a; Greenhill and Tye 2013; González-Martin 2019; González-Martin, Martínez-Rivera, and Otero 2022), though much work remains. Feminist folklore research has also included such divergent topics as the baking traditions of one woman (Tye 2010) and Mardi Gras traditions of groups of women (Ware 2007).

However, Ellen Stekert's 1987 words still apply today: "What sexism infects is difficult to disinfect. We must know that as a Society we are sexist. We must know that in our own deafness that we attack our very selves in the old ways. That I have lived to see a day of feminist scholarship celebrated in the AFS seems almost a miracle, and that it is almost a miracle is itself a pity. It is heartening to see changes beginning. But we must know that our stories do not yet have either a committed audience or a happy ending" (Stekert 1987, 585). Women—along with others who have been marginalized—have not yet come to a happy ending, though perhaps the committed audience has grown.

NOTES

1.   Betty Friedan's *The Feminine Mystique* (1963) is often credited with kick-starting second-wave feminism. Without diminishing the importance of the book, particularly for white middle-class American women, it is, of course, a more complicated story. Later works such as *This Bridge Called My Back: Writings by Radical Women of Color* (Moraga and Anzaldúa 1981) demonstrated that women of color were also deeply concerned with women's issues, if not the same issues with the same perspectives.

2. "National Women's Studies Association," accessed May 13, 2025, https://www.nwsa.org.

3. Parsons already held a doctorate in sociology when she met Boas (Zumwalt 1988, 86), and according to Rosemary Lévy Zumwalt, "Though Elsie was never literally a student of Boas', still, in the early years, he could well have been viewed as her mentor in anthropology" (1992, 164). "Benedict was first a student of Elsie Clews Parsons and then a student of Franz Boas" (Zumwalt 1988, 89–90). Interestingly, Parsons and Benedict were the first two women to serve as presidents of the American Anthropological Association; Margaret Mead (mentored first by Benedict and then by Boas) was the third (Brondo et al. 2009, 7). While Boas has received credit for bringing in and elevating women, the brief genealogy of these three women suggests a more complicated picture, as in this case women were bringing other women into the field.

4. See Stekert (1987, 583). In sharp contrast, from 1986 through 2022, there have been twice as many women presidents (fourteen) as men (seven).

5. See Clements (1988) for lists of the leaders in the first one hundred years of AFS, from which these numbers are calculated. "Established in 1960, the Fellows of the American Folklore Society is an honorary body of folklorists, whose election to the Fellows signifies their outstanding contributions to the field." See "AFS Fellows," American Folklore Society, accessed May 13, 2025, https://americanfolkloresociety.org/our-community/afs-fellows.

6. Richard Bauman and Beverly Stoeltje, interview with authors, August 1, 2021, Bloomington, IN.

7. During the research and writing of this book the #MeToo movement began in Hollywood and quickly spread to academia, including folklore studies. Activist Tarana Burke first used the term "Me Too" in 2006 as a show of support for survivors of sexual assault and harassment. It was not until 2017 that the term went viral as a Twitter hashtag and spread around the world, with men in powerful positions in entertainment, politics, and other realms publicly called out and, in some cases, charged (criminally or civilly) for their behaviors and actions (cf. "History & Inception," accessed May 16, 2025, https://metoomvmt.org/get-to-know-us/history-inception/; Daigle 2021). We return briefly to the #MeToo movement as addressed in folklore studies in the concluding chapter.

8. See "Our History," National Association of Commissions for Women, accessed May 13, 2025, http://www.nacw.org/history.html.

9. See "History and Mission," Committee on Women, Gender, and Sexuality in the Profession, accessed May 13, 2025, https://www.mla.org /About-Us/Governance/Committees/Committee-Listings/Professional-Issues/Committee-on-Women-Gender-and-Sexuality-in-the-Profession /History-and-Mission.

10. Minutes of Organizational Meeting of Women's Caucus, November 3, 1973. Unless otherwise noted, all references to AFS-related minutes and letters in this chapter are from American Folklore Society records, 1890–2011. (COLL MSS 206). Utah State University. Special Collections and Archives Department.

11. Minutes of Organizational Meeting of Women's Caucus, November 3, 1973.

12. Letter from D. K. Wilgus, AFS President, to Eleanor Long, Frank Hoffman[n], and Rayna Green, December 1, 1971.

13. During the writing of this chapter, the Supreme Court revoked the right to abortion in *Dobbs v. Jackson Women's Health Organization.* The right to contraceptives is considered threatened.

14. See "Timeline of Legal History of Women in the United States," National Women's History Alliance, accessed May 13, 2025, http://www.nwhp.org/resources/womens-rights-movement /detailed-timeline; and "A Brief History of Sexual Harassment in the United States," accessed May 13, 2025, https://now.org /blog/a-brief-history-of-sexual-harassment-in-the-united-states.

15. The executive board meeting and business meeting notes were largely verbatim until the late 1970s, as will be clear later in this chapter.

16. Annual Meeting: Business Meeting Minutes, 1972 (hereafter cited as AFS Business Meeting Minutes, 1972).

17. Susan Kalčik quoted from the recording of, "Her-Story: A Feminism and Folklore Retrospective 2016," forum, American Folklore Society Annual Meeting, Miami, FL, October 20, 2016, https://media.dlib.indiana.edu /media_objects/zw12z6651 (hereafter cited as "Her-Story" 2016).

18. AFS Business Meeting Minutes, 1972.

19. AFS Business Meeting Minutes, 1972.

20. AFS Business Meeting Minutes, 1972, 18.

21. AFS Business Meeting Minutes, 1972, 18.

22. AFS Business Meeting Minutes, 1972, 19.

23. AFS Business Meeting Minutes, 1972, 19.

24. AFS Business Meeting Minutes, 1972, 20.

25. AFS Business Meeting Minutes, 1972, 19.

26. AFS Business Meeting Minutes, 1972, 19.

27. AFS Business Meeting Minutes, 1972, 20.

28. AFS Business Meeting Minutes, 1972, 20.

29. AFS Business Meeting Minutes, 1972, 21.

30. AFS Business Meeting Minutes, 1972, 22.

31. AFS Business Meeting Minutes, 1972, 23.

32. AFS Business Meeting Minutes, 1972, 24.

33. AFS Business Meeting Minutes, 1972, 25.

34. AFS Business Meeting Minutes, 1972, 24–25.

35. AFS Business Meeting Minutes, 1972, 25.

36. In 2018, in the midst of the #MeToo movement, the University of Pennsylvania removed a portrait of Dell Hymes from the halls of the Graduate School of Education, where he had been dean for twelve years. The removal was a result of student actions related to their demands for improved sexual harassment policies, including posting a list of allegations rumored about for years. According to the *Daily Pennsylvanian*, "[In 1988] Hymes had reached out-of-court settlements with multiple [Graduate School of Education (GSE)] faculty who had filed sexual discrimination lawsuits against him and had been named in a court case involving the sexual harassment of a female GSE faculty member. After a 'going-away bash' hosted at the Penn museum, Hymes left Penn in 1987 for a research post at the University of Virginia. He retired from UVA in 1998 and died in 2009" (See "Penn Removes Portrait of Former GSE Dean with Alleged History of Sexual Harassment," accessed May 13, 2025, https://www .thedp.com/article/2018/04/gse-getup-sexual-harassment-dell-hymes -portrait-removal-upenn-penn-philadelphia). See the winter 2025 issue of *JAF* for a forum including fifteen essays that offer perspectives on the legacy of sexual harassment in the field (Gilman 2025).

37. An addendum to the report in the meeting agenda states, "More sophisticated and comprehensive follow-up studies are now in preparation under the direction of committee members Frank A. Hoffman[n] and Rayna Green; your cooperation in implementing those studies will be most welcomed by the committee." If such reports were completed, they appear to have been neither included in materials archived nor referenced in correspondence and other materials related to the committee that were archived. This is from the agenda of the 1973 annual business meeting of the American Folklore Society in Nashville, TN. Annual Meeting: Business Meeting, November 3, 1973.

38. Minutes, Annual Meeting: Business Meeting, November 3, 1973 (hereafter cited as AFS Business Meeting Minutes, 1973).

39. Agenda, Annual Meeting: Business Meeting, November 3, 1973 (hereafter cited as AFS Business Meeting Agenda, 1973).

40. AFS Business Meeting Agenda, 1973, 18.

41. AFS Business Meeting Agenda, 1973, 19. For instance, the Center for Folklore Studies at the University of Texas at Austin had just been established in 1967, the Department of Folklore at Memorial University of Newfoundland in 1968, and at Western Kentucky University the undergraduate minor was established in 1968 and the MA program in 1972.

42. AFS Business Meeting Agenda, 1973, 19–20.

43. AFS Business Meeting Agenda, 1973, 20.

44. AFS Business Meeting Agenda, 1973, 20. In this period, per the AFS Constitution, the executive board included the following: president, first vice president, second vice president, secretary-treasurer, recording secretary, and four at-large members. Cf. "Constitution and Bylaws" 1973, 156. This changed in 1976 with the new constitution.

45. AFS Business Meeting Agenda, 1973, 21.

46. AFS Business Meeting Agenda, 1973, 21.

47. AFS Business Meeting Agenda, 1973, 21.

48. AFS Business Meeting Agenda, 1973, 21.

49. AFS Business Meeting Minutes, 1973, 19.

50. AFS Business Meeting Agenda, 1973, 22.

51. AFS Business Meeting Agenda, 1973, 19.

52. AFS Business Meeting Agenda, 1973, 20.

53. AFS Business Meeting Agenda, 1973, 22.

54. AFS Business Meeting Minutes, 1973, 15.

55. AFS Business Meeting Minutes, 1973, 17.

56. AFS Business Meeting Minutes, 1973, 18.

57. AFS Business Meeting Minutes, 1973, 19.

58. AFS Business Meeting Minutes, 1973, 19. The minutes present this as a summary of his comment, not a direct quote.

59. AFS Business Meeting Minutes, 1973, 20.

60. AFS Business Meeting Minutes, 1973, 18.

61. AFS Business Meeting Minutes, 1973, 20.

62. AFS Business Meeting Minutes, 1973, 21.

63. AFS Business Meeting Minutes, 1973, 21.

64. AFS Business Meeting Minutes, 1973, 21.

65. AFS Business Meeting Minutes, 1973, 22.

66. AFS Business Meeting Minutes, 1973, 22.

67. AFS Business Meeting Agenda, 1973, 22.

68. AFS Business Meeting Minutes, 1973, 22.

69. AFS Business Meeting Minutes, 1973, 22.

70. AFS Business Meeting Minutes, 1973, 23.

71. AFS Business Meeting Minutes, 1973, 23.

72. Letter from Dell Hymes, AFS President, to Richard Bauman, July 29, 1974.

73. Also in Hymes's files are a copy of the minutes from the Women's Caucus formation meeting and a copy of the "Progress Report of the Chairwoman, Steering Committee of the Women's Caucus, AFS" that was to be published in the fall 1974 issue of the *FFC*, both with handwritten notes to Hymes from Virginia Briscoe (and it was published there). Presumably she sent them to Hymes either with her July letter or at some point after that and prior to the fall AFS Annual Meeting.

74. Letter from Eleanor Long, AFS CSWP Chair, to Dell Hymes, August 20, 1974.

75. Letter from Dell Hymes, AFS President, to Eleanor Long, September 10, 1974.

76. Letter from Dell Hymes, AFS President, to Eleanor Long, September 10, 1974.

77. It is beyond the bounds of this chapter to provide a detailed history of the AFS Women's Caucus, which later became the Women's Section, but some attention to how it began is germane because of the relationship with the Committee on the Status of Women in the Profession.

78. Rosan Jordan, interview with authors, July 3, 2021. Telephone.

79. Kay Turner, interview with authors, August 9, 2021. Zoom.

80. Kay Turner ("Her-Story" 2016). Turner listed Richard Bauman, Roger Abrahams, Américo Paredes, and Roger Renwick, as well as John Vlach and Archie Green, both of whom came later.

81. Chaired by Bess Lomax Hawes, this panel included papers by Mary Ellen B. Lewis (IU), Rosan Jordan de Caro (LSU), Robbie Johnson (UT Austin), and Marcia Herndon (UT Austin). Richard Bauman, program chair, apparently suggested this session and wrote to Hawes in July 1972 and asked her to chair it (de Caro 1975b, 4).

82. According to the 1973 minutes of the organizational meeting of the Women's Caucus, Rayna Green mentioned the 1972 "informal meetings of women" when asked to provide a "short history" of the women's committee.

83. According to Beverly Stoeltje and Richard Bauman, the Folklore Center at UT financially supported the reproduction and mailing of the *FFC*, and administrative support was provided by the center's secretary

Frances Terry (Richard Bauman and Beverly Stoeltje, interview with authors, August 1, 2021, Bloomington, IN).

84.   The abbreviation *FFC* (occasionally *ffc*) was an intentional reference to the *Folklore Fellows Communications*. According to Rosan Jordan, "So we started the *Folklore Feminists Communication*, which was kind of a parody of the *Folklore Fellows Communication*—the big publication—just in order to get people in touch with each other" ("Her-Story" 2016). The *Folklore Fellows Communication* was established in 1910 in Finland as a means of fostering international folkloristic research and communication, and it continues today as a monograph series. See https://www.folklorefellows.fi/folklore -fellows-network-2/, accessed May 13, 2025. While the *Folklore Feminists Communication* was more concerned with the Fellows of the American Folklore Society as a body that was dominated by white men than they were the *Folklore Fellows Communication*, in terms of their interest in addressing male power in the discipline, the *Folklore Fellows Communication* was no less male-centered.

85.   See de Caro (1975b). According to de Caro's chronology, Susan Kalčik, Claire R. Farrer, Joanne Krauss, Diane Meyerowitz, Rosan Jordan de Caro, and FA de Caro met at the de Caro home in Austin on July 19, 1973. Plans for both the *FFC* and the Women's Caucus were hatched at that meeting. Following the meeting, an announcement regarding the first *FFC* was sent out (he does not say to whom), and in August Camilla Collins was asked by Claire Farrer to arrange for the Women's Caucus organizational meeting (de Caro 1975b, 21).

86.   Rosan Jordan ("Her-Story" 2016).

87.   Minutes of the Organizational Meeting of the Women's Caucus, November 3, 1973. The program for the 1973 AFS meeting lists the organizational meeting of the Women's Caucus as taking place on the evening of November 2; however, not only are the minutes dated November 3, but the discussion includes the reports of the CSWP given at the business meeting on November 3, making it clear that is when it took place, for whatever reason. In 1978, the name of the newsletter was changed to the *Folklore Women's Communication,* following a very close vote by subscribers. This was in part due to the creation of the Women's Section and due to discussions that "women" might "attract more subscribers" than "feminist." See "On the Title Change" (Weigle 1978) and occasional mentions in subsequent issues (including Levin 1984). The name continued to be discussed periodically over the years, and it was changed back to *FFC* with the spring 1994 issue.

88.   Minutes of the Organizational Meeting of the Women's Caucus, November 3, 1973 (hereafter cited as AFS Women's Caucus Minutes, 1973), 4.

89. AFS Women's Caucus Minutes, 1973, 3.

90. AFS Women's Caucus Minutes, 1973, 7.

91. AFS Women's Caucus Minutes, 1973, 6.

92. AFS Women's Caucus Minutes, 1973. Although this occurred the following day, the November 3 minutes end by noting the officers who were elected by the steering committee on November 4.

93. Charge to the State of the Profession Committee of the American Folklore Society, 1976–77, October 21, 1977, Lynwood Montell Papers, Folklife Archives, Special Collections, Western Kentucky University (hereafter, WKU Montell papers).

94. State of the Profession Committee, Minutes of the Meeting, November 4, 1977; Report of the Status of the Profession Committee, August 29, 1978, WKU Montell papers.

95. The definition and directory didn't happen, and it is interesting to note that in 2021, AFS introduced a similar idea within the unveiling of a new website; anecdotally, this appears to have raised similar questions, though in conversation rather than public platforms. The code of ethics took ten years. See the "AFS Statement on Ethics: Principles of Professional Responsibility," accessed May 13, 2025, https://americanfolkloresociety.org/our-work/position-statement-ethics. See also AFS 1988, 8.

96. Kalčik, "Her-Story."2016

97. Eleanor Long (Mrs. D. K. Wilgus), interview by Luisa Del Giudice, October 13, 1986, Bloomington, IN, https://archives.iu.edu/catalog/InU-Ar-VAD8923aspace_829c5f7f630d892abfe4813e94f5c219. For the Women in Folklore Oral History Project, Indiana University Bloomington. At the time of the interviews, Long had married Wilgus "recently" after they had lived together for 5 years.

98. Sections were part of the new constitution as well, and the Women's Section and Applied Folklore Section were the first created in 1977.

99. Presenters included Claire R. Farrer (UT Austin), Kay F. Stone (University of Winnipeg), Danielle Roemer (UT Austin), Agnes Hostettler, Inez Cardozo-Freeman (OSU), Amy L. S. Pulver (Colorado Women's College), Susan Kalčik (UT Austin), and Nelia Templeton (Washington, DC). "Program for the Annual Meeting of the American Folklore Society," American Folklore Society, Nashville, 1973, https://scholarworks.iu.edu/dspace/items/77e646c6-51cc-4a81-b959-e17b4e8c3384.

100. "Program for the Annual Meeting of the American Folklore Society," American Folklore Society, Nashville, 1973, https://scholarworks.iu.edu/dspace/items/77e646c6-51cc-4a81-b959-e17b4e8c3384.

101.   Beverly Stoeltje has described the removal of a footnote from her article (Stoeltje 1975) without her permission during the editing of the issue. The footnote "acknowledged Richard Bauman's suggestions for the article" (Stoeltje 2025, 98) and, according to Stoeltje, "the support of a male scholar would have contributed legitimacy to my article, especially because it was the first article I published" (99).

102.   Nearly twenty years later, folklorist Alan Dundes repeated this sentiment in regard to folklore theory: "What precisely is the 'theory' in feminist theory?" (2005, 388). For a rebuttal to Dundes and an overview of folklore feminist theory, see Jorgensen 2010.

103.   Deemer was Barre Toelken's first graduate student at the University of Oregon. See "Polly Stewart papers," accessed May 13, 2025, https://libapps.salisbury.edu/nabb-archives/finding-aid.php?id=1637.

104.   Letter from Bruce Jackson to Tim Lloyd, October 25, 1986.

105.   Postcard from Bruce Jackson to Judith McCulloh at the University of Illinois Press, January 10, 1987.

106.   Memo from Bruce Jackson to Contributors of JAF #398, July 16, 1987.

107.   Kay Turner and Suzanne Seriff, interview with authors, March 23, 2023. Zoom. In his response to a letter from a group of the contributors, in which they detailed evidence of having been left out of the process and expressed strongly that a feminist should be the editor, Jackson wrote in part, "The logical core of the group letter of 21 July centers on the explicit notion (pp. 3–4 [of the group letter]) that only a person with female genitals can appreciate or utilize or work from a position informed by feminism." Memo from Bruce Jackson to Contributors of JAF #398, July 27, 1987.

108.   Linda Pershing, interview with authors, April 6, 2023. Zoom.

109.   Kay Turner and Suzanne Seriff, interview with authors, March 23, 2023. Zoom.

110.   Letter from Kay Turner and Suzanne Seriff to the Executive Board of the American Folklore Society, April 18, 1988.

111.   Minutes of the American Folklore Society Executive Board Question and Answer Session, October 28, 1988.

112.   American Folklore Society. Executive Board Minutes, New Series, No. 18, October 28, 1988, and Executive Board Minutes, New Series, No. 19, October 30, 1988, 4. Although it is beyond the scope of this chapter, Jackson also created conflict with the AFS Executive Board because he sought grant funding to support the extra pages and color printing of the cover without their approval. This resulted in numerous lengthy letters and

discussion by the board, making the decision to reappoint him even more surprising.

113.   Linda Pershing, interview with authors, April 6, 2023. Zoom.

114.   A comparison of the 1986 AFS program with the contents of the special issue and the two 1993 collections makes this clear; the vast majority of papers presented at the symposium and/or published in the special issue appear in Hollis, Pershing, and Young 1993. Pershing also stressed this difference between the two volumes to us.

115.   American Folklore Society Executive Board Minutes New Series #1, Detroit, MI, November 2, 1977, 3–11PM. This was the first time that the AAA handled the logistics of the meeting, led by AAA executive director Edward Lehman.

116.   Letter from David Hufford to the Executive Board of the American Folklore Society. Correspondence, March 10, 1978. Secretary Treasurer David Hufford wrote, "I hope that the form of the minutes meets with your approval. Past year's minutes have been in a rather lengthy narrative form and, from the point of view of the one who has to see that the items calling for action get done, have been quite difficult to use. I have therefore followed Ed Lehman's advice and stuck very closely to simple statements of action taken" (2).

117.   "Political" appears to be an insertion.

118.   "Other" is an insertion.

119.   Handwritten letter from Barre Toelken to David Hufford, "Fri-Sat 3am." While there is a day and time but no date on this letter, the content makes it clear that it was three a.m. on Saturday, November 5, 1977.

120.   "On" inserted.

121.   Handwritten letter from Barre Toelken to David Hufford, "Fri-Sat 3am."

122.   American Folklore Society Annual Business Meeting, New Series #1, Detroit, MI, November 5, 1977.

123.   Steering Committee of the American Folklore Society Women's Section 1978, 5–6.

124.   While a code of ethics had been part of Stekert's charge to the committee, this is much more specific.

125.   American Folklore Society Annual Business Meeting, New Series #1, Detroit, MI, November 5, 1977.

126.   American Folklore Society Executive Board Minutes New Series #2, Detroit, MI, November 6, 1978 [*sic*], 10 am–1 pm. Note that the minutes are incorrectly dated; there is no question that this was 1977 and not 1978.

127.   Letter from David Hufford to the Executive Board. Correspondence, March 10, 1978.

128.   Letter from Barre Toelken to the Executive Board, March 13, 1978.

129.   Letter from Barre Toelken to William A. Wilson, March 10, 1978. Although Toelken wrote that he was making this apology on behalf of the AFS, according to the minutes of the June 1978 board meeting, "There was consensus that Barre Toelken's letter of apology to Bert Wilson (March 10, 1978) is not a statement on behalf of the *whole* Board" (*emphasis authors'*). American Folklore Society, Executive Board Minutes News Series #3, June 5, 1978. This was further clarified at the October 1978 meeting, apparently due to the phrasing that the letter was not only not on behalf of the "whole board": "There was consensus that [the item in the previous minutes] does not imply that the letter was in part from the Board." American Folklore Society, Executive Board Minutes News Series #4, Salt Lake City, UT, October 11, 1978.

130.   Letter from David Hufford to the Executive Board, April 14, 1978, in which Hufford said that he was enclosing a transcript of the recording of the discussion at the November 6 board meeting; unfortunately it was not in the file.

131.   American Folklore Society, Executive Board Minutes News Series #3, Washington, DC, June 5, 1978.

132.   "Board Statement of Chronology," addressed "To: Members of the American Folklore Society," "From: The AFS Executive Board," 1978.

133.   Although the later meeting at University of Pennsylvania has been framed as having been in the planning as an alternative conference, the Call for Papers in FWC 16 doesn't mention the ERA issue.

134.   Green is referencing boycotts by many other scholarly, professional, and labor organizations; see "Cost of Convention Boycott to States That Have Not Ratified Equal Rights Proposal Put at $100 Million," *New York Times*, April 4, 1978, https://www.nytimes.com/1978/04/04/archives /cost-of-convention-boycott-to-states-that-have-not-ratified-equal.html.

135.   This letter is addressed to LDS church leadership bodies and the salutation reads, "Dear Brethren," indicating that this letter was addressed to male members of the church only (thank you to Barbara Lloyd for this clarification). The Church of Jesus Christ of Latter-day Saints, "Letter from First Presidency," *USU Digital Exhibits*, accessed December 10, 2024, http://exhibits.usu.edu/items/show/14166.

136.   Statement from Penn graduate students, May 8, 1978.

137.   Notice from Yvonne Milspaw, President, Middle Atlantic Folklife Association, WKU Montell Papers.

138.   Letter from the Folklore Student Association, Indiana University, John Bealle, Secretary, to Barre Toelken, March 21, 1978.

139.   Letter from the Folklore Student Association, Indiana University, Peter Voorheis, Secretary, to the Members of the Executive Board of the AFS and Members of the Status of the Profession Committee, May 4, 1978.

140. See Letter from Barre Toelken to David Hufford, May 22, 1978. See also American Folklore Society, Executive Board Minutes News Series #3, Washington DC, June 5, 1978.

141. Minutes of the Annual Meeting of the Committee on the State of the Profession of the American Folklore Society, 1978, Salt Lake City, UT; October 12, 1978, WKU Montell Papers.

142. Letter from David Hufford to Ellen Stekert, February 1, 1979.

143. AFS Annual Meeting Post Reports, 1975–78; AFS Annual Meeting Post Report, October 24–28, 1979, Los Angeles. From the collection of former AFS executive director Timothy Lloyd, used with permission. The attendance at the 1976 meeting in Philadelphia is significantly higher, perhaps because of the location in celebration of the US bicentennial.

144. Letter from Montell to Chuck Perdue, October 18, 1978, WKU Montell Papers.

145. Elliott Oring, interview with authors, March 15, 2022. Zoom.

146. AFS Executive Board Minutes, n.s.#4, October 11, 1978, Salt Lake City, UT. According to the meeting minutes, Dan Ben-Amos, Elliott Oring, and Judy McCulloh voted against the ballot.

147. American Folklore Society Board Meeting Minutes, October 4, 1983.

148. American Folklore Society Board Meeting Minutes, May 21–22, 1984, new series 36.

149. See "The Equal Rights Amendment: Recent Developments," Congressional Research Service, April 25, 2022, https://crsreports.congress .gov/product/pdf/LSB/LSB10731#:~:text=J.-,Res.,ratify%20the%20 ERA%20in%202020 for other action on the ERA, including both ratification by additional states (despite the passage of the deadline imposed by Congress) and attempts by states to rescind ratification.

150. See "Annual Meeting Policies," American Folklore Society, accessed May 16, 2025, https://americanfolkloresociety.org/our-work/meeting /annual-meeting-policies.

FOUR

"RIGHTEOUS MORALITY"

The Rise and Fall of the Tennessee-Tombigbee Waterway Folklife Project

IN CHAPTER 1, WE PROVIDED an abbreviated overview of the six-year lobbying effort that resulted in the establishment of the American Folklife Center (AFC) in 1976 at the Library of Congress. Following the passage of the American Folklife Preservation Act and the establishment of the AFC, Alan Jabbour was hired as the AFC's founding director. Jabbour, an accomplished fiddler, had previously headed the Archive of American Folk Song in the Library of Congress (1969–74) and the Folk Arts Program at the National Endowment for the Arts (1974–76). By the spring of 1979, the AFC had begun a concert series; sponsored its first conference; launched regional field projects (including the Chicago Ethnic Arts Project, the Southern-Central Georgia Folklife Project, and the Blue Ridge Parkway Folklife Project); begun the process of merging the Archive of Folk Song into the AFC; and more (see Jabbour 1996). By the winter of 1979, the young agency and its staff and board of trustees had also "found itself drawn into controversy within the field of folklore and folklife studies about whether accepting mitigation funds lent support to a public works project" (Jabbour 1996, 13) that was widely characterized as a "boondoggle." In the end, Jabbour made the decision to withdraw the AFC from the project rather than accept those funds.

This withdrawal prompted historic preservationist Thomas F. King (2003, 32) to write,

> Although I found it stimulating to work with the folklife people, they never seemed to me to relate to the rough-and-tumble world I was involved in—the world of Section 106—any better than the NPS archaeologists did. The archaeologists accepted the construction of destructive projects provided they could recover data from the sites such projects destroyed. The folklife people shied away from projects like the Tenn-Tom with righteous morality but did little to help the people whose traditional lives were upset by such projects—except to record their songs and stories for posterity, and to put on festivals to showcase their skills in the hope that they would thus be transmitted down the generations in some form or other. These are worthy enterprises, but they didn't engage the agents of change; they didn't confront the conflicts between tradition and modernity directly; they didn't help us with Section 106 review.

Some folklorists will read this passage as a devaluation of folklorists' important work of documenting for the sake of posterity or as a misunderstanding of the goals of the field. However, to those on one side of the 1979 debate, King offers a serious indictment: by backing out of a planned mitigation project in the region of the Tennessee-Tombigbee Waterway, folklorists missed an opportunity to get a foot in the door of mitigation projects and failed the local communities. Those on the other side might argue that they were right to insist that the project, despite any positive outcomes there might have been for communities, was not worth compromising the integrity of either the AFC or the field through association with the US Army Corps of Engineers' money. King's critique raises questions with which the field was grappling in the 1970s and 1980s: Can (should?) documentation also be advocacy? What impact, if any, do we hope to have in communities? This chapter also raises questions about the relationship between the work folklorists intend to do and the sources of funding we look to as well as how our work intersects with environmentalists and economic and community development initiatives. It raises questions specific to the times (What is the role of the newly established AFC?) and questions that are very much still with us (What does it mean to be "political"?). There has been "righteous morality" on all sides of such debates.

Most contemporary folklorists likely only vaguely know, if they know at all, the story of folklorists' near-involvement in 1979, through the AFC, in a folklife survey that would have documented the "living" cultures of the region in which the Tennessee-Tombigbee Waterway (known as the "Tenn-Tom") was being built by the Army Corps of Engineers. With the exception of those who were involved with the proposed Tenn-Tom folklife project or the debates about it and those who continue to work at the juncture of folklore and historic preservation or cultural conservation, it is likely that references to the controversy in three American Folklore Society (AFS) presidential addresses (Bulger in 2002 [Bulger 2003]; Ivey in 2007 [Ivey 2011]; and Williams in 2015 [Williams 2017a]) constitute the sum total of knowledge of the proposed project.

Peggy Bulger's presidential address to the AFS in 2002 is a stark reflection on "missed opportunities of the past," including debates over the legislation that eventually established the AFC and over AFC involvement in the Tenn-Tom. Bulger served as the director of the AFC from 1999 to 2011, and although she was not the director in the period of the Tenn-Tom, her perspective is still particularly informed by her position, making her address important to the discussions in this book. She described the cancellation of the Tenn-Tom folklife project due to "cries of protest" within the field (Bulger 2003, 385) as a missed opportunity for folklorists "to be central to the work of cultural conservation and the environmental survey work that is still going on today" (387). Her address was also a clarion call for folklorists to "fulfill our potential as a socially relevant, professional and scholarly society with the capacity to affect international policy and the future of cultural conservation across the globe" (389).

Michael Ann Williams, a folklorist with expertise in historic preservation, also described the Tenn-Tom survey as a missed opportunity. Williams worked in the region of the Tenn-Tom "as the first folklorist employed by the Historic American Buildings Survey [HABS]," documenting structures of those who were being relocated. "From that experience," she noted, "I came away with the strong belief that folklorists can and should act as advocates and witnesses in federal impact statements" (Williams 2017a, 140n17). For folklorists who work at the juncture of folklore and historic preservation, such as Williams, the Tenn-Tom folklife project was a missed opportunity for making a place for folklorists and their particular expertise in federal mitigation work, alongside archaeologists and preservationists (see Sommers 2013, 2019; Vidutis 2019; Williams 2017b). Yet folklorists, with the exception of Bulger, have not written about the failed Tenn-Tom folklife project in detail, and nonfolklorists who have written about it have not included the proposed folklife project; it is a story that needs to be told in fuller detail.[1] We tell a fuller version here.

First, because the magnitude of the waterway project and the communities affected is needed as context for understanding the story of AFC involvement, we provide an overview of the Tenn-Tom, including a summary of the history and planning of the waterway as well as the geography and demographics of the region. We then pick up the story of the AFC's involvement from start to finish based on the extensive record in the AFC archives, which includes notes and correspondence, planning documents, sound recordings, news clippings, and other ephemera. We also interviewed people involved in a variety of ways, ranging from direct involvement to astute observers. We quote extensively from this array of primary sources, the vast majority of which have not been published elsewhere.

The Tennessee-Tombigbee Waterway was one of the largest and most controversial US Army Corps of Engineer projects in history. According to Alabama folklorist Henry (Hank) Willett, "People called it the 'Biggest pork barrel project in the history of the nation.' It was a two-billion-dollar waterway that people weren't sure would ever pay for itself. Some of their concerns ended up coming true."[2] The construction of the Tenn-Tom Waterway has been framed by its major chroniclers as a "political" story at its heart (Stewart 1971; Stine 1993), so it is no surprise that it became a political story in the folklore world as well, even though many folklorists who voiced opinions argued that folklorists and/or the AFC should avoid being political. However, the archival record demonstrates that those on both sides of the debate used this argument, suggesting that the central conflict was in fact about what counted as political: Was it political to make a statement against the Corps of Engineers by not participating in the folklife survey, or was it political to accept Corps money and/or engage in a mitigation project? The argument among folklorists was not directly about whether the lives and traditions of those in the region were deserving of documentation; in part, the arguments came to be about who should do the documentation and with what money.

These questions and others raised during the debates over the Tenn-Tom folklife project remain important today. Those who opposed the project had a two-pronged argument: by agreeing to do the folklife project and by accepting money connected with the Army Corps of Engineers, folklorists would be supporting the waterway project and tarnishing the AFC and the field of folklore more generally by association. No one in the folklore world was arguing in favor of the waterway project, but those in favor of the folklife project argued that if the waterway was going to be completed, then the folklife of the region and potentially the very effects of the waterway project itself needed to be documented. From that perspective, the cancellation of the Tenn-Tom folklife project was a missed opportunity in two ways.

As we will discuss, the Tenn-Tom period was also the period of the passage of the National Historic Preservation Act (1966), the National Environmental Policy Act (1969), and the Moss-Bennett Act (1974), all of which impacted federal projects, including the Tenn-Tom. Section 106, previously referenced by King, refers to Section 106 of the National Historic Preservation Act of 1966, which "requires that federal agencies or their applicants consider the effects of their undertakings on historic structures and archaeological resources" (Sommers 2019, 362). Section 106 does not "stop demolition or other adverse impacts," but it requires that mitigation is considered (362). As folklorist and historian David Rotenstein has written, "Mitigation is an inelegant word. . . . According to regulations implementing NEPA, mitigation includes avoiding, minimizing, reducing, and rectifying impacts; it also includes 'Compensating for the impact by replacing or providing substitute resources or environments'" (2019). The term is ill defined in the relevant regulations, and according to folklorist and preservation expert Sydney Varajon, "Though mitigation varies greatly from project to project, at its base, mitigation involves the reduction (minimization) or removal (avoidance) of impact on any variety of natural, cultural, and social resources—from ecosystems and landscapes to historic sites and properties to living communities."[3] Because mitigation has been and still is most often understood in terms of tangible culture, particularly archaeological sites, this work is carried out primarily by cultural anthropologists and archaeologists in a career path known as cultural resource management. As we hope will become clear, folklorists engaged in historic preservation view the cancellation of the Tenn-Tom folklife project as a missed opportunity for folklorists to get a foot in the door of the mitigation process, which "all too often . . . emphasize[s] buildings, structures, and artifacts—and omit[s] the people who use them" (Sommers 2019, 362). The

Tenn-Tom project could have resulted in folklorist involvement in cultural resource management, they argue, which would have meant bringing their perspectives to the process as well as jobs for folklorists. The absence of folklorists from the mitigation process relates to the second way that the cancellation is understood as a missed opportunity: for communities of the region whose folklife was not documented.[4] While this second reason has not been the primary focus of those who have taken up this issue in print in the ensuing decades, it was a central part of the final debate leading to the cancellation, as we will discuss.

Peggy Bulger concluded her recounting of the events leading up to the cancellation of the project by arguing that folklorists should have been there from the start: "Protesting the displacement of communities and cultures would have been appropriate during the planning stage of the project" (2003, 387), and here she echoed the testimony of Black performing artist, professor, and activist Jane Sapp, discussed below, whose testimony to the AFC in 1979 included the refrain "Where were you then?" By "during the planning," Bulger likely meant when funds were appropriated for the Tenn-Tom in 1971, prior to when the digging began in 1972. However, the Tenn-Tom project had been discussed in some form for two centuries, and therefore some background is called for.

THE TENNESSEE-TOMBIGBEE WATERWAY: OVER TWO CENTURIES IN THE MAKING

Early eighteenth-century French colonizers are said to have been the first to dream of connecting the Tennessee and Tombigbee Rivers as the most direct way to get to the Gulf Coast from points too far to the east to easily access the Mississippi River (Stewart 1971, 1). "As early as 1790, promoters, merchants and evangelists began suggesting the possibility of commercial

Figure 4.1 One of the largest and most controversial US Army Corps of Engineer projects in history, the Tennessee-Tombigbee Waterway was a 234-mile-long waterway project along the border of Mississippi and Alabama. Though discussed for nearly two centuries, construction began in 1972. Map by Sydney Varajon.

transportation between Mobile, Alabama, and the Tennessee River via the Tombigbee River. Reliable and cheap transportation to supply commerce and defense needs was vitally important to the young and expanding nation" (Rodeffer 1981).[5] The Tennessee River flows from "the Great Smoky Mountains of Tennessee and North Carolina . . . southwest through Tennessee and northern Alabama," turning north in northeast Mississippi at "the rocky hills that separate its drainage from that of the Tombigbee River to the south" and crossing into western Tennessee and Kentucky, eventually joining the Ohio (Brose 1991, 3). The Tombigbee River begins in northern Mississippi, eventually flowing through central and southern Alabama to the Gulf of Mexico at Mobile. Although connecting the two rivers required the digging of a twenty-seven-mile canal through the rocky hills of northern Mississippi, it would save river traffic from traveling hundreds of miles from the Tennessee to the Ohio to the Mississippi before turning south to the Gulf of Mexico. Though early dreamers would not have known it, by the time the plan came into being, the Tombigbee also had to be widened, deepened, and straightened to allow for twentieth-century river transport.

The potential to connect the two rivers continued to be discussed over the next century by those in Kentucky, Tennessee, and Alabama, and in 1874, Congress called for a formal study of the possibility. The outcome of the first feasibility study was a determination by the US Army Corps of Engineers that "they could build a canal but they doubted whether there was enough commerce in the area to justify it" (Stewart 1971, 2). In the following decades, multiple cost-benefit analyses were conducted, and all determined that the costs outweighed the benefits of such a large project (Stine 1993, 13–14; Stewart 1971, 2–3). It was 1938 before the Corps of Engineers first "found the project's benefits to outweigh—if only slightly—its costs," but the Corps did not yet strongly support going forward (Stine 1993, 14). The project failed to gain support of the US Congress the following year, in part due to the railroad lobby. The head of the Association of American Railroads as well as representatives of labor unions testified before a congressional committee against the Tenn-Tom, with one union executive charging that "only well-to-do interests would benefit from expenditures for waterways, not the average consumer" (Stewart 1971, 11).

The proposal failed again in 1941 and 1943 (Stine 1993, 15), and it was not until after WWII that the Tenn-Tom received congressional approval, after a restudy estimated the benefit-cost ratio at 1.05 to 1 (Brown 1974, 2; Stewart 1971, 27–30), as part of the Rivers and Harbors Act of 1946; even then, actual construction was not yet funded. But planning began, and with it, the costs rose: between 1946 and 1950, cost estimates rose 45 percent to $169 million (Stine 1993, 16). The House Appropriations Committee began an investigation into the cost increases following the 1950 projections (Stewart 1971, 44; Stine 1993, 16), after which the project was formally put on hold (Stewart 1971, 48). The project was started and stopped for another twenty years, with funding allocations periodically provided for planning and further study only.

Two of the major factors that would be central to the fight against the Tenn-Tom, then, were already rearing their heads in the early planning stages: (1) the repeated dramatic cost increases prior to and during the construction phases, along with charges of perverse overstatements of the economic benefits of the project,[6] and (2) opposition from the Association of American Railroads—particularly the L&N, whose main line would be directly paralleled by the waterway, but others as well—because the waterway would open fierce competition for business from river travel. As Jeffrey K. Stine argued, however, one central piece was still developing: "the environmental movement that flowered during the middle of the Tenn-Tom's lengthy gestation" (1993, 33).

In 1970, the project was finally—though only partially—funded. The power of southern congressmen such as those representing Mississippi (Representative Jamie L. Whitten [D], Senator John C. Stennis [D], and Senator James O. Eastland [D]) and Alabama (Representative Robert E. Jones [D] and Senator John J. Sparkman [D]) ultimately led to inclusion of the Tenn-Tom in President Nixon's Southern Strategy: "By backing the Tenn-Tom, Nixon could demonstrate that he was not neglecting the South" (Stine 1993, 29). Though there was not full agreement within Nixon's White House, his budget for fiscal year 1971 included the first allocation of construction funding, to the tune of $1 million (30–31). Ironically, considering what was to come, this was the same year that Nixon signed the National Environmental Policy Act (NEPA) into law.[7]

"Tennessee-Tombigbee was dedicated in Mobile, Alabama, in May 1971, with President Nixon in attendance. In July suit was filed against the project by the Environmental Defense Fund" (Brown 1974, 6). When construction began on the Tenn-Tom in 1972, the 234-mile-long waterway project included "ten locks, five dams, extensive river widening, deepening, and straightening, and a 27-mile-long cut through hilly terrain" (Stine 1993, 1) and ultimately included the flooding of 40,000 acres of land and the excavation of "over 300 million cubic yards of earth … (more than was removed to dig the Panama Canal)" (Stine 1992, 8). The project was completed ahead of schedule in 1985 at a final cost of nearly $2 billion (Stine 1993, 9); the estimate in 1970 had been $323 million (Miller 1978, 2).

"As one of the first major water projects to be built entirely under the auspices of NEPA, the Tenn-Tom became an important early test case for the newly passed legislation" (Stine 1993, 85). NEPA meant two things: the introduction of the requirement of environmental impact statements (EISs), which included protection of the natural as well as the cultural environments, and increased and increasing national attention to protecting the environment. Over one hundred thousand acres of forest and farmland would be overtaken by the Tenn-Tom, including those

Figures 4.2–4.4 Aerial views of the divide cut section, joining the Tennessee and Tombigbee Rivers, of the Tenn-Tom Waterway under construction. US Army Corps of Engineers Digital Library.

flooded as well as acres given over for the deposit of materials dredged in the process (86) and for periodic drainage and flooding. "The 115 species of fishes supported by the free-flowing stretch of the upper Tombigbee made it one of the richest rivers in North America in terms of native fish fauna," and many questioned the "ecological consequences of mixing the waters" of the two rivers (87). "Numerous historic and archaeological sites would also be destroyed" (86). The Corps submitted the EIS in April 1971; in it, they concluded that there were no "detrimental effects significant enough to forgo development of the project" (as quoted in Stine 1993, 97). However, environmentalists argued that the EIS was not adequate on multiple grounds (98).

The first lawsuit, filed in 1971—consisting of seven allegations, including that the Tenn-Tom violated NEPA and the Historic Sites Act of 1960 (Stine 1993, 112)—was decided in the Corps's favor in 1974 (126). In November 1976, the Environmental Defense Fund and the L&N Railroad filed "separate but parallel" lawsuits against the Tenn-Tom (199), and by 1982, the Corps had won these suits too, "end[ing] nine years of litigation" and clearing the way for the completion of the project (217–18). The lawsuits and controversies swirling around the Tenn-Tom, from environmental concerns to continued criticism of the mounting costs of the project, had resulted in the Corps doing everything it could to complete the project as quickly as possible.

"A CRUEL HOAX": THE PEOPLE OF THE TENN-TOM REGION

Those living in the sixteen-county region directly affected by the Tenn-Tom Waterway were predominantly low income (60%), and 40 percent of the people of the region were Black; 75 percent of the Black population of the region was low income (Zippert 1977, 2).[8] The chief argument made by proponents of the Tenn-Tom was that it would bring economic opportunities to the region—"the waterway's backers portrayed it as a panacea for regional unemployment and underemployment" (Stine 1993, 6)—and for many Black residents, the project therefore offered hope. A study of the perceptions of the economic impact of the Tenn-Tom in eight West Alabama counties showed that three-quarters of the population was optimistic about the potential for the Tenn-Tom to "make things better" in the region, though whites were more optimistic than Blacks (Molnar et al. 1981, 14ff).

In the early 1970s, the Federation of Southern Cooperatives began to investigate what the Tenn-Tom would mean to people living in the direct region of the waterway (Zippert 1977, 1–2). Civil rights activists such as John Zippert, Carol Zippert, Hubert Sapp, and Jane Sapp played central organizing roles. The First Peoples Conference on the Tennessee-Tombigbee Waterway was held in January 1974, and out if it came the Minority Peoples Council on the Tennessee-Tombigbee Waterway (MPC), "a coalition of people, organizations, elected officials and others organized to insure [*sic*] that Black and poor people are fully involved and receive a fair share of all benefits of the Waterway during construction and in the subsequent development phase" (4). The MPC lobbied for a range of outcomes, including minority representation in the planning and development of the Tenn-Tom and access to employment for Black people and other poor people in both the development of the waterway and jobs that were promised as a result of its completion.

In 1977, the MPC issued "The Tennessee-Tombigbee Water Project: A 'White' Paper," authored by John Zippert of the Federation of Southern Cooperatives and Robert Valder of the NAACP Legal Defense Fund. According to the MPC, "Once completed in the 1980s, the Waterway will stimulate increased industrial, agricultural, and recreational growth in Southwest Alabama and Northeast Mississippi, an area which includes some of the poorest counties in the South with the highest percentages of blacks in the nation."[9] However, the report was meant to express that the MPC was "deeply distressed that the Federal Government, which funds the Waterway, has ignored the civil rights statutes and executive orders at its disposal to mandate the participation and involvement of black citizens."[10] Further, the paper argued, "A cruel hoax is being perpetrated against the minority and poor people of the Tennessee Tombigbee Waterway area. Their economic plight is being manipulated to justify the construction of a major development project which will serve local, regional and multinational economic interests, but whose benefits the people themselves may never enjoy."[11] The "'White' Paper" was submitted to the Army Corps of Engineers, but the MPC also saw "a larger audience . . . The President, the Congress of the United States, numerous Federal agencies, state and local officials, the private sector, and environmental groups."[12]

The inclusion of "environmental groups" in this list points out that many civil rights activists saw their concerns as in opposition to those of the environmentalists who were then in the midst of suing to end the Tenn-Tom project. For instance, in the early 1970s, the county probate judge of Greene County, Alabama— one of the earliest counties affected and "one of the nation's poorest counties and the county with the highest percentage of African-Americans (73 percent)" (Stine 1993, 180)—was an outspoken opponent of the environmental groups. For instance, he charged "national environmental groups with caring 'more about wildlife than the desperate needs of suffering poor people'" (181).

In a paper presented to the Southern Association of Agricultural Scientists in 1977, Zippert wrote that "The MPC Legal Committee plans to intervene in law suits filed by the environmentalists opposed to the Waterway, to assert and protect the interests of minority and poor people in the TTW area" (Zippert 1977, 6). According to Jeffrey Stine, "African-American community leaders became enthusiastic supporters of the Tenn-Tom, taking at face value the promises of plentiful employment opportunities and job training, but their hopefulness gradually soured after construction got underway" (1993, 177).

Arguments made by the MPC, however, suggest that the MPC did *not* take these promises at "face value" but rather as an opportunity to fight to ensure that the waterway—which seemed inevitable to the people of the region if not to those who were suing to stop it—would benefit local Black and poor people as much as possible.[13] In her testimony to the AFC Board of Trustees in February 1979, discussed later in this chapter, Jane Sapp described the fact that not only was it clear that there was no way to stop the waterway, it was already in progress. She continued,

> And as we weighed those concerns, and as we looked at the
> people with whom we worked and the people with whom we
> were concerned, it seemed to me, that as we looked at that, if this
> project was indeed going to happen, which in our mind was in
> fact a reality, that it was going to happen, then we needed to be-
> gin to fight with the Army Corps of Engineers, and with whoever,
> and to say that if it is going to happen, then let's make sure the
> people along this area have some kind of economic benefits from
> this waterway project.[14]

According to Stine, those involved in the MPC "shared a common perception among African-American activists that the mainstream, predominately white environmental organizations valued outdoor recreational amenities over basic issues of social justice and economic equity" (1993, 180). Jane Sapp clearly articulated this as the position of the Minority Peoples Council in February 1979: "We have never seen the environmentalists as being on the side of preserving the people's culture."[15]

The activists successfully garnered minor concessions for the Corps, including the appointment of Black members to the Tennessee-Tombigbee Waterway Development Authority (Stine 1993, 177) as well as the establishment of affirmative action goals for the hiring of contractors and employees in the construction of the waterway (188).[16] However, according to Stine, the "concessions, which ultimately had little or no effect on the cost or quality of the waterway, may well have saved the entire project.

Thus, for a very small price, the Corps and its political backers were able to achieve their goal" (197).

THE MOSS-BENNETT ACT AND THE MITIGATION OF CULTURAL RESOURCES IN THE TENN-TOM REGION

The 1974 passage of the Archeological and Historic Preservation Act (Pub. L. No. 93–291), widely known as the Moss-Bennett Act, expanded the Reservoir Salvage Act of 1960 "to include *all* Federal or Federally-licensed projects, activities, or programs resulting in the alteration of terrain" (Reaves 1976, 35) and "allow[ed] Federal agencies to transfer to the Secretary [of the Interior] up to 1% of project funds for salvage, or to assist the Secretary in salvage," among other things (36). The Interagency Archeological Services (IAS) was created to oversee archaeological projects external to the National Park Service (36), with three field offices. According to a report written by Bennie Keel, then chief of IAS-Atlanta (IAS-A), "some salvage work in the lower portion of the [Tenn-Tom] project" had been undertaken by the predecessor to the IAS and by the Corps of Engineers.[17] In 1977, however, Keel and Jerry Nielsen of the Mobile District of the Corps of Engineers[18] agreed "that the Tennessee-Tombigbee project was too large and complex to deal with in the traditional construction project by construction project fashion."[19] They went on to initiate and obtain a listing on the National Register of Historic Places for a 135-mile stretch of the Tenn-Tom as a multi-resource district in September 1977, thus avoiding the listing of individual sites throughout the region.

Once the Tombigbee River Multi-Resource District was established, Keel worked in consultation with Nielsen to create a mitigation plan. In October 1977, a four-day Cultural Resource Planning conference was held in Atlanta that included interested parties from the archaeological and historic preservation offices and university programs in Alabama and Mississippi and a range of federal agencies. According to Keel, "Insofar as I know, this was the first instance in which such a wide variety of interests ever met to develop a comprehensive, programmatic plan to deal with cultural resources in a Federal project."[20]

Although earlier studies along the waterway had been oriented toward the prehistoric archaeological record of the area, the Moss-Bennett Act "required a broader approach" (Stine 1992, 25). According to Stine, in the summer of 1977 Kathleen Pepi of the Advisory Council on Historic Preservation and Sarah Bridges of the National Register of Historic Places "criticized the Corps for neglecting historic cultural resources (such as extinct river towns, standing antebellum plantations and folk houses, barns, ferry sites, bridges, and railroad stations) along the waterway, which raised questions about the Corps's full compliance with historic preservation legislation" (26). Preservationists present at the October 1977 meeting, including representatives from HABS and the Historic American Engineering Record (HAER), voiced their concerns regarding the lack of attention to historic sites. One result of the meeting is that in the following year, HABS and HAER both were contracted to survey the district and make recommendations for the National Register.

Through what Stine described as "helicopter reconnaissance," "HABS and HAER officials identified fifty structures and twelve bridges as worthy of recording through measured drawings, photographs, and historical research" (1992, 27). Ultimately, HABS "found few structures of architectural significance" and between the two, HABS and HAER made recommendations to the National Register for only fourteen structures and one bridge (28).

This was the project Michael Ann Williams worked on while in graduate school. Writing to AFC Folklife Specialist Howard ("Rusty") Marshall[21] in October 1978, following her work on the HABS project, Williams noted, "By far the greatest restriction on our work this summer, however, was the insistence that we only study structures in the Army Corps' 'take.' As the river is only being widened in the southern area of the project, this included only a narrow strip in the flood plain on which very few structures, mostly modern fishing camps, were built. All the structures were inventoried, but there were fewer worth drawing than anticipated. Furthermore, this restriction impeded a broader regional study of the architecture."[22]

She went on to name the three communities where the work primarily centered, and then she commented, "I strongly feel that all three could warrant further study, and I would love to return to the areas in more depth. In regard to our project, I feel that although much was left undone because of the very restricted nature of the project, we did succeed in documenting with some thoroughness the architecture that will be destroyed by the waterway, and I personally feel that it was a rewarding, though often frustrating, experience."[23]

The amalgamation of legislation passed in this period—the National Historic Preservation Act (1966), NEPA (1969), and the Moss-Bennett Act (1974)—changed the federal government's approach to cultural resource management dramatically, and the Tenn-Tom, "the largest navigation project ever built by the US Army Corps of Engineers" (Stine 1992, 8), just happened to be underway as these changes were tested and implemented. Bennie Keel described this as an exciting time, as "this was very early in the program after the Moss-Bennett legislation was passed and there weren't a lot of ground rules and it was an exciting time because we were going as far as we wanted to, thought we should go, and nobody was telling us 'no, we shouldn't be doing this.'"[24] "The ultimate outcome was that the elements for a [Section] 106 Case report and Mitigation Plan were identified through this [October 1977] meeting.... Briefly, the mitigation plan set forth the goals and called for investigation of all elements of the cultural fabric within the Tombigbee River Multi-Resource District. These investigations require a thorough footing in current theory of a range of disciplines."[25]

"MAYBE WE SHOULD TALK TO A FOLKLORIST": PLANS FOR A "FOLK LIFE STUDY" ARE HATCHED

It appears that the idea to approach the AFC was born, or at least moved to the potential planning stage, during the Cultural Resource Planning conference in October 1977, because although he was not in attendance, Alan Jabbour was listed as the principal investigator of a "Folk Life Study" in the conference notes. On November 10, 1977, Marshall noted a phone call from John Burns of HABS about a potential "comprehensive mitigation" project that he thought should include folklorists and the documentation of "local history—cultural landscape—folk buildings, etc." The first brief notes in the AFC files on the Tenn-Tom make it clear that the AFC staff was aware from the very beginning that the waterway project was surrounded by controversy; Marshall noted, "This project was on Pres. Carter's 'hit list.' Volatile issue; Sierra Club, etc. vigorously against the project."[26] By November 14, 1977, Marshall and Jabbour had apparently spoken of the potential project and determined they "may pursue it." Marshall's planning wheels were turning, as he was already envisioning a "folklife museum for the region," which would include "a living historical farm . . . research center for continuation of work we start with the folklife SURVEY . . . teaching."[27] These initial plans reflect the times, as with the introduction of the Scandinavian folklife model by Don Yoder and others beginning in the 1960s came interest in the development of folklife museums.[28] It also suggests that from the very start, Jabbour and Marshall had intentions for not only documentation but also for making lasting contributions to the region.

Jabbour and Marshall met with Bennie Keel on December 4, 1977, regarding the interest from the IAS of contracting with the AFC to "do a folklore mitigation project for the Tennessee-Tombigbee Project."[29] Keel said in a 2019 phone interview that "Jerry [Nielsen] and I talked about it and with that impact on those communities, a lot of the things that were going to be lost, and so we decided 'well maybe we need to have a study done,' I don't know, I just can't remember how I came up with the idea of 'maybe we should talk to a folklorist.'" He went on, "Because we had already had historical research done by a professor at the University of Alabama who wrote a nice report over—a typical historical report of dates and who did what, and what happened and so on and so forth in the local histories. Jerry and I felt like we were still missing the kind of human side of it."[30]

By March 1978, Marshall was talking with potential local partners, including Alabama folklorist Hank Willett, who had heard about the project planning from Jane Sapp and others and had contacted Alan Jabbour. On March 23, Marshall spoke with Nielsen, and they discussed possibilities including a "cooperative project with H. Willett's Alabama folklife office and someone in Mississippi, using mostly Corps mitigation monies. . . . We could design a hefty, long-range project with a fulltime field coordinator there for a year or so, with the payoff in two years being the initiation of a folklife museum. (The Corps has to establish visitor centers along the project anyhow—so, why not a folk museum?)"[31]

On May 16, 1978, a meeting was held in Columbus, Mississippi, to discuss the feasibility of such a project. Participants included Jabbour and representatives of the IAS, including Bennie Keel; the Corps of Engineers, including Jerry Nielsen; the Alabama State Historic Preservation Office (SHPO), Historical Commission, and Council on the Arts & Humanities (Hank Willett); and the Mississippi Department of Archives and History. A memorandum from Jerry Nielsen summarized the meeting, including the plans that the AFC was in the process of developing, and he stressed that such a project would be led by the AFC in partnership with state agencies in Mississippi and Alabama as well as community organizations. "Thus the program could have a twofold purpose; to serve the interests and responsibilities of the Federal and State parties and consequently laying the ground work for continued public interest and involvement."[32]

Figure 4.5 November 1978 meeting in Columbus, Mississippi, between the Tenn-Tom folklife project planning team and members of groups representing the interests of minorities living in the region. Photo by Carl Fleischhauer, courtesy of the American Folklife Center, Library of Congress.

Representatives of local communities were explicitly not included, much to the distress of members of the Minority Peoples Council. The MPC leadership knew of the May meeting from Hank Willett and wrote a joint letter to Alan Jabbour on May 4, 1978, in which they described their struggles to get the Corps to work, and work fairly, with minority people in the region. Within this context, they wrote, the fact that a meeting was to take place regarding the documentation of the culture of the region without them was a sign of disrespect.[33] However, they go on to express the desire to negotiate with the AFC to involve local people in the project, signaling, as with other aspects of the Tenn-Tom, that they were willing to be involved in order to make the best of it for local communities. Willett's correspondence with Jabbour during the period—as well as his recollections in 2019—demonstrate that he continued to advocate for the inclusion of local communities and for the creation of a "local-state coalition,"[34] which he suggested at the May meeting and mentioned repeatedly in correspondence with Jabbour. In a letter back to Willett in August 1978, Jabbour stated that he remained "fuzzy about the precise nature of the coalition you envision."[35] Willett said in 2019 that in hindsight this was likely Jabbour's way of politely saying that such a "coalition" wasn't going to happen. According to Willett, "Again I remember I think I was particularly pushing for involving the local population. And, no one was expressing open opposition, but I didn't feel like it was enthusiastically embraced at that point either. By any of the parties." Early the following fall, Willett arranged for an informal meeting and a tour of the region with Jabbour, Zippert, and Jane and Hubert Sapp.[36]

TO "PRESERVE THE CONTINUITY OF CULTURAL LIFE": FORMALIZING THE TENN-TOM FOLKLIFE PROJECT

Following the May meeting in Columbus, a preliminary budget and proposal were drawn up, and Alan Jabbour presented the Tennessee-Tombigbee Folklife Project to the Projects Committee of the AFC Board of Trustees, followed by the full board, at their meeting in late May 1978. The minutes and notes of the board meeting reflect a discussion dominated almost entirely by concerns about the potential negative repercussions of the project. Alan Jabbour, in fact, was the first to point out that the project was risky for some of the very reasons that would later lead to the cancellation of the project, including the central issue: the political implications and potential effect of involvement on the image of the AFC. Janet Anderson,[37] who was new to the board, expressed her concerns about negative associations with the Corps of Engineers and the environmental impacts of other Corps projects, and she wondered about the feelings of people in the region about the Tenn-Tom. A discussion ensued about whether or not the AFC would be "doing a Corps of Engineers project," with Jabbour stressing that the money was really coming through the Department of the Interior, not the Corps—a point he made in other contexts as well as an attempt to rhetorically separate the money and therefore the project from the Corps of Engineers. The discussion ended with Jabbour's assurance that he would not commit to the project without further discussions with the board, both individually and as a group.[38]

Planning continued through the summer and fall, and the AFC Board of Trustees approved the project at their November 1978 board meeting. The minutes do not suggest a lengthy or a contentious discussion.[39] However, Ralph Rinzler, representing Secretary S. Dillon Ripley of the Smithsonian, whom he described as "a leader in the field of protection of natural species," "abstained because of uncertainty about the Secretary's position." According to the minutes, Rinzler expressed Ripley's concerns about "the Center's becoming involved with an environmentally controversial waterway project." The brief discussion of the project as summarized in the minutes ends thus: "[Alan Jabbour] said that he would proceed with the project with the Board's approval but that he would call it off if things emerge that he did not anticipate."[40]

Jabbour and AFC folklife specialist Carl Fleischhauer,[41] who had been brought in on the project by this point, returned to Columbus November 27–29, 1978, and during this trip they began looking at real estate space for the team and held a meeting that included representatives of the MPC and Jane and Hubbert Sapp. It is clear from correspondence both prior to and following the meeting and from the meeting notes that Jabbour needed to work hard to persuade local activists to place their trust in the AFC. According to Carl Fleischhauer's handwritten notes, the concerns raised (particularly from Jane Sapp) included the selection of the project director and the team, the importance of the inclusion of local people, the long-term impact of the research (researchers not merely taking pictures and leaving), and the importance of training local people in order to assure long-term impact. Fleischhauer's notes capture an important discussion of the value of local versus outsider "experts" as well as the heterogeneous nature of "local"—not all communities in the region are the same—that is ongoing in folklore studies.[42]

The November 1978 issue of the MPC newsletter summarized the meeting and voiced tepid support of the AFC project.

> MPC, the Federation [of Southern Cooperatives], and Miles College-Eutaw expressed concern that local individuals and institutions have a more direct role in this project. Suggestions range from forming an advisory board made up of representatives of the local communities to involving local people in some of the important "research" and planning work. Mr. Jabbour seemed receptive to these suggestions and promised to give them full consideration.
>
> MPC has long been aware of the cultural implications of the TTW. The effort of the American Folklife Institute [*sic*] should be supported. However, care must be taken to insure [*sic*] that the lives of people in the Waterway area, many of whom are black and poor, are represented in a balanced and accurate way. It also seems fair that Waterway area residents share some of the employment opportunities and research experiences such a project creates (MPC 1978).

At the February 1979 AFC board meeting discussed later in this chapter, Jane Sapp described her support of the project in this way:

> And to me, one of the plusses of this particular project, as I understood it, and as I was enthusiastic about it, and as other institutions in the area were enthusiastic about it, was that it not only spoke to just coming in and doing documentation, but that it also spoke to assisting people along those counties in the Tennessee-Tombigbee Waterway area. If for nothing else, one it brought national attention, to the people along those areas. Two, to say that there was a governmental agency that was interested in coming along those 16 counties, along the Tennessee-Tombigbee

> Waterway area, to say that "I think that what you are and what you are about is important enough for me to document" was enough to generate some enthusiasm from those people in terms of who they are and what they are all about. To me that was a plus. Because as I understood it, from the American Folklife Center, they were not interested in coming in and documenting, taking whatever they were going to do as—excuse my prejudice towards a lot of folklorists, documenting and running away and writing a book, and the people never know anything about it. But there was a sincere interest in generating, with the people, in those areas, and sharing with the people the materials that had been developed, that had been documented, that you would have a copy of the video tapes, that you would see the films, that you would see the photographs, that you would see the written material that had happened.[43]

The final project proposal is dated October 4, 1978, and it lays out the goals of the project to "preserve and present the cultural traditions of the region, past and present."[44]

> "Preserve and present," the key phrase of the American Folklife Preservation Act, suggests a useful approach to comprehensive cultural work in the area. Federal cultural research should consciously and carefully adopt the mutually compatible goals of service to research and scholarship, and service to a wider public in the region itself and throughout the nation. Adoption of these goals should yield "preservation" both in the documentary and archival sense and in the sense of nourishing the continuity of cultural life and expression in a region coping with the currents of change.
>
> . . . The project will locate, document, study, and disseminate salient features of the traditional life, thought, and cultural expression of the people of the region.[45]

The proposal goes on to list the goals, which include amassing an archival collection to be housed at the AFC as well as products potentially including publications, recordings, films, and educational materials. Importantly, the final goal was to "seek to establish a useful model for future cultural undertakings by the federal government."[46]

The strategies of the project included a broad folklife survey of the 135-mile Tombigbee River Multi-Resource District, followed by more in-depth focus on four communities to be selected based on the broad initial survey. In addition to the employment of folklorists to carry out the work under the leadership of the project director, an internship program was planned to "train seriously interested citizens, folklore and folklife students, or students from disciplines in folk cultural research methods."[47]

An Interagency Agreement between the LOC/AFC and the Department of the Interior / IAS-A / Heritage Conservation and Recreation Service was signed on December 14, 1978. The funding was to originate with the Corps of Engineers and flow through the IAS to the AFC, totaling $483,261.[48] According to the AFC board meeting minutes of November 1978, "The Center will add a mix of cash and in-kind services which brings the total [budget] to $550,000."[49]

The Interagency Agreement began, "Whereas, the IAS-A on behalf of the Mobile and Nashville Districts, Corps of Engineers under the authority of Public Law 93–291 requires reliable information on the folklife traditions of people living along the course of the Tennessee-Tombigbee Waterway to prevent loss of significant local and regional cultural data, and preserve the continuity of cultural life in the region." And here is where the regrets of those who see the failed project as a missed opportunity become clearest: the Corps of Engineers, an arm of the federal government, required folklife data in order to "preserve the continuity of cultural life."

The preliminary work was to begin immediately, with the core team in place by May 1979 and fieldwork to take place through May 1980, followed by product development. Project staff job descriptions and contracts had been drafted. Members of Congress in the region had been sent a draft press release for their use in announcing the project, dated February 5, 1979. Folklorist Neil Rosenberg, then a faculty member at Memorial University of Newfoundland (MUN), had been selected to serve as the project director and had received an eighteen-month leave of absence from MUN in order to carry out the work, which would be directed from Columbus, Mississippi, due to its proximity to the project. Beginning in December 1978, Rosenberg had made several trips to the AFC and had begun to search for project fieldworkers and other staff. He wrote in retrospect, "We were moving into a region which had both Anglo- and African-[American] populations. Our fieldwork team particularly required specialists in African American folklore. There weren't many, and, as I found in the unsuccessful campaign to recruit Bill Wiggins, they were much in demand."[50] The search was made public by early 1979, as the January 1979 *Folklife Center News* includes a brief article on the project and invites applicants for the team to contact Alan Jabbour (American Folklife Center 1979), and Lynwood Montell, director of what was then the Center for Intercultural and Folk Studies at Western Kentucky University, circulated a memo to former and present folklore graduate students advertising the positions and instructing interested candidates to contact Neil Rosenberg.[51] However, Rosenberg had begun to sense a change in attitude from potential project staff he was working to recruit: "And it became clear that there was opposition building, and it became harder and harder, for me to get people to commit."[52] Elsewhere he stated, "Indeed, as soon as Archie [Green]'s opposition to the project became known, support for the project was itself impacted. Some people previously interested, like Judy McCulloh, quickly withdrew."[53]

At some point, Jabbour drafted a list of issues and questions raised by the project:

 I. Ethical Issues
  a. Is the waterway an accomplished fact? If not, will a folklife study contribute to its completion?
  b. If building the waterway is wrong, should the Government assume nevertheless a responsibility for mitigation of its impact on the cultural resources of the region?

   II. Professional Issues
- a. Should folklorists be involved in federally funded studies in the future?
- b. If such involvement is likely, what should the Center's role be?
- c. If there is uncertainty on these professional issues, will a demonstration project help crystallize the issues for future professional debate? Will it help to set standards?

  III. Administrative Issues
- a. Is our financial relationship to the other agencies a proper reflection of the folklife project concept?
- b. Is the Center capable of administering the project? The Library?
- c. Is the contract to the project director appropriate?
- d. Will it take too much Center staff time?[54]

By early 1979, every one of these questions was being asked.

"THE WATERWAY PROJECT IS SO HEAVILY TAINTED . . .": OPPOSITION TO THE FOLKLIFE PROJECT MOUNTS

By January 1979, after the folklife project had been approved by the AFC Board of Trustees and as the planning continued, opposition was growing, coming from two primary sources: S. Dillon Ripley, secretary of the Smithsonian, and Archie Green, who was and is considered the father of the AFC because of his tireless leadership in the work to establish it through the passage of the American Folklife Preservation Act.

In a January 25 letter to AFC chair Raye Virginia Allen,[55] Secretary Ripley asked that the board "reconsider its commitment" to the folklife project. His primary concerns were "the adequacy of management experience" (that the AFC could not handle such a large budget) and "the tarnish of ecological and natural conservation issues."[56] In her reply, Allen committed to devoting a portion of the upcoming board meeting in February to discussion of the project.[57]

Meanwhile, Archie Green had been making his opposition known in conversations since early 1978.[58] Neil Rosenberg told us,

> Archie . . . pretty early on took me aside and said, "Look, I don't agree with this project, I'm gonna oppose it, because . . . I don't think that the Folklife Center should be seen as being in bed with the Army Corps of Engineers." It was a bad association is what he thought. And, I have to say that, you know, I looked at the legislation [such as the Moss-Bennett Act] and there wasn't just one piece of legislation, it was a series of things. And, it seemed to me that the legislation was meant to send that message anyway. You know, that—to keep the Army Corps of Engineers from destroying culture. So I didn't really see why he had a problem with that.[59]

On January 30, 1979, Archie Green wrote a letter to AFC chair Raye Virginia Allen describing his ardent opposition to the project. His central arguments included that the Tennessee-Tombigbee Waterway was a wasteful pork barrel project and harmful to the environment, folklorists should be allied with conservationists, the project would benefit the Corps of Engineers, the AFC's association with the Corps would serve as a signal to the nation about the AFC's priorities, and the AFC should not be carrying out model projects around the country as it had been doing (i.e., field documentation projects in Chicago, Georgia, and the Blue Ridge region).[60]

Alan Jabbour sent copies of Green's letter to Allen, along with a letter he wrote in reply, to the executive board of the AFS, chairs of graduate programs in folklore, and other folklorists who had expressed interest.[61] His brief cover letter asked for "thoughts about the subject," and the AFC Tenn-Tom correspondence files include a collection of letters he received in response as well as summary notes from phone calls he and Carl Fleischhauer received. For instance, Fleischhauer summarized the opinion of Kenneth Goldstein in this way: "Professor Goldstein said he wished to express his firm and complete support of the position outlined by Alan Jabbour in his letter to Archie Green. He said he felt Archie's argument was not cogent, and said that if sensitive, thinking folklorists did not perform these tasks that probably the 'Army' would with disastrous results."[62] Brief handwritten notes summarize Jabbour's conversations with Alan Lomax, Polly Stewart, Worth Long, and David Hufford, all of whom were in support of the project, as well as Richard Bauman, who was not.[63]

The majority of the letters in the files express the opinion that the AFC should go ahead with the folklife project, even as they agree with many of Green's arguments.[64] Many state that they agree with Green's opinion on the Corps in general and that the Tenn-Tom Waterway was indeed a "boondoggle," but they express various opinions on why, despite this, the project should go ahead. Hank Willett's reflection in 2019 on his own letter at the time is apt.

> Archie was not only a hero of mine, but he was a pretty good
> friend actually too. . . . And I shared almost all of Archie's politi-
> cal views, regarding the way things happened in Washington
> and everything else. In fact the—I think I gave you a copy, but
> the fairly long, two or three pages, letter I sent to Alan Jabbour,
> in response to reading the Archie communications and so on
> and so forth. Reading that over, for the first time in many many
> years, I can see where I'm basically supporting the project
> and singing Archie's praise at the same time. Which I don't
> think was a real disconnect, because I agreed with almost all
> of Archie's objections to the Tennessee-Tombigbee Waterway.
> What I did not agree with was his objections to folklorists
> getting involved with doing something I considered mitigating,
> you know.[65]

Many argued that AFC involvement would not change the fact that the waterway was being built, and at least this project would document what would be lost. Richard Dorson, who infamously testified in opposition to the creation of the AFC (see chap. 1 and Bulger 2003), wrote a brief letter to Jabbour in support of the project, on the grounds that he found Jabbour's position more convincing than Green's.[66] Barre Toelken sent Jabbour a lengthy letter of support, writing in part:

> Folklorists can, as Archie suggests, keep themselves aloof from such nasty considerations as these and pretend by not being there on the spot that they bear no political responsibility for what our government does. They can take safe jobs in Washington and argue blue collar interests while wearing white shirts and ties. They can construct delicate coordinative networks with bureaucratic interchanges of folkloristic interest and pretend that their taxes are not paying for Tenn-Tom or some similar abomination. But I see no reason, moral or professional, why they should.
>
> In fact, I feel the greatest mistake we could commit at this point in history would be to allow such a project as the Tenn-Tom to take place <u>without</u> folklorists being present.[67]

Bert Wilson wrote as well, and his letter is an articulation of the difficulties of choosing a side in this debate, particularly in regard to negotiating the arguments invoked by environmental conservationists and cultural preservationists. He urges Jabbour to keep the AFC out of such political issues. Richard Bauman also articulated the difficulties, as he wrote, "I have long thought that impact assessment would be a highly appropriate and productive activity for folklorists to undertake"; however, "the waterway project is so heavily tainted that I fear the Center will not be able to avoid being tainted itself by association with it." He concludes, "Other cleaner and more appropriate opportunities will present themselves for the Center to undertake a pilot impact assessment."[68] The arguments for and against the Tenn-Tom folklife project that had been expressed in letters and very likely in many undocumented conversations culminated in a meeting of the AFC Board of Trustees on February 23, 1979.

"PITTING SNAIL DARTERS AGAINST POOR PEOPLE": THE FEBRUARY 1979 MEETING OF THE AFC BOARD OF TRUSTEES

By the time of the meeting, according to Rosenberg, "Archie had called in his chips, is the way it looked to me."[69] The portion of the meeting dedicated to discussion of the Tenn-Tom folklife project was open to the public, and a number of folklorists and other interested parties were in attendance. The recording of this portion of the meeting totals approximately 240 minutes, and it includes impassioned speeches and remarks by those on both sides of the question.[70] In contrast to the letters Jabbour received, however, the majority of those who spoke expressed opposition to the project. Obviously, in this chapter, we cannot recount all that was said by all who spoke in this four-hour period; we will describe the framing of the meeting by Board of Trustees chair Raye Virginia Allen and the central arguments made by some of the most vocal participants. This includes those who spoke in opposition to the project, including Archie Green along with AFC board members folklorist Wayland Hand, Janet Anderson, and Ralph Rinzler on behalf of Dillon Ripley, and those who spoke in favor of it, including Vice Chair Edward ("Ned") Danson and the only person who was in attendance to speak for the people of the sixteen counties of the Tenn-Tom region, Jane Sapp.[71]

The meeting began with introductions by all present, including members of the AFC board and those there to speak. Chair Raye Virginia Allen began by outlining the structure of the meeting, which was to begin with presentations from those there to speak for or against the project followed by questions from the board. She noted that the board had received copies of the letters sent in response to Jabbour's request for comments, and she framed the meeting in this way: "I don't think this has been easy for any of us, as I wrote to Archie Green in a letter, to receive protest from a man who's a one-man institution in folk culture, has been very difficult for us all, for us all to respond to. And equally it's been difficult to find that Secretary Dillon Ripley is opposed to this project called the Tennessee-Tombigbee Folklife Project. And I'm sure that Ralph can answer questions for us when we get to that part of the presentation." She then called for a motion, which was made by Wayland Hand and seconded by Ned Danson. Allen then called on Archie Green as the first on the agenda. However, Green responded that while he was "prepared to speak strongly against the survey," he would prefer to speak "after there is at least one statement by a board member in favor of the survey and one statement by a board member against the survey. That would give me an opportunity to focus my remarks in terms of the position of the board." Green effectively reversed the meeting structure that Chair Allen had just described.

Wayland Hand was the first AFC board member to speak, and he spoke for about thirty minutes, including some back and forth with others, against the project. He described reading materials that had been made available to him in the prior two weeks, presumably by Archie Green, including packets of information such as brochures, news clippings, and opinion pieces put together by the Environmental Policy Institute and the Louisville and Nashville Railroad (both of whom had lawsuits pending to stop the waterway). He laid out questions this material raised for him, stating that he had not previously understood the implications of the project. "So I am here today, asking myself some questions, 'what am I doing and why am I doing it?' And 'why this eleventh-hour stand?' It would have been a lot better if we could have treated this early on." He spent several minutes on criticisms of the Corps of Engineers and the effects of the waterway on the environment, and then he came to the issue of mitigation.

> If I were going to do this myself, I think it would be nice to ascertain the feelings of the people who've been wrenched from their whole lives and from their anchorage. And there'll be a lot of folklore, they'll be quoting a lot of Biblical proverbs to you and a lot of Elizabethan things that will be worth taking. But more interesting would be if you could trace these people down in ten

years, if you could find them which would be close to impossible to—the follow up would be "How Green Was My Valley?" as they went back and they contemplated what had happened. So there's nothing we can do about that unless the waterway is stopped. And I think if we take action against it there's a fair chance that it may be stopped. If we go along and say "Well we can't do anything about it, we're sorry, but we think the record should be made" then maybe it will not be stopped. Someone must do this work, it's very important, no one doubts—we all believe it should be done but it mustn't be the American Folklife Center.

He went on to say, as others following him also did, that local people should be called on to do the folklife survey work. He said again in conclusion, "I think had we looked at this calmly earlier on with full information we'd not be in the quandary we are today. We have had an Army Engineer Corps briefing from the beginning, help and urging from the Interior. It could have been nice if we'd had the environmental policy people come to us and the Tombigbee River people."

Following Hand, Allen deferred back to Green, who said that he wanted to hear a board member speak in favor of the project before he spoke, and Ned Danson, vice chair of the board and anthropologist in the western US, provided a brief defense. Danson spoke for less than ten minutes, primarily about his own experiences of having worked in mitigation and his beliefs in conservation and in the duty to do mitigation when governmental projects are destroying a place. "If Tombigbee is going to go ahead, then I do not feel that the Center is being criminal, rotten, bad, doing wrong things, if they try to pick up and learn as much as possible—pick up the pieces and learn as much as possible about what is being ruined, dispersed. And that is why I feel this is a perfectly legitimate program."

Once he'd heard a board member on each side, Green spoke for close to a half hour, including a short question and answer exchange with Ned Danson. Archie Green's opposition to the project was well known. In addition to his letter to board chair Allen, sent out by Alan Jabbour, comments on the record and in our interviews suggest that he talked with many members of the field about his strong feelings against it. Green's argument, broadly speaking, was that the folklife project would taint the AFC by linking it to the Corps of Engineers.

> Now here's the problem on linkage. It has been suggested that "We're not involved in Tenn-Tom. We're not digging through the mountains. We're not moving people out of their homes. We're not pulling Mississippi into modernity. We're just making a survey." Well that's a form of sophistry. These projects are linked. The survey flows from the project. The survey is perceived by the Army Corps of Engineers metaphorically as a bucket of whitewash. We don't need the Corps, but the Corps needs us. . . . It wants surveys that suggest that the damage is not as great as it seems.

This was undoubtedly true. Much as Jeffrey K. Stine has argued in his histories of the waterway that the Corps made low-cost concessions to the Minority Peoples Council, the Corps likely saw the spending of a mere half million dollars on a folklife survey as a cheap means of public relations.

Green argued vehemently—as did others who followed him, particularly Janet Anderson—that there was a very good chance that the waterway project would be stopped any day, either by the courts (through lawsuits, one of which failed less than a month later and all of which had failed by 1982) or by the US Senate. He believed that canceling the folklife project would bolster the efforts to cancel the waterway itself. "We ought to encourage local preservationists—cultural, physical, historic—in the state of Mississippi to fight to the best of their abilities, and we ought to support them morally. And to me, returning the contract to the Interior is the first visible sign to the Corps of Engineers that there are some preservationists who understand the issues." A short time later in her remarks, Jane Sapp laughed wryly at the references to the Tenn-Tom as something that was "going to happen": "as it has happened, ten miles from me in terms of the Gainesville Lock and Dam, that's already happened." In fact, an estimated one-third of the waterway project was complete by this time (Sinclair 1979).

Figure 4.6 AFC Board of Trustees meeting on February 23, 1979, at which the Tenn-Tom folklife project was debated. Archie Green, pictured here, argued against the project. Photo by Carl Fleischhauer, courtesy of the American Folklife Center, Library of Congress.

Green saw the waterway as "pulling Mississippi into modernity." He argued that mitigation made sense for archaeologists but not the folklorist because

> he-the-archaeologist gives us knowledge about our past and gives us a sense of our future. One of the important distinctions, however, is that as folklorists, we deal with certain aspects of the past, but those aspects as they operate in society today. And we cannot, we cannot salvage living culture. You see, folklorists by definition are drawn to marginal society, are drawn to enclave

people, and we have a special obligation to deal with the folk as mediators between—not as mitigators, Wayland [Hand], but as mediators, mediators between the folk and the pressures that grind up and destroy folk society.

In the conclusion to the prepared portion of his remarks, he critiqued the approach of the young AFC, as led by Alan Jabbour, to conducting multiple folklife surveys in different parts of the country as stretching the small staff too thin.[72] He then compared this to "the old BAE [Bureau of American Ethnology] approach" and went on:

And I want really to appeal to my colleagues here on the board, to think just this thought about the history of ethnography in the United States, to take you back in time. When the Jesuit priests and the Moravian missionaries began working with American Indians, those early ethnographers in our colonial period were faced with an existential dilemma: did they pull Indians into Western European modes, into Christian styles, into learning and to literacy, or did those ethnographers those missionaries, those men of God, did they see their roles as mediating between the harsh effects of industrialization, of modernization and commercial process and Indian life? And we know that those ethnographers were constantly caught. That was the dilemma faced by Major Powell, it's a dilemma faced by all of us now. And if we're conscious of that dilemma, if we're conscious of the, of the path that we have to follow between antiquarianism and advocacy, we will then choose projects where we can reach out to peers, where we can symbolize to the American people that we stand for land ethic and community. We cannot, we cannot permit our ethnographic studies to be tainted by the politics of destruction and disaster.

Here, he compared the work of the AFC to that of our very problematic past. The history of the linkages between colonialization and ethnography are very real, and it is crucial to keep that history in the forefront, as Green argued, as we approach ethnographic research today (along with linkages with romantic nationalism, cf. Abrahams

1993; Roberts 2008). However, his continued references to the people of the Tenn-Tom region as somehow premodern and ethnographic research in the region as a means of introduction of modern industrialization and literacy demonstrate that this perspective was still in transition in this period, as reflected elsewhere in this book.

Individuals have told us in conversations and interviews about the project that part of Archie Green's fervent opposition to the Tenn-Tom folklife project was based in his feelings that after working for years for the passage of legislation that established the AFC, he had lost control of it. It is widely understood that he was not pleased with Jabbour's leadership. While that is not the subject of this chapter, it is important to note that aspects of his argument against the folklife project reflect his critique of the work of the AFC up to this point. For instance, he expressed anger that Jabbour had not heeded his opinions: "I must say though that it was very distressing for me, to have talked to the director of the Center for nearly a year, expressing my deep opposition to the project and to find that as recently as two or three weeks ago, some of the members of the board had not read a single piece of literature critical of Tenn-Tom" (*emphasis his, with the sound of his hand hitting the table on each word*). He pointed out that this material was available within blocks from where they sat, and "it seems to me that we had a minimum obligation to flood the board with this kind of literature, and that would have helped people like Wayland, and other members of conscience, to thread some kind of path through controversy."

Here he was getting to the environmental decimation resulting from the Tenn-Tom Waterway, which was a primary issue in his letter to Chair Allen, in which he argued that folklorists should be allied with conservationists and preservationists, and as individuals, folklorists should join the lawsuits filed by environmental groups to stop the Tenn-Tom. Rosenberg recalled, "I remember him saying, 'We want to be seen as allies of the Sierra Club, not the Army Corps of Engineers.' That was his argument."[73]

Jane Sapp spoke not long after Green, and she began by say-ing that she felt nervous. She then said, "There's a gospel song that says, 'We've come a long way to be here,' and I've come from a long, long way to be here. I've come from Alabama. And I've been journeying since 5:30 yesterday morning to be here." She described the "several constituencies" she was there to represent, including "number one, those of us who live along the Tennessee-Tombigbee Waterway project. Number two, those of us who are interested in folklife and culture along that area" as well as her institution, Miles College-Eutaw (Alabama), the Federation of Southern Cooperatives, and the Minority Peoples Council. "So I sit here in a sense representing those 16 counties . . . and to me that feels like a very awesome responsibility. But I also feel like it is absolutely necessary to sit here and say this." She spoke for approximately forty minutes, saying about halfway through,

> As you know I live in the Tennessee-Tombigbee area, so for me to come to Washington . . . to deal with people who haven't even *been there*, who haven't even *looked* at that area, *who do not even know the kind of poverty* that exists in that area, *do not even know that people there*—and I hope you don't think I'm crying the blues because that's not even what it's about. I don't want you to bring out your violins, and I don't even want you to bring out your guitars. Because that's not what I'm about. But what I'm saying is that, from what I've heard thus far, I'm listening to a lot of folks who haven't even *been there*, who don't even know what's happen-ing in those 16 county areas. And I haven't even heard anybody talk about community development along those areas.

She said at another point that she's not here to support the Corps of Engineers or the waterway or the AFC: "I'm simply here to talk about: what are the interests of the people along that area." As previously discussed in this chapter, Jane Sapp was quite clear about the opinions of the MPC and others in the region that conservationists and preservationists were not allied with poor people and Black people in terms of interests.

And our interests are, and our questions are—when it comes
down to human concerns, human conditions along those areas, for
those who talk about ecological concerns, for those who talk about
environmentalist concerns, our question is "Where were you, a long
long time ago? Why were you not there screaming then? Why are
you screaming now? Where were you five years ago? Where were you
when the project was first instituted? Where were you when people
were walking along that area with picket signs, saying 'this is going to
do such a thing, it's going to destroy our' whatever?"

The MPC was working to intervene in opposition to the lawsuits filed by environmental groups—which they saw as choosing
wildlife over poor people—while Green was urging folklorists to
support the lawsuits and ally with preservationists and conservationists. Sapp asked, "And are we concerned about the poverty
conditions of human beings consistently, and systematically? Or
are we more concerned about whether a snail darter or an old
antebellum house survives?" To which Green seemed to reply—
without mentioning her name—about thirty minutes later, "The
forces in our civilization that are destructive of the autonomy of
the folk and destructive of people's autonomy, destructive of vi-
able community life, constantly pit snail darters as one symbol
against poor people as another symbol." He continued,

> I can't push folklorists into political advocacy, but individuals can
> support good causes. But I have suggested that folklorists ought to be
> mediators in that process. That is a way to make a synthesis of black
> and white, of snail darters and of poor people, and unless we begin
> to think through redevelopment for stranded people, for marginal
> people, for enclave people, whether they're on Indian reservations or
> on the Tombigbee, or in the slums of Chicago. You know unless we
> think very very hard, about the politics for the next 30 or 40 years for
> the end of this century, then we're all in deep trouble.

Archie Green's opposition to the AFC folklife project was
grounded in vital big-picture issues of who we were as a field, who
we accept money from, and whose side we choose. This project

seems to have symbolized for him the very worst alliances the field could make and how alliances could taint the AFC and the field. In his statements of opposition, however, he had to ignore the consequences of canceling the folklife project for the people of the region; he was choosing, however unintentionally, to side against documenting the folklife of poor and Black people of the Tenn-Tom region—documentation supported by many of those very same poor and Black people. In a sense, Green and Sapp were making completely irreconcilable arguments, even as they considered similar issues.

As another example, Green described the effects of the post-WWII mechanization of cotton production as it forced "surplus people off the land."

> We exported surplus folk off the land and turned them into welfare families. We have three generations of welfare families . . . from Mississippi in Illinois. We have Appalachians in Cincinnati who have never worked since they left the rural South. So what I am suggesting is a, a—really a dramatic rethinking on the politics of development. We ought to take this two billion dollars away from the engineers, and we ought to turn it into units in [the Department of] Agriculture and [the Department of the] Interior that have a special sensitivity in working with rural people in the area. We can't arrest change entirely, but politically as folklorists, we can opt for that form of development that's the least destructive of community. That's the basic distinction between a salvage mentality and a preservation mentality.

Jane Sapp talked about this history as well, continuing the series of questions quoted above that emphasize the lack of attention to the historical conditions of the region.

> Where were you many years before that, when industrialization and mechanization was taking place in those rural and economically depressed areas? Where were you when the large landholders along that area said, "*We* have the money, *we* can mechanize, *we* can industrialize"? And the people were *indeed* uprooted,

and this is aside from the whole TTW project. Our question is, "Where were you then?" And "why are you now, why are you now raising these questions?" If indeed—and like I said, as the Minority Peoples Council saw this, this was a tradeoff. We have never seen the environmentalists as being on the side of preserving the people's culture. . . . We have not seen you there, where were you then? And as I said before, "Where were you when the large landholders in those sixteen counties or more, began to move in terms of mechanizations, because they had the money, and the small farmers did not have the money, and Black people and poor people in those areas did not have the money and did not have the means to begin to say, 'Yes we can begin to buy the machinery. Yes, we can begin to stop the out-migration in this area because we have the economic facilities to do that'? Where were these people then, screaming against all of this stuff?"

Sapp and the MPC supported the Folklife Center project because they saw it as having the potential to positively impact community and economic development in the region and therefore the people of the region—a region that had historically been ignored and in which systemic racism had long served to ensure that poverty prevailed. Green, too, was cognizant of this history; however, he saw canceling the project and creating a new system as the answer. They—Green, Sapp, and most others in the room—really didn't disagree on the big picture but on the role of the folklife project in addressing immediate versus long-term problems.

Other speakers attempted to mediate between the big picture Green offered and the effects on the ground as described by Sapp. Bennie Keel made an appeal: "What I'm saying to folklorists, as an anthropologist, not a dirt archaeologist because I don't get to dig in the dirt anymore, is that irrespective of how you may feel about the Tenn-Tom or any other project, I think you have to face up, that you do have a responsibility, there is a responsibility there, and there is a responsibility to do the best job you can do on good projects and there's, it seems to me, a responsibility, to do the best job you can do on bad projects until the bad projects

Figure 4.7 AFC Board of Trustees meeting on February 23, 1979, at which the Tenn-Tom folklife project was debated. Jane Sapp, pictured here, argued in favor of the project. Photo by Carl Fleischhauer, courtesy of the American Folklife Center, Library of Congress.

are stopped." He suggested that loss won't be fully mitigated even if the project is stopped: "In making your decision you need to consider that until that point in time, if the Tenn-Tom is stopped, what will be lost? What has already been lost?"

Toward the end of the discussion, David Hufford summarized his observations of what had been said, getting to what was truly irreconcilable about the positions represented by Green and Sapp.

> It occurs to me that everyone here is voting in favor of doing good
> folklife projects in areas *like* the Tenn-Tom area, that will both
> have academic and community development impact. And also is
> in favor of opposing the forces which steamroller culture. And,
> what is still not clear to me is whether it is absolutely necessary
> to do, at this point, only one or the other- whether we are faced
> with the kind of choice that Dave Whisnant[74] was describing,
> being based in those places themselves. Is it not possible to do
> both simultaneously? And I ask this as a question, I'm not trying
> to answer it myself. One way of doing both simultaneously was
> suggested by Janet. Say "no we won't take the money from the
> Interior, but we will still do the project." It appears to me that a
> major problem there is I don't see where the money is coming
> from if it doesn't come from Interior—

After a brief interruption in which Green points out that the
money isn't coming from the Department of the Interior but from
the Army Corps of Engineers, and Jabbour then says that in fact it
is the public's money, demonstrating the different ways each rhetorically framed the source of funding, Hufford continues,

> It's painful, I'm sure to everybody, to think of having to say "you
> can keep that money, we are not going to do a project here even
> though we like the idea of the project, because we want to fight
> against these forces in a larger arena, and we have to sacrifice this
> project." I would like to hear someone *for* the project argue how
> it is possible to do it *without* supporting the Corps and the cause
> of that kind of steamrolling, and then I would like to hear Archie
> explain why that argument is not correct. It may be an unreason-
> able request, but I think that that's the basic choice.

Though there is not a move made for direct responses to Hufford, as Allen moves on to call on people in order of hands raised,
there are two seemingly indirect responses. After a couple of
other speakers, Jane Sapp says, regarding the Corps's money,
that "if you don't take it, we'll take it"; in effect, she says she
doesn't care where the money is coming from because the need
outweighs such concerns. "Because we are very interested in, as

I said before, coming back to this theme, culture as it relates to community development, as it relates to our educational development, as it relates to our economic development." However, she goes on to say, the people of the region need the AFC to come in and do this project "Because if you've got a half million dollars to do it, certainly, you know that we're not gonna get a half million dollars to do that kind of survey—though we're interested in getting a half million dollars to do that kind of survey. But we're not gonna get it. That's the bottom line." This seems a reply to one aspect of Hufford's question as well as to the many speakers who had suggested that local people should do the project, and perhaps an answer Hufford was anticipating as he juxtaposed the larger fight against the forces of big government and the reality on the ground in the Tenn-Tom region as it was being lived by those Sapp was there to represent. Sapp's statement provides a stinging reality check: it was ludicrous to think that either the Corps of Engineers or the Department of the Interior would consider handing a half-million-dollar budget over to local people to conduct the project, and while we don't know how it landed on people in the room, from a historical distance we have to wonder how it is that so many folklorists thought that they might—or at least suggested it in that room in ways that implied that they thought it might.

Second, though directly responding to Ralph Rinzler's points on behalf of Dillon Ripley (discussed below), is a point made by Bennie Keel. Keel assures those present that he looked at other options before moving forward with the planning of the project with the AFC. He spoke with folklorists in Alabama and Mississippi, he spoke with William Ferris regarding the Center for the Study of Southern Culture, which was preparing to move to the University of Mississippi, he spoke with Jane Sapp and others, but "while all were willing and interested in participating in the program, none were able to take on the program in terms of the needs."[75] This seems to both answer Hufford's question and demonstrate Sapp's point: local people and organizations would not be considered as a backup plan if the AFC backed out.

Keel was more directly responding to a point made by Rinzler on behalf of Secretary Ripley. Ripley did not have confidence that the AFC could handle a budget of the size of this project, and he, too, had suggested that someone in the region should conduct the project. While some today may remember the impact of Archie Green's opposition, opposition from the secretary of the Smithsonian was strong and was likely equally responsible for the cancellation of the project. Ralph Rinzler, Ripley's representative, didn't speak until near the end. As he began, Rinzler spent nearly three minutes making the "record clear" that Ripley's opinions were his own: "no one ghost writes his letters." It seems likely that this comment was intended for those who thought that Ripley's opposition was heavily influenced by Rinzler.[76]

The issues that Rinzler articulated on behalf of Ripley were intertwined. He questioned whether Rosenberg could handle a project with forty fieldworkers and whether either Rosenberg or the AFC itself could handle a half-million-dollar budget. Ripley's letter had focused in part on his concerns about the environmental impact of the project, and in our interview Keel recollected that Ripley's vote against the project was primarily for that reason. However, Rinzler mentioned the environmental impact really only in noting that Wayland Hand's assumption, in his remarks, of that as the basis of Ripley's opposition was an oversimplification. Rinzler argued that while the project should be done, it should not be managed from Washington; instead, people and institutions of the region should take on the project with the support and expertise of the AFC. This would include the developing Center for the Study of Southern Culture, Hank Willett in Alabama, and Jane Sapp. Rinzler said, "And I think we should be able to depend upon people in that region. We should commit ourselves to enhancing their efforts, to developing them, but not to managing, maintaining, and directing them from a

Washington base." He said that "we" should "encourage people in that region to muster the forces that are there, rally the organizations and the grass roots people and make them be responsible for doing the work and making the decisions and deciding how this is to be done. I think that would be an appropriate way of interpreting what the Secretary has put down" in his letter. This is the point to which Keel responded that this had been explored and was not feasible, as discussed above.

Eventually, the vote was called. The final vote was 5–4 in favor of the folklife project, with two abstentions[77] and several members absent, but this was not the last word.[78] Within a week, Alan Jabbour made the decision to cancel the project. Bennie Keel said in our interview, "I must say at the time I really didn't understand why he did not . . . proceed with the project. Then I realized, well that was a board he had to get along with. And that since the opposition was so strong he felt it was probably in the best interest of the folklife center not to proceed."[79] According to Jabbour, in his 1987 interview with Jeffrey Stine, he did so "because it had clearly become so controversial" within the board and the folklore community, but also in public.[80]

Rusty Marshall described his take on the meeting and decision in this way: "I think we were all surprised by the 1979 Board of Trustees meeting where the Tenn-Tom project was so contentiously debated, as well as the level of vitriol that seemed to be aimed at Alan himself by certain board members and interested scholars who lobbied against the Tenn-Tom. The board meeting and the heavy politicking that preceded it were remarkable. I was relieved that Alan decided to cancel the project. Ending the project was a defeat for him, and I think he was grieved by the furor and criticism, and I think he took it personally."[81]

The day following the board meeting, an article in the *Washington Post* by Ward Sinclair entitled "Corps Offer Roils Folklife Center" caught the attention of Congressman Bevill of Alabama, and Jabbour had to "go around and calm things down" by writing a statement explaining that the derogatory remarks about the Corps of Engineers had not been made by members of the AFC board or staff but by a private citizen.[82] According to Peggy Bulger, "Perhaps it was this article that sealed the deal" (2003, 387)—or *broke* the deal, more accurately, between the Department of the Interior and the AFC. A letter from Bennie Keel to Jabbour dated March 9, 1979, officially terminated the agreement and canceled the Tenn-Tom folklife project.[83]

FAILED HOPES AND MISSED OPPORTUNITIES

In a letter to the AFC Board of Trustees following the cancellation of the project, with which he sent copies of letters he had received following the board meeting, Jabbour communicated optimism: "To me this correspondence is far and away the most promising outgrowth of our Tennessee-Tombigbee debate. It reveals a profession for the first time seriously engaged by the issues we raised, thoughtful and reflective, ready to examine the matter in its every aspect in preparation for further action."[84] For Jabbour, this further action included the 1980 amendment to the National Historic Preservation Act, which mandated that the Department of the Interior in partnership with the AFC provide a report and recommendations "on preserving and conserving the intangible elements of our cultural heritage such as arts, skills, folklife, and folkways" (Loomis 1983, 1).[85] This resulted in the 1983 report *Cultural Conservation: The Protection of Cultural Heritage in the United States* (Loomis), which in turn led to the *National Register Bulletin No. 38: Guidelines for Evaluating and Documenting Traditional Cultural Properties* (National Park Service 1990) and, more broadly, to the widespread usage of the terminology—and arguably, new perspective—of "cultural conservation" in AFC projects and by folklorists and those in allied fields.[86] However, though understood to have been "foundational to the evolution of folklore and historic preservation policy and projects, facilitating the introduction of intangible cultural heritage into national discourse" (Sommers 2019, 365), *Cultural Conservation* and its results have been critiqued as "timid" and as having done "little to create a structure to ensure that intangible culture was protected by federal environmental and preservation law" (Williams 2017a, 139n16).

Ultimately, no one involved in the Tenn-Tom folklife project debates saw their hopes achieved. The waterway completion was not affected by the cancellation of the folklife project, the waterway did not bring economic prosperity to the region, the living traditions of the region were scarcely documented, we have not since dismantled and rebuilt the system in which living folk culture is considered prior to federal projects, and folklorists have not become central actors in impact assessments or mitigation projects.

The Tennessee-Tombigbee Waterway itself did not live up to the hopes of those who dreamed of it for decades (even centuries). A 2019 Associated Press article provides one of countless updates on its failures, noting that the Tenn-Tom "has never come close to traffic projections used to sell it to the public, and poverty rates have increased in most of the counties it flows through in Mississippi and Alabama" (Reeves 2019). According to Hank Willett,

> It did very little of what was sold to us or what they tried to sell to us. In terms of what it's done for the Alabama counties that are affected, it's basically nothing. There's a few places where you can go camping or launch your boat, which you didn't used to be able to do. Because there's a little bit of inland pleasure traffic, there might be a couple little gas, stock-up places along the river, but basically the barges just slide right on through. A handful of jobs to operate the locks and to maintain the waterway but not much. It didn't do much for the Port of Mobile, because actually the barge traffic is not much there either. And 70 percent of what goes down the Tenn-Tom, is timber and coal. And the timber—God, they haven't run out yet? And the coal, we're trying to shut down our coal industry completely, and so there's no future in shipping anymore coal to Mobile.[87]

By the time of the completion of the Tenn-Tom Waterway in 1985, "Over 900 archaeological sites, buildings, and bridges had been studied by more than 20 universities, museums, public agencies and private companies" (Brose 1991, 7). However, the communities—the folklife of the people—of the region had been documented only in very small pockets.

There were multidisciplinary mitigation projects conducted in the Tombigbee River Multi-Resource District, and in the summer of 1979, two of the projects involved Indiana University folklore graduate students, though both were employed as oral historians as Williams had been in the HABS project the previous summer.[88] Stephen Poyser was part of a team contracted to conduct research in and around Bay Springs, in north Mississippi, which was the site of the largest and northernmost lock and dam of the waterway. The divide section of the waterway, which included the twenty-seven-mile connection between the two rivers, began at the Bay Springs lock, going north from the Tombigbee to the Tennessee. Where once there was a town of Bay Springs, there is now Bay Springs Lake (Poyser 1991).[89]

Betty Belanus, who has since spent her career at the Smithsonian Institution Center for Folklife and Cultural Heritage, was part of the team on a mitigation project at the former plantation of Waverly and the surrounding community, near which the Waverly Ferry Recreation Area was planned along the Tenn-Tom.[90] Waverly itself, "one of the most elegant and significant houses in the South" (Adams 1980, 7), was not in danger; however, the construction of the recreation area would impact archaeological sites between Waverly and the river. The ethnoarchaeological project at Waverly was "the first systematic study of tenant farmers in the late 19th and early 20th centuries making use of material culture, oral testimony, and written documents" (iii) and included historical archaeologists, historians, and oral historians. Oral histories were conducted with eighty-nine people living in the region (46), which had once been largely populated by descendants of former slaves who then became tenant farmers, though by the 1930s, white residents had begun moving into the area as Blacks migrated away.

In March 2019, Belanus recalled being mostly unaware of the controversy surrounding the AFC's aborted project at the time, though she did recall that Richard Dorson, who reviewed the oral history portions of the final published report about the project (Adams 1980), commented to her afterward that "the trouble with tainted money is 't'ain't enough of it."[91] Poyser was more familiar with the controversy, as he had heard Jabbour speak about it shortly after it had been canceled, at a conference on public sector folklore held in the spring of 1979 at Western Kentucky University (Poyser 1991, 2).[92]

In a broad sense, proponents of the folklife project expressed support for it because they saw it as an opportunity to include "living" culture in mitigation efforts, rather than only archaeological sites and historic structures. At the May 1978 AFC board meeting, when Jabbour first presented the project to them, Bess Lomax Hawes commented that the only advantage she saw was the potential recognition of the value of living culture in addition to historic sites and buildings.[93] In his February 1979 letter to Archie Green, just before the board meeting that led to the cancellation of the project, Jabbour wrote, "Our project along the Tombigbee River would for the first time implement that responsibility [of the mitigation of cultural resources] on behalf of living folk cultural traditions."[94] Hank Willett described it this way: "My big argument in favor of doing the Tennessee-Tombigbee project was, here folklorists, for the very first time, could sneak in the tent a little bit, and actually be applying Moss-Bennett to living breathing cultures, living breathing people. And I think a lot of people saw that."[95]

For this reason, there are many who saw and continue to see the AFC's aborted Tenn-Tom folklife project as a missed opportunity for the field. There's no question that this was Alan Jabbour's vision: he viewed it as a model project with the potential to open the door for folklore work in mitigation, and he very purposefully developed and framed it in this way. Neil Rosenberg described Jabbour as "hoping to use it as a proof and example for extension of the mandated impact assessment legislation to include intangible culture. Thus this project fell, strictly speaking, outside of the ambit of the legislation. It was a gamble for future jobs in the field."[96] In a memo to the Projects Committee of the AFC Board of Trustees during the early planning stages, Jabbour wrote, "If we were to carry out the Tenn-Tom project successfully, we could reasonably hope for regular consideration of folklore within HCRS [Heritage Conservation and Recreation Service of the Department of the Interior, in which the IAS was housed]-administered projects in the future. It is even possible to hope for amendment of the Moss-Bennett Act in its next authorization round to include the word 'folklife' or some comparable keyword, thus making folklife projects less marginal in Moss-Bennett funding."[97] In hindsight these were lofty goals. More prescient was a fear expressed by Jabbour in this same letter: "I fear that if we were to decline this serious overture, it would suggest to them [HCRS] that people in folklife are 'all talk, no do.' Such an impression would make it hard to argue our case in the future."[98]

In a twenty-year retrospective on the AFC in the *Folklife Center News*, Jabbour wrote, "'Cultural resources' were generally understood to consist of historic buildings and archeological sites; the Center saw the project as an opportunity to broaden the concept to include living cultural traditions. But though construction was already underway, part of the project was not yet funded. Some environmentalists continued to oppose it, and the Center found itself drawn into controversy within the field of folklore and folklife studies about whether accepting mitigation funds lent support to a public works project the ultimate fate of which was not yet determined. In the end, the Center withdrew" (Jabbour 1996, 13). Karen Jabbour, wife of Alan, confirmed that he saw the cancellation of the project as a missed opportunity. She also noted that it was important to him that the AFC board voted in support of the project in February 1979 (though by just the one vote), but a major part of what he also had to consider is that funding for the AFC had to be regularly reauthorized by Congress. Members of Congress wanted projects that were about collection in their states but not projects that were political.[99]

Those on both sides of the Tenn-Tom debate voiced support for folklorist involvement in mitigation projects. Richard Bauman, as discussed above, was one. Janet Anderson is another; she spoke against the project when Jabbour first presented it in May 1978, and she continued to speak against it in February 1979.[100] However, she said during the debate, "*Of course*, as part of the American Folklife Center, there will be projects involving mitigation, that the Center must be involved in. But hopefully those will be projects the Center has a hand in from the very beginning in terms of being able to decide whether the total impact of the project is something that they want, they really want to share."[101]

The feeling that the Tenn-Tom was a missed opportunity was expressed in retrospective statements by others involved. Hank Willett said, "if it had been done well, and done right, I think right now you could be sending your graduate students to do impact work on major federal projects of one kind or another."[102] When asked if this was a missed opportunity for folklorists, Benny Keel said, "I often felt like that if we had gone on with that study, that it would have been the basis for studies in all kinds of federal projects, particularly reservoir projects, and maybe highway projects."[103] When asked what he thought about the cancellation of the project, Neil Rosenberg—who would have been project director—said, "Well, I think it was an opportunity missed." He continued, "So, if that had gone ahead, it's certainly possible that, you know, we could've seen much more extensive projects by the Folklife Center that would reflect this. And it would be ameliorative, but in a good sense, I think. That was how I looked at it then."[104] According to Carl Fleischhauer, "So, the Tenn-Tom project would have been one more, you know, block in the foundation of sort of building the edifice of bringing together ethnographic and tangible culture studies in some way."[105]

Those involved in ongoing efforts to integrate folklore and historic preservation continue to see the aborted Tenn-Tom project as a missed opportunity (cf. Sommers 2013, 2019; and Vidutis 2019 for mention of the Tenn-Tom as a missed opportunity), as do at least three former presidents of the AFS (see Bulger 2003; Ivey 2011; Williams 2017a, 2017b). Peggy Bulger, who succeeded Jabbour as head of the AFC, said in her AFS presidential address, "Although I can see both sides of the argument, I feel strongly that, despite well-meant impulses, folklorists missed an opportunity to be central to the work of cultural conservation and the environmental survey work that is still going on today. By demonizing powerful institutions such as the Army Corps of Engineers and refusing to deal with their agendas, our outraged sensibilities have kept us on the fringes of this important work" (2003, 387).

In addition to the missed opportunity for the field, canceling the project affected the lives of the people of the region in ways that we will likely never know. During the February 1979 AFC board meeting, Janet Anderson said,

> When this topic came up in May at the board meeting, I rather incoherently talked about the people in the Tennessee-Tombigbee region, and about my concern for the devastation in their lives, wrought by the Corps here and in other similar projects. At that time, it was pointed out to me, that this project was important *not* because of the people in the Tennessee-Tombigbee area, but because it was the biggest, most ambitious budget that the Center had ever been handed. In addition, it was pointed out to me, that this was an important project in terms of developing relationships in Washington, and that establishing a good rapport with Interior and other departmental agencies. Until today, I had not heard the proponents of the Tennessee-Tombigbee issue speak with such passion about the personal lives and the personal devastation of the area.[106]

The minutes of the May 1978 meeting at which Jabbour first proposed the project to the board support her assertion. Jabbour presented the project in terms of the opportunity presented by Moss-Bennett, and the focus of the discussion was on the political implications of the project; little is recorded in the minutes about the people of the region.

Hank Willett said further regarding the cancellation of the folklife project, "If anything, [for] people like the MPC, it just confirmed what they'd thought all along anyway. That people really don't give a shit about us over here. And they were probably right."[107] Perhaps because, like Willett, she had firsthand experience in the region, Williams has described the missed opportunity not only for the field but for the people of the region: "Many of these people through legacies of poverty and illiteracy (and in the southern portion of our study area, virulent racism) could not establish clear title to their land and lost their homes and means of sustenance. Would the folklife survey have stopped the waterway? No. Would it have made a difference? I believe yes it could have. We could have borne witness, we could have advocated" (2017b, 7). Due to the "righteous morality" on all sides of the debate, we don't know what might have been.

NOTES

1. Historian Jeffrey K. Stine, whose work is cited frequently in this chapter, interviewed Alan Jabbour on January 6, 1987, about the AFC's folklife project for a history project for the Corps of Engineers but, as far as we can tell, has not written about it other than a brief mention in a footnote (Stine 1992, 29n59). The interview was conducted as part of a project for the Corps of Engineers by History Associates Incorporated of Rockville, Maryland. The associated release form signed by Jabbour provides open-access "to all who seek access."

2. Henry (Hank) Willett, interview with Ann K. Ferrell, September 14, 2019, Fort Payne, AL.

3. Sydney Varajon, email communication, March 28, 2024. Varajon's parenthetical use of *minimization* and *avoidance* references 40 CFR 1508.20 of the NEPA regulations.

4. For an important and often-cited example of what folklorists could have offered in a different context, see Camitta 1988.

5. Paper found in Tennessee-Tombigbee Waterway Folklife Project collection (AFC 1985/035), Archive of Folk Culture, American Folklife Center, Library of Congress, Washington, DC (all materials from this collection are hereafter cited as AFC 1985/035).

6. Accusations of hidden costs and dishonesty on the part of the Corps continued throughout the entire project and were central to the labeling of the project by many as a "boondoggle." See Miller 1978; Stine 1993; Stewart 1971.

7. Nixon signed the NEPA of 1969 into law on January 1, 1970, and the 1971 budget was passed by Congress in October 1970.

8. According to John Zippert, citing US census data, "These percentage figures of the poor and Black composition of the TTW impact area population remain relatively constant as the impact area is expanded to include the 165 counties in the 'tributary impact area of the TTW' recognized by the US Army Corps of Engineers as the primary impact area of the Waterway in southeast Alabama, northwest Mississippi, east Tennessee and western Kentucky" (1977, 2). Paper found in AFC 1985/035.

9. John Zippert and Robert Valder, 1977, "The Tennessee Tombigbee Water Project: A 'White' Paper," unpublished paper submitted to the Secretary of the Army, AFC 1985/035 (hereafter cited as Zippert and Valder 1977, AFC 1985/035), 1.

10. Zippert and Valder 1977, AFC 1985/035, 2.

11. Zippert and Valder 1977, AFC 1985/035, 5.

12. Zippert and Valder 1977, AFC 1985/035, 2.

13. The Auburn study by Molnar et al. supports this as well, suggesting that Blacks in the eight West Alabama counties surveyed were generally positive about the potential benefits, but not thoroughly convinced. Although 71.4 percent of Black males and 65.3 percent of Black females (as compared with 75.3% of white males and 74.9% of white females) responded "better" to the question "Do you think the Tombigbee River Canal will make things better or worse in the years to come?" (Molnar et al. 1981:15) one conclusion of the report was that "most blacks and low income individuals were fatalistic about the potential for dramatic shifts in their daily lives resulting from the Waterway's impact on the area" (88). Respondents were also asked about the "effect of the waterway on minorities," and "Blacks were least optimistic about benefits" (19).

14. Recording of the public portion of the February 1979 Meeting of the American Folklife Center Board of Trustees, transcribed by the authors.

Tennessee-Tombigbee Waterway Folklife Project collection (AFC 1983/002), Archive of Folk Culture, American Folklife Center, Library of Congress, Washington, DC (hereafter cited as February 1979 Meeting, AFC 1983/002).

15. February 1979 Meeting, AFC 1983/002.

16. See also Zippert 1977, 5.

17. Bennie C. Keel, n.d., "Evolution of the Historic Preservation Program in the Tennessee Tombigbee Waterway, Alabama and Mississippi," unpublished paper, Interagency Archeological Services-Atlanta, AFC 1985/035 (hereafter cited as Keel n.d., AFC 1985/035), 1.

18. Nielsen was hired in 1975—the first archaeologist hired by the Army Corps of Engineers—and he "single-handedly managed the cultural resources program for the Tenn-Tom and all the [Mobile] District's many other projects for over a year before the Corps hired a second archaeologist" (Stine 1992, 13).

19. Keel n.d., AFC 1985/035, 1. According to Stine, the controversies surrounding the completion of the Tenn-Tom drove the Corps "to build the waterway as rapidly as it could," in part by working on multiple sections of the project at a time, which further complicated and hampered the efforts of archaeologists—who "often found themselves working only a few hours ahead of the bulldozers' blades"—and preservationists (1992, 14). Stine cites examples of Nielsen's struggles with the Corps personnel as discoveries of Native American archaeological sites—artifacts, burial sites—often went unreported. Stine writes that once Keel was hired in 1976, "it took him little time to conclude that the Tenn-Tom's problems were too great to overcome through the existing, traditional approach" (19).

20. Keel n.d., AFC 1985/035, 3.

21. Howard ("Rusty") W. Marshall was a folklife specialist at the AFC from 1977 to 1981. He worked with Jabbour on the early development of the folklife project. Carl Fleishhauer was pulled into the planning as well and became more involved than Marshall as he traveled with Jabbour to the region as the media specialist, taking photos and recording meetings. Marshall shared that he was never fully comfortable with the project, due at least in part to witnessing the devastating results of a Bureau of Reclamation water project in Colorado in the 1940s (Howard W. Marshall, email correspondence with Ann Ferrell, June 18, 2021).

22. Letter from Michael Ann Williams to Howard ("Rusty") W. Marshall, October 24, 1978. AFC 1985/035. Quoted with permission of Williams.

23. Letter from Michael Ann Williams to Howard ("Rusty") W. Marshall, October 24, 1978. AFC 1985/035. Quoted with permission of Williams.

24. Bennie Keel, interview with Ann K. Ferrell, July 31, 2019. Telephone.

25. Keel n.d., AFC 1985/035, 4.

26. The AFC Tenn-Tom files include a combination of handwritten and typed notes titled "First notes, proposal, budget," AFC 1985/035 (hereafter cited as Notes 1977–78, AFC 1985/035). See Stine (1993, 167–72) for discussion of President Jimmy Carter's review of "water resources development policy" and projects, dubbed his "hit list," which included the Tenn-Tom. Following a public meeting about the waterway in Columbus, Mississippi, in March 1977 attended by "over five thousand people, the majority of them waterway enthusiasts" (169), Carter decided to continue Tenn-Tom funding.

27. Notes 1977–78, AFC 1985/035.

28. Cf. Yoder 1963. The open-air museum Skansen, founded by Artur Hazelius in Sweden in 1891, provides the earliest and most cited model.

29. Notes 1977–78, AFC 1985/035.

30. Bennie Keel, interview with Ann K. Ferrell, July 31, 2019. Telephone.

31. Notes 1977–78, AFC 1985/035.

32. Jerry Nielsen, 1978, "Memorandum for the Files," June 22, 1978. AFC 1985/035, 5.

33. Letter signed by Wendell Paris, Chairman, MPC; John Zippert, Director of Programs, Federation of Southern Cooperatives; Hubert E Sapp, Director, Miles College-Eutaw; Jane W Sapp, Director, Community Based Arts Education Program. AFC 1985/035.

34. Jerry Nielsen, 1978, "Memorandum for the Files," June 22, 1978. AFC 1985/035, 6.

35. Letter from Alan Jabbour to Hank Willett, August 16, 1978.

36. By August 1978, William Ferris was involved as well, as plans were underway for the establishment of the Center for the Study of Southern Culture at the University of Mississippi. Ferris met with Jabbour, Keel, and Nielsen at the AFC that August (1978), and correspondence between him and Jabbour suggest complicated conversations around the role of the new Center in the project. Letters, AFC 1985/035.

37. Janet Anderson had been an aide to Senator Mark Hatfield of Oregon, a key supporter of the eventual passage of the American Folklife Preservation Act, which established the AFC. Anderson is remembered as a central part of the work (see Gross Bressler 1995; Green's 1976 pamphlet reprinted in Feintuch 1988a). She was also married to folklorist Roger Abrahams.

38. Minutes of the Meeting of the Board of Trustees of the American Folklife Center, Library of Congress, May 23, 1978, and Notes of the same meeting. AFC Files: AFC Board Meetings.

39. Minutes of the Meetings, Board of Trustees, American Folklife Center, Woodstock, VT, November 19–20, 1978. AFC 1985/035. The notes on the discussion run less than two pages (6–7).

40. Minutes of the Meetings, Board of Trustees, American Folklife Center, Woodstock, VT, November 19–20, 1978. AFC 1985/035, 7.

41. Fleischhauer, folklorist and visual documentarian, was hired as a folklife specialist at the AFC in 1976.

42. Handwritten notes of meeting of November 28, 1978, AFC 1985/035.

43. February 1979 Meeting, AFC 1983/002.

44. Proposal for a Folklife Project along the Tennessee-Tombigbee Waterway, October 4, 1978, American Folklife Center, Library of Congress. AFC 1985/035 (hereafter cited as Folklife Proposal 1978, AFC 1985/035), 1.

45. Folklife Proposal 1978, AFC 1985/035, 1.

46. Folklife Proposal 1978, AFC 1985/035, 4.

47. Folklife Proposal 1978, AFC 1985/035, 5.

48. Interagency Agreement between Library of Congress American Folklife Center and the Department of the Interior Interagency Archeological Services-Atlanta Heritage Conservation and Recreation Service, signed on December 14, 1978. AFC 1985/035.

49. Minutes of the Meetings, Board of Trustees, American Folklife Center, Woodstock, VT, November 19–20, 1978. AFC 1985/035.

50. Diary of Neil Rosenberg, August 18, 2017. Copy provided to authors, used with permission.

51. Memo from Lynnwood Montell, Director of the Center for Intercultural and Folk Studies, to "All Former and Present Graduate Students." n.d. AFC 1985/035.

52. Neil Rosenberg, interview with the authors, October 21, 2017, Minneapolis, MN.

53. Diary of Neil Rosenberg, August 18, 2017. Copy provided to authors, used with permission.

54. This typed list is a single sheet of paper, untitled and undated, described in the finding aid as "Ethical Issues Posed by Alan Jabbour." AFC 1985/035.

55. Raye Virginia Allen was from Temple, Texas, was a cultural historian and civic leader, was a founding trustee of both the AFC and the Fund for Folk Culture, and served on an impressive range of boards and commissions in both Washington, DC, and her home state of Texas (see "Raye Virginia Allen Collection, 1925, 1938, 1964–1978, 1997," accessed May 22, 2025, https://txarchives.org/utcah/finding _aids/01015.xml).

56. Letter from S. Dillon Ripley, Secretary, Smithsonian Institution, to Mrs. Raye Virginia Allen, Chairman of the Board of Trustees, American Folklife Center, January 25, 1979. AFC 1985/035.

57. Letter from Mrs. Raye Virginia Allen, Chairman of the Board of Trustees, American Folklife Center, to S. Dillon Ripley, Secretary, Smithsonian Institution, January 31, 1979. AFC 1985/035.

58. He details points at which he offered his opinion to Allen, Jabbour, and Rosenberg in his January 1979 letter to Allen and says that they'd obviously chosen to ignore him, since they had not halted the development of the project.

59. Neil Rosenberg, interview with the authors, October 21, 2017, Minneapolis, MN.

60. For an overview of the early AFC projects and other work in its first twenty years, see Jabbour 1996.

61. Jabbour listed these categories of recipients in a letter to the Board of Trustees dated March 8, 1979. AFC 1985/035.

62. Memo, "Telephone Call Received by Carl Fleischhauer," February 23, 1979. AFC 1985/035.

63. Handwritten notes titled "Comments on Tenn-Tom Rec'd since Letter Mailed Out." AFC 1985/035.

64. Nine out of thirteen letters in the file—received before and after the February 23 board meeting—are in favor of the AFC continuing the Tenn-Tom folklife project; of the remaining four, one (William A. Wilson) doesn't quite pick a side, two are entirely opposed (Dan Ben-Amos and Judy McCulloh), and one supports folklore involvement in impact assessment but thinks that Tenn-Tom is just too controversial (Richard Bauman). In a January 1987 interview with Jeffrey R. Stine, Jabbour says that he sent "maybe 20 copies" out (Transcript of interview of Alan Jabbour with Jeffrey Stine. AFC 1985/035, 16). However, there is no complete list of those to whom Jabbour sent his letter, and there is no way to know whether there were letters or notes on phone calls that did not make it into the file. However, copies of the letters were given to members of the board in their packets for the February 1979 meeting, and a letter in March 1979 from Roger Abrahams (AFS president) to Jabbour includes a list of those carbon copied, and a letter from everyone on the list is in the AFC files, suggesting that the file is complete. With the exception of David Hufford, who was the secretary treasurer of the AFS at the time, none of those who wrote letters were in attendance at the meeting, according to the recording.

65. Henry (Hank) Willett, interview with Ann K. Ferrell, September 14, 2019, Fort Payne, AL.

66. Letter from Richard M. Dorson, National Humanities Center Fellow, to Alan Jabbour, February 20, 1979. AFC 1985/035.

67. Letter from Barre Toelken, University of Oregon, to Alan Jabbour, February 16, 1979. AFC 1985/035. Quoted with permission of Kaz Toelken.

68. Letter from Richard Bauman, University of Texas at Austin, to Alan Jabbour, February 15, 1979. AFC 1985/035. Quoted with permission from Richard Bauman.

69. Neil Rosenberg, interview with the authors, October 21, 2017, Minneapolis, MN. Though careful in his word choices, Alan Jabbour made it clear in his 1987 interview with Jeffrey Stine that from his perspective, the "divisions" that developed among the board members about the project were fostered by Green. "There was no opposition to it when it was first brought up as an idea at the board of trustees meeting" (Transcript of interview of Alan Jabbour with Jeffrey Stine. AFC 1985/035, 14).

70. February 1979 Meeting, AFC 1983/002. All quotations from the meeting that follow were transcribed from this recording by Ferrell.

71. According to Alabama folklorist Hank Willett, Sapp had taken folklore classes as a student at Chapel Hill, so she was familiar with folklore studies through that and through association with folklorists such as Willett (Henry [Hank] Willett, interview with Ann K. Ferrell, September 14, 2019, Fort Payne, AL). Sapp is also listed as a participant in the first conference of the Association of African and African American Folklorists in 1974, discussed in the introduction, which further demonstrates her engagement with folklore studies in the 1970s.

72. He lists model projects completed or in process at the time including those in Georgia, Nevada, Chicago, and the Blue Ridge Mountains in addition to the Tenn-Tom region.

73. Neil Rosenberg, interview with the authors, October 21, 2017, Minneapolis, MN.

74. In his comments during this meeting, David Whisnant drew parallels between the Tenn-Tom region and what he had witnessed in Appalachia: "They were asked to choose between alternatives, both of which were, in human terms, unacceptable and in ethical terms unacceptable. And, having no other alternatives, they have to choose one of those: do you want to starve or do you want to work on a strip mine? Do you want to move to Cincinnati where there are no jobs or do you want to stay here where there are no jobs?"

75. As he describes this, Keel is referencing a calendar of events that the board members have in their packets. It is important to point out that this (and other evidence) suggests that he talked with all of these people and

institutions after he was already in conversations with Alan Jabbour and the AFC. However, William Ferris did in fact express interest in taking the project after the AFC cancelled it, as evidenced in correspondence (AFC 1985/035), and as Keel said in our interview.

76. For instance, Neil Rosenberg suggested that Rinzler drafted the letter sent to Raye Virginia Allen in opposition to the folklife project. Diary of Neil Rosenberg, August 18, 2017. Copy provided to authors, used with permission.

77. This included Bess Lomax Hawes, who was there in place of the chair of the NEA, Livingston L. Biddle Jr., stating that she could not vote because the chair was out of the country: "I have my own ideas but [*laugh*] I am uninstructed and therefore I can't vote."

78. Even the circumstances of the vote itself were controversial, as there followed a lengthy dispute over what had actually been voted on. The issue was whether they had voted, as though for the first time, to approve the contract—Green pointed out that the American Folklife Preservation Act required approval of contracts by a two-thirds vote of the board—or whether they were voting to reaffirm their previous vote, which would have required a simple majority. This was sent to the LOC's general counsel for resolution, and our attempts to follow this trail failed; it is unclear whether it was ever resolved or if it just became a moot point and was dropped (likely).

79. Bennie Keel, interview with Ann K. Ferrell, July 31, 2019. Telephone.

80. Transcript of interview of Alan Jabbour with Jeffrey Stine. AFC 1985/035, 23.

81. Email from Rusty Marshall to Ann Ferrell, June 21, 2021.

82. Transcript of interview of Alan Jabbour with Jeffrey Stine. AFC 1985/035, 23. A March piece in the *Congressional Record* included Rep. Bevill's statement of "shock" at the report of the meeting, particularly a comment from Archie Green: "The Corps needs us—they need a bucket of whitewash. They need to buy us because they want surveys that suggest the damage is not as great as it seems." It also included a letter from Jabbour in which he assured the congressman that the AFC was in no way "passing judgement upon" either the Tenn-Tom or the Corps of Engineers (Bevill 1979, H 6334).

83. Letter from Bennie C. Keel, United States Department of the Interior, Interagency Archeological Services-Atlanta, to Alan Jabbour, March 9, 1979. AFC 1985/035.

84. Letter from Alan Jabbour to the Members of the Board of Trustees, March 8, 1979. AFC 1985/035.

85. For Jabbour's discussions of this as a direct next step, see, for instance, his 1987 interview with Jeffrey Stine as well as Jabbour 1996.

86. For instance, AFC projects that followed such as the cultural surveys in Grouse Creek, Utah, and the New Jersey Pinelands (see Sommers 2019). Important publications also engaged with this perspective; see Feintuch 1988a; Hufford 1994.

87. Henry (Hank) Willett, interview with Ann K. Ferrell, September 14, 2019, Fort Payne, AL.

88. Ferrell also interviewed Kentucky archaeologist Kim McBride about her work beginning in 1979 as a graduate student at Michigan State University on a large multidisciplinary project at the sites of the communities of Culbert, Barton, and Vinton near West Point, Mississippi. Kim McBride, interview with Ann K. Ferrell, January 26, 2022. Zoom.

89. Poyser went on to write his doctoral dissertation based on his work there. The county in which Bay Springs was located, Tishomingo County, "traditionally had had one of the smallest percentages of blacks of any county in Mississippi largely because the area's physiography precluded plantation-type operations characteristic of the 'black prairie' and the Delta to the south" (Poyser 1991, 71). Poyser's dissertation provides an overview of the history of Bay Springs, which had once been largely centered around a cotton processing factory. However, the factory burned in the mid-1880s, and the town slowly declined following the fire. Poyser provides this description of the former Bay Springs following the completion of the waterway:

> The last remaining structures still standing in Bay Springs, the old lodge building and the general store, were bulldozed over by contractors working on the waterway in early 1979. Later that year, just before the contract archaeologists were to begin excavation of the factory site, a bulldozer cut a wide swath through the site, thus relieving the archaeologists of the necessity or possibility of conducting a lengthy and detailed examination of the archaeological record in situ.
>
> Today, the physical remains of Bay Springs lie fifty feet under water, inundated by a huge lock and dam constructed by the Corps of Engineers. The landscape has been forever altered by construction of the waterway, and the large tracts of pine trees where visitors to the reunions once spread their pallets and which later served as a source of livelihood for area residents have also disappeared, a victim of technology. Many former residents whose property was located in the right-of-way of the waterway were forced to sell their land, either by mutual purchase agreement or through condemnation proceedings initiated by the Corps of Engineers through right of Imminent Domain.

Ironically, the Corps decided to construct a visitor's center adjacent to the dam at Bay Springs where tourists might come together to picnic and interact with one another, just as the community's residents had done nearly a century before. The center also includes a plaque which presents visitors with an overview of the history (85) of the area. But for the people who once lived in Bay Springs, its history lives on—to be recalled on occasions when memories of the past bring smiles and, for some, tears. (Poyser 1991, 86)

90. Waverly was built in the 1840s–50s; was vacant from about 1913 to the 1960s when it was purchased, renovated, and opened to visitors; and was placed on the National Register of Historic Places in 1974 (see Adams 1980, 2–3). Ferrell lived in Columbus as a child in the early 1980s and visited Waverly many times. The narrative of the tour stressed that the population of enslaved people had been very large, enabling the plantation to be self-contained, with all the services and resources needed supplied by the enslaved population. Secondarily, the tour focused on the long period in which the mansion remained abandoned and the efforts of the new owners to rehabilitate it and open it to the public. Also, of course, there was a ghost of a little girl.

91. Betty Belanus, interview with Ann K. Ferrell, March 5, 2019, Washington, DC.

92. This was the first conference ever held that focused on public sector folklore, organized by Burt Feintuch and Camilla Collins, who were then faculty members at WKU.

93. "Meeting of the Board" notes, May 23, 1978. AFC Files: AFC Board Meetings, 48. Hawes also wrote to Jabbour in August 1978 to caution him about the political impact of the project and to offer suggestions for improving the project plan. Letter from Bess Lomax Hawes, National Endowment for the Arts, to Alan Jabbour, August 14, 1978. AFC1985/035.

94. Letter from Alan Jabbour to Archie Green, February 5, 1979. AFC 1985/035, 2. Jabbour also wrote, "My first goal in undertaking the project is to broaden the definition of the word 'culture' and the phrase 'cultural resources' within HCRS [Heritage Conservation and Recreation Service of the Department of the Interior]. The agency has tended up to now to define 'cultural resources' in terms of things past and things artifactual. Folklife as a complementary concept would in my opinion strengthen and enrich their vision of their cultural mission" (2).

95. Henry (Hank) Willett, interview with Ann K. Ferrell, September 14, 2019, Fort Payne, AL.

96. Diary of Neil Rosenberg, August 18, 2017. Copy provided to authors, used with permission.

97. Memo from Alan Jabbour to the Projects Committee, Board of Trustees, July 10, 1978. AFC 1985/035, 1.

98. Memo from Alan Jabbour to the Projects Committee, Board of Trustees, July 10, 1978. AFC 1985/035, 2.

99. Karen Jabbour, unrecorded interview with the authors, August 10, 2021. Zoom.

100. Anderson was not present at the November meeting when the project was approved by the board, and Hand remarked that had she been there and not absent due to illness, the vote might have gone differently.

101. February 1979 Meeting, AFC 1983/002.

102. Henry (Hank) Willett, interview with Ann K. Ferrell, September 14, 2019, Fort Payne, AL.

103. Bennie Keel, interview with Ann K. Ferrell, July 31, 2019. Telephone.

104. Neil Rosenberg, interview with the authors, October 21, 2017, Minneapolis, MN.

105. Carl Fleischhauer, interview with Ann K. Ferrell, March 3, 2019, Washington, DC.

106. February 1979 Meeting, AFC 1983/002.

107. Henry (Hank) Willett, interview with Ann K. Ferrell, September 14, 2019, Fort Payne, AL.

"CORPORATE CULTURE" VERSUS "THE SHOP FLOOR"

The Organizational and Occupational Folklore "Controversy" in Retrospect

IN A LETTER TO THE editor in the December 1984 issue of *The American Folklore Society Newsletter*, Robert McCarl suggested that he and Michael Owen Jones engage in a "debate concerning the relative merits of our contrasting approaches to occupational folklore" (McCarl 1984, 5). According to McCarl, this letter reflected comments he had made in the question and answer session with the executive board and at the business meeting at the recent American Folklore Society (AFS) Annual Meeting. McCarl's challenge followed on the 1984 publication by the AFS of a booklet entitled *Folklore/Folklife*, which provided a brief history of the field and overviews of major areas of concentration for folklorists, including "Folklore and Organizational Life" (Jackson, McCulloh, and Weigle 1984, 14).[1]

According to the description in *Folklore/Folklife*, "The stories that people tell, the ways they decorate their work space, ceremonies in which they take part, and ritualistic interaction provide data essential to understanding human concerns and the culture of an organization. Forms of expressive behavior and aspects of organizational culture may play an important role in clarifying and communicating organizational philosophy and objectives, enhancing managerial styles and methods, and improving life in the workplace. In years past, corporations occasionally employed folklorists

Folklore and Organizational Life

14

SOME OF THE NOTABLE collections in the twentieth century have been of occupational folklore, especially the lore of miners, loggers, and the oil industry. Recent years have witnessed the growth of a field focusing on the study of organizational symbolism and corporate culture. In 1983, for example, the Center for the Study of Comparative Folklore and Mythology and the Behavioral and Organizational Science Group at UCLA jointly sponsored a conference on organizational folklore. In 1984, the Faculty of Commerce and Business Administration at the University of British Columbia directed a major symposium on organizational culture and life in the workplace; members of the American Studies Department and the Work-Learn Center at the University of California at Davis organized a conference on corporate culture; and the European Group on Organizational Symbols held an international conference on organizational symbolism at the University of Lund in Sweden. Participants in those conferences were folklorists, management theorists, and business leaders.

The stories that people tell, the ways they decorate their work space, ceremonies in which they take part, and ritualistic interaction provide data essential to understanding human concerns and the culture of an organization. Forms of expressive behavior and aspects of organizational culture may play an important role in clarifying and communicating organizational philosophy and objectives, enhancing managerial styles and methods, and improving life in the workplace. In years past, corporations occasionally employed folklorists to help prepare corporate oral histories; folklorists now are more likely to help corporate executives understand the dynamics of the institutions they direct.

Young Irish-American step Dancers at the Rhode Island Ceilidhe Club, Cranston, Rhode Island. (Michael E. Bell/ American Folklife Center)

Figure 5.1 The 1984 AFS publication *Folklore/Folklife* included an essay devoted to a new area of study, "Folklore and Organizational Life," setting off a debate between proponents of occupational folklore and this new approach. Courtesy of the American Folklore Society.

to help prepare corporate oral histories; folklorists now are more likely to help corporate executives understand the dynamics of the institutions they direct" (Jackson, McCulloh, and Weigle 1984, 14).

McCarl objected vehemently in the *AFS Newsletter* to both the inclusion of "organizational folklore" in *Folklore/Folklife* and to the approach itself: "From the early days of the discipline, folklorists with such varied backgrounds as [J. Frank] Dobie and [John] Lomax, through [Benjamin] Botkin, [George] Korson, [Mody] Boatright, [Wayland] Hand, and [Archie] Green were fieldworkers who went to the workplace and negotiated with workers face-to-face to collect their stories, songs, and skills. Although not necessarily pro-union, these fieldworkers approached work from the bottom up—the shop floor, the mine shaft, the oil derrick—not from the corporation down" (McCarl 1984, 2). He went on to argue that the engagement in "organizational folklore" meant "getting corporate support to study work culture in order to further control the working lives of those on the shop floor" (5).

This chapter returns to this debate between these two folklorists, and although as we describe below, our interest is the issues relevant to the field that underlie the debate, our discussion requires that we closely examine and quote from the arguments made by these two men. Robert McCarl and Michael Owen Jones were and still are prominent folklorists, well known for their work in their particular areas of folklore study. McCarl was a key organizer of the Working Americans programs of the Smithsonian Festival of American Folklife (now Smithsonian Folklife Festival) in the 1970s, and he was and is well known as a folklorist central to the development of occupational folklore studies away from a primary focus on strictly oral genres such as folk song to what he called a "canon of work technique" (McCarl 1986, 71–72). A former firefighter himself, much of his work is based on ethnographic fieldwork with firefighters (see McCarl 1985a). By the early 1980s, Michael Owen Jones was well known for his fieldwork-based publications in a range of areas, including belief studies (1972), folk art (1975), and foodways (Jones, Giuliano, and Krell 1981), and he continues to make important contributions in these and other areas. He led the development of the study of organizational folklore/culture in the early 1980s along with colleagues and students at the University of California, Los Angeles (UCLA). Jones is a former president of the American Folklore Society (2004–05).

Attention to folklore of organizations began in earnest in the early 1980s, as Michael Owen Jones and other folklorists collaborated with scholars and practitioners in business and public administration, behavior and organizational science, and related fields to pursue what was described as a new field of study. Though based out of UCLA, this effort reached much further. This new field proposed to apply the "diagnostic uses of folklore research" to a wide range of folklore genres found within organizations—including "celebratory events, foodsharing, and play"; "stories about dramatic events or critical incidents"; "rumor, gossip . . . Xeroxlore"—as well as "what is professed and what is signaled through actual behavior" within an organization (Jones 1988, 20).

Though Jones declined McCarl's invitation to debate,[2] his lengthy "Reply" was published in the *AFS Newsletter* in April 1985. He discussed the two approaches and argued that in fact "While there are conceptual differences between the two sub-fields of occupational and organizational folklore studies—why else would two different terms have evolved?—they are complementary" (Jones 1985b, 5). Further, "That McCarl in his Letter to the Editor is willing to freely admit that folklorists 'should be mindful of who we are attempting to serve' ('the worker') is chilling, for this commits the discipline to identifying with one group over another. Folklorists do not and should not serve the interests of one person or group but rather the broader aims of understanding how and why individuals make use of expressive forms in organizational life" (5). There were further exchanges in the *AFS Newsletter* and in *Western Folklore* as well as in unpublished letters, and they and others commented on the disagreement in other publications in their respective areas of research well into the 1990s. While the exchange between Jones, McCarl, and a few others is obviously important and therefore central to this chapter, our interest here—like all the chapters in this book—is not limited to the individuals who engaged in this debate, nor are we interested in picking a side. Rather, we are interested in how this controversy is indicative of questions being asked in folklore studies in the 1970s and 1980s. Broadly speaking, this debate is reflective of different and changing perspectives on the concepts of "folk" and "group" in this period in which American folklore studies as an independent field was still establishing a disciplinary identity. From there, this debate raises questions about representation: Who *do* folklorists represent? Do folklorists represent anyone but themselves? Perhaps surprisingly—at least upon first glance—it raises questions about the fundamental differences between applied folklore and folklore as advocacy. And it raises contrasting understandings of the soul of a folklorist. Getting to the disagreement and to the questions within the context of the debate first necessitates an overview of both organizational and occupational folklore studies up to and in the period of the debate as well as contemporaneous discourses among folklorists. We begin with organizational folklore because its introduction set off the debate, and then we discuss an overview of long-standing approaches to occupational folklore.

"STUDYING ORGANIZATIONAL FOLKLORE AND CORPORATE CULTURE"

In a paper Michael Owen Jones presented at the AFS Annual Meeting in 1987 about a pilot project in a tutoring center at UCLA, he explained, "By documenting and interpreting expressive behavior, we can uncover problems in organizations. We may be fortunate on some occasions to discover supportive traditions and positive relations between management and staff. Undoubtedly we would want to report and explain both situations: the issues and dilemmas that plague so many organizations—as well as the traditions, positive practices and pleasant ambiance that might serve as models for solving some of the problems that abound in other units and organizations" (1987, 9–10).[3]

This new approach was intended to be interdisciplinary. In multiple publications, Jones described the 1970s as a time in which two parallel things were happening. For one, fields examining organizations (e.g., organizational development, organizational behavior) had become interested in the role of "symbols" in organizations, by which they meant stories, rituals, and other "expressive forms and research questions similar to those dealt with in folklore studies" (Jones 1994b, 165). Jones argued that such fields were using terms like "culture" and "symbolism" without adequate definitions (cf. Jones 1988, 24–27) and lacked guides to conducting qualitative research (cf. Jones 1988, 27–28).[4] Kurt Dewhurst, a folklorist who participated in conferences and publications dedicated to this approach, described it in these terms: "You know, it was an interesting time for our field. . . . It was a period where there was concern about the field of folklore being isolated, and concern about the hard barriers between disciplines. And it was a period with a lot of discussion about multidisciplinarity, crossing lines."[5]

At the same time, folklorists were broadening the boundaries of previous approaches to occupational folklore to include, "for example, occupational role as artistic performance, initiation rituals among smokejumpers as ritualized communication, the pervasiveness of photocopier lore in modern offices, the functions of beliefs of commercial fisherman, the themes and ambiance in industrial factory lore in the North and a hosiery mill in the South, and rodeo as symbolic performance" (Jones 1994b, 165).

Looking back on what led to the study of organizational folklore, Jones listed these and other factors, including the increased move to jobs outside of academe. He noted in sum, "Nearly 40 years later I cannot reconstruct my thoughts at that earlier time other than to assume that I likely wondered why as folklorists we seemed to document only the traditional expressive behavior of those on the shop floor, behind typewriters, and in primary industries such as logging, railroading, mining, etc.; why we tended to ignore the lore of others in organizations; and why we had to adhere to a single model of working in organizations as an arena of inevitable hostility and conflict."[6] According to Jay Mechling, in those days the folklore program at UCLA shared a building with the Graduate School of Management, and "before long Michael Owen Jones discovered in casual conversation that the management faculty who studied the symbolic lives of corporate cultures in essence did what folklorists do when they study the symbolic culture of a group, including groups of workers" (Mechling 2023, 59).

In the 1980s and early 1990s, Jones and other folklorists joined with scholars and practitioners in organizational studies to bring together these disciplinary approaches in a new area of study, resulting in a proliferation of organized panels at AFS annual meetings, conferences in other academic fields, and conferences organized around the topic as well as publications and the creation of an interest section on organizational folklore within the AFS. A symposium by and for folklorists was held at UCLA in 1982,[7] followed by a multidisciplinary conference in 1983 entitled "Myth, Symbols, and Folklore: Expanding the Analysis of Organizations."[8] Jones described the 1983 conference in the *AFS Newsletter* as "the first to bring together folklorists, organization behaviorists in business and management, and corporation personnel (managers of industrial relations, personnel, training and development, etc.)" (Jones 1983, 4). He quoted a human resources manager who spoke at the conference—"I'm sharing with you a rich lore of stories that I'm coming to appreciate as stories that tell us about our company"—and he described the stories this HR manager shared: "Most of the narratives treated motivation to excel, commitment to quality, and concern about safety. Some were humorous, others frightening, and some inspirational" (4). According to Jones, the "applications" this manager saw for "studying organizational folklore and corporate culture" included "new employee orientation, management development (improving leadership and decision making), and executive assessment" (4). As reflected here, central to Jones's approach to organizational folklore is the idea that an analysis of the folklore within an organization could provide a means for management to make changes for the better within the organizational culture.

A comparison Jones made between two 1970s dissertations on occupational folklore, those of Bruce Nickerson and Camilla (Cam) Collins, provides a useful example of this approach. Jones characterized Nickerson's description of the urban factory he studied as a workplace in which "the machinists had developed a strong work-group culture opposed to and distrustful of management; and rightly so, for apparently there were instances of deception and exploitation" (Jones 1987, 2). In contrast, Collins described the hosiery mill of her research as contrasting with assumptions about industrialized workplaces as always characterized by distrust of management by workers; instead, she witnessed a "patent lack of antagonism in the folklore of the mill hands" (Collins as quoted in Jones 1987, 2). Unlike the factory studied by Nickerson, in the hosiery mill, workers shared food and celebrated holidays and birthdays, and they welcomed new employees rather than hazing them, as in Nickerson's study (Jones 1988, 10). Jones attributed at least part of this difference to the "management attitude, philosophy and values as well as behavior"; the managers "set the tone" (1987, 3).

He argued that the environment in the factory studied by Nickerson emphasized the hierarchy of the workplace, while in Collins's hosiery mill, there was less emphasis on a rigid differentiation between workers and management in terms of dress, communication expectations, and so forth (Jones 1988, 10). However, Jones also described the contrasts in compensation between the two factories; while both factories operated on a piecework system, workers in the hosiery mill studied by Collins "received lower pay" and "did not have formal retirement, insurance, or other benefits programs" (10).

Jones asked, "Is there danger, then in advising managers about folklore?" (1988, 18). In other words, might putting a spotlight on the role of folklore in fostering a positive workplace give management more power over workers? Might the use of folklore to create a sense of community in a workplace lead to worker acceptance of lower pay and no benefits? He provided examples in which the actions of managers cause a sharp turn toward a distrustful and antagonist work environment, and he concluded that "while it is unlikely that they actually 'create' or even really 'manage' the culture, as we have seen they certainly can bring about distrust and divisiveness quickly, or, more slowly and with the need for constant effort at this, help stimulate in people a sense of personal satisfaction, self-esteem, and fellowship" (19–20).

Foundational to Jones's approach to the folklore of organizations was his assertion that while folklorists have tended to focus on unofficial/informal contexts and have not taken "organization," understood broadly, into account (1988, 31), "textbooks on organization behavior tend to assume that the phenomenon of 'organizations' is exclusively that of formal organization" (5). Jones's intent seems to have been to bridge these gaps, and although he described this at times as an extension of occupational folklore, he also described it as broader than the workplace, to encompass unofficial symbolic expression in any context of organizations, including but not limited to occupational organizations (e.g., a softball team [33]).

Case studies by both folklorists and nonfolklorists such as those in the 1988 collection *Inside Organizations: Understanding the Human Dimension* (Jones, Moore, and Snyder 1988) provide additional examples that help to demonstrate what was meant by organizational folklore. Occupational contexts include a health-care organization (Christensen) and a military hospital (Wolfe), a public utility company (Hanford), restaurants (Fine), automobile (Runcie, Dewhurst) and airplane (Snyder, Tommerup) factories, a software company (Martin), and a university committee (Arora). Nonoccupational contexts include a Girl Scout camp (Atkinson Wells), the Los Angeles Olympics Organizing Committee (McDonald), a dance troupe (Evanchuk), a university public event (Mechling and

Wilson), and church/religious communities (Moore, Wilson). On the one hand, the inclusion of organizational contexts beyond occupational settings demonstrates one obvious difference between this and occupational folklore studies. On the other hand, some of the chapters in *Inside Organizations* are concerned with topics that occupational folklore researchers were engaged with as well, particularly art in the workplace, the categories of work and play, and particular genres of folklore. For instance, folklorist Kurt Dewhurst described his ethnography of "aesthetic solutions among workers in Michigan's foundries, factories and small businesses" (Dewhurst 1988, 246), such as autoworkers making belt buckles out of trunk lock ornaments and jewelry from excess paint. Folklorists and nonfolklorists alike were interested in challenging the dichotomy of work and play. Gary Alan Fine, a sociologist with deep engagement with folklore studies, discussed his fieldwork in three restaurants and argued that "the work culture may directly contribute to productivity by supporting values that, in turn, support the conditions of work" (Fine 1988, 120). However, he argued, the relationship between work and play is context dependent; not "all expressive behavior in the workplace is constructive and supportive of the organization" (126). Thomas C. Dandridge (described as having joint appointments in a school of business and a college of public affairs and policy) provided examples from his research at Mattel and a Hyatt Regency Hotel that challenge the dichotomy of work and play. He described events like coffee breaks and birthday parties that take place in the workplace and argued that while they may appear to be play, they in fact might lead to something like Victor Turner's concept of "'communitas' or a sense of a common bonding emerg[ing] from the event" within the workplace (Dandridge 1988, 255). Shirley L. Arora examined the use of proverbs by members of an academic committee, finding that "skillful use of proverbial language can help to provide" a necessary ambience for finding common ground, "an ambience conducive to effective interaction, an ambience characterized by cordial relations and, if possible, good humor" (Arora 1988, 189).

Those in the volume who examined occupational spaces differ somewhat from more typical occupational folklore in terms of their interest in such things as the structure of a workplace and the relationships between levels of employees and between the officially sanctioned aspects of a workplace and the more unofficial aspects. Some of the authors in *Inside Organizations* are interested in "dysfunctional" (Wells 1988) or "deviant" (Runcie 1988) behaviors within organizations both occupational and nonoccupational. For the most part, this work is meant to be applied in some way, whether directly or indirectly, toward making organizational changes, linking it to the applied folklore efforts of the previous decade discussed in chapter 2.

In another example, the perspective is clearly very different from the labor-oriented approach of conventional occupational folklore studies. Jodi Martin, a graduate student in the UCLA Folklore and Mythology program at the time, provided an analysis of the process through which a software firm laid off 10 percent of its employees (including Martin herself). Her purpose seems to have been to show how the actions of management resulted in the remaining employees contending that "in hindsight, the layoff had its virtues—in reducing expenditures, making people more cost and revenue conscious, and reminding everyone of the dangers of complacency. Perhaps, too, it generated an increased sense of commitment or community among people who, having confronted a crisis and survived, came to have more clearly defined goals and a greater awareness about themselves" (Martin 1988, 224). While layoffs may be an inevitable part of doing business, this chapter does raise questions about whether this approach might be used to teach management how to approach layoffs with efficiency while ensuring that the remaining employees remain loyal and satisfied with the decisions of management. One wonders whether an alternate reading could suggest that the layoffs in fact created an environment in which employees feared that if they did not change their work practices, they, too, could face layoffs.

While the publications of the period and conversations with Jones and others make it clear that this was not the goal, Kurt Dewhurst suggested that there were concerns "below the surface" among folklorists at the time about the potential for misuse of ethnographic material but said it "really was not front and center in that initial conference as I recall."[9] Similarly, Patricia Atkinson said, "And I think that our own professional ethics prevent us from providing anything to the organization that would be hurtful or disadvantageous to the workers." When asked whether she recalled these ethical questions being discussed at the time, she responded, "No, they weren't, because it was really just sort of the beginnings of the recognition of organizational culture."[10]

Jones maintained that the goal of organizational folklore was to create better workplaces for all: "If we can discover what the symbolic forms and processes are as well as when and how they are generated, then we are that much closer to understanding how to utilize them and capture the assumptions and values they express in order to redesign organizations to work for, rather than against, people" (Jones 1988, 34). He was interested in what it is about an organization that promotes "spontaneous" folklore, and he saw this is an "extension" of occupational folklore because such knowledge could then be applied to foster folklore in organizations where it does not exist. Embedded in his assumption is that because folklore serves as a barometer for conditions, folklore within an organization that is positive suggests that the organization is a positive place to be. An idealistic extension of this—one that we think Jones subscribed to—is that in order for management to successfully encourage the growth of positive symbolism, conditions in the workplace must be positive.

In addition to applied ethnography within an organization, Jones also defined organizational folklore as "folklore *about* organizations" (1988, 32, *emphasis ours*). As such, he analyzed expressive critiques of "organizational culture" such as workplace cartoons that, for example, "juxtapose concern over human welfare with a climate of autocracy, self-interest and fear" (Jones 1989, 18).[11] Like occupational folklorists, Jones and other folklorists interested in organizational folklore were interested in the subversive uses of folklore.

The study of occupational folklore has focused on folklore as shared between and among members of an occupation; less attention has been paid to how it is created or to the comparative study of differences between workplaces. In an interview, Malachi O'Connor—a folklorist who has long worked as an organizational consultant—described a difference between the approaches of occupational folklore and organizational folklore: "occupational folklore, in terms of 'the study of,' and the looking at ways in which expressive culture plays itself out in organizations—and, you know, norms, and how culture works in an organization—began to then take on, 'Well, what if we applied folkloristics to the solution of practical problems?'"[12] As we will return to, this suggests organizational folklore as a form of applied folklore, in marked distinction from most occupational folklore, at least at the time. As Jones noted in the introduction to *Putting Folklore to Use*, "Application, then, is a value-laden concept" (1994a, 13). This, as well as questions about who folklorists should represent and more basic but related questions such as those about "the folk" and "folk groups," was embedded in the core of the debate.

"WHAT YOU NEED TO KNOW TO DO THE WORK"

The beginnings of occupational folklore study are most often traced to the broadening of American folklore studies in the early twentieth century. As Roger Abrahams argued in 1993, the European roots of the field in the preceding centuries inherently involved "class struggle," as the period to which the field traces its origins is also the period in which "official enclosure polic[ies]" led to "dislocating much of the peasant populations from the country landscape. There are manifest ironies involved in this process of sentimentalizing a way of life only after those who once practiced it have been taken from the land" (1993, 4). As students of folklore quickly learn in their introductory courses, as the study of folklore later developed in the nineteenth-century US, it had to be reinvented to fit a new context, for, as Regina Bendix writes, "In the European case, a native Other in the form of the folk had been embraced as an organic or familial link to a pure origin" (1997, 71). The historical center of the study of folklore in eighteenth- and nineteenth-century Europe had been the peasant class, a category that didn't exist in the same way in the US. Introductory textbooks reference the list of the "fast-vanishing remains of Folk-Lore in America" created by William Wells Newell and published in the first issue of the *Journal of American Folklore* to guide folklore collection and publication in the journal (Newell 1888, 3). The list represents our founders' struggle with the central question "Who are the folk in America?" and includes the lore of Southern Blacks, American Indians, French Canadians, and Mexicans, along with "Relics of Old English Folk-Lore."[13] The conceptualization of the folk that was both reflected in and shaped by this list in turn both contributed to and shaped the development of interest in the folklore of occupations, if only particular genres of folklore and particular occupations.

THE JOURNAL OF

AMERICAN FOLK-LORE.

VOL. I. — APRIL–JUNE. 1888. — No. I.

ON THE FIELD AND WORK OF A JOURNAL OF AMERICAN FOLK-LORE.

A PROPOSAL to establish a Folk-Lore Society in America was made in the form of a circular letter, dated at Cambridge, Mass., May 5, 1887, and subscribed with seventeen names. This invitation was repeated in a second letter, issued in October, bearing 104 signatures, representing various parts of the United States and Canada. In consequence, the number of signers having reached the necessary number, the American Folk-Lore Society was organized at Cambridge, January 4, 1888. In the proposals in question, the objects to be accomplished are stated in the following terms : —

It is proposed to form a society for the study of Folk-Lore, of which the principal object shall be to establish a Journal, of a scientific character, designed : —

(1) For the collection of the fast-vanishing remains of Folk-Lore in America, namely :

    (*a*) Relics of Old English Folk-Lore (ballads, tales, superstitions, dialect, etc.).

    (*b*) Lore of Negroes in the Southern States of the Union.

    (*c*) Lore of the Indian Tribes of North America (myths, tales, etc.).

    (*d*) Lore of French Canada, Mexico, etc.

(2) For the study of the general subject, and publication of the results of special students in this department.

In the first number of a journal established in conformity with this definition, it may be proper briefly to outline the services which a journal of American folk-lore may hope to accomplish in each of the departments above indicated.

As to Old English lore, the early settlers, in the colonies peopled from Great Britain, not only brought with them the oral traditions of the mother country, but clung to those traditions with the usual tenacity of emigrants transported to a new land. It is certain that up to a recent date, abundant and interesting collections could everywhere have been made. But traditional lore was unprized: the

Figure 5.2 In the first issue of the *Journal of American Folklore*, editor William Wells Newell set out the collection goals for the journal and, through it, the early ideas of who counted as "folk" and what counted as "lore" in the US. Courtesy of the American Folklore Society.

As American folklorists struggled to define the "folk"—the nature of which is of course "contingent and constructed" (Moody-Turner 2013, 13)—in a nation in which collectors lacked ancestral ties to those who had worked the land generation after generation, the folk remained *them* to *us* (with the exception of the "relics" of *our* ancestral survivals, such as English ballads, a category most similar to the European approach to folklore—and the one category in Newell's list that was a *what* and not a *them*). According to Shirley Moody-Turner, "While Newell may have found innovative ways to adapt European folklore studies to the American context, his identification of certain groups as 'folk,' which he variously equates with savage and primitive, marked the groups as a less evolved other to the mainstream, 'civilized,' whites" (2013, 27). These categories are racialized, and they also reflect assumptions about the economic and social class of the folk, suggesting a closer affinity to the European category than is often acknowledged, even as the new field engaged in the ongoing search for the American folk.[14]

At the same time that categories of folk were being defined, many Americans were engaged in a quest for what it meant to be American. For instance, as Bendix described, in "the literary discourse and Transcendentalist movements of the first part of the nineteenth century, the effort to formulate a distinctively individualistic American legacy free from European inspirations manifests itself strongly" (Bendix 1997, 69), and this was intensified following the Civil War (cf. Bendix 1997, 119). The founding membership of AFS included not only museum- and university-based folklore collectors and scholars but also "popular writers who used folklore" (Bronner 1986, 16), particularly those who contributed to the overlapping literary genres known as "local color" and "regionalism," including Samuel Clemmons, Joel Chandler Harris, and Edward Eggleston.[15] Their presence demonstrates, at least in part, links between the search for a uniquely American conceptualization of folklore studies and a larger search for Americanness. This search for Americanness also included masculinities distinctly different from what were seen as elite and effeminate European ways (Kimmel 2006, 17), as the masculine hero became "the frontiersman of manly independence" (Axton 1975, 58; see also Kimmel 2006), a "common man."[16] From its beginnings, the study of occupational folklore reflected the dominant conceptions of this American masculinity.

American folklorists began collecting folklore—particularly folk song[17]—from occupational groups in the first decades of the twentieth century, expanding the categories of "lore" as well as "folk." The recounting of the historiography of occupational folklore nearly always begins with John Lomax's 1910 *Cowboy Songs and Other Frontier Ballads* in part because this work represented an expansion of "folk" as well as of "folk song." It is also no mistake that the American cowboy—pictured as white, of course—is among the most iconic images of American masculinity. As Patrick Mullen has written, citing Jerrold Hirsch, "Lomax was one of the first American folklorists to romanticize masculine outdoor occupations as an appropriate context for folklore" (2008, 68). Other men who are credited with pioneering the study of occupational folklore include Phillips Barry, whose folk song collection included songs of Maine lumberman (Bendix 1997, 144, 149); George Korson, who began collecting Pennsylvania mining songs in the 1920s (Taft 2004); followed later by Wayland Hand in the 1940s, who also collected the folklore of miners; and the folklorist who is perhaps the most synonymous with occupational folklore, who gave us the term *laborlore* and who documented the laborlore of miners, pile drivers, tinsmiths, and others: Archie Green (see Burns 2011, 107 for Green's development of the term *laborlore*).[18] Over the course of decades, the occupational folk were limited to iconic, predominantly white, American men who worked with their bodies and their hands, away from the worlds of women and children, in circumstances of danger from the forces of nature and other men.

The introduction to a 2006 special issue of *Western Folklore* on occupational folklore attributed the male bias "to the work experiences of the folklorists and other cultural workers who conducted the research, in addition to the romanticized and *epic* nature of the predominantly *frontier* occupations they have been drawn to" ("Introduction" 2006, 9, *emphasis in original*). McCarl's work as a smoke jumper and firefighter and Green's work as a shipwright are included as examples. While it is certainly likely that the work experiences of early occupational folklorists influenced their focus on such male-dominated occupations, even with the broadening of the scope of such research to blue-collar workers, discussed below, women working outside the home continued to be too frequently excluded. In addition, women's work, particularly but not exclusively in the domestic sphere (Levin 1993), has often not fit definitions of "work," and therefore, until recent decades, women were not fully understood as "workers." The feminist folklore scholarship of the 1970s and '80s, discussed in chapter 3, made important contributions to our understanding of a range of women's work in the domestic sphere in general (Lanser 1993; Levin 1993) along with such domestic-based work as quilting and other textile traditions (Ice 1993; Johnson 1985; Pershing 1993a, 1993b; Roach 1985; Yocom 1993) and healing work (Mulcahy 1993). Such topics fit easily into genre-based folklore study of the time, and inarguably attention to each was needed. This work was also important because, as Judith Levin pointed out, it had been difficult for 1970s feminists to argue that women's place was not just in the home while simultaneously calling attention to the undervaluing of women's work in the home (Levin 1993, 288), and this work did just that. Levin did so directly, of course, but all of this research contributed to the valuing of work that has traditionally been done by women. It is, however, of note that the collections of the period are nearly devoid of women's work outside the home for pay. Exceptions include Cheryl Keyes on women rap artists (1993), Barbara Babcock on the pottery of Helen Cordero (1993), and Elaine Lawless on women pastors (1993), but even these are not framed as "occupational" even though they deal with women in occupations.[19]

It is instructive to compare editions of Jan Brunvand's popular textbook, *The Study of American Folklore: An Introduction*, because he edited it ever so slightly over time to reflect changes in the field. In the first edition, in 1968, Brunvand introduced a "concept that has grown out of recent collecting . . . the theory of recognizing 'folk groups'" (Brunvand 1968, 21), which included four major types: groups based on occupation, age, region, and ethnicity/nationality.[20] His discussion of occupational groups is in large part consistent over all four editions, including:

> Among occupational groups in the United States, we immediately associate the old rugged callings with vigorous oral traditions: ax logging, raft and barge freighting, sailing before the mast, and running cattle were all activities rich in folklore. The long exposure of small bands of toughened men to the elements led them all to fall back on their stocks of stories and songs for entertainment, and the dangers inherent in the work produced superstitions like the "Flying Dutchman" and the "ghost herd." But the present has its comparable groups too with their own folklore, as studies of mining, railroading, oil pumping, and other industries have shown. (Brunvand 1968, 22; 1978, 29; 1986, 42; 1998, 53)

He went on to list other "all-male labor groups," such as pilots, journalists, clergymen, the armed forces, and even computer programmers. There was no change in the second edition (1978), but by the third edition, he had added mention of "the domestic scene and other usual workplaces of American women" (Brunvand 1986, 42).[21] The fourth edition (1998) retained all of the above with only very minor changes in wording (though "clergymen" was changed to "clergy"). Interestingly, then, the only change made by Brunvand over the course of four editions published over four decades is the minutest possible acknowledgment that women, too, work, though he provides no specific examples beyond the domestic sphere.

Folklorists have always collected the lore of groups, of course—whether the *Märchen* of German peasants, the ballads of the descendants of the English immigrants living in the Appalachian Mountains, or the songs of cowboys or prisoners. But until folklorists broadened beyond the collection of texts to include people and contexts, they were not thinking so much about the groups to which those texts belonged. The concept of "group"—ideas about which Dorothy Noyes has described as "the most powerful and the most dangerous" (2010, 7)—came into sharper focus with the new folkloristics of the early 1970s (and the many precursors that influenced the new perspectives), with the turn to context over text, the individual performer within the group, folklore as communication, and so forth. Writing about the "New Perspectives" questioning of the "folk" in 1993, Amy Shuman and Charles Briggs noted, "The politics that shape who counts as the folk became a key question. Folklorists were once content to accept the category of 'folk' as traditional, peasant, working class, rural, poor, self-trained, or marginal; the heightened concern with situational contexts evident in the 1970s went hand-in-hand with an expansion of who counted as 'folk.' Soon *any occupational group* or the shared knowledge (in some artistic form) of any collectivity became the province of folklorists" (Shuman and Briggs 1993, 123, *emphasis ours*).

Occupational contexts were expanding, but not quite "any occupational group" yet counted, as the focus of occupational folklore studies remained solidly on blue-collar men. Richard Dorson wrote in *America in Legend* in 1973, "Folksongs and folktales celebrate the cowboy but not the insurance salesman, the lumberjack but not the factory worker, the railroad engineer but not the chairman of the board" (Dorson 1973, 127). Just a year later, Bruce Nickerson asked in the *Journal of American Folklore*, "Is there a Folk in the Factory?"; in other words, do blue-collar workers have identifiable shared folklore and therefore constitute a folk group (Nickerson 1974)?[22] He considered this question through examples from his fieldwork in a factory near Boston and elsewhere,[23] and he concluded that although expressions in the factory may not conform neatly to the traditional genre-based approach, these workers do have folklore and should be studied by folklorists. Nickerson continued the traditional approach to occupational folklore, excluding the work of women, and all of his examples are of men.

The search for the American folk and lore was a key theme in the writing of the most ardent advocate for folklore studies as an independent discipline, Richard M. Dorson.[24] Dorson frequently offered up his ideas on the state of the field in the US, including numerous book-length works as well as special issues of the *Journal of the Folklore Institute*, such as "Folklore in America versus American Folklore" (1978) and "The American Theme in American Folklore" (1980). According to Dorson in his posthumous 1982 "The State of Folkloristics from an American Perspective," "If the United States lacked a peasantry in the classical European sense, it could [in its early days] find an equivalent in the marginal folk living in southern Appalachian and Ozark mountain hollows or in the slave-descended black population or in fringe groups of occupational workers such as cowboys on the plains, lumberjacks in the woods, and miners underground" (Dorson 1982, 71). However, as Dorson noted, folklore studies had changed over the previous decade: "from the marginal to the mainstream . . . country to the city . . . past to the present . . . text to context . . . lore to folk . . ." and so on (71–72). Among the major themes in the "the current folkloric scene in the United States" (72) described by Dorson is "occupational-industrial folklore," signaling his acknowledgment that the study of occupational folklore had shifted from a mostly exclusive interest in the folk songs of groups such as cowboys and miners to the folklore— with expanded genres—of men in factories. "Folklore collectors originally sought occupational folklore in the outdoor and extractive industries that gave rise to folksongs. Cowboys, lumberjacks, sailors, and miners yielded volumes of ballads, work songs, ditties, chanteys, love songs, and protest songs. The collectors showed little interest in narrative or other genres and no interest in mechanized industries. A turning point came in 1963 with the publication by Mody Boatright of *Folklore of the Oil Industry*, a study which considered an industry that, while outdoors and underground in its extractive phase, did rely on technology" (77).

The existence of folklore among workers in factories may seem obvious today, but we must recall that the motivation for the beginnings of folklore studies, and those that collected folklore for the generations that followed, was saving folklore "from the fire," as metaphor for the threat first from modernity and then from industrialization. The study of "occupational-industrial folklore" signifies acceptance of the idea that folklore continues in new forms, despite profound changes such as industrialization.

Dorson drew attention to another turning point: the 1978 special issue of *Western Folklore* entitled "Working Americans: Contemporary Approaches to Occupational Folklife" (Byington 1978c). This issue, introduced by Robert Byington, was motivated by the "growing interest in occupational folklife and the consequent demand for appropriate materials and courses to satisfy that interest" and the growing collection of recordings in the Smithsonian Institution's Office of American and Folklife Studies resulting from the "Working Americans" programs of past Festivals of American Folklife (Byington 1978b, 143).[25] The "contemporary approach" to occupational folklife study represented in this special issue was grounded largely in the study of the folklore of men working in skilled blue-collar jobs. Folklorists had, however tentatively, widened the scope beyond the rural to include the factory floor and beyond primarily folk song to genres of narrative and to informal learning; however, although the context changed, the "folk" had not. Occupational folklore continued to be exclusively approached as the sphere of working-class men.

In the 1978 special issue, Robert McCarl presented "a definition and theoretical justification" (McCarl 1978, 145) of his now well-known approach to occupational folklore as "technique" ("what you need to know to do the work" [148]) along with gesture, oral expression, and custom, and Jack Santino discussed themes in occupational narratives of "workingmen" (201)—railroaders, airline employees, telephone company workers—particularly as they related to "hostility toward authority" (Santino 1978, 201).

Byington presented a guide to conducting fieldwork in occupational contexts. In his discussion of "getting in," he argued that "in almost every instance the entryways are two: through management or through organized labor" (Byington 1978c, 188); both have their problems, as all involved will be suspicious. He argued that when there is a union involved, "the sponsorship of management . . . is the kiss of death to the elicitation of cooperation from the workers themselves," but working through a trade union to achieve management sponsorship can be a means of gaining entry, as "they tend to respond more sympathetically to suggestions that in-depth ethnographies focused on workers' skills can do their industry no harm and might possibly be of some benefit"[26] (189). There is no suggestion that folklorists would seek lore from anyone but the workers, so while the spaces in which occupational folklore might exist had broadened, the category of occupational "folk" had really not. This is made explicit by Archie Green in this special issue.

Green argued for attention to "industrial lore," a term he credits to Benjamin A. Botkin (A. Green 1978, 229): "I am concerned that industrial work not be overlooked as we probe for change. Because industry is still bizarre or mysterious to many American folklorists, I ask these questions: Are workers to be seen as members of folk society?" (A. Green 1978, 214). Green grappled with questions he called "troublesome":

> Even if we grant that the factory is a field, what are proper
> standards for inclusion, both for worker and lore? Is the well-paid,
> highly-educated sophisicated [*sic*] airline pilot a member of folk
> society and a carrier of folk tradition? Does he perceive himself
> as a wearer of a blue or white collar? Commercial pilots and
> municipal bus drivers are both service tradesmen in their shared
> function of public transportation. Are bus drivers more "folk"
> than pilots? What do pilots, bus drivers, bracero farm laborers, or
> miners toiling in danger hold in common, if anything? When we
> turn away from the nature of folk society to the work sequence

and structure in which cultural data surfaces, we must reformu-
late these questions. Do bus drivers have more or less lore than
pilots? (A. Green 1978, 223–24)

He continued, "It was with some reluctance that ballad scholars
trained in the nineteenth century came to accept cowboy com-
positions as folk songs, and it is with similar reluctance today that
scholars view as folklore the expressions of assembly line and
service workers. Yet it is far easier to tag the word folk onto the
wearer of a blue collar than to do so for his white collar brother
or sister. The factory hand is still 'low' or 'isolated,' not unlike
the peasant, formerly favored by gentlemen scholars" (A. Green
1978, 224).

Also in this special issue, Roger Abrahams wrote, "In all low
status jobs, but especially those in which the worker 'serves'
(whether it be a master, a customer, or even one's community
or nation), one can witness traditions passed on from worker to
worker, ways in which the recurrent problems of the interactions
occasioned by the job are routinely solved" (Abrahams 1978, 176).
Abrahams engaged questions about "folk group," pointing out the
recent move from the focus on communities to smaller groups as
part of the new perspectives on folklore; he was interested in
shared experiences as they lead to a feeling of groupness—even
in brief encounters like standing in line. He pointed out that occupational folklore studies had long favored groups that work
together in isolation and therefore create more folklore together,
particularly "high-risk male occupations" (169–70).

As Abrahams's discussion reminds us, it had not been long
since Dan Ben-Amos defined folklore as "artistic communication
in small groups" (1971, 13), stressing the small group: those who
interact "face-to-face" as part of the "same reference group": "a
family, a street-corner gang, a roomful of factory workers, a village, or even a tribe" (12), marking a shift from the implicit question "who are the folk?" to "what groups count as folk groups"?
Alan Dundes's oft-quoted "any group of people whatsoever who

share at least one common factor" (Dundes 1965, 2) aside, "folk" continued to be class-based[27] and implicitly gender-based. This questioning of folk groups was explicitly noted by Abrahams and also evidenced by Green's questions.

Abrahams wrote, "We have been collecting and analyzing lore from those many small groupings who are either 'folk' (i.e., peasant) or folk-like inasmuch as they share language, attitudes and values. With regard to the occupational groups which we have studied, the groups make up a unit of socio economic behavior, inasmuch as groups like cowboys and loggers carry on both economic and social activities together; that is, both working with and entertaining each other" (1978, 182). Taking Abrahams's point a step further, a workplace such as a factory includes multiple categories of workers (not just managers but others—including perhaps women—who work in the factory office) or multiple "unit[s] of socio economic behavior," suggesting a place in which there are groups with potentially competing interests, providing a challenge to the traditional study of occupational folklore. Though technology was a reason for hesitancy regarding industrial lore to Dorson and others, perhaps the heterogeneity of such workspaces in contrast to the woods or the ranch was also a challenge.[28]

While Richard Bauman introduced the term "differential identity" (1972), he was partly describing what Américo Paredes had previously demonstrated in *With His Pistol in His Hand: A Border Ballad and Its Hero*. Paredes had pointed out the existence of folklore on both sides of the border: folklore among the Texas Rangers about Mexicans, which he summarized in six points as the "Anglo-Texan legend" (1958, 16), as well as folklore among Mexicans about the Texas Rangers. His focus was, of course, the latter, as he was most interested in the Mexican *corrido* tradition rather than the lore of the Texas Rangers. The folkloristic emphasis on marginalized groups is complicated by "differential identity" when there are power disparities, and occupational contexts demonstrate this particularly clearly. Though there are multiple groups within many workplaces, it was the folklore of *workers*—assumed to be gendered male—that was of interest to those interested in occupational folklore. Yet the 1970s was a time in which the category "folk" was being questioned and, at least for some, expanded. Alan Dundes concluded his essay "Who Are the Folk?" with "Who are the folk? Among others, we are!" (1977, 19).

In his essay in the 1978 special issue, Green seems openly troubled with the expansion of the category of "folk" beyond the working class while grappling with what even counts as *work*: "Clearly soldiers share an ancient body of tradition—is it to be categorized as occupational? Many athletes now figure among the highest paid employees in the United States. Is a football star less a worker than a pilot, a television anchor woman, or a Broadway actor?" (A. Green 1978, 227). "The museum art curator enters his place of work every morning as does the janitor or sanitation engineer. At times the curator is joined by a wealthy collector or patron who works with him on a special project. Does this shared activity of curator and patron link them as workers?" (228). He concluded,

> In essence, I want to see all workers' culture studied, but I am not comfortable with enlarging the term "folk." As a scholar I have long accepted limited views of folk society and traditional behavior. Similarly, I have felt at ease with conventional methods in research. As a citizen I have wanted to see marginal or overlooked persons, including industrial workers, achieve their "place in the sun." I continue to be partial to people labeled "folk" and treasure their lore. In examining the twin roles of study and action, I know also that scholarly conduct does affect the identity and esteem of the subjects of my research. Accordingly, I am not immune from responsibility beyond the academy. Hence, the kinds of questions asked here about bus drivers, boat builders, airline pilots, and television anchor women, are not only conceptual, but are also civic and moral in nature. Scholarly choices of field or method do have consequence in the larger society. It seems to me that our sensitivity is heightened and our reports strengthened if we can articulate and face openly the dilemma posed by the cliché, "scholarship *versus* activism." (A. Green 1978, 238)

Green's passionate approach to folklore as activism is a primary reason that many have long admired and emulated him and his work. For Green, maintaining a limited definition of "folk" was a moral decision that he maintained even as he grappled with questions that challenged the very core of the idea that the folk are a particular class of people.

At the time that organizational folklore was introduced as a new approach to studying workplaces, occupational folklore was understood by those closely studying and theorizing about it as a field of study that was most interested in the folklore of primarily working-class men, even as "folk" was in flux within the broader field of folklore studies. This would be a central point underlying the ensuing debate about organizational folklore study.

THE (PUBLIC) DEBATE PLAYS OUT

The debate between Michael Owen Jones and Robert McCarl, as well as a small number of others who voiced their positions, played out very publicly. In 1983 and 1984, Jones contributed articles to the *AFS Newsletter* in which he described the beginnings of organizational folklore as discussed in conferences (Jones 1983, 1984a). The first sign of a debate to appear in the newsletter, however, was in the report of the 1984 annual meeting: "A motion was passed at the business meeting: 'That the AFS Board explore the financial possibilities of resetting the section of *Folklore/Folklife* entitled "Folklore and Organizational Life" and that the purpose of that revision be to provide a means through which a statement that more completely and accurately reflects the historical approach of folklorists to occupational life take its place'" (AFS 1984, 1).[29]

In this and subsequent issues of the newsletter, McCarl, Jones, and a supporter of each exchanged letters. The debate spread briefly to the pages of *Western Folklore* in the early 1990s, it was referenced in publications by Jones and others late into the 1980s and the 1990s,

The American Folklore Society Newsletter

Editor: *Charles Camp*
Production Editor: *Christopher Laxton*

President: *Jan H. Brunvand*, Department of English, University of Utah, Salt Lake City, UT 84112. **Past-President:** *Bruce Jackson*, 96 Rumsey Road, Buffalo, NY 14209. **President-Elect:** *Rayna Green*, Room 5119-NMAH, Smithsonian Institution, Washington, DC 20560. **Secretary/Treasurer:** *Charles Camp*, Maryland State Arts Council, 15 West Mulberry Street, Baltimore, MD 21201. **Executive Board:** *Bill Ivey* (1985): Country Music Foundation, 4 Music Square East, Nashville, TN 37203. *Michael Owen Jones* (1985): Folklore—1037 GSM, University of California, Los Angeles, CA 90024. *Marta Weigle* (1986): 1127 Old Santa Fe Trail, Santa Fe, NM 87501. *William A. Wilson* (1986): Folklore Program, UMC 32, Utah State University, Logan, UT 84322. *Jay Anderson* (1987): Folk Studies, Ivan Wilson Center, Western Kentucky University, Bowling Green, KY. *Meg Brady* (1987): Department of English, University of Utah, Salt Lake City, UT 84112.

Nominating Committee: *Kathleen E. B. Manley*, Department of English, University of Northern Colorado, Greeley, CO 80639. **State of the Profession Committee:** *Jan Brunvand*, Chair, Department of English, University of Utah, Salt Lake City, UT 84112. **Program Committee:** *Tom and Elizabeth Adler*, Department of English, 1215 Patterson Office Tower, University of Kentucky, Lexington, KY 40506. **Editor, Publications of the American Folklore Society:** *Larry Danielson*, Department of English, English Building, 608 S. Wright St., University of Illinois, Urbana, IL 61801.

Editor, Journal of American Folklore: *Richard Bauman*, Center for Intercultural Studies in Folklore and Ethnomusicology, University of Texas, SSB 3.106, Austin, TX 78712. **The AFS Newsletter Editorial Address:** *Charles Camp*, Maryland State Arts Council, 15 W. Mulberry St., Baltimore, MD 21201 **Dues, Address Changes, Forms:** American Folklore Society, 1703 New Hampshire Ave., N.W., Washington, DC 20009.

The American Folklore Society Newsletter (ISSN 0745-5178) is published six times annually for $10 a year by the American Folklore Society, 1703 New Hampshire Ave. NW, Washington, DC 20009. 2nd class postage paid at Washington, DC. POSTMASTER: Send address changes to the American Folklore Society at the above address.

Copyright © 1984 by the American Folklore Society

Members having business with the American Folklore Society are encouraged to direct their letters to the proper officer for action rather than overloading the president or executive secretary/treasurer. Carbon copies of correspondence should, however, be sent to those two officials for informational purposes.

Editor's Note

This year's annual meeting in San Diego broke a few patterns. First of all, it was far better attended than any other West Coast meetings in recent memory, with more than 400 preregistrants and nearly another 100 walk-ins. Second, the much referred-to and seldom substantiated "closed-door" meetings at which, legend has it, the Society's business is truly transacted were convened at poolside, rather than in more traditionally sequestered quarters. Fourth, a spirited discussion actually took place at the business meeting, concerning the newly published Society booklet *Folklore/Folklife* (see below). And fifth, the reunification of the annual banquet and the presidential address in the program came off without hitch or complaint. At least I haven't heard a complaint as yet—letters invited and space on this page reserved.

Speaking of broken, John West appeared at the gathering after all, choosing not to entrust his task of moving adjournment of the business meeting to a lesser colleague. It was good to see him in the front row again, body on the mend, spirit intact. To those members unable to attend the San Diego meeting, here's hoping this issue of the *Newsletter* gives some idea of what happened. And on behalf of the Board, members present, and myself, another round of thanks is hereby extended to Carol Edwards and Steve Jones for engineering a meeting so roundly enjoyed.

Letter to the Editor

I made the following comments at the question and answer section of the annual meeting in San Diego, and presented a similar argument at the actual business meeting itself. For the benefit of members of the society who were not at the meeting and as a reinforcement and focusing of my side of the issue, I provide the following:

I would like to make a comment about the section of the AFS publication *Folklore/Folklife* entitled "Organizational Folklore." The reason that I am concerned about this section stems not only from its self-serving posture—unlike other portions of the book, it is essentially a commercial for those graduate programs that train students in corporate folklore—but more importantly because it misrepresents virtually the entire subfield of occupational folklore. From the early days of the discipline, folklorists with such varied backgrounds as Dobie and Lomax, through Botkin, Korson, Boatright, Hand and Green were fieldworkers who went to the workplace and negotiated with workers face-to-face to collect their stories, songs and skills. Although not necessarily pro-union, these fieldworkers approached work from the bottom up—the shop floor, the mine shaft, the oil derrick—not from the corporation down. A current generation of folklorists including Santino, Stoeltje, Lloyd, Bell, Mullen, Collins, Hunt, Gonzalez, myself and others have continued this approach in the field. We have (and I am speaking from my personal point of view here) accepted the notion that workers' folklore—the informally passed means through which workers control techniques and information in the workplace is (1) covert and often in opposition to the subcultural and organizational goals of management; and (2) that this material should either remain under the control of the work group or its dissemination should be conducted with their cooperation. I am not arguing that all research done in work settings is supported by labor unions or that that is always desirable, merely that there is a necessary and healthy difference between the goals of workers and managers and that we should be mindful of who we are attempting to serve. This predominant concept in the area of occupational folklore is not only overlooked in the article, it is disregarded in favor of a diametrically opposed point of view. The author would have the reader believe that folklorists tend to work as agents of scientific management and that the expressive dimensions of work "may play an important role in clarifying and communicating organizational philosophy and objectives, enhancing managerial styles and methods and improving life in the workplace." This is nothing new—it is the same approach taken by F. W. Taylor, the Gilbreths, the human relations school of management and the current QWL approach to organizational conformity borrowed desperately from the Japanese to replicate their success in auto plant management.

What I am objecting to is a shift apparently condoned by members of the executive board and those readers listed in the acknowledgments, away from

(Continued on page 5)

Figure 5.3 The debate about occupational and organizational folklore studies took place in multiple forums, including the *AFS Newsletter*. "Letter to the Editor" by Robert S. McCarl. *The American Folklore Society Newsletter* 13 (6): 2, 5 (1984). Courtesy of the American Folklore Society.

and it was raised by McCarl as recently as the business meeting during the 2016 annual meeting of the AFS in Miami, Florida.

In a letter to the editor published in the *AFS Newsletter* in 1984, McCarl provided the comments he made "at the question and answer session of the annual meeting in San Diego" that year (1984, 2). He argued that the organizational folklore section in *Folklore/Folklife* "misrepresents virtually the entire subfield of occupational folklore," which he went on to describe in the terms with which we began this chapter: "Although not necessarily pro-union, these fieldworkers approached work from the bottom up—the shop floor, the mine shaft, the oil derrick—not from the corporation down" (2). These categories also reflect the shifts pointed out by Dorson, as the "shop floor" had become a central symbol of occupational folklore now that the focus had widened beyond those working in forests and mines, on horseback, and so forth to those laboring in factories, reflecting the changes in American work as well.

McCarl wrote that he and others of his generation of occupational folklorists continued the traditional understanding of "workers' folklore" as "covert and often in opposition to the subcultural and organizational goals of management; and . . . material [that] should either remain under the control of the work group or its dissemination should be conducted with their cooperation." He emphasized that "there is a necessary and healthy difference between the goals of workers and managers and that we should be mindful of who we are attempting to serve" (McCarl 1984, 2). He was objecting to what he saw as the acceptance by the discipline more broadly as "a shift . . . away from community control of cultural materials" (2, 5) which meant that folklorists were now promoting the study of organizations "in order to improve their efficiency. That means getting corporate support to study work culture in order to further control the working lives of those on the shop floor. I think that is ethically wrong and misrepresents my approach and that taken by a number of occupational folklorists" (5). "The bottom line is this: as folklorists move increasingly into the public sector they will be asked to deal with a variety of organizations that may have diverse and even conflicting goals. In the work setting, the lack of funds to support research that is documented and presented from the worker's point of view will make the support and the promises of corporate sponsors incredibly attractive" (5).[30] He ended the letter with his first and only mention of Jones by name in the letter, calling for a public debate.

Letters by two other folklorists were printed in the newsletter. First, Robert Byington described the essay in *Folklore/Folklife* as "a picture of folklore in the service of corporate management which smacks of F.W. Taylorism at its starkest"; "It reads like a CIA pamphlet" (1985, 2). A couple of issues later, Alf Walle commented on Byington's letter, calling it a "hyperbolic attack of organizational folklore" (1985, 2) and arguing that folklorists have the skills to help "business professionals better understand the complexity of human behavior" (3).

Meanwhile, Jones submitted a lengthy reply to McCarl, in which he defended the study of organizational folklore in part by describing McCarl's work with firefighters as essentially organizational folklore. In regard to McCarl's *Good Fire/Bad Night: A Cultural Sketch of the District of Columbia Fire Fighters as Seen through Their Occupational Folklife* (1980), which Jones described as "an applied ethnographic study of fire fighters' work culture" supported by a National Endowment for the Arts grant, he wrote that while "approximately half of his monograph is devoted to describing life in the firehouse and work techniques in fighting a fire," the other half is largely focused on relationships and conflicts as they affect the "fire fighting performance and the effectiveness of the fire fighting force" (Jones 1985b, 8). According to Jones, "All of these are very real and significant *organizational*—not just occupational—concerns" (8, *emphasis in original*). He continued, "In other words, McCarl is using folkloristic research of one kind of work among one group of workers to recommend to higher administrative levels how they might train supervisors of those workers in order to improve life in the workplace and the effectiveness of the organization in meeting some

On Folklorists Studying Organizations: A Reply to Robert S. McCarl

The lives of all of us are affected daily by organizations and their representatives, policies and procedures, and products or services. Schools, universities, governmental agencies, utilities companies, religious institutions, manufacturers and retailers, special interest groups, charities, institutions of banking and commerce, healthcare centers, agencies in the business of enforcing laws and fighting fires and so on are dominant aspects of contemporary American society. For the 90% of us who are not self-employed, some organizations are vital to us as the workplace, which in turn may constitute a large part of our social life and expressive world. If our lives and livelihood—not only materialistically but also socially and spiritually—depend on organizations, then it seems appropriate to study organizations in order to understand them, and, if necessary, to recommend ways of improving them.

Earlier folkloristic research of occupational life has laid a foundation for organizational studies. While there are conceptual differences between the two subfields of occupational and organizational folklore studies—else why would two different terms have evolved?—they are complementary. To understand both the similarities and differences between the fields, we may consider some of Robert S. McCarl's works.

In an unpublished essay entitled "Describing the Critical Center: Approaching Work Cultures from an Applied Ethnographic Perspective" (n.d.), McCarl defines workers' culture as "the vast repertory of actions, gestures, and techniques which are based on a shared concept of appropriate behavior or generated through collective interaction on the job. When performed in the presence of fellow workers, the terms used, techniques exhibited or stories told are both a model of and a model

The American Folklore Society Newsletter

Copy Deadlines	Mailing Dates
April 12	May 16
June 11	July 16
August 13	September 17
October 14	November 18
December 4	January 16
February 14	March 18

8

for the knowledge one must possess to exhibit competence in the occupational group" (n.d.; p. 12). To illustrate, McCarl describes an informal teaching relationship between an officer and a rookie fire fighter in which the chief tells a story about a lesson in fire fighting that he learned, early in his career when driving a hose truck, from a captain leading a squad into a burning building. For McCarl, a basic concept emerged, that of the "critical center": the core values and concerns of a culture that can be inferred by the researcher from recurrent scenes and incidents. But the focus of McCarl's interest is fire fighting per se. He is aware that officers at various levels lead, supervise, administer, manage; but the *work* culture, as he treats it, is not managing but fighting fires. Indeed, McCarl distinguishes between fire fighters and officers, and considers "occupational folklore" as the knowledge, techniques, and stories related to fire fighting only. Extinguishing blazes may be one of the purposes, goals, or objectives for which the larger organization (the city fire department) exists, and controlling fires may be one task of some organizational participants; there are other goals and objectives and other tasks, as well.

A second concept that McCarl sets forth in this essay is that of "applied ethnography." Early in his research, he became aware of dramatic changes taking place in the constituency of engine companies and departmental administration, and of tensions and conflicts. As McCarl viewed it, therefore, his task was to write an ethnography of fire fighting to give to those concerned with this endeavor. For, as he concludes his paper, "Change is inevitable and it is our job to document and present our conception of a particular cultural reality based on our research so that those experiencing the change can make some informed decisions concerning its direction and impact on their lives" (n.d.; p. 14). Although he writes ostensibly *for* and *about* fire fighters—the "workers," in his view—his comments for change are directed *to* upper-level administration in the city department, as apparent in his monograph.

One of McCarl's objectives in publishing his monograph *Good Fire/Bad Night: A Cultural Sketch of the District of Columbia Fire Fighters as Seen Through Their Occupational Folklife* (1980) was to present "a perception of work" (i.e., fighting fires) to "both fire fighters and outsiders"; one of

the goals was to make some recommendations for action. McCarl had been hired by the D.C. Fire Fighter's Association, Local 36, with the assistance of an NEA grant, to conduct an applied ethnographic study of fire fighters' work culture. Approximately half of his monograph is devoted to describing life in the firehouse and work techniques in fighting a fire. A third chapter, comprising the second half of the study, focuses on relationships among some people associated with the enterprise of fire fighting. As McCarl reports, there are conflicts because of the hiring of blacks and women, for whom fire fighting has sometimes been little more than a "job," in an occupation once dominated by men of Italian and Irish descent for many of whom fire fighting was a "way of life" that integrated work, family, and community. There are also tensions between some of the lower-level employees—the "fire fighters"—and some of the officers, because of an ambivalence in the role of officer or because of what appears to be an insensitivity at times of officers toward those whose activities they direct, supervise, or administer. Sometimes racial and administrative tensions are combined: "Although white fire fighters are still in the majority, they feel threatened by a black administration which they feel is discriminating against them because they are white" (1980; p. 60). Whatever their origins, the tensions and conflicts appear to undermine morale, erode "the basic fibre and cohesiveness of the occupation," and diminish the quality of fire fighting performance and the effectiveness of the fire fighting force (1980; p. 60). All of these are very real and significant *organizational*—not just occupational—concerns.

Throughout the latter portion of his monograph, McCarl recommends ways of reducing some of these tensions or of resolving some conflicts. He suggests, for example, that an independent body of advisors be established to "openly discuss and advise the Department concerning the various points of view within this increasingly heterogeneous occupational group" (1980; p. 102). McCarl also observes that there is no educational program preparing officers for a leadership, supervisory, or administrative role. Such training, if instituted, "might not only improve the performance and satisfaction of the officers, it might also improve the morale and performance of the companies they administrate" (1980; pp. 73–74). Potential officers, writes McCarl, should be taught more about human motivation and psychology; sensitized to the needs of minority groups and attitudinal differences toward work

(continued on page 5)

Figure 5.4 The debate about occupational and organization folklore studies took place in multiple forums, including the *AFS Newsletter*. "On Folklorists Studying Organizations: A Reply to Robert S. McCarl" by Michael Owen Jones, *The American Folklore Society Newsletter* 14 (2): 5–6, 8 (1985). Courtesy of the American Folklore Society.

of the purposes, goals, and objectives for which the organization had been formed and perpetuated" (5).[31] According to Jones, the contrasts between the two approaches as characterized by McCarl were a "misunderstanding" of the aims of organizational folklore.

Jones made two additional arguments in this reply. First, that within his research and writing on firefighting, McCarl saw only firefighting as work and firefighters as workers, while in that very same workplace, "there are other goals and objectives and other tasks" related to management that McCarl did not count as part of "the *work* culture" (Jones 1985b, 8, *emphasis in original*). Jones questioned the strict differentiation between workers and managers elsewhere as well: "Some researchers insist on distinguishing workers from managers and labor from management. The conceptual implications are that managers and executives do not work, and workers do not manage or execute" (1985a, 250), which he disputed. Second, as quoted at the start of this chapter, Jones described McCarl's stance as "chilling" because he was attempting to commit "the discipline to identifying with one group over another," a position that Jones was unwilling to accept (Jones 1985b, 5).

In McCarl's published reply he stated, "I am a firm believer in the right of any folklorist to study anything and everything he or she wants to study"; his outrage was instead prompted by the essay in *Folklore/Folklife*, which he argued misrepresented the history of the study of occupational folklore (1985b, 2). He described his approach to occupational folklore in contrast to organizational folklore, in which, he argued, "the data become part of a larger, decision-making process that places cultural information in the hands of the most powerful members of the social organization" rather than protected, as he attempts to do (5). He concluded by stating that he would present his "views on this important philosophical and methodological question in papers and juried journals" in order to further the discussion in a more scholarly realm (5).

Although this was the end of the debate in the pages of the newsletter, it continued elsewhere. In a 1985 memo to the AFS Executive Board, accompanied by a collection of documents chronicling what he titled the "Alleged Controversy" about organizational folklore and *Folklore/Folklife*, Jones wrote that he did "not insist that there be a passage in the [*Folklore/Folklife*] booklet" on organizational folklore, and he did not demand that it not be changed, but he wanted the board to consider that only two members of AFS (McCarl and Byington) had spoken out against it.[32] The documents accompanying this memo included the pieces previously published in the newsletter, correspondence between McCarl and Jones, and an excerpt from a letter Byington wrote to Bruce Jackson (who had coedited *Folklore/Folklife*), which Jones noted had been distributed by Jackson at the May 1985 AFS Board Meeting. In the excerpt, Byington wrote that although he stands by his letter in the newsletter, he was under the impression that a firestorm of letters was being sent; he felt that the fact that his was the lone letter overemphasized his objections.

The AFS celebrated its centennial in 1988–89, in part through publications about the field.[33] Though published well in advance of the centennial, *Folklore/Folklife* was the first such publication, followed by *100 Years of American Folklore Studies: A Conceptual History* (Clements 1988) and *Time & Temperature* (Camp 1989). These publications are as indicative of the time in which they were published as they are of the history of the discipline. *Folklore/Folklife* had featured what was then a brand-new area of folklore studies, the folklore of organizations; it was not included in either of the centennial publications published just five years later. *Time & Temperature* included short essays by sixteen folklorists on categories of what folklorists do, including "The Folklorist as Dramatist" by Robert McCarl, in which he described the pitfalls of presenting occupational folklore in festival contexts—or, as he phrased it, "the arrogance of this type of public contextualization which relies on the museological conventions of item-oriented display within which the worker is simply installed like another item" (McCarl 1989, 30).[34]

The third section of *100 Years of American Folklore Studies*, "The Concept of 'Folk,'" included McCarl's "The Folk as Occupational Group: From the Cow Camp to the Shop Floor," which provided an overview of the history of the study of occupational folklore from Lomax's *Cowboy Songs* through the "ideological disagreement among folklorists who study the workplace regarding the contextual frame of their investigations" (1988a, 42). McCarl concluded,

> These two divergent approaches to occupational folklife (the "shop-floor" folklorist and those who maintain an "organizational" approach) reflect the importance of careful documentation and presentation of occupational folklore in a capitalistic society. Both approaches require the combination of fieldwork and analytical skills generated in the academy with the ability to present collected material to audiences outside the workplace. As long as the dialogue between these two points of view continue in full view of the people being presented, the study of occupational folklore will mature both as a part of our discipline and as an important aspect of public education. (42)

Although this seems to suggest that McCarl had come to see occupational and organizational folklore as different perspectives, signaling the end of the debate, it surfaced again in *Western Folklore* in the 1990s.

Some of the essays in *Time & Temperature* reflect a serious dissatisfaction with where the field had gone and was going, suggesting, at the time of the centennial of the official establishment of the field in the US, the very growing pains that we are addressing in this book.[35] This dissatisfaction continued in a 1991 special issue of *Western Folklore* edited by Robert A. Georges: "Taking Stock: Current Problems and Future Prospects in American Folklore Studies." In his introduction, Georges described disappointment with the centennial celebrations, particularly the 1989 annual meeting, which, he said, "did not live up to its advanced billing" as a chance to "look ahead and consider what the future was likely to hold" (1991a, 1). As a result, Georges, along with Robin Evanchuk and Stephen Stern, had organized two sessions on this theme at the 1990 annual meeting, resulting in the special issue.

The essays in the volume included topics ranging from both the appropriation and concealment of "folklorist" as professional identity (Georges 1991c), public misunderstandings of what folklorists do (Evanchuk 1991), and an essay by Michael Owen Jones entitled "Why Folklore and Organization(s)?" (Jones 1991). Jones argued that those in organizational studies need a folklore perspective and folklorists need to study organizations as "a fundamental human endeavor" (33). He wrote that folklorists would find some of the approaches to folklore genres by organizational studies "misinformed or misguided" (35) and the language of some of the work "inherently manipulative and intellectually dubious" (36). He made a distinction between work within organizational studies that is top down and work that "insists on including in a project's planning and implementation the direct participation of a variety of members who represent different levels and functions of the organization" (37). According to the transcription of the discussion that followed, included in the issue, Jones clarified that he was proposing that "we take folklore studies to other fields" rather than bringing other fields to folklore studies (Georges 1991b, 97).[36]

When asked in 2021 whether he thought one of Michael Owen Jones's goals was for folklore to offer something to fields such as organizational studies, Kurt Dewhurst stressed that Jones's goal was not for folklore to surrender to another field but rather "he really thought we could bring something. This would enrich our field. It would put us in higher standing within not just the eyes of [academic] administrators, but as a discipline around the world. If we could figure out a way to translate our knowledge and experience in a constructive way that benefitted the worker, the occupation, the traditions, without in any way undercutting them."[37] Jones reiterated his critique of McCarl's work with DC firefighters in this 1991 article, and in an issue of the journal that followed, McCarl responded, essentially with his earlier critiques (McCarl 1992). At this point, it is quite clear that the two were in fact shouting past each other, so grounded was each in his own position. The way in which this debate had gotten deeply personalized suggests irreconcilable positions between the two, but more importantly for our purposes, it suggests differing perspectives in the field more widely.

WHAT EVER HAPPENED TO ORGANIZATIONAL AND OCCUPATIONAL FOLKLORE?

The petition for an organizational folklore interest section of AFS was successfully initiated in April 1983 by Richard Raspa of Wayne State University, who then served as convenor of the section. According to a review of annual meeting programs, the section met annually from 1984 through 1989, and it was closed in 1993.[38] Meanwhile, the Occupational Folklore Section (sometimes called the Occupational Folk*life* Section in the program) was created in 1988, initially convened by Robert McCarl, and it met regularly through 2000 (it appeared in the list of AFS sections each year through 2007).[39]

For some, the intervening time since this debate played out has brought reflection. For instance, Patricia Atkinson described her take on the two today as interwoven: occupational folklore is at least in part the ways in which workers "operate within an organizational culture that may be somewhat at odds with their own beliefs or behavior" as well as "the contrast between the stories the organization chooses to tell them about the culture, and their own experience of that organizational culture." She went on to add, "I think other people saw these as oppositional. But I saw the occupational culture within the organizational culture as really survival mechanisms and ways that people had with dealing with a disconnect between what they were told, and what was actually enacted, what they actually had to do, what their job actually was."[40] For the most part, rather than reaching a resolution, the debate about organizational folklore mostly faded away, though references to it continued.

In a 1987 article, Archie Green wrote, "Recently, a few teachers in the humanities have forged links with management, and have placed occupational lore under the rubric 'corporate culture' and 'organizational theory.' These trends carry a potential danger—the subversion of workers' needs to managerial privilege" (Green 1987, 168). In the introduction to a 1988 special of *New York Folklore* on "Folklore in Industry," Mia Boynton pointed to "a rather unsettling lack of connection to current methodologies and theories" in occupational folklore and went on:

> A 1978 attempt to retool the subfield (Byington 1978) did partially jar some of us out of our sleep, but a more recent dispute between two important theorists of work, Robert McCarl and Michael Owen Jones (see *American Folklore Society Newsletter* vol. 13 #6, 1984; and vol. 14 #2 and 3, 1985) indicates that a great drowsiness still afflicts us. There has been a recent tendency by some folklorists to bypass important industrial workplace models in the name of "organizational folklore." The organizational model, in my view, ignores the existence of genuine worker attitudes—ways of thinking which spring from a long history of working class life—and thus fails to fully report upon the richness and meaning of worker expressivity. (Boynton 1988a, 1)

The 2006 *Encyclopedia of American Folklife* (Bronner 2006) included separate entries for "Occupational Folklife" and for "Organizations, Corporate and Work," and "Organizations, Voluntary and Special Interest." The entry for Occupational Folklife provided an overview of the topic, from the early work of George Korson through the broadening of the field of study to include industrial settings. It also included a subsection on "Organizational Folklife and Corporate Culture," which described it as a by-product of growing interest in modern and urban folklore, leading to an expansion of the conception of folk groups to include office personnel and management and included lists of genres that can be found in workplaces (Scully 2006, 903–06). The entry for "Organizations, Corporate and Work" also provided an overview of the area of study, much as it was described in the 1980s. However, author Richard Raspa expanded it by describing corporate organizations that were once "run like family systems" in which supervisors would happily leave a birthday party on a Sunday afternoon to address a problem at the assembly plant to a changed world in which "globalization has eroded the covenant between business organization and managers by expanding the competitive marketplace" (Raspa 2006, 923). The controversy was not mentioned in any of these entries (and McCarl is not listed in the sources, though Jones and Green are), and frankly such entries seemed out of date by 2006, when even Jones had moved on. The entry for "Organizations, Voluntary and Special Interest" began by noting that membership organizations based on shared interests differ "from the kind of corporate entities commonly studied in organizational folklife by being membership driven and typically established for the purpose not of making profits but of advancing a cause" (Nusbaum 2006, 924–25). Nusbaum went on to describe examples of the folklife of voluntary associations such as the Polka Lovers Club of America and associations of veterans, musical traditions, and fishing; essentially, he was describing recreational folklore, yet it seems even in 2006 either he or the editor felt the need to acknowledge organizational folklore.

Since 2010, the American Folklife Center has awarded Archie Green Fellowships each year, which "support new, original, independent field research into the culture and traditions of contemporary American workers and/or occupational groups found within the United States."[41] Examples of occupational categories that have been supported by these fellowships suggest that the boundaries of "occupational folklore" have indeed expanded to include workers—including women workers—such as doulas, teachers, psychiatric nurses, personal home aides, entrepreneurs, funeral directors, and park rangers. However, the majority remain "workers" in the sense of those occupational folklorists have long studied: those on the waterfront, in waste management, and in kitchens; cowboys, automobile workers, and those in the building trades; tugboat captains and engineers, machinists, harbormasters, drydock workers, and locktenders; taxi drivers and domestic workers.[42]

Though there are certainly exceptions, much of occupational folklore today is still focused on "workers" and is still largely shaped by class as well as race and ethnicity, though it is somewhat more inclusive of women. We don't believe this is because folklorists do not recognize that even those who work in upper management have folklore but because many continue to apply the label *folk* to those for whom they wish to provide what Green called a "place in the sun."

According to Jones's 2018 reflection, "The greatest impact of my directing the conference [on organizational folklore] in 1983, participating in organizational behavior and organization development meetings, and publishing several essays and books has been on scholars outside the field of folkloristics in the area of organization studies." He continued, "Some folklorists began to think about work life and institutions, including their own, in a new way." He had long moved on, however, to other things, particularly foodways: "Also, by 1996 I felt I had made sufficient inroads for folklore studies into the realm of organization studies and organizational theorizing. I had likewise tired of sparring with McCarl over the concept of organizational folklore."[43]

According to public comments made by Robert McCarl in 2016, he believes that the debate itself had lasting consequences within the field. As we will discuss in the concluding chapter, prior to, during, and after the 2015 AFS Annual Meeting in Long Beach, California, there was a labor dispute as members of the hotel housekeeping and food service staff were attempting to hold a vote to unionize and the hotel was using stalling tactics in their attempts to stop unionization. Among those calling for AFS to cancel the contract was Robert McCarl; he and others boycotted either the entire meeting or the hotel by coming to the conference but staying elsewhere. McCarl was invited by the AFS leadership to attend the meeting the following year to express his views, and he spoke at the business meeting. His comments framed the debates about the Long Beach meeting as tied directly to the organizational/occupational folklore debates, presenting what he saw as a direct line between the "willingness of folklorists to explicitly accept organizational folklore" to what he described as "the decision by the AFS Board and individual folklorists to cross the picket line[44] and patronize the hotel":

> Before 1983, most folklorists approached the workplace via the shop floor. Certainly it was necessary to seek managerial permission to gain access to the workers, but once there, the emphasis of most workplace studies were bound in some way within the values, traditions and expressive culture of workers themselves. After 1983, and with the AFS support and publication of *Folklore/Folklife*, this was no longer the case. The willingness of folklorists to explicitly accept organizational folklore sent a signal to labor and working class scholars (as well as scholars of color who share many of the same values) that the discipline was at worst hostile, and at best, ambivalent, about the lives of working people. This hostility, expressed in both overt and covert ways, was the reason that Archie Green and other labor scholars rarely attended AFS meetings.[45]

The discussion and disagreements surrounding the 2015 AFS Annual Meeting represent a recent dispute within the field that demonstrates that the issues we describe in this volume are far from resolved.

IN RETROSPECT

Looking back from the vantage point of nearly four decades, it seems that McCarl and Jones were shouting past each other because they were coming at similar questions from very different directions. What might have seemed a debate between two men, in retrospect, highlights changing understandings of the "folk" and differences between folklorists coming from an activist tradition and some of those engaged in applied folklore. Jones saw organizational folklore as applied folklore that had the potential to improve the workplace—including for workers—but he argued against McCarl's position that folklorists are, by default, activists or that, as a field, we must choose a side. McCarl appears to have seen his work with DC firefighters as at least in part applied folklore, but he, along with other occupational folklorists, viewed the recognition and celebration of workers and their creativity, skills, and occupational knowledge as activism. McCarl articulated this in 1988 while distinguishing between his goals and those of organizational folklore: "What must not happen is the documentation of one group (workers on the shop floor) for another (managers) in the naïve hope that this process will result in a more humanized workplace" (McCarl 1988b, 139). He continued,

> As intervenors into the political fabric of work culture, we can recognize the necessary dialectic between overt and covert expressions of cultural identity in the workplace and use the insights of the workers themselves to shape public perception in a direction of their choosing. If we fail in that regard, we run the risk of documenting and presenting work culture without considering the implications of our depictions or the impact that this information might have if it is simply turned over to outsiders without any concern for community control. Rather than preserving and celebrating work culture, this latter approach (like that taken by time/motion experts, industrial engineers, and organizational folklorists) will result in the development of public sector folklorists

> who improve the products and streamline the processes of work
> with little concern for the lives of those involved.
>
> When cultural material leaves the direct control of the pri-
> mary work group of face-to-face workers, our role as researcher
> and academic specialist is traded for that of activist or informer.
> (McCarl 1988b, 149–50)

McCarl raises questions here about representation that were increasingly under consideration by folklorists and those in adjacent fields at this time. Centuries of assuming that the products
of collection and publication could and should be disconnected
from and have no impact on (or be read by) the "folk" were being challenged, and a "crisis of representation" took hold in folklore and anthropology in the mid-1980s (cf. Clifford and Marcus
1986). This was driven in part by contemporary acceptance that
folk did not denote a separate category of humanity based on
class, race, ethnicity, or other factors.

Meanwhile, Jones and others involved in organizational folklore
were looking at the folklore of a workplace with goals that included
understanding an organization in order to improve it. Certainly, he
saw organizational folklore as an applied approach, a means of "putting folklore to use," as he would later title a collection he edited
(Jones 1994c). To Jones, "The study of organizational folklore was
a logical extension of research on occupational folklore and folklife.
As valuable as previous research on workers' tradition was, something seemed to be missing. Some of the research was informed by
an earlier notion of folklore as a survival and 'the folk' or 'a folk' as an
isolated group" (1988, 30). He goes on, in regard to the 1980s, "Folklorists' research of occupational folklife and workers' culture tended
to dwell on lower-level employees following an historical dichotomy
between 'workers' and 'management,' and tended to ignore the lore of
managers or of the organization as a whole" (31). According to Jones,
"Many folklorists attempt to divide an institution's population into
two camps, workers and managers, thereby distorting the complex
interrelations, loyalties, and interests of both those with and those

without supervisory responsibilities and erroneously concluding that workplace traditions are *always* in opposition to 'management' or 'the company'" (1991, 35 *emphasis in original*). Jones, too, is pointing to the closing distance between the scholar/researcher and the folk.

Although both perspectives exhibit changing definitions of "folk," discussions happening in other fields of study are echoed here, as McCarl represented a perspective in which there can be no separation between being a scholar and an activist—he seemed to argue that folklorists had already chosen a side— while Jones represented those who argued that as a field we should not take sides. In some ways, however, folklorists were choosing a side as they developed the discipline; after all, the category "folk" had from its beginnings included only Others on the margins. "Folkloristics ostensibly focused on the poetics and politics of a vanishing social class, the folk, and this concern has forced practitioners from the very beginning of this discipline to continually address and redress the notion of who the folk/Volk are" (Bendix 1997, 155). It is tough to argue—and we are not—that our early disciplinary ancestors were advocates for the folk, as the folk were all too often seen as vessels containing the lore in need of harvesting before it vanished. As Bendix reminds us, "the Grimms' efforts were dedicated to uncovering and understanding an anonymous or collective authenticity" (1997, 67). Arguably, however, something like advocacy grew out of the persistent equation of folk with marginalized groups, including examples that we look back on with regret (e.g., Alice Fletcher's role in the passage of the Dawes Act and John Lomax's paternalistic attitude toward his Black informants). As we've been reminded by those such as Shuman and Briggs, "Folklore is always already a politics of culture" (1993, 112). By the 1980s, certainly there had been a turn toward a fuller acceptance of the premise that, in the words of William A. Wilson, "we are all the folk" because, most simply, we all engage in folklore (Wilson 1989, 97). By advocating for studying all of those within an organization—managers as well as workers—Jones was demonstrating this broadening of the category "folk." So, too, was McCarl, as he expressed concerns about the potential consequences of publicly presented products of documentation.

At the same time, to enlarge the category "folk" to all, to include those in positions of power in a workplace, opens many questions, particularly for those, like Green and McCarl, who explicitly connected their scholarly work with activism. Kurt Dewhurst described this moment:

> Some of the other issues that came up, related to that, were certainly the fact that—who was being interviewed? . . . Our field was known for particularly focusing on yes, everyday life, but also capturing the voices of those whose voices hadn't been heard. And the sense of our civil and social responsibilities being front and center. Many people came to the field of folklore because of our [social and] political perspectives. And then all of a sudden you find yourself not interviewing a chairmaker in western Kentucky, but you're interviewing somebody who is an office worker . . . the folklore of the middle class or folklore of the business world. Those were big jumps and . . . there were questions about whether it was [ethically] appropriate . . . Could we really afford to spread out without giving up the long and hard-earned reputation for folklorists for doing responsible ethical fieldwork, being a model for how you value and build relationships and sustain relationships, and trust?[46]

While we often point to the early 1970s as the moment at which folklorists challenged central concepts and broadened categories, it is not as though a switch was flipped. As Amy Shuman argued not long after the debates about organizational folklore, "What we have seen since the period in which *Toward New Perspectives* was published is a *gradual* displacement of the field of folklore. The displaced elements included . . . the identification of 'the folk' with either peasants, male risk-taking occupational groups (loggers, whalers, etc.), or 'native,' tribal, or otherwise authentic others" (1993, 349, *emphasis ours*). Her use of "gradual" serves to remind us that the 1970s and '80s were a transitional period in the establishment of American folklore studies as an independent field. The thing about transition periods is that multiple, even incompatible, ideas coexist. Discussing changing paradigms in folklore studies in regard to both folk and group/community, Roger Abrahams points out, "Semantic drag sets in . . . and our thinking drags along with it" (1993, 22).[47] Though folklore studies is a small field, it is difficult to impossible for any folklorist to make a claim that truly represents the field as a whole. Jones and McCarl were each accusing the other of doing just that.

For some folklorists who recall this debate, it may be remembered as a disagreement between Robert McCarl and Michael Owen Jones, and it undoubtedly was that. But it was bigger than the two of them; viewed in retrospect, they each stood in for perspectives in the field in a time in which the disciplinary identity regarding social responsibility was still in the making. As we describe in chapter 2, the decade prior had seen debates about applied folklore, and although the plans for a Center for Applied Folklore were dropped, applied folklore itself was not, and many folklorists came to see their work as applied to some degree or another, including both Robert McCarl and Michael Owen Jones. Jones went on to edit *Putting Folklore to Use*, which included a range of ways in which folklore research was being applied by the 1990s (1994c). Meanwhile, there were folklorists who were increasingly understanding themselves as advocates for the communities with which they were working—whether "applied" or not. While McCarl critiqued organizational folklore as essentially divulging the secrets of workers without their permission or their control over it, Jones stressed that the best practice was for all involved to be aware of the goals of a project. Both felt the weight of social responsibility, as we think all those with the soul of a folklorist do. This debate demonstrates that, though shared, the weight is differently felt and carried.

NOTES

1. *Folklore/Folklife* also included essays entitled: "Folklore in Education," "Fieldwork," "Archives," "Material Culture and Folklore in Museums," "Folklore and the Federal Government," and "State and Local Folk Cultural Programs." It is surprising that a very new area of study was included in this short list of arenas in which folklorists had long worked (though state programs were somewhat new as well). None of the essays in the publication have a named author, though a lengthy list of contributors to the volume includes Michael Owen Jones.

2. Letter, Michael Owen Jones to Robert McCarl, March 28, 1985. From American Folklore Society records, 1890–2011. (COLL MSS 206.) Utah State University. Special Collections and Archives Department hereafter, "AFS Archives."

3. We thank Michael Owen Jones for generously providing a collection of both published and unpublished papers authored by him on the topic as well as a thorough bibliography.

4. Jones wrote such a guide; see Jones 1996.

5. C. Kurt Dewhurst, interview with the authors, July 2, 2021. Zoom.

6. Michael Owen Jones, email communication with the authors, October 9, 2018.

7. According to Michael Owen Jones, Robert McCarl attended the 1982 conference, and he recommended that representatives of labor unions be included in the larger conference planned for the following year. They were not included in the 1983 conference, and McCarl "declined to take part." (Email communication with the authors, October 9, 2018.) A special section entitled "Works of Art, Art as Work, and the Arts of Working" of *Western Folklore* 43 (3) was devoted to papers presented at this conference. See Jones 1984b; MacDowell 1984; Dewhurst 1984; Lockwood 1984; and Bell 1984.

8. According to the conference program, participating folklorists included Richard Raspa, Robert Georges, Sue Samuelson, Gary Alan Fine, Jay Mechling, Marsha McDowell, Kurt Dewhurst, Yvonne Lockwood, William A. Wilson, Patricia Atkinson Wells, Barbara Kirshenblatt-Gimblett, and others. On the organizational side, participants ranged from representatives of corporations such as Mattel and an aerospace company to those affiliated with schools of management, business, public administration, and organizational behavior. (Myth, Symbols, & Folklore: Expanding the Analysis of Organizations [conference program], March 10–12, 1983. Conference sponsored

jointly by the UCLA Center for the Study of Comparative Folklore and Mythology and Behavior and Organizational Science Group, Graduate School of Management, UCLA [AFS Archives]).

9. C. Kurt Dewhurst, interview with the authors, July 2, 2021. Zoom.

10. Patricia Atkinson, interview with the authors, March 16, 2022. Zoom. As noted in chapter 3, the AFS code of ethics was developed over a ten-year period by the State of the Profession Committee and was completed in 1988. See "AFS Statement on Ethics: Principles of Professional Responsibility," accessed May 23, 2025, https://americanfolkloresociety .org/our-work/position-statement-ethics.

11. This work by Jones is not unlike that found in *Work Hard and You Shall Be Rewarded: Urban Folklore from the Paperwork Empire* (Dundes and Pagter [1975] 1978). While Thomas Burns's review of *Work Hard and You Shall Be Rewarded* in the *Journal of American Folklore* is fairly critical, he does not question the study of folklore in an office: "Office personnel have repertoires of traditional materials, graphic and otherwise, that relate to the office" (1977, 86).

12. Malichi O'Connor, interview with the authors, August 10, 2021. Zoom.

13. Much has, of course, been written about this list and its implications. See, for instance, introductory folklore textbooks such as Brunvand (1998, 4) and Oring (1986, 8–9) as well as disciplinary histories including Bendix 1997, 126; Bronner 1986, 16; Moody-Turner 2013, 18; Roberts 2008; and Zumwalt 1988, 14. Also see essays on "The Concept of 'Folk'" in *100 Years of American Folklore Studies: A Conceptual History* organized around this list (Clements 1988).

14. For more on Newell, see Moody-Turner 2013, Zumwalt 1988, and Bell 1973, 1979.

15. For a list of the founding members, see Camp 1989, 10. The terms *local color* and *regionalism* are sometimes used interchangeably and at other times are used exclusively; they are frequently debated and contested.

16. See Bendix on the differing "construct of the American 'common man' . . . from the German *Volk* construct" (1997, 74).

17. See Bendix (1997, 142–43) on the special place of "song" in the early field.

18. Zora Neale Hurston's well-known fieldwork in Florida in the 1920s and '30s included folk song and narrative collection in lumber and turpentine camps and among other Black male occupational groups, yet she is not among the collectors most often listed as early pioneers of occupational folklore.

19. Of course there has been work focused on women's occupational folklore. See, for instance, Boyd 1997; Boynton 1988b.

20. By the fourth and most recent edition, he expanded these major groups to also include family and gender-differentiated groups, and he added religion to groups based on ethnicity and nationality (Brunvand 1998).

21. Interestingly, this is the same year of the folklore and feminism conference described in chapter 3, during which Judith Levin presented her paper arguing that folklorists should study housework, later published in *Feminist Theory and the Study of Folklore* (Levin 1993).

22. As McCarl (email communication with the authors July 12, 2021) and others have pointed out, Benjamin Botkin and other early folklorists had already demonstrated that of course the answer is "yes." Nickerson echoes the title of Richard Dorson's 1970 article, "Is There a Folk in the City?"

23. This included the factory in which his dissertation was based, as noted above as discussed by Jones.

24. According to Bendix, "Dorson saw himself as uniquely predestined to carry the banner of a newly focused and exclusively academic legitimized folkloristics" (Bendix 1997, 189) as he worked to build the discipline of folklore studies in the US, through the Folklore Institute at Indiana University in 1963 and the many folklorists he trained.

25. The ongoing "Working Americans" festival theme began in 1973, although "The presentation of working peoples' skills, crafts, and lore began in 1971 and continued in 1972 when the Union Workers programs featured ten member unions of the AFL-CIO." See "Working Americans," accessed May 23, 2025, https://festival.si.edu/past-program/1973/working-americans.

26. It's interesting to consider this argument, coming as it did in the years just prior to deep questioning of the consequences of ethnographic fieldwork in folklore and anthropology. Yet, even before the increasing attention to reflexivity, the writing of ethnography as a rhetorical act, and the "poetics and politics of representation," it is difficult to come up with ways that fieldwork might benefit a group that includes sharing that group's folklore without inadvertently sharing it with those with more power (i.e., management in this case). Further, if such collection is to lead to improved conditions, the results must somehow be shared.

27. The 1970s also saw a turn to the "ethnic group." According to Barbara Kirshenblatt-Gimblett, "The focus on ethnicity during the 1970s was, in its time, such a frontier, because the more interesting work challenged the

construct of folk group as a bounded social entity coterminous with its traditions, explored the socially situated nature of identity, applied sociolinguistics to the notion of multiple cultural repertoires, and offered concepts of tradition as a construction rather than an inheritance" (1983, 180). The focus on ethnic groups is also signified by Elliott Oring's chapter in his introductory textbook *Folk Groups and Folklore Genres*; "Ethnic Groups and Ethnic Folklore" is the only chapter devoted explicitly to "group" (1986).

28. Of course, these spaces were not as homogenous as the ideal might suggest, including in terms of race. For instance, despite the popular images of the American cowboy, "historians estimate that one in four cowboys were black" (Nodjimbadem 2017).

29. The motion would have been a vote by the membership present at the AFS Business Meeting. See Article XI, Section 5 of the AFS by-laws: "Five (5) percent of the Members in good standing shall constitute a quorum for transacting business at the Annual Business Meeting. The business of this meeting shall be transacted by a simple majority of those voting" ("Bylaws [2017–2022]," last updated 2017, https://americanfolkloresociety.org/about/bylaws). The annual AFS Business Meeting takes place during the annual meeting (Article XI, Section 4 of the AFS bylaws), and it has often been a place of discussion and debate as, for instance, discussed in chapter 3. According to the AFS Executive Board Minutes of May 21, 1985, "It was agreed that when supplies of the booklet were exhausted an editorial committee under the direction of PAFS editor Larry Danielson will be appointed to undertake revisions for the next edition" (5). The booklet was never reprinted.

30. Interestingly this was only about five years after the controversy involving the American Folklife Center's planned folklife project in the Tennessee-Tombigbee Waterway region, discussed in chapter 4, and suggests similar underlying tensions about folklorists taking "dirty money."

31. Jones offers additional critiques of McCarl's published work on DC firefighters here and elsewhere that are beyond the scope of this chapter. One example is the critiques offered by McCarl's major inside sponsor of this work, David A. Ryan, president of the Fire Fighters' Association of the District of Columbia, Local 36. McCarl published Ryan's critique in an expanded version of his original *Good Fire/Bad Night* (1980), and it is interesting because in some ways Ryan's description of the project supports Jones's argument that aspects of McCarl's work were essentially organizational folklore. For instance, Ryan wrote, "Although I felt Bob's image of the DC fire fighters was idealistic, I thought I could see the opportunity to get answers to some basic questions about the community to which I had

dedicated my life. If these answers could be established, there would be wide application in public relations, training, community relations, employee counseling, and even labor relations" (Ryan in McCarl 1985a, 30). Ryan also described a process in which he and others reviewed McCarl's draft and shared their thoughts with McCarl, who then made changes, particularly to one section (33). By asking members of the department to review his draft, making changes based on their comments, and even including Ryan's voice in his final product, McCarl was essentially experimenting with what would later be called reciprocal ethnography (cf. Lawless 1991; thanks to Jim Leary for pointing this out, personal communication.)

32. Memo from Michael Owen Jones to the AFS Executive Board, Subject: Revisions in *Folklore/Folklife*, October 15, 1985 (AFS Archives). In a letter dated 10 December 1984, AFS president Jan Brunvand asked if Jones was "interested in revising page 14, or at least having some input in the job" (AFS Archives).

33. The Centennial Coordinating Council was established in 1983; for details, see Camp 1989, 4.

34. This period saw reflection on the pitfalls of folklife festivals. Cf. Camp and Lloyd 1980 and, more broadly, Whisnant 1983.

35. See, for instance, along with McCarl's essay, Bob Byington's "What Happened to Applied Folklore?" and Lydia Fish, "The Folklorist as Community Organizer." Timothy Lloyd has edited a much expanded and updated collection modeled on *Time & Temperature, What Folklorists Do: Professional Possibilities in Folklore Studies* (2021), which includes over six dozen examples of the many things that folklorists do.

36. Elliott Oring served as the panel discussant, and his response begins, "Almost everyone seems to agree that something is wrong with folklore and that the future of folklore studies in the United States depends upon something being fixed or otherwise improved" (Oring 1991, 75). He goes on to argue that the answer is not "the forging of alliances" (79) with fields such as organization studies (or communication studies, as argued by Jay Mechling) but—as Oring had argued previously and continues to argue today (cf. Oring 1976, 2019)—that we have not made a distinct theoretical contribution; instead we seem "to draw willy-nilly from any and all scholarly traditions" (Oring 1991, 80).

37. C. Kurt Dewhurst, interview with the authors, July 21, 2021. Zoom. Insertions in brackets are clarifications requested by Dewhurst.

38. The creation and closure of these sections are documented in the Index of Executive Board Actions of the AFS, which includes actions taken by the board from 1987 through 2017 (See https://web.archive.org/web

/20250000000000*/https://cdn.ymaws.com/www.afsnet.org/resource
/resmgr/executive_board_minutes/Index_of_Board_Actions-FINAL
.pdf, accessed May 23, 2025). Annual meeting programs are available digitally through Indiana University Libraries.

39. The Index of Executive Board Actions of the AFS, which includes actions taken by the board from 1987 through 2017, does not include a record of the official closure of the section (See https://web.archive.org/web/20250000000000*/https://cdn.ymaws.com/www.afsnet.org/resource/resmgr/executive_board_minutes/Index_of_Board_Actions-FINAL.pdf, accessed May 23, 2025). There have been attempts to revive the section, including at least one meeting, during the 2011 AFS meeting.

40. Patricia Atkinson, interview with the authors, March 16, 2022. Zoom.

41. "Archie Green Fellowships," accessed May 23, 2025, https://guides.loc.gov/american-folklife-center-fellowships-internships/archie-green-fellowship.

42. See "Previous Archie Green Awardees," accessed May 23, 2025, https://guides.loc.gov/american-folklife-center-fellowships-internships/green-previous-awardees. The fellowships provide particularly important examples because while archived at the American Folklore Center and perhaps showcased through public presentation, much of this work does not necessarily make it into publication.

43. Michael Owen Jones, email communication with the authors, October 9, 2018.

44. As we describe in more detail in the conclusion, workers and members of the union were periodically holding what AFS referred to as "informational demonstrations" outside the hotel, and AFS argued that there was no "picket line" as the workers were not on strike. Through negotiations with the AFS staff, the union agreed not to hold demonstrations during the meeting itself.

45. Report and critique of AFS Focus on Social Justice Issues, October 2016, Miami, Florida. Robert McCarl.

46. C. Kurt Dewhurst, interview with the authors, July 21, 2021. Zoom. Insertions in brackets are clarifications requested by Dewhurst.

47. In his 2020 Francis Lee Utley Memorial Panel during the AFS Annual Meeting, folklorist Anand Prahlad pointed out that we are still dragging on this issue in a manner quite relevant to this chapter: "If folklorists really believed that everyone is the folk, where are all the articles and books about the 'non-exotic people,' for example, white professionals in business, law, the tech industry, politicians, the entertainment industry, suburban enclaves, and so on?" (Prahlad 2021, 260).

ONE STEP BACK AND TWO STEPS FORWARD

The Controversy over the Bills to Designate the Square Dance the American National Folk Dance

IN 1984, FOLKLORISTS FOUND THEMSELVES in a situation they had not been in before, mounting a challenge to a congressional effort to promote a form of expressive culture. Folklorists had spoken as a group to Congress some years earlier, in the years prior to and during the 1976 effort to pass the American Folklife Preservation Act (AFPA). But this time, we were opponents, writing and speaking to Congress to block a bill seemingly brought to Congress on behalf of tradition bearers. Why and how folklorists mounted opposition in 1984 and again in 1988 tie directly to folklore's commitment to cultural diversity in the face of melting pot Americanist ideology. This chapter explores the effort to make the square dance the national folk dance, how we came to be involved, the concerns folklorists had with that initiative, and the opposition to the effort that we presented to Congress in 1984 and 1988.

BACKGROUND TO THE EFFORT

Beginning in the early 1970s, square dance enthusiasts began pressuring Congress to make the square dance the American national dance. Petitions came from all over the country, describing the square dance as "clean and wholesome," "a traditional form of family recreation," and "a popular tradition in America since early colonial days" with "a revered status as part of the folklore of this country" (Pub. L. No. 97–188). Between 1971 and 2003, legislation was introduced to make square dancing the national folk dance in virtually every Congress. Most of the petitioners were associated with Western-style square dance clubs and associations with names like the Polka Dots, the Silver Buckles, Krazy Daizies, Ankle Knockers, See Saws, Curli Qs, Circle Squares, Surf Twirlers, Peat Dusters, Highland Hillbillies, Stanislaus Stumblers, Bootjack Stompers, Squarenaders, Squares & Flares, Boots & Bloomers, Skirts & Flirts, and Swing Ding Dandies. Western-style square dance organizations across the nation collaborated on these efforts organized largely by the California-based National Folk Dance Committee, which later became the American Folk Dance Committee of the United Square Dancers of America, Inc. Originally introduced as a bill to pass full designation of the square dance as the national dance, the bill later became limited in both time and scope. In 1982, S. Res. 59, a joint resolution designating the square dance the "national folk dance of the United States of America" sponsored by Senator Robert Byrd of D-West Virginia, was passed by the Ninety-Seventh Congress[1] *as amended.* The amendment to the original resolution, approved in the House with the Senate in agreement, stipulated that the square dance would serve as the national *folk* dance (rather than the national dance) and only temporarily, for 1982 and 1983. Two hundred and sixty-five members of Congress supported the amended legislation. Although Western square dance enthusiasts had won a significant battle in that 1982 resolution, the win was limited, and proponents were acutely aware that once 1984 arrived, the United States would once again be without a national dance, folk or otherwise. As a result, in 1984, Representative Norman Mineta of California, home to the largest of the enthusiast clubs, once again brought forward a square dance designation proposal, H.R. 1706.

Representative Mineta and others argued that square dancing represented the best of American history and heritage, promoting American values and etiquette. In his opening statement of the hearings[2] before the Subcommittee on Census and Population, Committee on Post Office and Civil Service, Congressman Mineta said,

> You will hear later on about whether or not the square dance is really representative of being an American dance. And you will [hear] testimony that the polka may be traditional for Balkan Americans, the hora for Jewish Americans, the Scottish country dance for Scottish Americans, and I will apologize because I am not really sure of the pronunciation of the word, but I believe that it is czardas for Hungarian Americans. But believe me, the square dance is indeed uniquely American. It is American American. It has been in our repertory of dances for over 300 years from the first colonies on into the formation of the union and to present day America. Square dancing has brought all Americans together in an activity which all groups in our society can participate. As the many ethnicities which comprise our great nation developed common life styles, customs, and visions, they have shared in this common expression of patriotism.[3]

Mineta also argued, "HR 1706 would designate the square dance as the national folk dance of America. Not the national dance, but to designate it as the national folk dance of America."[4] The Bill H.R. 1706 read,

> Be it enacted by the Senate and House of Representatives of the United States of America in Congress assembled, That the Congress finds that—
> (1) square dancing has been a popular tradition in America since colonial times
> (2) square dancing is a joyful expression of the vibrant spirit of the people of the United States,
> (3) the American people value the display of etiquette among men and woman which is a major element of square dancing,
> (4) square dancing is a traditional form of family recreation which symbolizes a basic strength of this country, namely the unity of the family,

(5) square dancing epitomizes democracy because it dissolves arbitrary social distinctions, and

(6) it is fitting that the square dance be added to the array of symbols of our national character and pride.

Following the hearing, H.R. 1706 died in committee with, as the chair noted, "insufficient support to mark up H.R. 1706 in its present form,"[5] only to be revived again in 1988 as H.R. 2067. Both hearings for H.R. 1706 and H.R. 2067 involved folklorists, and both revolved around similar sets of arguments on both sides of the issue. Advocates for the bills who were called as witnesses included principally leaders of Western square dance associations and square dance "callers." Opponents to the bills called to testify included African American, Latin American, and Native American dancers; dance historians; and professional folklorists. By 1988, folklorists had refined their opposition, and although the campaign by square dance clubs and enthusiasts to make the square dance a national dance continued until 2003, they made little headway, eventually turning their efforts to state legislatures to argue that the square dance be named the state dance, thus attempting to conquer the issue one state at a time.

ENTER THE FOLKLORISTS

So how did folklorists get to the table? Every legislative effort by Congress is appointed, if needed, temporary research assistance from the Library of Congress. On May 8, 1984, the Honorable William D. Ford, chairman of the Committee on Post Office and Civil Service of the House of Representatives, wrote to Daniel J. Boorstin, librarian of Congress, requesting the assistance of the American Folklife Center (AFC) in preparing for a hearing to be held June 28 on a bill designating the square dance as the national folk dance of the United States. Ford noted that Chairwoman Katie Hall particularly requested the assistance of folklorist Gerald Parsons, research librarian at the Archive of Folk Culture. Hall's

Hearings Held on the "Square Dance Bill"

On June 28, 1988, the Subcommittee on Census and the Population of the U.S. House of Representatives conducted hearings on H.R. 2067, a bill designating the square dance as the American folk dance of the United States. Members may recall that a hearing on a similar bill (H.R. 1706) was held on June 28, 1984, and that the American Folklore Society was one of several parties testifying in opposition to its adoption (see October 1984 *AFSNL*, p. 1). I am pleased to report the outcome of this year's hearing on H.R. 2067 is the same as that for H.R. 1706, and that the subcommittee has not recommended the resolution to the full Committee on the Post Office and Civil Service.

Last summer, after the resolution had been introduced and its proponents (principally members of Western square dance associations) had gathered sufficient support to schedule a hearing, I volunteered to organize opposing testimony on the Society's behalf. I took two actions that helped to set the course for the Society's efforts to successfully oppose the bill, first requesting that the AFS Executive Board adopt a resolution regarding the legislation, and second asking LeeEllen Friedland to help organize testimony.

The Society's resolution was approved by the Board on September 20, 1987 and is reprinted below. LeeEllen, whose writings on the square dance and folk dance in general, including the entry on square dance for the forthcoming *International En-*cyclopedia of Dance* had mapped the complex historical terrain on this issue, brought together the varied and complementary points of view of dance scholars, folklorists, and tradition bearers that comprised the case against the bill.

Those who testified against H.R. 2067 were folklorists Friedland and Rayna Green, ethnomusicologist Laura Courtney, Baltimore square dance caller Robert Dalsemer, tap dance master Honi Coles, and musician and Hispanic cultural activitist Juan Gutierrez. As in 1984, the scheduling of the hearing during the Smithsonian Institution's Festival of American Folklife enabled the Society to bring to the hearing representatives of culture groups participating in the Festival as well as local scholars.

Those who had supported the resolution were disappointed in the outcome of the hearing, but found much in the testimony—particularly that of LeeEllen Friedland—to illuminate the history of the dance forms they practice and enjoy. It may be that a learning relationship can be built between members of square dance associations and the folklorists and other scholars who study folk and popular dance. It was clear that without further mutual education the likelihood of similarly regrettable legislative proposals remains strong.

H.R. 2067 was not recommended by the subcommittee because of the strengths of the testimony LeeEllen and I organized in

(Continued on page 4)

Figure 6.1 "Hearings Held on the 'Square Dance Bill.'" The *AFS Newsletter* reported on the efforts of folklorists and the American Folklore Society to defeat the bills to designate the square dance the American national dance. *American Folklore Society News,* New Series 17 (3): 3 (1988). Courtesy of the American Folklore Society.

letter to Ford, also written on May 8, 1984, said, "I understand there is an individual within the American Folklife Center, Mr. Gerald E. Parsons, Jr. who is an expert in American folk culture. Mr. Parsons's assistance to my subcommittee until the time of the hearing would prove invaluable."[6]

Katie Beatrice Hall was the Indiana representative, African American, from Mississippi, and a longtime resident of Gary, Indiana, a steel mill town roughly twenty-five miles from downtown Chicago. Hall was a social studies teacher who served as US representative for Indiana from 1982 to 1985. Raised under segregation laws and unable to vote before the civil rights era, Hall was the first Black woman from Indiana elected to the US House of Representatives and only the fifth African American representative in US history. Although in the House only a short time, Hall led the drive to make Martin Luther King Jr.'s birthday a national holiday.

Many of Hall's comments and questions at the hearing suggest that she knew that the square dance was likely of little consequence to much of nonwhite America and also knew that a folklorist would be oriented toward providing a cultural diversity framework for understanding national symbols. Chairwoman Hall might have simply picked Parsons's name out of the phone book, and the paper trail provides little information on how the two met or if Hall was aware beforehand of Parsons's opposition to the bill. Certainly, Parsons's research files and questions he suggested for both proponents and opponents of the bill demonstrate the normal neutral stance required of the research assistance provided by the Library of Congress. Nevertheless, Representative Hall's specific request for Parsons combined with his engagement with the issue call into question Hall's prior knowledge of Parsons, his perspective, or the field of folklore. Since both are now deceased, we are unlikely to know for sure, but Margaret (Peggy) Parsons, Gerald's widow, thought it was likely that Hall either knew her husband or knew of his opposition to the national dance designation. Asked if she had any insight into their relationship before Hall requested Parsons, Margaret replied, "I'm quite certain that Katie Hall knew of Gerry because he was very vocal, behind the scenes, about resisting the designation of the square dance as the national folk dance. Gerry probably even wrote to Katie Hall to express his adamant point of view, though I do not know for sure. He talked and even wrote about this issue a lot during the '80s. The fact that Hall requested Gerry is not surprising. This was not a random choice."[7] What we do know for sure is that Hall requested Parsons's assistance in compiling research on the square dance issue, and Parsons, together with Charles (Charley) Camp, executive secretary-treasurer of the American Folklore Society (AFS), brought folklorists to the table.[8] Camp immediately contacted folklorist, dance historian, and convener of the AFS's Dance and Movement Analysis Section, LeeEllen Friedland. Not a dance scholar himself, Camp asked Friedland to help prepare the testimony and recruit speakers for the hearing. Friedland described the effort by saying, "There were assumptions . . . that were unspoken between Gerry and Charley and Charley and I that there were lots of cultural issues that needed to be brought to Congress' attention to consider this bill and whether or not it was worthwhile to support it . . . and of course we understood what they were and why they mattered."[9]

On June 18, 1984, the executive board of the American Folklore Society passed a resolution in opposition to the square dance bill.[10] The resolution provides a sense of how the executive board understood the issue and their responsibility to respond to the national folk dance initiative. It read,

> As an international organization of scholars and students of America's traditional life, the American Folklore Society approaches its centennial in 1988 with a proud record of professional interest in and commitment to the nation's folk songs, stories, customs, arts, music and dance. In the ninety-five years since our Society's founding folklore has become a recognized

and respected field of scholarly endeavor which has rigorously maintained the importance of interpreting the arts of a community or a culture according to the values and standards held by those who practice such arts. Through the efforts of its more than 1500 members, the Society today strives to honor the intellectual legacy formed by its founders: a profound respect for America's traditions and the varied cultures within our national boundaries which sustain them.

The value which our discipline places upon the spoken word, the observed gesture, and the repeated custom is based upon the belief that America's folk traditions are defined by the informal, community-based processes by which they are passed down within families, among co-workers, or between people whose lives are joined by a common faith, locale or national origin. America's traditions flourish in great part because Americans respect the languages which enable steelworkers or Polish-Americans, or Texans to express their shared cultural bonds. It is the respect Americans have for their neighbors' shared cultural bonds. It is the respect Americans have for their neighbors' culture which nourishes and protects the varied traditions which folklorists study and all Americans celebrate.

The American Folklore Society's commitment to these principles moves us to speak in opposition to House Resolution 1706, which designates the square dance as the national folk dance of the United States. The designation of a "national folk dance" serves neither those Americans for whom square dancing may be a traditional form of entertainment and social activity, nor those whose cultural background and upbringing have nurtured a preference for other types of traditional dance. America's cultural diversity may be directly attributed to the ability of our communities to practice in a spirit of freedom and mutual celebration those customs and arts which are uniquely their own. The identification of one dance as "the national folk dance" undermines the true meaning of the term "folk" and the degree to which all Americans may equally and proudly use it to draw attention to the traditional aspects of their lives and communities.

Americans justifiably take great pride in all of the traditions which express our cultural variety. The democratic spirit in which these traditions flourish also provides their greatest source of vitality and continuity, and it is that spirit which the American Folklore Society urges the congress to respect and maintain.[11]

Folklorists who testified in 1984 included Charley Camp, executive secretary of the AFS; Ralph Rinzler, assistant secretary for public service, Smithsonian Institution; Joe Wilson, executive director, National Council for the Traditional Arts; Bernice Johnson Reagon, director, Department of Black Culture, Smithsonian Institution; Thomas Vennum, Folklife Program, Smithsonian Institution; and John Vlatch, American Studies Department, George Washington University. Letters were also submitted by Archie Green, Rayna Green, Bess Hawes, Bruce Jackson, and Alan Lomax as well as by a few ethnomusicologists and dance ethnologists. The 1988 hearings included LeeEllen Friedland, independent folklorist and dance historian; Laura Courtney, folklorist and member of the Makah Indian Tribe; and Rayna Green, past president of the AFS and Cherokee, as well as tradition bearers—African American tap dancer and teacher LaVaughn Robinson and Juan Gutierrez, Latinx cultural activist and teacher.

AN AMERICAN SYMBOL

The 1984 bill was also framed initially by Congressman Leon Panetta of California and cosponsoring Congressman Earl Hutto of Florida, who argued that it was a dance that was "vital to American tradition," "a dance that celebrates the ideals of the country," and that the square dance evoked "a deep sense of patriotism in the hearts of all Americans."[12] For those who cosponsored the bill, it was important that patriotism be seen as the underlying argument, thus making the square dance appear to be a symbol, perhaps *the* symbol of American culture. Panetta argued, much like Mineta's earlier comment, "The Square Dance is indeed uniquely American. It is American American."[13] Chairperson Hall was more cautious in her opening statement:

One can look to an array of objects that are symbols of the United States. The log cabin, the pine tree, the coonskin hat, and the Kentucky rifle, all representative of our rich history. Even foods like corn on the cob, roast turkey, ice cream, apple pie and others are all natural wonders. Even the Grand Canyon, Niagara Falls and many other things team up to symbolize what our nation is all about. I am sure that you will agree with me that in this brief survey, we have barely scratched the surface of the wealth and the profusion of such elements. In our culture, they call forth the sense of the larger American experience. The purpose of this moment of reflection on America is to point out that among all of the things we have named, and that we Americans recognize as insignia of our existence among the family of nations, that there is not one that has been officially designated as such by the Congress of the United States.[14]

She questioned, "Should this American symbol, the square dance, be designated by such law by the United States Congress, and thus receive the stature that this nation has conferred upon the Anthem, the great seal, the flag and so many other of our standing symbols?"[15] Chairwoman Hall requested of those who testified that they "present information concerning the appropriateness of the square dance form as a symbol of the history and values of the American people."[16]

Numerous letters from proponents of the 1988 bill take the lead from Representative Hall's questions and either state directly or suggest the symbolic nature of the square dance as an essential American tradition. Ralph Case, leader of the Ralph Case Square Dancers and Cloggers, ended his letter to the committee saying, "In a world filled with so many trying times, passage of H.R. 2067 would represent a positive step in substantiating a cultural identity that is shared by millions of Americans."[17]

In the 1988 hearing, Congressman Leon Panetta concluded his opening remarks by replying to Representative Hall's questions:

> We have great diversity, but we also have a number of symbols that give us unity. These of course include our flag, our national

anthem, and our national bird, the eagle. Recently two other specific designations were made: one of the rose as the American Flower, and earlier in this Congress, of the Stars and Stripes by John Philips Sousa as the National March. Square Dancing, which, as I mentioned, incorporates a variety of dance forms, deserves national recognition as much as these other symbols. It is truly, I feel symbolic of the vitality, diversity, and wholesomeness of this country. For these reasons, I hope that the Committee will favorably report H.R. 2067 and that Congress will then adopt it.[18]

Opposition writers and speakers also addressed the national symbol issue by opposing the idea of there being a single dance that could stand as a symbol of the United States. Ralph Rinzler, assistant secretary for public service at the Smithsonian Institution and panelist in the 1984 hearing, said,

> The term folk means a traditional dance originating among the common people of a nation, or a music accompanying such a dance, or a social gathering at which such dances are performed. The common use of the term folk implies the existence of a particular ethnic group or subculture, or the inhabitants or a given regional group or regional culture, if you will. Given the subcultural connotations of this term folk—and the point has been made several times this morning that this would not be the national dance, but the national folk dance—I as a folklorist find it difficult to comprehend, especially in a multicultural society like ours, how one could have a "national folk dance."[19]

Folklorist Joe Wilson, longtime executive director of the National Council for the Traditional Arts, testified in 1984 that "the strength of our nation's folk culture lies in its diversity. . . . Pressures toward standardization and official status should always be resisted. In order to make such a selection, the congress would have to pass over many dances that are older and have deeper roots in this nation." He continued, "My organization sees no good reason for the Congress to make what in essence is a value judgment about the folk dances of the United States by selecting one as the national folk dance."[20] Echoing Rinzler and Wilson, Charley Camp told us, "Any public folklorist will tell you, there is no National anything when it comes to folklore."[21] Camp wrote,

> The designation of an "American" or "National" folk dance serves neither those Americans for whom square dancing is a traditional form of entertainment and social activity, nor those whose cultural background and upbringing have nurtured a preference for other types of traditional dance. . . . The identification of one dance as "the American Folk Dance" undermines the true meaning of the word "folk" and the degree to which all Americans may equally and proudly use the word to draw attention to the traditional aspects of their own lives and communities. (Camp 1988, 3–4)

While the "no one dance" resistance to the bill featured in the comments of folklorists, this was more a way to lead into important issues of pluralism and diversity than a concern with the sanctity of designated symbols.

In both 1984 and 1988, in addition to the folklorists who addressed Congress in person, numerous letters were submitted to the House committee concerning the issue of designated symbols. In June 1984, the National Council for the Traditional Arts under the leadership of John Holum submitted a draft resolution to Chairwoman Hall arguing in part, "Many Americans, ourselves among them, are particularly proud of our nation's remarkable diversity. For us it is of special symbolic value that our government grants to no craft, no dialect, no music style, no drama, no folktale, no region, no trade, no sport, and no dance a status that raises it above the others. With this in mind, we ask the congress not to reject square dancing (an activity that we ourselves have fostered for more than five decades) but rather to preserve a greater symbol of this nation's genius for diversity."[22] Like Holum and Camp, several folklorists tried in their submissions to the committee to stress that the notion of a single national dance ran counter in every way to the diversity at the heart of the very concept of folk culture.

NOT YOUR MAMA'S SQUARE DANCE

As Chairwoman Katie Hall looked around room 311 of the Cannon House Office Building as the national folk dance hearings began in June 1984, she was clearly struck by a somewhat more colorful audience of spectators than was typical of congressional hearings. Hall commented, "This morning, we will start by hearing some of the most colorful testimony in America's history. And we are very pleased to have you with us. One word that comes to my mind when I think about this proposal is colorful costumes. Certainly, when I look around the room, I see a lot of beautiful colors, beautiful costumes."[23]

The audience Chairwoman Hall saw before her was filled with what are sometimes called "club square dancers," those associated with Western-style square dance clubs and associations. Club square dancers commonly wear Western-style square dance outfits or "square dance attire," costumes that are frequently regulated by club dress codes. Inspired by Western movies and popular styles of the 1950s and 1960s, club square dance attire includes Western-style shirts, cowboy boots, cowboy hats, and bolo ties for men and colorful wide skirts or dresses, puff-sleeved blouses, and multiple layers of crinolines (or petticoats) for women.

The *Square Dancing Indoctrination Handbook* published by *Sets in Order* magazine included details of the dancers' expected costume. The booklet was cited in the 1984 hearing[24] as a publication issued to the learners and membership of the United Square Dancers of America and articulated what the volume noted was "a minimal standard of performance which should be acquired before being able to dance." On the issue of women's costumes, the book, which emphasized femininity and modesty, said, "Square dance dresses give a truly feminine look and through various patterns, materials and trims complement any lady's figure. Petticoats come in many choices of fabrics, colors and fullness. Some type of pettipant is worn to add an appreciated decorum to the activity."[25] The images in the book emphasized the flouncy skirts and poufy undergarments associated with modern Western square dance, costumes that, like the 1950s poodle skirts they were based on, emphasized teenage femininity.

In March 1996, Bess Lomax Hawes, retired director of the Folk and Traditional Arts Program at the National Endowment for the Arts, responded by letter to an article on square dancing in the February 1996 issue of *Smithsonian Magazine*, reflecting on the costumes illustrated there. The cover showed a somewhat childlike woman, dressed in square dance costume with numerous crinolines and an apron, smiling and winking over her shoulder. The caption read, "A frisky modern square dancer shows off her elaborate costume" (Hubbell 1996, 92).

The cover picture was more than Lomax Hawes could take. In an unpublished letter to Don Moser, editor of *Smithsonian Magazine*, Hawes wrote,

> *Dear Sir:*
>
> *It takes a lot to get me to put my feminist hat on these days—there are so many other things to get outraged about—but the February 1996 issue of the Smithsonian has finally done it.*
>
> *The cover is sexist and condescending, the photographs illustrating the lead article (pps 94–99) no better. I was so irritated; I almost didn't read the article itself. When I did, it turned out that Maggie Steber had done a professional piece on a complicated situation, but those cutesy illustrations distorted her research and didn't suggest a truly serious conflict that is going on.*
>
> *The fact is that the National Square Dancing Convention has dedicated itself to a cause that has engendered nation-wide concern: to make the square dance (their version, complete with baby-doll skirts) "the national dance of the United States." I myself, along with*

Figure 6.2 Women's square dance wear. Flouncy skirts and poufy under-garments associated with modern Western square dance, from "What to Wear," Square Dancing Indoctrination Handbook, *Sets in Order* magazine, The American Square Dance Society.

> *folklorists from the Smithsonian and the Library of Congress, have,*
> *in several previous years, testified before Congress in opposition to*
> *their bill. Our view was and is that no single dance form can represent*
> *our complex national unity. The election of national symbols is a*
> *complex task: consider the polka, tap dance, round dance, hip hop,*
> *mambo, hula, etc., each identifying varied American populations. Is*
> *the square dance to be elevated above all these others to the status of*
> *the national anthem, the American flag?*
>
>   *Don't you folks ever consult your own experts within your own*
> *institution? Any folklorist at the Center for Folklore Programs*
> *and Culture Studies could have filled you in on the complex issues*
> *involved in this "amusing" little article.*[26]

While Hawes was deeply irritated by the over-feminized, child-like portrayal of women in the cover photograph and in women's modern Western square dance clothing in general, her comment "*their version,* complete with baby-doll skirts" illustrates the tie between the clothing Chairwoman Hall saw in front of her at the hearings and one of the central problems that created the intensity of folklorists' opposition to the square dance bill. The square dance put forward by proponents of the bill was the modern Western square dance also known as the "club square dance." According to LeeEllen Friedland, "Following the Second World War there was an explosion of interest in organized Western square dancing and clubs formed all over the country" (Friedland 1998, 689).

Unlike the dance that some of our mothers learned at barn dances or at the town dance hall or even the one many of us were forced to learn in elementary school, the modern Western square dance was a more complicated matter. Julianne Mangin ([1995] 2017) writes that the modern Western square dance put forward by the clubs required that dancers become competent and certified in sixty-six different square dance figures, involve knowledge of one hundred square dance "calls," and use recorded music rather than live music. By contrast, the traditional square dance, the one your mother might have danced and the one we learned in school, required learning only a few dozen calls; lessons and certification were not necessary, although a "walk-through" might take place at the very beginning of the dance; and recorded music was a rarity at traditional events. Mangin also notes that there is a whole industry associated with club square dancing, which includes the selling of a variety of products and services, costumes, amplification, and recording and dance paraphernalia while traditional square dancers wear street clothes and require very little in the way of accoutrements.

Putting forward the club dance as the national folk dance made no sense at all to folklorists. Furthermore, dance historians were puzzled by the historical record put forward by the square dance enthusiasts. As dance historian Gretchen Adel Schneider told the hearing,

> As a scholar in American dance, I do not see what they allege. What I do see is that organized, recreational, and professional- ized square dancing is a remarkable phenomenon that has grown since the 1920s. Participants in the form have mythologized and created "an American folk dance" in the absence of one. Such a creation has virtually nothing to do with historical traditions or traditional community life, but popular culture. Such a modern creation is not trivial, it is a significant and vital development in our culture. Like Santa Claus and the Easter Bunny, the desire for some Americans to have an American folk dance has been strong and cannot be ignored. . . . The essential point is that there is no relation between the creation of the modern Square Dance (a created American Folk Dance) and the colonial and early nineteenth-century history of dance in America. The modern Square Dance is not a hybrid of historical dance from three centuries of life in the United States, but it is a vital twentieth- century hybrid created by well-meaning enthusiasts.[27]

Traditional dances practiced in the US have been catego- rized, according to Friedland, choreographically into three main regional groupings: the Northeastern square dance, largely derived from nineteenth-century quadrilles; the Southeastern form, an "Americanized form developed from shared European patterns and aesthetics that were shaped by immigration and frontier experience in the New World" and that was essentially circular in formation; and the Western square dance, which developed from a confluence of these Northeastern and Southeastern forms in the nineteenth century as the territories west of the Mississippi were peopled by settlers from these regions (Friedland 1998, 687).

Modern Western square dance, on the other hand, was developed in the 1930s. An educator from Colorado, Lloyd Shaw, began teaching square dance patterns and calls from his region to his own students. Eventually Shaw became more ambitious and began to train exhibition dance teams, taking them to festivals, contests, and conferences around the country to demonstrate their "cowboy dances" (Friedland 1998, 689). Shaw used the framework of the traditional Western square dance but introduced the idea of all four couples dancing throughout a dance with no inactive time. From there Shaw introduced more and more complicated routines danced to an increased tempo. Before long he began offering training seminars. In the late 1940s, according to Friedland, square dance recreational clubs sprang up in many parts of the United States, initially drawing on regional dance forms but increasingly using Shaw's version of the modern Western square dance. By the early '50s, square dance clubs were growing in popularity, and products and services developed for the clubs flooded the market. The modern Western square dance repertory expanded quickly, eventually making it impossible for occasional dancers to keep up with the expanding number of figures and eventually grouping dancers into a variety of levels of achievement (Friedland 1998).

Bob Dalsemer, the square dance caller who testified in opposition to the 1988 bill, argued that Congress was being asked to adopt the entire lifestyle, including classes, costumes, badges, and levels of complexity, things that square dancers outside of the Western movement do not choose. Dalsemer testified as both a traditional square dancer and caller and someone who had been trained in a club. He testified,

> However, you must realize that in order to dance in a modern Western square dance club, you must take lessons for up to forty weeks. The class that I attended began in September and ran through May. I took two and a half hours of weekly lessons per week in order to graduate from a class in order to be able to dance in the club. And even then, the club that I was to dance in required one to learn 25 or 30 more figures in order to be able to comfortably dance. Modern square dancers must know a hundred calls approximately. This is at the plus level. Approximately a hundred calls, of which I would say only 25 existed before 1955.[28]

Opening comments of the bill's sponsors, who conflated both traditional square dance and modern Western square dance, suggested that being asked to adopt the entire lifestyle was indeed a part of the effort and reflected what Charley Camp referred to as a "campaign" by the clubs to promote their form of square dance. Representative Panetta, in his opening statement in 1984, specifically cited the dance clubs, saying about the square dance,

> We are talking about a dance that has been a vital American tradition since something like 1651. And it has evolved into, I think, the most popular participatory dance in the United States today. It is reflected by the number of square dance clubs[29] and the number of people that are a part of it. I think that something like 8500 square dance clubs exist throughout the nation in the United States. And something like 6 million dancers are parts of those clubs, not to mention obviously the millions of school children that participate in square dancing on a daily basis in their schools.[30]

Mineta said, "If the square dance is formally made our national folk dance, it will become even more visible in our society, and will give schools and other institutions further impetus to teach this rewarding activity."[31] Ironically Dalsemer ends his formal statement with a quote from the 1936 book *Cowboy Dances* by Lloyd Shaw: "Shaw wrote, 'One last word. Please do not teach these dances to little children. Grade school pupils may enjoy them, but it will mark the dances forever in your community with the stigma of kid stuff.'"[32]

STIRRING THE DANCING MELTING POT

Crucial to the proponents' case for the square dance as the national folk dance was a series of assertions about both the historical provenance and cultural representativeness of square dance. David and Dorothy Borchard testified, "With the roots of Square Dancing coming from all over the world and having been modified to fit our culture; and the interest and participation of dancers counting in the millions in the U.S.; we can think of no better designation as the National Folk Dance of the United States of America than the American Square Dance."[33]

The supporters of H.R. 1706 frequently asserted 1651 as the origin date for the square dance and virtually the whole world as the geographical source of the dances. The Borchards told the hearing,

> Since 1651 the Square Dance has consistently been the one dance traditionally recognized by the American people as a dignified and enjoyable expression of American Folk Dancing. Square Dancing is a part of our history, the history of our settlers. Like everything else, when the settlers came to this country they brought their dancing backgrounds with them from Europe, Africa, and north and south of our borders. The elegant quadrille got involved with the country dance of the backwoods area, the lilting Quebec Swing got all mixed up with the uproarious New Hampshire "contry"; a circle mixer from Maine made an alliance with a "longways dance" from New York State.[34]

The bill's supporters clearly felt that inclusivity approaches would assist in their legislative goals. Representative Panetta underscored inclusivity in his opening statement by emphasizing the square dance as an amalgam of other dance traditions:

> It also, I think, celebrates some important ideals of the country in the sense that it is really a dance that includes people of all ages, all races, all colors, all creeds. It includes the handicapped now, and the healthy. It includes all of those that are now part of the broad spectrum of American life.
>
> In addition to that, square dancing, I think, is the one dance which incorporates the folk dance traditions of a large number of ethnic and cultural groups in this country. It evolved really as an amalgamation of the Morris and Maypole dances of England, the ballroom dances of France and the Spanish church dances.
>
> And later as immigrants from all over the world came to our shores, the square dance incorporated the folk traditions of nations like Ireland, Germany, Poland, Austria, Italy, Mexico, to name but a few.
>
> The term square dancing, it should be pointed out, also includes a number of other folk dances that are popular in specific regions of the United States. Round dancing, contra dancing, clogging, line dancing and the Virginia Reel have all been designated as square dancing by State and national square dance conventions.[35]

Opponents of the bill continually pointed to the amalgam theory as based on a fictionalized genealogy. As Colin Quigley writes, "The mythologized genealogy of modern Western square dancing, although listing a good many dance forms showing morphological and structural relationships and including a few instances of demonstrable historical genetic connection, was constructed to culminate in 'today's square dance' in a way that both authenticates its roots in ancient folk practice, and demonstrates a democratizing Americanization process leading to an inclusive American amalgam" (2001, 149).

Indeed, the approach by proponents of the bill to criticisms of the square dance bill as representing only a slice of American pluralism and diversity was to create a genealogical narrative, illustrated in a family tree of dance, a family tree intent on showing inclusiveness. Friedland notes, "They sought to construct an argument toward equity, a version of equity. Which I think they elaborated as they . . . tried to strengthen their presentations to Congress."[36] A genealogical chart of dances from around the world from 1450 to the present and representing everything from Morris dancing to French Ballroom dancing to Play Parties and Mexican Court dancing, leading to the (modern Western) square dance, was entered into evidence at the hearing. The chart, one of many that evolved over time, according to Friedland, was likely created (at least originally) by Dorothy Shaw,[37] wife of Lloyd Shaw (Quigley 2001, 148). According to Friedland, testifying in opposition and challenging the historical narrative directly, the genealogy "inherits and perpetuates . . . grievous errors and outdated misconceptions."[38] The genealogical chart exemplifies a square dance origin narrative meant to demonstrate a focus on diversity, pluralism, and inclusivity illustrated as a historical and global melting pot.

BACKDROPS AND A SOMEWHAT UGLIER HISTORY

In May 2018, a member of the folklore LISTSERV Publore posted a YouTube video called "the secret racist history of square dancing,"[39] noting the flawed nature of the film and opening up a discussion of the links between square dance and racist ideology.[40] The film was making the rounds at the time, not just in folklore circles but in dance and race and culture circles as well. The argument put forward by many of those replying to the Publore post was that the square dance revival of the early and mid-twentieth century had racist undertones and motivations, and thus efforts

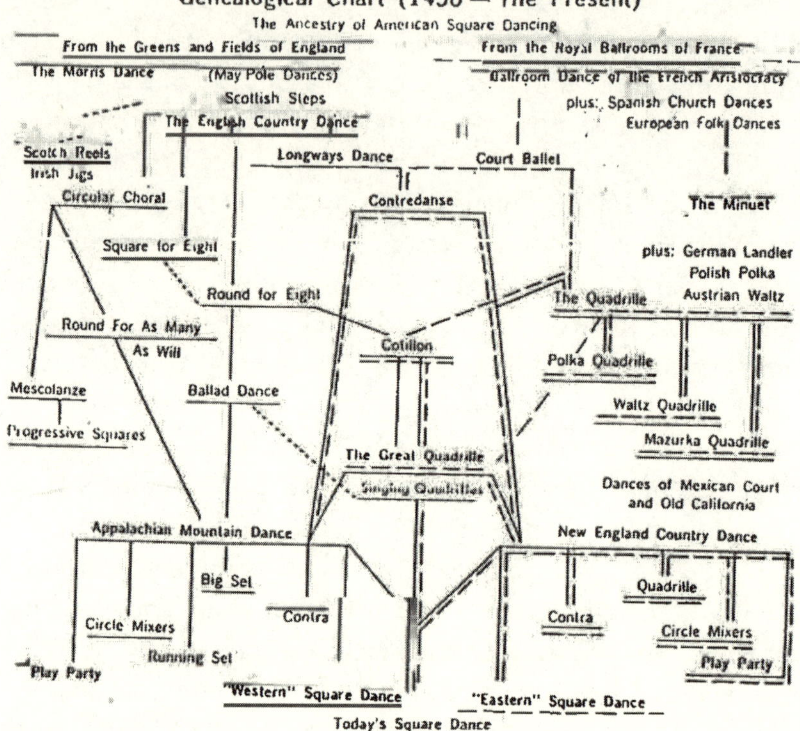

Figure 6.3 Genealogical chart (1450–the present) depicting the ancestry of American square dancing from the point of view of the modern Western square dancers. From Ninety-Eighth Congress, H.R. 1706, public hearing, "A Bill to Designate the Square Dance as the National Folk Dance of the United States" June 28, 1984.

to grant it official status should be denied. Although these issues did not explicitly enter the hearings, concerns about the connections of the square dance to racist and antisemitic ideology, particularly through the promotion of the square dance by Henry Ford, are frequently mentioned in relation to the square dance bill both casually online and in publications, suggesting it likely existed as a backdrop to concerns about the national folk dance effort.[41]

Many people associate the politics of square dance with the efforts of Henry Ford, the car maker and philanthropist. In 1924, Henry Ford founded the Ford Motor Company Music Department, intending to revive "old fashioned dancing and early American Music." From 1923 until his death in 1947, Ford poured enormous amounts of money into reviving what he called "Old American" music and dance, hiring a full-time dance master who stayed on Ford's payroll for over twenty years, underwriting the salaries of an old-time dance orchestra, paying for the dance education of hundreds of university students and thousands of Michigan schoolchildren, covering the costs of writing and production of several dance manuals, financing more than twenty old-time musical recordings, buying and restoring three historic inns that he transformed into dance venues, building a large dance hall in Dearborn, Michigan, and creating numerous radio broadcasts and film shorts of old-time music and dance (La Chapelle 2011, 30).

Ford was intent on promoting the music and dance that he associated with nineteenth-century agrarian America. He deplored the popular music of the early twentieth century, especially jazz music and dancing, which he saw as creating the atmosphere for alcohol, tobacco use, and sexual license. Society, according to Ford, was being damaged by those who promoted jazz, African Americans, recent immigrants, and especially the Jewish people (Warnock 2009, 79). In his pamphlets and volumes, which Ford titled *The International Jew*, Ford railed against Jews particularly on topics of organized labor unions, Jewish control of the press, and Jewish influence on the American arts. As Warnock notes of Ford, "His well-documented anti-Semitic beliefs and writings influenced his promotion of early American folk music and dance" (80). Ford's vision was to create a more perfect society through American folk dance and music. In *The International Jew*, Ford accuses Jews of distorting the music industry in America and of ruining Anglo-Saxon Americans' taste for their own cultural music heritage. In chapter 11, "Jewish

Jazz Becomes our National Music," Ford writes about how the American Jewish community monopolized, culturally and economically, contemporary American popular music.

> It is the purpose of this article to put people in possession of the truth concerning the moron music which they habitually hum and sing and shout day and night, and if possible to help them to see the invisible Jewish baton which is waved above them for financial propaganda purposes. Just as the American stage and motion picture have fallen under the control of Jews and their art-destroying commercialism, so the business of handling "popular songs" has become a Yiddish industry. The Jews who captured it in the early days of exploitation were for the most part Russian-born Jews, some of whom had personal pasts which were unsavory as the past of many Jewish theatrical and movie leaders have been exposed to be. (Ford 1921, 1)

In 1925, Ford began to explicitly reeducate the dancing public. He used his antisemitic ideas to denounce jazz and promote round and quadrille (square) dances. He wrote,

> The modern dances with their lesser demand for skill and spirit, their tuneless music, their tendency to jazz, their essential unsociability, are losing vogue everywhere. Unless a dance be sociable it cannot live long, unless it promote the spirit of play it will soon weary its devotees, and it is just here that dances requiring eight or twelve or sixteen persons as the unit for their performance make their appeal. More persons thrown together, the spirit of grown up play is irresistible, and besides there is a wider scope and a stronger demand for skill and style. The bane of the modern dance was its almost utter lack of grace, style and skill. (Ford 1926, 30)

Not only did Ford promote square dance and old-time music to local dancing audiences, but he also saw dance and music as crucial to creating a productive workforce. Katherine Brucher argues that "dance hall reform emerged from a broader movement" by Ford "to reform workers' leisure time" (2016, 476). As part of Ford's "industrial paternalism" (471), which sought to remake workers' "hygiene, factory routine, citizenship" and leisure, in 1914 he opened the Ford English School to teach immigrant workers about Anglo-American culture. Brucher describes Ford's approach to American culture as tied figuratively and literally to the notion of the American melting pot.

> The graduation ceremonies of the Ford English School quite literally staged a performance of assimilation to Anglo-American culture, foreshadowing Ford's belief that by changing appearance and comportment, one could be remade as an "American." At one such event, the stage featured a large cauldron—a melting pot—stirred by Ford executives. One hundred and fourteen graduates entered the cauldron from one side wearing clothing emblematic of their home country and exited the other side dressed in suits and waving American flags. The spectacle and symbolism signaled Ford's belief that assimilating immigrants to Anglo-American culture would produce better workers. (478)

The foundations of melting pot theory are generally tied to a French immigrant, J. Hector de Crevecoeur, who, in 1782, first used the metaphor to discuss a completely new race he envisioned for America. In 1908, playwriter Israel Zangwill popularized the notion in a play entitled *The Melting Pot* that explored the then-booming immigration from northwestern Europe (Berray 2019, 142). The metaphor rose and fell over the years, particularly in relation to changing concepts of the importance of homogeneity. While it is completely discredited today, at the beginning of the twentieth century "the melting pot" was supported by some liberals as well as those who strove to preserve America from foreign influence.[42]

MOSAICS, NOT MELTING POTS

For folklorists, the challenge of the hearings was to make it clear that a melting pot ideology applied to expressive culture was both not accurate and not respectful of the nation's traditions. As the AFS's resolution argued, "America's cultural diversity may be directly attributed to the ability of our communities to practice in a spirit of freedom and mutual celebration those customs and arts which are *uniquely* their own" (*emphasis ours*).[43]

For both the 1984 and the 1988 hearings, Friedland and Camp looked not only to folklorists to testify as experts but also to tradition bearers to illustrate the relationship of their own communities both to their own dance traditions and to the square dance. As Camp said, "When a group of private citizens are seeking some kind of blessing from the government the best approach to denying them that is not to have representatives of a bunch of federal agencies saying that they don't deserve it." Speaking of the tradition bearers who testified, he continued, "they spoke with a lot of articulation about how important their dance was to them. And that's the same thing that the square dancers said. . . . How could we give this honor to one dance and thereby shut out these others, these many others?" [44]

The scheduling of the hearing both years during the Smithsonian Institution's Festival of American Folklife[45] enabled the AFS to bring to the hearing representatives of culture groups participating in the festival (Camp 1988). Introduced in 1984 by Ralph Rinzler, two traditional dancers were brought forward. Rinzler was brief in his own comments, putting his longer written testimony into record. He noted in part,

> Such a term [national folk dance] appears to us to be a self-contradiction, as folk is usually associated with a subculture, and national indicates belonging to or representing all. To make something national would from the point of view of folklorists, and I think from the point of view of many people in traditional communities around this country numbering several million, strip the tradition of its folk characteristics.
>
> For example, if we assume that a certain Anglo-American dance tradition is representative of the whole society, we overlook the multifarious dance traditions of Africa, Europe, Asia, the

Middle East and Native American origin, in which millions of Americans like the two gentlemen with us this morning actively participate.[46]

Rinzler continued his argument, using the hearing as an opportunity not only to educate those present but also to promote the festival.[47] He said,

> And as one who is interested in the study and preservation of customs and traditions and all of their appealing diversity, as we see them on the Mall today, and may I respectfully invite you and members of the committee to join us at the Folklife Festival in the next two weeks—it will be closed Monday and Tuesday; but through the 8th of July, otherwise it will be running full-time—there you will see a variety of different kinds of dance, each one passionately practiced by people like those who have joined us here today, eloquent not only with their voices, but with their bodies, hands and feet.[48]

The statements from the two dancers were very brief. Paul Tiolono, from the King Island Eskimo Group of Alaska, said in part, "I never remember hearing or seeing any square dancing in my area. . . . And I would highly recommend the committee to study more about Anupiak dancing before you make a decision on which is going to be the national dance for America. Because our Anupiak dancing was done before the Europeans came to America."[49] LaVaughn Robinson, tap dancer from Philadelphia, Pennsylvania, and instructor at the Philadelphia College of the Performing Arts, said, "One of the main things I would like to say is to say that to make folk dancing a national dance would be a slap in the face to other arts as far as dance is concerned. The Afro-American dance, the Indian folk dance, and other dances of that sort."[50]

The perceived impact of the words of tradition bearers on the hearing, illustrating the importance of both recognizing diversity and celebrating distinctiveness, inspired Camp and Friedland to pursue this same strategy when, after the 1984 bill died in committee, it arose again in 1988. Friedland indicated that by 1988, it was clear to the folklorists involved that the right strategy to challenge the bill was not to rely on academic experts but instead, as they did in 1984, to select community members who could speak eloquently on behalf of their communities and their traditions. Friedland explained,

> I felt for the 1988 testimony that I wanted to assume that the members of Congress and their staffers would know about those things or would know about it in a way that they could relate to. You know, to read a statement summarizing what you just said is one thing but to see, hear, hear someone in front of you from this person's district or that person's district and talk about what happened to them, to their parents, to their community, is a different thing. And I felt that that's where the power lay and the potential for us to counter the view of the proponents for this, for the bill where we didn't have to say, "You proponents of the bill are bad people or what you're promoting is worthless or you care about it and nobody else does."[51]

Once again, the Smithsonian Institution's Festival of American Folklife assisted in bringing the speakers to Washington. This time the tradition bearers were given longer to speak.

Charles "Honi" Coles, actor, past president of the Negro Actors Guild, manager of the Apollo Theater, singer, tap dancer, and teacher,[52] spoke. He began,

> I would like to preface my main statement by saying that I have nothing against square dancing. I think it is very, very well done. It looks gorgeous, and it is a very, very family associated dance. I have yet to hear—I hear about where square dancing came from, its origin, and all I hear is Europe and England. I don't hear anything else. And I am here representing black people. I assure you; I could walk up and down 125th Street and shout, "Square dance! Square dance!" And nobody would have the faintest idea what I would be talking about. Consequently, I can't for the life of me realize square dancing becoming recognized as the national

American dance. I love it and all of that, but I just can't see that
at all. And that is just about what I have to say. If there is nothing
black-oriented in the world, and when you say dance, automatically you think of black. You think black when you say dance. You
think joy. You think happiness. You think abandon.... But I am
a tap dancer and there are more tap dancers in the United States
than there are square dancers.[53]

Congressman Mervyn Dymally, a Caribbean American, was
chairing this part of the hearing and made it clear that he knew of
Mr. Coles's distinguished reputation. He indicated after Coles's
testimony, "I saw you at the Apollo many times and I read the
story about the Capezio Award."[54]

Perhaps the most moving of the witness testimonies came
from folklorist, former president of the AFS, and representative of the Cherokee Nation of Oklahoma, Rayna Green. Green
highlighted the comparative provenance of Native American
dance traditions and the importance of diversity within those
traditions.

> I have heard people say they represent over 200 years of Ameri-
> can dance tradition. I represent 30,000 years of American dance
> tradition. Should the national dance be the oldest? If that was the
> truth, the round dance as it is practiced by Native peoples would
> be the dance. It would be the round dance, the true round dance,
> not a ballroom form practiced by couples.... However even our
> tribal peoples would have difficulty choosing whose round dance
> Smithsonian Institution's Festival of American Folklife if that
> standard were to be applied. Would it be a Cherokee, a Sioux, a
> Makah, a Navajo, Crow, Cree or Seneca dance?[55]

Green continued,

> I speak about this passionately because of the strange history we
> have in America. When my grandmother was a girl and when
> my great-grandmother was a child, they were forbidden to speak
> their language, forbidden to dance their dances by the American
> government and by missionaries in this country. They were

forbidden to have our ceremonies. They were forbidden to wear our ceremonial clothes. How ironic I think it would be if my grandmother, who danced the square dance in school—the only place she ever danced it—but could not dance her own tribal dances, were now to be dishonored, and all of our ancestors were to be dishonored, in fact, with the designation of a dance that represented the overturn and the repression of our own dances. It was a miracle to us that those laws were repealed forbidding our forms of dance, even as African dance and the African drum was forbidden in slave days. It would be a dishonor to us to have one dance now designated as the American folk dance when, in fact, for so long our dishonor was that we were forbidden our dance.[56]

Green's comments increased the stakes substantially, so much so that Congressman Dymally noted, "Now, to the proponents of this legislation, you see the dilemma that the subcommittee is faced with; there is strong opposition to this measure."[57]

Despite the battle lines implied by the language of *opponents* to and *proponents* of the square dance bill, folklore's campaign was as much about education as it was about the square dance. Two write-ups of the key points of opposition to the bill in 1984 illustrate the learning curve dance club leaders faced in trying to understand folklore's perspective. The National Folk Dance Committee summarized opposition testimony as focusing on three points:

1) No one dance should be designated the National Folk Dance.
2) Ethnic dance groups may feel slighted.
3) Might stop or slow down the development of other folk dances. (National Folk Dance Committee 1984)

While the listed points demonstrated a significant gap in understanding for the National Folk Dance Committee representatives, William Ford, chairman of the Committee on Post Office and Civil Service of the House of Representatives, responded to letters with a different list, demonstrating that congressional leaders were beginning to understand the case made by folklorists.

Three major concerns were expressed about designating the square dance (or any other dance) as this country's official dance.[58] They are as follows:

1) The possibility of offending those who do not feel themselves to be a part of the America that is represented by square dance;
2) The possibility of creating a perceived standard form of folk dance that will inhibit the natural, creative evolution of American dance traditions; and
3) The possibility of setting up barriers to our ability to represent the cultural diversity of America to audiences.[59]

The 1988 bill was ultimately defeated, in large part because of the testimony of folklorists and tradition bearers illustrating the difference between cultural diversity and melting pot ideology. Friedland and Camp both felt that the 1988 testimony from community members ended the continual fight for a national dance, and indeed there has not been a national hearing on the topic since that date. Today the designation effort has moved their campaign to the state level.[60] Currently over half of the country have so far adopted the square dance as their official state dance.

While seeming to argue against an expressive form was likely not ever an entirely comfortable position for folklorists, the point was never to pit some traditions against others. This was a debate by folklorists about tradition, representation, and diversity—a debate not with ourselves but rather with lawmakers and the country. The square dance bill controversy was an extension of lessons learned during the efforts leading to the eventual successful passage of the AFPA about our role in educating Congress and the country about folk culture. It was an extension of the folklife festival educational efforts undertaken by Ralph Rinzler and the Smithsonian folklorists. It was an extension of not just who we were coming to be but also our growing understanding of our role as public educators and the power of community members' voices. By the 1988 hearing, nearly all folklore opponents to the bill were careful not to portray modern Western square dance as itself a bad thing (although authenticity, commercialism, and other concerns remained in the background). Folklore's opposition was not to the dance but rather to a world where a dance, any dance, would stand out over and above others in a nation rich in diversity and tradition.

NOTES

1. The House of Representatives approved an amendment to the resolution, and the Senate agreed, stipulating that the square dance would serve as the national folk dance only temporarily, specifically, through 1983. On June 1, 1982, President Ronald Regan signed Senate Joint Resolution No. 59, *as amended*, naming the square dance the national folk dance of the United States of America . . . *for a limited time only; 1982 and 1983*. Vol. 127 (1981): September 23, considered and passed Senate. Vol. 128 (1982): May 11, considered and passed House, amended. May 19, Senate concurred in House amendment. June 1, 1982, Approved. Resolved by the Senate and House of Representatives of the United States of America in Congress assembled, That the square dance is designated the national folk dance of the United States of America for 1982 and 1983.

2. *A Bill to Designate the Square Dance as the National Folk Dance of the United States: Hearings on H.R. 1706, Before the Subcommittee on Census and Population, Committee on the Post Office and Civil Service*, 98th Cong. (1984). Retrieved from Square Dance Legislation collection (AFC 1984/024), Archive of Folk Culture, American Folklife Center, Library of Congress, Washington, DC. AFC Collection hereafter cited as AFC 1984/024. Public hearing for H.R. 1706 hereafter cited as *H.R. 1706 Hearing*, AFC 1984/024.

3. *H.R. 1706 Hearing*, AFC 1984/024, Norman Pineta, 6–7.

4. *H.R. 1706 Hearing*, AFC 1984/024, Norman Pineta, 6.

5. Letter from Representative Katie Hall to the Honorable William D. Ford on behalf of the Committee on Post Office and Civil Service Subcommittee on Census and Population, May 8, 1984, AFC 1984/024 (hereafter cited as Hall 1984, AFC 1984/024).

6. Hall 1984, AFC 1984/024.

7. Margaret Parsons, personal communication with authors, June 26, 2021.

8. It also resulted in the existence of a thorough collection of materials in the collection of the AFC, making this chapter possible.

9. LeeEllen Friedland, interview with authors, June 19, 2018, Washington, DC.

10. Three board members voted against the resolution, but there is no evidence of a debate. Charley Camp indicated that there was no opposition from members of the AFS (Interview with the authors, October 16, 2019, Baltimore). The vote was held by mail ballot. It is possible that the members thought they were voting against the square dance bill rather than against the resolution since because of the wording, a yes to the resolution meant a no to the bill and vice versa. On the other hand, the three members who voted against the bill were from western states. The bill's sponsors and proponents come from that region of the country, as did many of the square dance clubs.

11. AFS Executive Board, 1984, AFC 1984/024.

12. *H.R. 1706 Hearing*, AFC 1984/024, Rep. Earl Hutto, 20.

13. *H.R. 1706 Hearing*, AFC 1984/024, Rep. Leon Panetta, 6–7.

14. *H.R. 1706 Hearing*, AFC 1984/024, Rep. Katie Hall, 3–4.

15. *H.R. 1706 Hearing*, AFC 1984/024, Rep. Katie Hall, 3–4.

16. *H.R. 1706 Hearing*, AFC 1984/024, Rep. Katie Hall, 3–4. The congressional record dates these statements to June 16, 1984, but the hearing actually occurred on June 28, 1984.

17. *H.R. 2067 Hearing*, AFC 1984/024, Letter from Ralph Case to the Honorable Marvyn Dymally June 28, 1988, 44.

18. *A Bill to Designate the Square Dance as the American Folk Dance of the United States: Hearings on H.R. 2067, Before the Subcommittee on Census and Population, Committee on the Post Office and Civil Service*, 100th Cong. (1988) (hereafter cited as *H.R. 2067 Hearing*, AFC 1984/024). Statement of Rep. Leon Panetta, sponsor of the bill, 4.

19. *H.R. 1706 Hearing*, AFC 1984/024, Ralph Rinzler, 29–30.

20. *H.R. 1706 Hearing*, AFC 1984/024, Joe Wilson, 49.

21. Charles Camp, interview with authors, October 16, 2019, Baltimore.

22. Resolution from the National Council for the Traditional Arts, AFC 1984/024.

23. *H.R. 1706 Hearing*, AFC 1984/024, Rep. Katie Hall, 2.

24. *H.R. 1706 Hearing*, AFC 1984/024, Gerald Parsons, 47.

25. *Square Dancing Indoctrination Handbook* (revised), 1980. Sets in Order, American Square Dance Society.

26. Letter from Bess Lomax Hawes to Don Moser, March 2, 1996, AFC 1984/024. Quoted with permission from Naomi H. Bishop.

27. *H.R. 1706 Hearing*, AFC 1984/024, Gretchen Adel Schneider, 12.

28. *H.R. 2067 Hearing*, AFC 1984/024, Bob Dalsemer, 56.

29. Differences in capitalization of modern Western square dance clubs is a result of different hearing stenographers.

30. *H.R. 2067 Hearing*, AFC 1984/024, Rep. Leon Panetta, 13.

31. *H.R. 1706 Hearing*, AFC 1984/024, Rep. Norman Mineta, 8.

32. *H.R. 2067 Hearing*, AFC 1984/024, Bob Dalsemer, 58. From Lloyd Shaw, *Cowboy Dances* (Toledo, OH: The Caxton Printers, 1936).

33. *H.R. 1706 Hearing*, AFC 1984/024, David and Dorothy Borchard, 3.

34. *H.R. 1706 Hearing*, AFC 1984/024, David and Dorothy Borchard, 3.

35. *H.R. 2067 Hearing*, AFC 1984/024, Rep. Leon Panetta, 14.

36. LeeEllen Friedland, interview with authors, June 19, 2018.

37. In 1961, Dorothy Shaw published "The Story of Square Dancing: A Family Tree," *Sets in Order* 13 (11), making a similar case.

38. *H.R. 2067 Hearing*, AFC 1984/024, LeeEllen Friedland, 250.

39. The Publore LISTSERV was launched in December 1996 by the late Claude Stephenson of New Mexico Arts, and at the time of this writing has long been administered by Arkansas folklorist Mike Luster. The LISTSERV is an active forum for issues of concern to public folklore, requests for information or assistance, job postings, and announcements of events, exhibits, and publications.

40. See "The Secret Racist History of Square Dancing," accessed May 18, 2025, https://www.facebook.com/MicMedia/videos/the-secret -racist-history-of-square-dancing/1747317361957713/.

41. See Friedland 1998 and Quigley 2001 in this regard.

42. We are grateful to our reader for IU Press for this point. They also noted, "Race in this period corresponded with nationality as well as color, so for example Italian Americans were not white but members of the Italian race and so on."

43. AFS Executive Board, 1984, AFC 1984/024. The phrasing ("mosaic") in the section title here was not directly used in the hearing but is based on Canada's metaphor for pluralism: not the melting pot but the mosaic— ethnicity, culture, identity, and language existing distinctly side by side, not as an amalgam.

44. Charles Camp, interview with authors, October 16, 2019, Baltimore.

45. It should be noted that in 1984, the hearing also coincided with the annual convention of the American Square Dance Association in nearby Baltimore.

46. *H.R. 1706 Hearing*, AFC 1984/024, Ralph Rinzler, 29–30.

47. This tactic, of using the hearing to invite Congress to the festival to see for themselves the cultural diversity and artistry presented there but also the work of folklorists, was also used during the hearings for the AFPA, as discussed elsewhere in this volume.

48. *H.R. 1706 Hearing*, AFC 1984/024, Ralph Rinzler, 31.

49. *H.R. 1706 Hearing*, AFC 1984/024, Paul Tiolono, 36.

50. *H.R. 1706 Hearing*, AFC 1984/024, LaVaughn Robinson, 34. The congressional record misspells his name as "Levon."

51. LeeEllen Friedland, interview with authors, June 19, 2018.

52. Coles was awarded the Dance Magazine Award in 1985, the Capezio Award for lifetime achievement in dance in 1988, and the National Medal of the Arts by President George H. W. Bush in 1991.

53. *H.R. 2067 Hearing*, AFC 1984/024, Charles "Honi" Coles, 22.

54. *H.R. 2067 Hearing*, AFC 1984/024, Rep. Mervyn Dymally, 23.

55. *H.R. 2067 Hearing*, AFC 1984/024, Rayna Green, 37.

56. *H.R. 2067 Hearing*, AFC 1984/024, Rayna Green, 39.

57. *H.R. 2067 Hearing*, AFC 1984/024, Rayna Green, 39.

58. This letter predates the 1984 hearing but demonstrates Ford's understanding of the issues based on information supplied by the Archive of Folk Culture.

59. Letter from William Ford to Mr. and Mrs. Robert L. Stranaham, March 15, 1984. House of Representatives, Committee on Post Office and Civil Service. AFC 1984/024.

60. The list of state dances can be found here: "Official State Dances," accessed May 18, 2025, https://www.netstate.com/states/tables/state _dances.htm.

SEVEN

CODAS, COMPLEXITIES, AND ONGOING CONVERSATIONS

The Continuing Weight of Social Responsibility

A CODA

Most folklorists are familiar with William Labov's model of narrative analysis (Labov and Waletsky 1967). Labov provides six main parts to narrative structure, the last of which is the "coda." The coda points out the relevance of the story by connecting it to everyday life or with other actions and events that fall outside the frame of the story. The coda, quite often, brings the audience from the story to the current moment—it bridges the gap between where we were and where we are currently. This is our coda, an attempt to bring at least some of our story into the present. As noted in the introduction to this volume, our efforts to understand and embrace new and different ways of thinking about equity, inclusion, advocacy, change, and political representation don't stop. They propel us forward as we attempt to understand where we have been and where we are going. So, in this chapter, we revisit some themes that appeared here earlier, themes that continue to demand from us, as folklorists and those in allied fields, better ways of thinking and doing.

The contexts of life and the discipline seem so much more complex today in terms of issues of political representation than in the '70s and '80s. But we suspect that is only because we are living them now. The assaults on women's health, race and ethnicity, the right to vote, the right to love who we want to love, to identify how we identify, justice reform, human rights and democracy, economic justice—those assaults make what we do, how we represent, feel like we carry the weight of the world in each representation. And perhaps we do. These are *our* growing pains. And they mirror those felt by our colleagues as they experienced the earlier civil rights movement, the antiwar movement, the women's movement, the gay and lesbian movement, and the environmental justice movement. Our coda is by necessity only a tiny slice exploring the gap between where we were, where we are, and where we are going. But here we pick up a few of the threads that we addressed in earlier chapters and bring them closer to the moment in which we now find ourselves.

OUR CHANGED CONTEXTS

Folklore is different today, thanks in part to colleagues, events, and debates we describe here. Public folklore now employs more than half of our field, with jobs in arts and humanities councils and commissions, museums, universities, federal government, historical associations, parks commissions, nonprofits, communication and media, public health, social work, and gerontology, to name just some of the contexts (see Lloyd 2021). Our colleagues have served as chairpersons of National Endowment for the Humanities (NEH) and the National Endowment for the Arts (NEA), president of the Guggenheim Foundation, and presidents of universities. They have won McArthur Awards, Grammy Awards, and even Oscars. We have more graduate programs (see Sawin and Zumwalt 2020), although it is fair to say they have risen and fallen over the years. Folklore courses are now taught in hundreds of universities at the undergraduate level, and our colleagues teach throughout the country in graduate and undergraduate folklore programs, and in allied departments, from Ivy League universities to small liberal arts schools to community colleges. Dorson's concerns about our profile as a discipline, while it still worries us, certainly look different now. Nevertheless, we worry about the stability of our programs, courses, jobs, and funding, and we strive to meet and exceed the best practices of contemporary humanities, social science, and arts fields.

Our worries are not without reason; the larger political context we work in is fraught with fights that involve the people and things we care about; the arts and humanities themselves are being attacked in universities and funding agencies throughout the country. And, more recently, the far right has increased its attack on American education, particularly in relation to culture, diversity, and inclusion; teachings about race in the classroom; critical race theory; and policies toward gender identification and sexual orientation. Today, throughout the country, we are witnessing banned books, restricted courses on race and racism, silenced educators and students, eroded institutional independence, banned drag shows, and school gender policies and dress codes that defy human rights. Attacks on women's rights, particularly reproductive rights, add to this dystopian landscape, changing decision-making about where one can safely study or work. Our current political context engenders fears similar to those experienced by our collegial ancestors concerning McCarthyism. Just as our colleagues from the 1970s and '80s thought about their disciplinary responsibilities to political representation in the context of the times—feminist, civil rights, and labor movements, anti-Vietnam war protests, and so forth—so today's folklorists contemplate those responsibilities in light of our national and global moment.

As we were nearing completion of this volume—after many years of conversations that led to travel to archives, interviews with colleagues, and contextual research from a wide range of secondary sources—discussions were taking place among American Folklore

Society (AFS) members regarding the plans for the 2022 annual meeting in Tulsa, Oklahoma. Because Oklahoma was among a growing number of states passing anti-transgender and antiabortion legislation, on social media and in private discussions there were calls for boycotting the state and canceling the meeting, and there were arguments against boycotts and in favor of engaging with local communities about their needs from us as visitors.[1] The meeting went forward as planned. This is only the most recent case since the 1978 Utah meeting in which AFS members debated the location of the annual meeting; we discuss others below. The discussions concerning Tulsa are an example of the ways our thoughts about political representation today continue to reflect our earlier debates.

Although this volume reaches far beyond the AFS to other arenas and institutions in which folklorists do our work—and it covers territory familiar to those in other fields—the AFS plays an important role in the evolution of how American folklorists see themselves as collectors of folklore, as applied folklorists, as scholars, as advocates, as activists. We center our overview of recent events and debates largely in AFS, as the organization that brings the largest number of our colleagues in the US together virtually, in real time at our meetings, and through our journals, newsletters, and events. In addition to debates about holding meetings in locations in which politics are at issue, members have debated the role of the AFS in issuing statements in response to social and political issues, made efforts to diversify the AFS membership (and, it is hoped, that through it the field of folklore studies), and discussed both gender-based and minority discrimination and violence.

POLITICS AND POLICY

Just as our colleagues in the 1970s and '80s struggled with if, how, and when to assert the political/social justice concerns of our field, our position on articulating our political ideology has matured over time. A clear view of that growing maturity could be seen in the development of pathways for making statements and taking policy positions on behalf of the field.

It could be argued that the first real foray into the courage needed for a wide-scale statement of where we, as a field, stand on social justice matters began with the development and publication of a disciplinary code of ethics. In the late 1980s, AFS, like its sister organization the American Anthropological Association (AAA), established a code of professional ethics. The AFS Statement on Ethics was a result of ten years of work by the State of the Profession Committee, as mentioned in chapter 3, and finally at its October 1987 meeting, the executive board approved a final draft created by the committee with the help of the membership. The preamble of the code noted, "Because folklorists study issues and processes that affect general human welfare, they are faced with unusual complexities and ethical dilemmas. It is a major responsibility of folklorists to anticipate these and to plan to resolve them in such a way as to do least damage to those with whom they work and to their scholarly community" (AFS 1988, 8). Intended to clarify the professional responsibilities of folklorists, the code of ethics addressed a number of issues that arose out of the case studies addressed in this volume, not the least of which is the first declaration in the statement: "In research, folklorists' primary responsibility is to those they study. When there is a conflict of interest, these individuals must come first. Folklorists must do everything in their power to protect the physical, social, and psychological welfare of their informants and to honor the dignity and privacy of those studied." Several portions of the statement reflect on specific areas of concern—for example, on unintended consequences (see intro.) the statement notes, "There is an obligation to reflect on the foreseeable repercussions of research and publication on the general population being studied." In relation to concerns about quality of research, our disciplinary reputation, and applied work (see chaps. 2, 4, and 5), "Folklorists bear responsibility for the good reputation of the discipline and its practitioners." And in relation to the issue of ethical questions regarding sources of funding (see chap. 4), "They face the obligation, prior to entering into any commitment for research to reflect upon the purposes of their sponsors in terms of those sponsors' past behavior and what the likely uses of their research data will be."[2]

The AFS code of ethics was one of a number of position statements adopted and published by the society prior to the 1990s. As the intertwining of social justice issues with the work of the society and its members became progressively more visible to a growing number of members, calls for AFS to take a stand on issues by releasing statements became more frequent. While the executive director and the president of the AFS are most clearly authorized to speak on behalf of the society, some society members sought an official means for member involvement in the development and release of position statements with increased urgency in the early 2000s—though the idea goes back further (see chap. 3 for such calls in the 1970s).

In March 2003, the George W. Bush administration initiated an attack on Iraq that it claimed was part of the response to the attacks on the US on September 11, 2001. The war in Iraq was polarizing in the US and around the world, and the AFS membership was not immune from this polarization. At the 2003 AFS Business Meeting, members of the Politics, Folklore, and Social Justice Section as well as the Cultural Diversity Task Force requested that the AFS issue a statement condemning the war. Throughout the United States scholarly societies were dealing with the same issue: whether to, and how to, pass a resolution or a position concerning the war. The American Sociological Association (ASA), for example, put forward a contentious resolution calling for an immediate end to the war against Iraq.[3] In the ASA and AFS, the decision to issue a statement or resolution hinged on two central matters: members' attitudes toward the war and

A Statement on Ethics for the Society

At its October 1987 meeting, the Executive Board of the Society approved a final draft of a Statement on Ethics for AFS. Though the Statement printed below has gained the approval of the Board, this should not be considered the final word on the subject. The Board expects and in fact urges members to explore the abstract and practical implications of this Statement and, most important, to communicate their descriptions of and opinions on matters of ethical concern in the *Newsletter* and the *Journal of American Folklore*.

The Board would like to extend its thanks to all members of the State of the Profession Committee and the membership at large, whose thought, effort, comments and criticism have gone into the making of this Statement. Particular thanks are due to Frank de Caro, Lynwood Montell and William Nicolaisen, who were active in early discussions of the Statement; to Rayna Green, who prepared early drafts for Committee and Board discussion; to Jack Santino, who drafted the version of the Statement distributed to the membership for comment in *AFSNL* 15:5; and to Yvonne Milspaw, who prepared a text based on Santino's draft for Board consideration in October 1987.

STATEMENT ON ETHICS:
PRINCIPLES OF PROFESSIONAL RESPONSIBILITY

Preamble:

This statement of principles is intended to clarify the professional responsibilities of professional folklorists. Folklorists, more than most other professionals, work with peoples from many different communities and socioeconomic backgrounds. Their professional situation is therefore particularly varied and complex. They are involved in different ways with their discipline, their colleagues, their students, their sponsors, their own and host governments, the particular individuals and groups with whom they conduct their fieldwork, and other populations and interest groups in the nations where they work. Because folklorists study issues and processes that affect general human welfare, they are faced with unusual complexities and ethical dilemmas. It is a major responsibility of folklorists to anticipate these and to plan to resolve them in such a way as to do least damage to those with whom they work and to their scholarly community.

The following principles are deemed fundamental to the responsible, ethical pursuit of the profession.

1. Relations with those studied:

In research, folklorists' primary responsibility is to those they study. When there is a conflict of interest, these individuals must come first. Folklorists must do everything in their power to protect the physical, social and psychological welfare of their informants and to honor the dignity and privacy of those studied.

a. Where research involves the acquisition of material and information transferred on the assumption of trust between persons, the rights, interests and sensitivities of those studied must be safeguarded.

b. The aims of the investigation should be communicated as well as is possible to the informant.

c. Informants have the right to remain anonymous. This right should be respected both where it has been promised explicitly and, as much as possible, where no clear understanding to the contrary has been reached. These strictures apply to the collection of data by means of cameras, tape recorders and other data-collecting devices, as well as to data collected in interviews.

d. There shall be no exploitation of individual informants for personal gain. Fair return should be given them for all services.

e. There is an obligation to reflect on the foreseeable repercussions of research and publication on the general population being studied.

f. The anticipated consequences of the research should be communicated as fully as possible to the individuals and groups likely to be affected.

2. Responsibility to the public:

Folklorists are responsible to all presumed consumers of their professional efforts. To them they owe a commitment to candor and truth in the dissemination of their research results and in statements of their opinions as students of human behavior.

3. Responsibility to the discipline:

Folklorists bear responsibility for the good reputation of the discipline and its practitioners.

4. Responsibility to students:

In relations with students, folklorists should be candid, fair, nonexploitative and committed to the students' welfare and progress. Folklorists as teachers have the responsibility of instruction in the professional ethics of academe in general and of folklore in particular in addition to their duties of instruction in the field, career counseling, academic supervision, evaluation, compensation and placement.

a. Folklorists must alert students to the ethical problems of research and discourage them from participating in projects that employ questionable ethical standards.

b. Folklorists should acknowledge in print the student assistance used in their own publications; give appropriate credit (including coauthorship) when student research is used in publication; encourage and assist in publication of worthy student papers; and compensate students justly for the use of their time, energy and intelligence in research and writing.

5. Responsibilities to sponsors, including one's own and host governments:

In relations with the sponsors of research, folklorists should be honest about their qualifications, capabilities and aims. Thus, they face the obligation, prior to entering into any commitment for research, to reflect upon the purposes of their sponsors in terms of those sponsors' past behavior and what the likely uses of their research data will be. Folklorists should be especially careful not to promise or imply acceptance either of conditions contrary to their professional ethics or of competing commitments, and they should demand assurance that they will not be required to compromise their professional responsibilities and ethics as a condition of the sponsors' permission to pursue research.

Epilogue:

Folklore research is a human undertaking for which the individual bears ethical as well as scientific responsibility. This statement provides guidelines to the accepted professional standards of research and the presentation of that research. When folklorists by their actions jeopardize peoples studied, professional colleagues, students or others, or if they otherwise betray their professional commitments, the American Folklore Society, through its State of the Profession Committee, may legitimately inquire into the propriety of those actions and take such measures as lie within its legitimate powers.

8

Figure 7.1 The AFS code of ethics was a result of ten years of work by the State of the Profession committee. The executive board approved a final draft at its October 1987 meeting. *The American Folklore Society Newsletter,* New Series 17, no. 1 (1988). Courtesy of the American Folklore Society.

the relationship between such a statement of condemnation and the standing of the organization and the field in terms of possessing particular insight and related expertise about the matter at hand. The debates that occurred at the AFS Business Meeting were heated, with some members opposed to any statement due to disputes in perspectives on the Middle East as well as opinions that only statements anchored in both knowledge and evidence directly related to matters central to folklore studies should be made. The statement condemning the war never was adopted, but two initiatives were: that there would be a clear process and policy for members wishing for statements to be made and that AFS would establish a working group to gather information concerning the impact of the war on Iraq's tangible and intangible cultural heritage. By 2005, the task force to explore the cultural impact of the war in Iraq had still not issued a report, in part due to a lack of resources to do the job effectively. Executive board members suggested that AFS might consider investing in a variety of policy issues, not just those requiring immediate responses to emergency situations.

In April 2007, the AFS Executive Board passed a set of guidelines for requests that AFS issue a statement on a particular issue. According to the guidelines, "Some people make a clear distinction between expertise and advocacy. However, participating in the formation of public policy is always, explicitly or implicitly, a political act. Endorsement of a policy statement demonstrates support for a particular point of view intended to inform a process in which many points of view and many interests will be voiced. The Society's contribution to the policy process is not simply to declare what is right or wrong, but to provide a folkloristic point of view that can be used in the context of informed advocacy." Among the things the board requested in the guidelines was a discussion of connecting any proposed position with disciplinary expertise. The list of requirements for a proposed statement includes "a description of the issue's relationship to existing folklore research and understanding. Policy statements endorsed by AFS should reflect a distinctively folkloristic perspective. The request for a statement should include a well-argued brief on expert grounds for the position being sought. This section of the proposal must demonstrate the thorough weighing of the range of folklore evidence and must then demonstrate why the preponderance of folkloristic judgment favors the requested position."[4]

The AFS now had a pathway to request position statements, although such statements do not indicate their provenance, so it is not possible to tell if they were initiated by the membership or the executive board or the staff. The recent statements reflect both social justice concerns and matters of disciplinary work/study conditions. For instance, statements on the AFS website at the time of this writing included a stand against race-based violence and injustice (undated), a statement on fair compensation for self-employed folklorists (dated 2001), a statement on the revision of the human subjects review process (dated 2011), and a statement on promotion and tenure standards and review (undated);[5] other statements issued during this period included a statement condemning "the invasion of Ukraine and support[ing] Ukrainian folklore and heritage scholars" (March 1, 2022) and a statement in solidarity with those impacted by the earthquakes in Syria and Turkey (March 3, 2023).[6]

In response to the ad hoc committee on cultural impacts of the war in Iraq and the resulting suggestion that the society invest in a variety of folklore and policy issues, not just those requiring immediate responses to emergency situations, the AFS created a series of seed-funded policy groups. In 2009, the AFS began putting out calls for proposals for six-member working groups that would create a series of products designed to articulate the contributions that folklorists have made to the development, implementation, and evaluation of public policy in a particular area and highlight future areas of application. In its calls for proposals for this initiative, the AFS acknowledged folklorists' contributions to public policy in areas such as historic preservation, intangible cultural heritage, intellectual property, health, education, labor, the environment, immigration, poverty, violence, language rights, and land rights. Working groups were asked to produce a minimum of an article on the topic likely to reach those in public policy work, resource materials for the AFS website, professional development activities or sessions for the annual meeting in that area of policy, and at least one other public presentation. The earliest groups focused on health policy and historic preservation.[7]

DIVERSITY, EQUITY, AND INCLUSION

As mentioned in the introduction to this volume, in 1992 President Barbara Kirshenblatt-Gimblett "charged the State of the Profession Committee of the American Folklore Society with the task of developing recommendations for 'enhancing minority participation' in the field of folklore" (Roberts et al. 1994, 9). The committee was chaired by John Roberts (who went on to become the first African American president of AFS, 1997–98) and included Robert Baron, Gerald Davis, Cheryl Keyes, Mario Montaño, Kirin Narayan, and Beverly Robinson. They produced a report on minority participation in the field of folklore, submitted April 8, 1994, and published in the subsequent *AFS Newsletter*. The committee "identified several areas of need that, if addressed, could lead to enhanced minority participation within the field. These areas include training, professional opportunities, networking, publications and scholarship, and institutional stability. In addition, [they] identified three constituencies toward whom recommendations in those areas should be directed: academics (including students and individuals holding academic appointments), community scholars, and public folklorists" (Roberts et al. 1994, 10). The report began to address issues of barriers in the field and AFS that inhibit minority participation. Subsequent years

Report of the State of the Profession Committee of the American Folklore Society on Minority Participation in the Field of Folklore

Background

Throughout its history, folklore as a discipline has largely involved the study of "others." Unlike anthropology, which, until recently, defined "otherness" primarily in spatial terms (i.e., as those who live in cultures geographically removed from that of the investigator), folklore, in its earliest configurations, defined its "other" primarily in temporal terms (i.e., the folk were conceptualized as those individuals who lived as anachronisms, in most cases, in the society of the investigator and who participated in a mode of creative cultural production [folklore] that was also anachronistic). This conception of the folk and folklore had an early impact and, to some extent, continues to influence the study of American folklore. In the United States, this concern with the "other" as the focus of folkloristic investigation was perfectly evident in William Wells Newell's conception of the field in the first issue of the *Journal of American Folklore*. In his statement on the work and scope of a *Journal of American Folklore*, Newell identified groups defined primarily by race and ethnicity as the bearers of a "fast vanishing" lore. Although Newell identified "remnants" of Old English and Scottish ballads as an additional area of study, he did not indicate the distinction between "lore" and "remnants" or the different conceptions of or relationship to community that this distinction might have implied. Nor was he apparently ever called upon to do so, thus suggesting that to his 19th-century audience this distinction was both clear and understandable.

Today, most of the groups specifically identified by Newell would be included under the rubric "minority." We would argue that in specifically identifying racial and ethnic groups as the focus of American folklore study in his initial conception of the field, Newell made an implicit and important distinction productive of the creation of a conception of the American folk. Certainly, the American concept of the folk today is closely identified with groups whose difference is defined primarily by race and ethnicity, and especially those racial and ethnic groups perceived as most marginal to some accepted social and political center within the society. Furthermore, the vernacular traditions of such groups continue to be subject to intense folkloristic investigation. While it would probably be inaccurate to attribute the continuing interest on the part of folklorists in these groups to a 19th-century view of the folk, it undoubtedly continues to contribute to our sense of what constitutes folkness in American folklore society. Although folklorists have in recent years expanded their sense of folkness to include groups whose vernacular traditions reflect such factors as gender, sexual orientation, and even disability, many continue to view racial and ethnic groups as the perennial folk in American society.

While the development of a concept of "folk" based primarily on racial and ethnic difference reflected social and political realities as well as power relations in late 19th-century America, this concept of the folk remains problematic for those groups subsumed under the rubric folk and for the theoretical development of the discipline. We would suggest that the conception of the folk and folklore as anachronistic has contributed historically to a sense of alienation for members of already marginalized minority groups. Their supposed difference from some mainstream standard has, in many cases, already stereotyped them as backward, and their incorporation into a discourse of folkness is perceived as only contributing to the perpetuation of their stereotype in the society. Therefore, it should not be surprising that many members of minority groups find it extremely difficult to embrace folklore as either an academic discipline or as a profession. The problem for many minorities is only exacerbated by the fact that despite continuing folkloristic interest in the vernacular traditions of these groups, members of these groups have historically constituted a very small percentage of those involved in folklore study.

While we do not feel that there is anything inherently wrong with outsiders studying the folklore of minority groups, we do believe that expanded minority participation can only help the field by broadening perspectives on culture and folklore. In addition, we would suggest that expanded minority participation would also enhance the discipline's credibility and expand its impact upon such fields as African American Studies, Native American Studies, Chicano Studies, Puerto Rican Studies, Asian American Studies, Gay and Lesbian Studies, and

Figure 7.2 AFS president Barbara Kirshenblatt-Gimblett's 1992 charge to the AFS State of the Profession Committee resulted in a 1994 Report of the State of the Profession Committee of the American Folklore Society on Minority Participation in the Field of Folklore. *The American Folklore Society Newsletter* 23 (3): 8–12 (1994). Courtesy of the American Folklore Society.

added incrementally to the diversity initiatives. In 1994, after the publication of the Roberts report, AFS created a Task Force on Racial Minority Participation Initiative in the Field of Folklore.[8] In 1999, these efforts were enhanced by the creation, in the long-range planning process under President Joan Radner, of an ad hoc "cultural diversity committee" (CDC).[9] The CDC initiatives began with brown-bag lunches and events for new members at the annual meeting as well as some programming of diversity-focused sessions and research into minority participation in the meetings. In 2011, incoming president Diane Goldstein and outgoing president Kurt Dewhurst strengthened the AFS's commitment to diversity enhancement by making the CDC a standing committee, no longer having the temporary status of AFS ad hoc committees. In 2023, the CDC listed its initiatives as including engaging with local communities at annual meeting sites, experimenting with meeting structure to more broadly initiate conversations on diversity, facilitating conversations about race and privilege within the AFS and the field, working in solidarity with those fighting racism and homophobia in our communities, and equipping "graduate students, new professors, and public sector workers with the tools they need to explore folklore theory and history at the intersection of critical race theory, queer theory, transnational, feminist theory/praxis, disability, and performance theory."[10] In 2017, President Kay Turner formed the Curriculum Opportunities Working Group to create a bank of resources for expanding the teaching of folklore theory and method to include more work related to diversity and inclusion.

Beginning in 2015, the CDC established for each meeting a group of diversity-related sessions. In 2019, the CDC sponsored a large group of sessions including a reception in recognition of twenty-five years of diversity efforts. Forums and panels focused on teaching intersectionality, the critical work of folklorists and community scholars of color, Black storytelling and cultural preservation, disability in folklore, African American dollmaking and puppetry, a cultural diversity retrospective, and the future of cultural diversity.[11]

By 2018 and '19, the push for diversity programming and educational opportunities moved substantially forward, in part as a result of the rise of both the #MeToo and Black Lives Matter movements. The AFS sponsored sessions at annual meetings for the discussion of each (and members also presented papers, outside of sponsored sessions).

Forums devoted to #MeToo were held in 2018, 2019, and 2022, each intended to promote conversations about #MeToo within folklore studies.[12] The first, led by Elaine Lawless, was intended as a forum for the discussion of the "#MeToo movement and issues of harassment within our field as a space of professional power brokering."[13] The session was packed and highly participatory. In 2019, Diane Goldstein was asked by the AFS to lead a continuation of this conversation by chairing a follow-up session, "#MeToo, Take Two," and she asked panel members to prepare open statements focused "on an aspect of folklore scholarship that either provides insight into #MeToo, or conversely, explores where #MeToo might challenge folklore perspectives."[14] After a two-year break, the AFS sponsored a third session in 2022, "How Folklorists Can Address the #MeToo Movement"; though sparsely attended, this session continued this important conversation.[15] Essays on the issues raised by #MeToo within folklore studies were published in a forum in the *Journal of American Folklore* (Gilman 2025).

Meanwhile, in 2020, we all experienced what some came to call a *double pandemic*: the COVID-19 pandemic and the pre-existing pandemic of systemic racism that came to the fore in the early months of the virus following the killings by police of George Floyd, Brianna Taylor, and countless others around the nation. We also witnessed a surge in anti-Asian hate crimes traceable to the rhetoric of blame for the origins and spread of COVID-19 espoused by former president Donald Trump and others; like the killings of Black people in the streets and in their homes, this surge served as a spotlight on preexisting racism and racist violence.[16] This dual pandemic was also evident in the disproportionate numbers of COVID-19 infections and resultant deaths in communities of color. This period brought systemic racism to the forefront of conversations not just within the justice and health-care systems but throughout all spheres of society, including academia, nonprofit organizations, arts agencies, museums—all the spheres in which twenty-first-century folklorists do their work. Though fully virtual due to the pandemic, the 2020 annual meeting was organized around examining and questioning folklore studies in terms of both historical and present-day racism and white privilege. There were many sessions, but some that were highlighted included the Francis Utley Memorial Lecture Panel on Race and Racism in the Practice of Folklore, Latinx Authors Recentering the Periphery, A Decolonizing Workshop on Reclaiming and Re-Envisioning Intellectual Space in Folklore Practice, Recentering the Periphery in African American Storytelling, breakout sessions on Race and Racism, and a session on African American Traditional Music Practitioners.[17] This focused programming continued in 2021 and 2022.

From the time of the submission of the Report on Minority Participation, the AFS undertook to increase minority participation at all levels of governance but most especially on the executive board, the AFS Fellows, and AFS standing and ad hoc committees. These efforts ran into difficulty, largely due to the dearth of minority members of the AFS, a lack of opportunities for minority networking, and a lack of funding for minority scholars to attend meetings. In order to increase the input and visibility of BIPOC members of the field, in 2012 the board created an appointed position to increase diversity (a strategy that was suggested in the report [Roberts et al. 1994, 12]), and the nominating committee began to periodically introduce slates of largely or

Figure 7.3 "Notable Folklorists of Color, Remembering Our Ancestral Legacies" exhibition at the 2019 Annual Meeting of the American Folklore Society. Photo depicts on the left, Phyllis M. May-Machunda and Olivia Cadaval, curators. On the right, Sojin Kim, contributor. Photo courtesy of the American Folklore Society.

entirely BIPOC candidates. In 2022, the executive board added two more appointed positions to the board to further this effort.

Included in the constituencies to whom the recommendations in the Report on Minority Participation were directed were community scholars (Roberts et al. 1994, 8). The committee noted in particular, "We recommend that the annual meetings include more artists, community scholars, cultural activists, and others whose work is folkloristic in the broadest sense of the term. That is, we need to recognize that the field is broader than the profession. At any rate, we need to encourage minority participation as other than entertainment" (12). The report suggested numerous paths for expanding connections to other constituencies, but their discussion also addressed issues of enhancing visibility.

Figure 7.4 The "Notable Folklorists of Color, Remembering Our Ancestral Legacies" exhibit was displayed at the 2019 Annual Meeting of the American Folklore Society. Photo courtesy of the American Folklore Society.

The AFS Notable Folklorists of Color project had its beginnings in 2019, "springing from conversations at a 2019 AFS Board meeting about creating a tangible commemoration to honor the 25th anniversary of the AFS Cultural Diversity Committee and the long-term and ongoing efforts of previous AFS boards and staff to diversify AFS membership and participation in the field. To do this, the project's curators planned to honor the truth that the field is and has been more diverse than the visible and established (or canonized) record suggests" (Turner 2022, 5).[18] To that end, a series of exhibit panels was created and displayed at the 2019 meeting. Since then, the project has expanded to two online exhibits that include a growing number of BIPOC scholars and their accomplishments.[19] Such work represents needed steps in both recognizing these scholars, and, more broadly, recognizing that the issues of representation that folklorists are deeply engaged in must begin with an examination of our own historiography with an inclusionary lens. Publications in the field have also recently devoted entire issues to BIPOC cultural expressions (see Boucicaut and Gilman 2021; González-Martin, Martínez-Rivera, and Otero 2022).

Broadening our contacts with community scholars also prompted increased place-based engagement with communities and events at the locations of our meetings. AFS had for a very long time planned pre-meeting excursions to local sites of interest to members, involved local performers in panels and opening ceremonies, and invited local traditional artists to display and sometimes sell their work. Though beginning with the meeting in Eugene, Oregon, in 1993 discussed below, following the Long Beach meeting, place-based engagements became more focused on social justice issues of concern to the local population in the regions of our meeting sites.

MEETING LOCATIONS AND POLICY STATEMENTS

An article published in *Inside Higher Ed* in February 2023 entitled "Should Conferences Stay Put or Relocate? It's Complicated" noted that the Association for the Study of Higher Education was moving its planned 2024 meeting out of Louisiana because of the state's laws restricting access to abortion and the participation of transgender people in sports. The article asserted, "Every Association . . . is grappling with this"; "if you're going to go, you have to exercise your voice." "The question for groups like [ours] . . . is whether it can be more impactful to cancel or to be there and voice our concerns" (Adame 2023). AFS has struggled with this same issue numerous times since the Utah ERA meeting in 1978 (see chap. 3). While each one of the troubled meetings has required hard decisions, each demonstrates the slow growth of representational competence as the AFS has learned how to respond to meeting locations that challenge our beliefs in inclusion and equity, arguably beliefs that are shared by the vast majority of members of the field, even if there is not agreement on the relationship between beliefs and scholarship as it relates to decisions about where meetings are held.

In 1992, "the strongest anti-homosexual measure ever considered by a state" (Egan 1992, 1), known as Measure 9, was on the ballot in Oregon. Measure 9 asked voters to consider amending the state constitution "to require that all governments discourage homosexuality, [along with] other listed 'behaviors,' and not facilitate or recognize them."[20] The summary provided by the petitioners of this amendment read, "Amends Oregon Constitution. All governments in Oregon may not use their monies or properties to promote, encourage or facilitate homosexuality, pedophilia, sadism, or masochism. All levels of government, including public education systems, must assist in setting a standard for Oregon's youth which recognizes that these 'behaviors' are 'abnormal, wrong, unnatural and perverse' and that they are to be discouraged and avoided. State may not recognize this conduct under 'sexual orientation' or 'sexual preference' labels or through 'quotas, minority status, affirmative action, or similar concepts.'"[21] Not surprisingly, "Oregon saw a wave of anti-gay hate crimes in 1992" (Blazak 2022), resulting in widespread fear within LGBTQIA+ ("LGB" at the time) communities throughout the state. The 1993 AFS Annual Meeting was planned for Eugene, Oregon, which meant that Measure 9 was a topic of concern at the 1992 meeting, as the ballot measure was to be voted on in the weeks following.

Joseph Goodwin brought the issue to the AFS Executive Board on behalf of the AFS Gay and Lesbian Section, of which he was a cofounder. According to the minutes of their October 15, 1992 meeting, the executive board held a discussion "of whether the AFS should meeting [*sic*] in Eugene pending the outcome of Ballot Measure 9 which would legitimate anti-gay/lesbian discrimination."[22] Shalom Staub, executive secretary/treasurer, had been looking into the implications of canceling the meeting and informed the board that "practically speaking, the AFS would open itself to significant economic and legal risk by breaking a contract without a cancellation clause." As the measure itself was on the ballot in November 1992, and the question of whether it would pass would be known long before the 1993 meeting, "the Board discussion hinged on the issue being a climate of social injustice, not whether Measure 9 passes or not," and the discussion included "what activities the AFS could do *in* Eugene that would advance the Society's concerns"; the need for a focus of the AFS meeting on issues of "folklore, civil rights, and social justice in a broad manner"; and the need for a policy regarding site selection and contract cancellation (*emphasis in original*).

Based on this discussion, Joan Radner drafted the following resolution on behalf of the board for presentation at the Executive Board Question and Answer Session the following day: "The Executive Board of the American Folklore Society condemns the introduction of Measure 9 on the Oregon Ballot and the widespread backlash that threatens civil rights in the United States today. The Board resolves to engage the Society at the 1993 Annual Meeting in the examination and public discussion of issues of human rights and in particular of the cultures and concerns of gay men and lesbians, and further resolves that issues of social justice must continue to be in the forefront of the American Folklore Society's concerns."[23]

The following evening, this was the major topic of the Executive Board Question and Answer Session, according to the minutes. Goodwin spoke first, relaying two proposals from the Gay and Lesbian Section. The first stressed the "increase in the number of acts of violence against lesbians, gay men, and bisexual people" as a result of the measure and proposed that the AFS Executive Board "send a letter of strong opposition" to Measure 9 to the governor and other Oregon lawmakers prior to the vote. The second proposed that the AFS "declare the theme of the 1993 meeting in Eugene, Oregon to be 'Folklore, Civil Rights, and Social Justice'" and "donate display space in the book room for an exhibit of books addressing gay, lesbian, and bisexual culture."[24] Following a report of the board meeting and a reading of the resolution by outgoing president Barbara Kirshenblatt-Gimblett, a discussion commenced in which members offered additional suggestions. At least two members called for canceling the Oregon meeting in the spirit of an economic boycott of the state, but the majority appeared to agree with both the Gay and Lesbian Section and the executive board that more could be done by going forward with the meeting while making the society's position clear and working toward some positive effect.[25]

Following the 1992 meeting, the executive board passed, through mail ballot, all of the actions proposed by the section; although the theme of the meeting passed with eight out of eight votes, there was one vote to table the donation of display space for books and one vote against the AFS president writing letters to lawmakers.[26] In the letter to the governor of Oregon, newly seated president Sylvia Grider stressed concern for the safety of members of the Gay and Lesbian Section of the AFS and stated that there had been "serious discussion about breaking our hotel contract and boycotting the Oregon meeting in order to express our overwhelmingly negative reaction to Measure 9. However, because we believed that we could express our scholarly and ethical commitment better by coming to Oregon rather than staying away, we will honor our contractual agreement and hold our meeting as planned in Eugene." Additionally, the governor was asked for assurances of the safety and civil rights of AFS members.[27] In response, Governor Barbara Roberts wrote briefly that she agreed with the society's opposition, stating, "This destructive measure is a betrayal of the best in Oregon."[28] Although Measure 9 ultimately failed, a disturbing 43.5 percent of voters supported it.[29]

According to a letter from Goodwin to Grider immediately following the 1992 meeting, many plans were underway for the Eugene meeting.[30] During the meeting itself, there were five panels on gay and lesbian folklore,[31] a "Non-Gender Specific Dance Party" called "Are You the Man or the Woman," and three tables dedicated to "gay, lesbian, and bisexual issues."

Measure 9 prompted broader conversations about future AFS meeting locations and how AFS could prepare for such situations in the future. At the Executive Board Question and Answer Session, Nancy Nusz spoke on behalf of both the Women's and the Gay and Lesbian Sections, presenting a two-part resolution: (1) that the AFS "refrain from entering into contracts in jurisdictions that discriminate against any person based on gender, sexual orientation, race, or religion" and (2) that the AFS "include in all future contracts language that renders the contract 'null and void' if the jurisdiction subsequently passes such discriminatory laws."[32] This proposal was later passed unanimously by the executive board.

All of this played out in remarkably different ways from, and saw significant changes of positions from, the 1970s and '80s. Though surely the Utah meeting would have been on the minds of and likely discussed by some, none of the meetings' minutes mention it. However, the question and answer session minutes summarized comments by Barre Toelken, then a member of the executive board, that included "that there will be issues no matter where we go," which was essentially the stand he took regarding the Utah meeting, as noted in chapter 3. Former AFS executive director Tim Lloyd commented to us in an interview that the executive board's position on the Eugene meeting is representative of their decisions in most cases in the period since. Lloyd characterized this position as "let's advocate for the position that we believe in, while we're there. Let's take the opportunity of, you know, having six or seven—eight hundred of us in a place to make a point about" whatever the issue is.[33]

The only time that AFS made a declaration to boycott a state, there seems to have been little debate. In 2010, Arizona governor Jan Brewer signed two pieces of legislation into law: House Bill 2281, banning the teaching of classes in ethnic studies in Arizona public schools,[34] and Senate Bill 1070, considered to be the strictest anti-immigration legislation in the nation, requiring, among other things, "state law enforcement to ask those deemed suspicious of being undocumented to present proof of legal immigration status during routine traffic stops. It also made it a misdemeanor crime to be caught without those papers" (Reznick 2020).

After conferring with other learned societies and soliciting feedback from AFS members living in Arizona and from members of interest sections within the AFS (Chicano and Chicana; Folklore Latino, Latinoamericano y Caribeño; Politics, Folklore, and Social Justice), the executive board issued a statement in opposition to the bills. In this statement, the board noted that the AFS "has historically supported policies that prohibit discrimination based on ethnicity, gender, national origin, race, religion, or sexual orientation, and our field has long been concerned with the well-being of immigrant populations."[35] The statement concluded, "The Executive Board of the American Folklore Society resolves that the Society will not hold a scholarly conference in the State of Arizona until such time that Arizona Senate Bill 1070 and Arizona House Bill 2281 are either repealed or struck down as constitutionally invalid and thus unenforceable by a court."[36] HB 2281, banning ethnic studies, was struck down in 2017 (Associated Press 2017); the Supreme Court struck down portions of SB 1070 in 2012, but the core remains in place. The AFS has not met in Arizona.

The next major debate was truly contentious and remains fresh in the minds of many. In February 2015, the staff of the AFS learned that there was a labor dispute at the Long Beach, California, hotel where the annual meeting was scheduled to take place the following fall. This led to months of communications between the AFS and the hotel, the union, and AFS membership, and it led to the boycotting of the meeting—or, in some cases, the meeting hotel—by some AFS members. This situation involving the location of the annual meeting was the most contentious among the AFS membership since the 1978 ERA debates, and although it is difficult to judge, it may have been even more divisive. For Robert McCarl and perhaps others, it connected back to the debate over occupational and organization folklore (see chap. 5).

As the AFS worked to make clear, the hotel workers at the Westin Long Beach (and another Long Beach hotel) were not on strike. Rather, some were working with UNITE HERE! (a labor union representing workers in the "hotel, gaming, food service, manufacturing, textile, distribution, laundry, transportation, and airport industries"[37]) to unionize. As described by Tim Lloyd, executive director at the time, in a 2021 email to us, "The hotels were against unionization but fell back on a standard management stalling argument over which of two forms of voting would be used in such an election, one of them customarily supported by unions and the other customarily supported by management. The union and hotel workers were holding informational demonstrations from time to time outside each hotel. UNITE HERE! wanted AFS to boycott the Westin by cancelling our contract with them to hold our 2015 annual meeting."[38] Canceling a contract with a conference hotel is incredibly expensive—expensive enough to wipe out the finances of an organization the size of AFS.

Following the pattern established in 1992, the AFS Executive Board voted not to boycott but to instead take other actions in support of the union and to attempt to address this issue preemptively in the future when choosing site locations and signing hotel contracts. According to the first of many communications from the AFS to its members on the situation, backing out of the contract would have cost the AFS $99,000 or $132,000 in penalties, depending on when they did so. "Paying these penalties would eliminate almost two-thirds of our reserve fund, which in turn would significantly diminish our ability to hold this and future meetings and to carry out our other activities that support our members and our field."[39]

In the months that followed, UNITE HERE! contacted AFS members directly by email and phone as well as in person in ways that some members described as harassment. One folklorist living in the Los Angeles area at the time described her experiences in a post in the AFS Annual Meeting online public forum. In her post, she noted that she herself is a union member and supported their rights to unionize—but described what she called "intimidating tactics" to convince her and others to demand that AFS boycott the Westin Hotel, including picketing outside the Western States Folklore Society meeting and showing up at her office and at a public lecture she delivered.[40] Other members vehemently supported a boycott. Also in a post in the AFS forum, another person voiced her support of the boycott, writing in part, "UNITE HERE is a wake-up call: a chance to check ourselves and realign our practices with our values and principles. I urge us to take this as an opportunity to consider how we as a society connect with large issues of our time: fights for a living wage, the rights of immigrant and undocumented workers, income inequality, and climate change. How can we as folklorists be part of movements for change? What can we contribute? We can start by siding with workers and acceding to their demand that we boycott."[41]

Robert McCarl was among those in the membership who boycotted the meeting in its entirety. AFS supported McCarl's travel to the meeting in Miami the following year to use his expertise in occupational folklore to explore the society's response to labor disruptions; he spoke at the business meeting about "the decision by the AFS Board and individual folklorists to cross the picket line and patronize the hotel at a delicate time in the formation of the local union" and provided what he described as "a wider historical framework" in order to "use this incident as a vehicle for the consideration of future actions of the AFS." In contrast to the argument made by AFS that the Westin workers' actions outside the hotel did not constitute a "picket line," McCarl described the consequences of crossing a "picket line": "Violation of that space—crossing the picket line—constitutes a violation of the shared values and physical experiences of workers. Once that line has been crossed, it becomes extremely difficult to repair the damage. If the picket line defines a hallowed space of cultural values, then its violation constitutes a serious rejection of those values."[42]

Meanwhile, the AFS staff felt that the union was not communicative in helpful ways as they attempted to gain a better understanding of the situation until, according to Lloyd in an email to us, "Finally, in the month before our meeting in October, the union . . . contacted us and we began useful conversations. In the end, an AFS delegation agreed to speak directly with hotel management about our concerns during our meeting, and in return the union agreed not to hold any demonstrations outside the hotel during our conference."[43]

As we discussed regarding the boycott of the Utah meeting in chapter 3, it is difficult to ascertain through meeting attendance alone the number of those who chose to boycott the meeting. In a preliminary report of the meeting provided by the AFS, 7 percent of presenters cited the labor dispute as their reason for withdrawing after the program was released, "includ[ing] the withdrawal of five panels, as well as individual papers." Additionally, "two paper panels met elsewhere, and the three Cultural Diversity Committee-sponsored panels were rescheduled and moved off-site to avoid meeting in the hotel. The social program took a hit, too, as the university-sponsored receptions withdrew, and plans for the Saturday dance party were abandoned because of difficulties caused by the dispute." Hotel staff and union representatives participated in a panel sponsored by the AFS Cultural Diversity Committee, and both AFS and individual members expressed their support for unionization through letters and a face-to-face meeting.[44]

As a result of the Long Beach labor situation, AFS amended their "Criteria for Selecting Annual Meeting Sites" to prioritize conferences "in hotels where the labor force is unionized" (Leary 2021, 203). According to Lloyd, "By the time of the Baltimore AFS annual meeting in 2019, productive relations between AFS and UNITE-HERE! had strengthened to the point where AFS was able to take an active role in the resolution of a labor dispute at that year's conference hotel."[45] Indeed in 2019, the union with the help of AFS was able to use the conference as leverage to resolve their dispute with the hotel. The October 16, 2019, issue of *AFS Review* stated,

> *Dear AFS meeting attendees and members,*
>
> *We have spoken with the President of UNITE HERE Local 7 who represents workers at the Hyatt Regency Baltimore Inner Harbor. She informed us that contract negotiations are progressing and that the union appreciates the fact that the AFS has made a point of patronizing union hotels because of the expectation for fair labor practices. She also expressed disappointment that AFS had not been notified prior to arrival about this ongoing labor issue.*
>
> *She informed us that the union is not asking us to move our event, and no strikes or picket lines will occur during our conference. The heads of the affected units at the Hyatt thanked us for our support and encouraged us to continue with our meeting as planned.*
>
> *The Union bargaining committee also spoke to our executive director and thanks AFS for its support and is looking forward to welcoming us to the Hyatt Regency Baltimore Inner Harbor. In keeping with the wishes of the workers at the hotel, we will not move forward with our alternate plans. We are letting the hotel management know that we expect them to move forward with good faith negotiations and encourage them to treat their employees justly.*
>
> *Most Sincerely,*
> *The Executive Board of the American Folklore Society*[46]

As Jim Leary noted, "Staunch Commitment by AFS leadership to that tenet [prioritizing unionized hotels] was crucial . . . when the largely minority membership of UNITE HERE's Local 7 won their 'One Job Should Be Enough' strike with our conference hotel for better pay and working conditions" (2021, 203).

The issues and situations with which the AFS has dealt demonstrate difficulties experienced by membership organizations more generally. As an organization, the AFS has fiscal and membership concerns that complicate decisions such as whether to back out of a hotel contract or even issue statements on controversial issues. Reaching agreement by a large and diverse membership is never easy and is often impossible. In fact, this reflects understandings that folklorists were reaching in their own work by the 1990s: the groups we study cannot be assumed to be homogenous (cf. Roberts 1993; Shuman 1993); as a group, folklorists, too, hold a range of opinions and beliefs.

APPLIED FOLKLORE AND ADVOCACY

Despite opposition to seeing applied folklore (in the sense of using folklore to ameliorate community problems) as an approach distinct from public folklore (see chap. 2), it appears the notion of "advocacy" was less problematic by the twenty-first century, to at least some members. As we complete this volume, the home page of the AFS website announces the online version of the "Folklore Advocacy Toolkit," originally created in 2014 by folklorist Susan Eleuterio in collaboration with others.[47] The tool kit defines advocacy by saying, "We recognize advocacy as 'a wide range of activities conducted to influence decision makers at various levels,' including 'not only traditional advocacy work like litigation, lobbying, and public education, but also capacity building, network formation, relationship building, communication, and leadership development.'"[48] Although closely aligned, some folklorists seem to feel more comfortable with the notion of folklore and advocacy over applied folklore. In part, this may be because the sense of advocacy as influencing decision-makers (in lobbying, litigation, public education) fits better with the kinds of interventions that public folklorists find themselves facing. Many public folklorists work for governmental agencies or are funded by government and thus find themselves acting as, or mediating with, decision-makers. And indeed, the advocacy tool kit was created initially with the sponsorship of the Public Programs Section of the American Folklore Society with intentions of addressing all of the spheres in which folklorists work.

This is not to say that there are not folklorists who oppose advocacy work (see, e.g., Oring 2004), but the term *advocacy*, as defined above, describes in the most general terms a type of work that our field has become accustomed to, particularly in areas of cultural policy. It can be argued that William "Bill" Ferris who served as chairman of NEH (1997–2001) and Bill Ivey who served as chairman of the NEA (1998–2001) both worked in advocacy positions. As Frank Proschan notes with respect to the numerous senses of the term *advocate*, this sense refers to "one who pleads, intercedes, or speaks for, or on behalf of, another . . . sometimes [as] an administrator, sometimes an adjudicator and allocator of resources, sometimes a researcher, sometimes a solicitor, sometimes a producer, sometimes an entrepreneur" (2004, 272). The tool kit, and increasingly the field, use the term *advocacy* to refer to work with institutions to benefit, promote, or sustain cultural traditions. This is a far more specific use of the term than Carl Lindahl means when he writes that "the work of a folklorist is by definition a work of advocacy" and that "such advocacy requires us to attempt to put another's truth before our own, to try to make that truth as credible and palpable to our readers and ourselves as our own subjective truths are to us" (quoted in Proschan 2004, 269).

The term *advocacy* as it is used in the tool kit and increasingly in the field refers to a kind of folklore activity that has reached beyond local communities to affect the treatment by institutions and decision-makers of both tradition bearers and tradition.

Forms of advocacy in the sense suggested by the tool kit can include, for example, localized forms such as working with your school board to alter culturally insensitive dress codes or working with lawyers to intervene on behalf of marginalized individuals or communities (Lindahl 2004; Bohmer and Shuman 2007), working with regional government to ensure the preservation and conservation of environmentally threatened communities (Lawrence and Lawless 2018; Lindahl 2012), and working nationally (such as for or with the NEA and NEH) or internationally to foster and promote understanding of and respect for cultural traditions. Over the last twenty-five to thirty years, folklorists have become increasingly involved in debates concerning the formalized agendas of international forums that address and affect the cultures folklorists study and champion (Rikoon 2004, 325). Much of this involvement is critical of the way traditionality and authenticity are addressed (Hafstein 2004) as well as concerned with people-centered versus property-oriented policies and the needs and rights of communities versus one-size-fits-all systems (Rikoon 2004, 326) and how local communities engage with global decisions (Foster 2015a, 143).

International advocacy has involved numerous folklorists in recent years through the World International Property Organization (WIPO)[49] and the United Nations Educational, Scientific and Cultural Organization (UNESCO).[50] In 2000, the UN agency responsible for the promotion of intellectual property worldwide, WIPO, established the Intergovernmental Committee on Intellectual Property and Genetic Resources, Traditional Knowledge, and Folklore. The committee was established to address both the "policy and practical linkages between the Intellectual Property system and the concerns of practitioners and custodians of traditional cultures" (World Intellectual Property Organization n.d.). In 2004, the AFS issued a series of recommendations to WIPO, approved by the 2002 AFS Executive Board and later published in the *Journal of American Folklore*.

The recommendations were largely oriented toward the need for communication with communities to ensure equitable and meaningful participation in decision-making; incorporation of the needs of communities affected by the work of the committee; requesting the provision of technical assistance to communities on matters related to intellectual property, traditional knowledge, and folklore; requesting cultural impact assessment of existing intellectual property regimes; underscoring the fact that cultural interests are not the same as commercial interests; and addressing the importance of both informed prior consent and acceptable compensation (AFS 2004, 296–99).[51]

Hundreds of folklorists over the years have become engaged (in various ways) with UNESCO policies, particularly after the 2003 Convention for the Safeguarding of the Intangible Cultural Heritage (which was based on the 1989 Recommendation on the Safeguarding of Traditional Culture and Folklore) and its accompanying Representative List. While UNESCO is huge with many components, it is for the most part the conventions in the area of culture that engage folklorists—on intangible cultural heritage (ICH) and the 2005 Convention on the Protection and Promotion of the Diversity of Cultural Expressions. The convention seeks to raise awareness of the world's intangible heritage and the need to safeguard it. Masterpieces are defined by UNESCO as "a cultural expression or cultural space" demonstrating "outstanding value as a masterpiece of the human creative genius" (UNESCO 2001, 12). In addition to the Masterpieces list, the convention encourages countries to establish national inventories and to take legal and administrative measures for the protection of their oral and intangible heritage. Folklorists have been actively involved not only in assisting with inventories and the preparation of nominations but also in the creation, theorization, and implementation of UNESCO policy.

There is a nomination process for what the convention calls "Masterpieces of the Intangible Cultural Heritage" with each nomination requiring a technical and scientific review (Seeger 2015, 274). Nomination requires a large dossier including an action plan for safeguarding a particular tradition (Seeger 2015; Gilman 2015). Folklorists around the world have been involved in identifying traditions for safeguarding as well as preparing the nomination process and enacting and evaluating safeguard procedures.[52]

In addition to assisting in the nomination and preparation process, folklorists have generated a large number of ICH case studies that, as Foster notes, have "become a testing ground for negotiations between the global and the local (however defined) and all points in between, where responses can be highly nuanced and contentious" (2015a, 144). These studies have explored how people involved with or affected by ICH experience and respond to the initiatives (Kurin 2004; Bendix, Eggert, and Peselmann 2013; Foster 2015b). Anthony Seeger writes that "the contrast between the honor of being elected to the Representative List and the tangible rewards to local tradition-bearers has often been quite large" (2015, 274). Folklorists have also critiqued the policies and role of UNESCO as potentially making it an arbiter of culture (see also Noyes 2006).

WIPO and UNESCO are perhaps the international agencies that engage the largest number of folklorists, though folklorists are or have been also engaged with the World Health Organization (WHO), the World Bank, the United Nations Children's Fund (UNICEF), and other UN specialized agencies in advocacy roles that overlap with areas of our expertise.

CONCLUSION

The advocacy engagements discussed above demonstrate the growing commitment of folklorists to expanding and maturing our role in expressive culture and political representation. Representation, though, is understood quite differently than it was forty or fifty years ago. As Susan Ritchie noted in 1993, "a truly post-modern folklore presents a different task than the mere critique of totalizing master narratives" (368). Based on Gayatri Spivak's question "Can the Subaltern Speak?" (1988, 297), Ritchie calls into question "ventriloquist strategies of representation, where folklore presumes to speak on the behalf of some voiceless group or individual" (1993, 369). Ritchie notes that Edward Said has argued that disciplines share as our "point of departure an interest in restoring the right of formerly un- or mis-represented human groups to speak for and represent themselves in domains defined, politically and intellectually, as normally excluding them, usurping their signifying functions" (Said 1985, 15). While folklorists still feel an obligation to represent the un- or underrepresented, as can be seen in the more contemporary actions discussed in our coda, we have also learned that we can join the fight for them to have their own seat at the table.

We take seriously the urging of Fivecoate, Downs, and McGriff to "examine the narratives that we tell about our scholarly community—how they bring us together as well as how they separate us" (2021, 7). It is no surprise that many of the issues raised through the case studies examined in this volume are far from resolved. But folklorists have moved more and more toward what Kodish calls "public interest folklore"—"grassroots and community based folklife practice inspired by a vision of progressive social change, addressing inequalities, and working for the common good" (2011, 32). We have found new or different ways of thinking about equality, subordination, social change, policy, representation, and politics. We don't always get it right, but we know we can make a difference. We try harder, explore our positionality a little better, learn greater humbleness, empathize more, listen more. The weight of social responsibility has gotten no lighter, and our folklore souls are still fragile, but, as luck would have it, the end of this book is not the end of our story.

NOTES

1. AFS was not alone in regard to conversations about both boycotts and alternative solutions regarding holding conferences in states that have banned abortion. See, for instance, Goodman 2022.

2. The full AFS code of ethics can be found here: "AFS Statement on Ethics: Principles of Professional Responsibility," American Folklore Society, accessed May 19, 2025, https://americanfolkloresociety.org/our-work /position-statement-ethics.

3. American Sociological Association, "Proposed ASA Statement against the War on Iraq." *Footnotes*, April 2003, p. 3,. https://www.asanet .org/wp-content/uploads/fn_2003_04_april.pdf.

4. The guidelines for requesting AFS to issue a position statement can be found here: "Guidelines for Requesting AFS to Issue a Position Statement," American Folklore Society, accessed May 20, 2025, https://americanfolkloresociety.org/our-work/guidelines-for -requesting-afs-to-issue-a-position-statement.

5. These identified position statements can be found here: "Position Statements," American Folklore Society, accessed May 25, 2025, https://americanfolkloresociety.org/our-work/#position-statements.

6. These position statements on Syria and Turkey can be found here: "AFS Stands in Solidarity with Those Impacted by Earthquakes in Syria and Turkey," American Folklore Society, March 3, 2023, https://americanfolkloresociety.org/afs-stands-in-solidarity-with -those-impacted-by-earthquakes-in-syria-and-turkey; the posi- tion statement on Ukraine can be found here: "AFS Condemns the Invasion of Ukraine and Supports Ukrainian Folklore and Heri- tage Scholars," American Folklore Society, March 1, 2022, https:// americanfolkloresociety.org/afs-condemns-the-war-in-ukraine-and -stands-with-all-who-oppose-this-violence. The AFS also increasingly signs onto joint statements issued by others. Two examples announced during the time of this writing included an American Council of Learned Societies (ACLS) Statement in Support of Academic Freedom and New College of Florida (signed by AFS on February 15, 2023; " AFS Signs Statement in Support of Academic Freedom and New Col- lege of Florida," American Folklore Society, February 15, 2023, https:// americanfolkloresociety.org/afs-signs-acla-statement-in-support-of -academic-freedom-and-new-college-of-florida) and statements by the ACLS and the American Historical Association "opposing Florida

House Bill 999, which allows political appointees unprecedented oversight of day-to-day educational decisions" (signed by AFS on March 6, 2023; "AFS Signs Statements Opposing Florida House Bill 999," American Folklore Society, March 6, 2023, https://americanfolkloresociety .org/afs-signs-statements-opposing-florida-house-bill-999). Beginning in 2019, decisions regarding signing onto such statements are made by the AFS executive director, president, and president-elect / past president, not the full executive board.

7. See "AFS Folklore and Public Policy Working Groups," accessed May 20, 2025, https://wayback.archive-it.org/all/20200408225636 /https://www.afsnet.org/page/FLPubPolicyWG. Also see Sommers 2019 and Sommers 2013 for a description of the work of the working group on historic preservation, cited in chapter 4.

8. See "AFS Index of Executive Actions," accessed May 23, 2025, https://web.archive.org/web/20250000000000*/https://cdn.ymaws.com /www.afsnet.org/resource/resmgr/executive_board_minutes/Index_of _Board_Actions-FINAL.pdf.

9. Marilyn White noted in our Zoom interview on March 16, 2023, that this committee had many iterations over the years. It may be that this was more a name change than anything else. Former AFS associate director Lorraine Cashman (personal communication, March 18, 2023) indicated that the 2001 annual report has a report from the "Task Force on Cultural Diversity" (personal communication, March 18, 2023).

10. The AFS Cultural Diversity Committee's description from 2023 can be found here: "Cultural Diversity Committee," American Folklore Society, accessed May 19, 2025, https://americanfolkloresociety.org/our-work /committees-and-working-groups/cultural-diversity-committee.

11. See the program for the 2019 Annual Meeting of AFS: "2019 Program and Abstracts for the Annual Meeting of the American Folklore Society," 2019, 11, https://scholarworks.iu.edu/dspace/handle/2022/26481.

12. Activist Tarana Burke first used the term "Me Too" in 2006 as a show of supporting survivors of sexual assault and harassment. It was not until 2017 that term went viral as a Twitter hashtag and spread around the world, with men in powerful positions in entertainment, politics, and other realms publicly called out and in some cases charged (criminally or civilly) for their behaviors and actions. See the "Me Too" website ("History & Inception," accessed May 19, 2025, https://metoomvmt.org/get-to -know-us/history-inception) and Daigle (2021). The lasting impact of #MeToo remains to be seen.

13. Elaine Lawless, Rachel V. González-Martín, Debra Lattanzi Shutika, and Jessica A. Turner. 2018. "Folklorists and #MeToo." Forum abstract, Program for the Annual Meeting of the American Folklore Society, Buffalo, NY, 107.

14. Diane E. Goldstein, Ann K. Ferrell, Thomas A. McKean, and Evangeline C. Mee. 2019. "#MeToo, Take Two." Forum abstract, Program for the Annual Meeting of the American Folklore Society, Baltimore, MD, 117.

15. Rachel V. González-Martin, Constance Bailey, Thomas McKean, Claire M. Schmidt, Jessica Turner, and Marilyn White. 2022. "How Folklorists Can Address the #MeToo Movement. Program for the Annual Meeting of the American Folklore Society, Tulsa, OK, 46.

16. See You 2025.

17. Panels and sessions from the 2020 Annual Meeting can be found here: "Past Annual Meetings," American Folklore Society, accessed May 20, 205, https://wayback.archive-it.org/all/20210509125123/https://cdn .ymaws.com/www.afsnet.org/resource/resmgr/am20/AM20_Printable _Program.pdf.

18. AFS Executive Director Jessica Turner's contribution is one of several in the Notable Folklorists of Color exhibition guide (AFS 2022).

19. See "Notable Folklorists of Color," American Folklore Society, accessed May 19, 2025, https://notablefolkloristsofcolor.org.

20. "Measure No. 9: State of Oregon," Official 1992 General Voters' Pamphlet, which can be found here: "2: Ballot Measure 9," accessed May 19, 2025, https://noon9remembered.org/stories/ballot-measure-9.

21. "Measure No. 9: State of Oregon," accessed May 19, 2025, https://noon9remembered.org/stories/ballot-measure-9/.

22. American Folklore Society. Executive Board Minutes, New Series, No. 30, October 15, 1992, 5. All quotations from this paragraph can be found on page 5 of the minutes. Unless otherwise noted, all references to AFS-related minutes and letters in this chapter are from American Folklore Society records, 1890–2011. (COLL MSS 206). Utah State University. Special Collections and Archives Department.

23. American Folklore Society. Minutes of the Executive Board Question and Answer Session, October 16, 1992, 5–6. The minutes note that approximately two hundred members were in attendance.

24. American Folklore Society. Minutes of the Executive Board Question and Answer Session, October 16, 1992, 1.

25. The minutes note that approximately two hundred members were in attendance. In this period, the minutes had returned to including more

details, though not at the level of partial transcription that they had prior to the late 1970s.

26. Enclosure to a memo from Shalom Staub to the Executive Board of the American Folklore Society, December 8, 1992.

27. Letter from Sylvia Grider, AFS President, to Barbara Roberts, Governor of Oregon, October 26, 1992.

28. Letter from Barbara Roberts, Governor of Oregon, to Sylvia Grider, AFS President, October 29, 1992.

29. Retrieved from National Conference of State Legislatures, "Statewide Ballot Measures Database," accessed May 20, 2025, https://www.ncsl.org/elections-and-campaigns/statewide-ballot-measures-database.

30. Also during the 1992 meeting, the Politics, Folklore, and Social Justice Section was formed, and it was approved by the executive board that same year. See: "Politics, Folklore, and Social Justice," American Folklore Society, accessed May 20, 2025, https://americanfolkloresociety.org/our-community/sections/politics-folklore-and-social-justice/.

31. That same year, the publication of a special issue dedicated to representation of a silenced group would once again be challenged, though not by editors; this time, it was the landmark special issue of *New York Folklore*: "Prejudice and Pride: Lesbian and Gay Traditions in America." At least one member of the board of directors of the New York Folklore Society objected to the issue, as indicated by a note below the board list in the front matter, which states, "Peter Voorheis considers certain material in this issue to be obscene and has requested that his objections to the publication of this material be recorded herein" (Blincoe and Forrest 1993b). According to editors Deborah Blincoe and John Forrest in the editorial essay that begins this special issue, the "outrage and anxiety communicated by advance critics of this special issue have been entirely focused upon the sexual aspects of the proposed (or imagined) contents. Of course, oppositional reactions to the concept of the special issue are situated within the very cultural matrix which has created that which is feared" (Blincoe and Forrest 1993a, 5).

32. American Folklore Society. Minutes of the Executive Board Question and Answer Session, October 29, 1993.

33. Timothy Lloyd, interview with authors, March 18, 2022. Zoom.

34. The language of this bill is very similar to laws enacted in a number of states during the writing of this book regarding the teaching of "critical race theory." See Stephenson 2021.

35. Final draft of the AFS statement on Arizona, provided by former executive director Timothy Lloyd.

36. Final draft of the AFS statement on Arizona, provided by former executive director Timothy Lloyd.

37. See https://unitehere.org/who-we-are/industries, accessed May 20, 2025.

38. Timothy Lloyd, email to authors, July 22, 2021.

39. Executive Board of the American Folklore Society. 2015. "Westin Long Beach: A Message to AFS Members from the Executive Board." AFS Review: News, March 14, 2015. https://web.archive.org/web/20210612161941/http://www.afsnet.org/news/221501/Westin-Long-Beach-A-Message-to-AFS-Members-from-the-Executive-Board.htm.

40. S. Magliocco. "My Experience with UNITE HERE." AFS Forum, 2015 Annual Meeting, May 22, 2015. https://web.archive.org/web/20160913235629/http://www.afsnet.org/forums/Posts.aspx?topic=1111920.

41. Comment posted to AFS Review: News post "AFS Executive Director Reaches Out to UNITE HERE." May 26, 2015. https://web.archive.org/web/20160913235502/http://www.afsnet.org/news/233451/AFS-Executive-Director-Reaches-Out-to-UNITE-HERE.htm.

42. Robert McCarl. Report and Critique of AFS Focus on Social Justice Issues, October 2016, Miami, FL.

43. Timothy Lloyd, email to authors, July 22, 2021.

44. "Preliminary Report on the 2015 Annual Meeting: Response and Outcomes." AFS Review: Reports, November 19, 2025. https://web.archive.org/web/20210310031436/http://www.afsnet.org:80/news/261134/Preliminary-Report-on-the-2015-Annual-Meeting-Response-and-Outcomes.htm.

45. Timothy Lloyd, email to authors, July 22, 2021.

46. Executive Board of the American Folklore Society. 2019. "UNITE HERE Local 7 Invites AFS Annual Meeting to Proceed." AFS Review: News, October 16, 2019. https://web.archive.org/web/20210412021635/https://www.afsnet.org/news/474305/UNITE-HERE-Local-7-Invites-AFS-Annual-Meeting-to-Proceed.htm.

47. See "Folklore Advocacy Toolkit," American Folklore Society, accessed May 20, 2025, https://americanfolkloresociety.org/our-work/folklore-advocacy-toolkit.

48. See: "Why Advocate," American Folklore Society, https://americanfolkloresociety.org/our-work/folklore-advocacy-toolkit/why-advocate. The tool kit cites Innovation Network 2009 for this quotation.

The publication produced by Innovation Network and Atlantic Philanthropies, "Pathfinder: A Practical Guide to Advocacy Evaluation," can be found here: "Pathfinder: A Practical Guide to Advocacy Evaluation," accessed May 20, 205, https://alnap.org/help-library/resources/pathfinder-a-practical-guide-to-advocacy-evaluation/.

49. WIPO is the global forum for intellectual property. It is a self-funding agency of the United Nations with 193 member states. The WIPO Convention was established in 1967.

50. UNESCO was founded after WWII in November 1945 to contribute to peace and security, encouraging collaboration among nations. It is headquartered in Paris and has 190 member states.

51. Submitted to WIPO the same month.

52. For representative lists, see: "Browse the Lists of Intangible Cultural Heritage and the Register of Good Safeguarding Practices," UNESCO, accessed May 26, 2025, https://ich.unesco.org/en/lists.

WORKS CITED

Abrahams, Roger D. 1978. "Towards a Sociological Theory of Folklore: Performing Services." *Western Folklore* 37 (3): 161–84.

Abrahams, Roger D. 1989. "The American Folklore Society Centennial 1888–89 to 1988–89." *Folk Music Journal* 5 (5): 608–19.

Abrahams, Roger D. 1993. "Phantoms of Romantic Nationalism in Folkloristics." *Journal of American Folklore* 106 (419): 3–37.

Adame, Jaime. 2023. "Should Conferences Stay Put or Relocate? It's Complicated." *Insider Higher Ed*, February 6, 2023. https://www.insidehighered.com/news/2023/02/07/should-conferences-stay-put-or-relocate-its-complicated.

Adams, William Hampton, ed. 1980. "Waverly Plantation: Ethnoarchaeology of a Tenant Farming Community." Submitted to the Heritage Conservation and Recreation Service. Bloomington, IN: Resource Analysts.

AFS (American Folklore Society). 1975. "Proceedings of the Annual Business Meeting." *Journal of American Folklore* 88:4–23.

AFS (American Folklore Society). 1979. "AFS Affairs." *The American Folklore Society Newsletter* 8 (2): 1–2.

AFS (American Folklore Society). 1983. "Board Identifies Key Issues for Nashville Meeting." *The American Folklore Society Newsletter* 125:1.

AFS (American Folklore Society). 1984. "Report from the 1984 Annual Meeting." *The American Folklore Society Newsletter* 13 (6): 1.

AFS (American Folklore Society). 1988. "AFS Statement on Ethics: Principles of Professional Responsibility" *AFS News*, New Series 17(1). https://americanfolkloresociety.org/wp-content/uploads/2021/05/Ethics.pdf.

AFS (American Folklore Society). 2004. "Recommendations to the WIPO Intergovernmental Committee on Intellectual Property and Genetic Resources, Traditional Knowledge, and Folklore." *Journal of American Folklore* 117 (465): 296–99.

AFS (American Folklore Society). 2022. *Recentering the Periphery, Coloring the Discourses, and Expanding the Frames: A Guide to the American Folklore Society Notable Folklorists of Color Exhibitions.* Bloomington, IN: American Folklore Society.

Agozzino, Maria Teresa. 2012. "American Folklore Society." In *Celebrating Latino Folklore: An Encyclopedia of Cultural Traditions*, edited by Maria Herrera-Sobek, 43–45. Santa Barbara, CA: ABC-CLIO.

American Folklife Center. 1979. "Tennessee-Tombigbee Folklife Study." *Folklife Center News* 2 (1): 1, 3.

American Folklore Society Records, 1890–2011. (COLL MSS 206). Utah State University. Special Collections and Archives Department.

Anttonen, Pertti. 2005. *Tradition through Modernity: Postmodernism and the Nation State in Folklore Scholarship.* Studia Fennica, Folkloristica, no. 15. Helsinki: Suomalaisen Kirjallisuuden Seura.

Arewa, E. Ojo, and Alan Dundes. 1964. "Proverbs and the Ethnography of Speaking Folklore." *American Anthropologist* 66 (6): 70–85.

Arora, Shirley L. 1988. "'No Tickee, No Shirtee': Proverbial Speech and Leadership in Academia." In *Inside Organizations: Understanding the Human Dimension*, edited by Michael Owen Jones, Michael Dane Moore, and Richard Christopher Snyder, 179–90. Newbury Park, CA: Sage.

Associated Press. 2017. "Arizona Judge Declares Ban on Ethnic Studies Unconstitutional." *NBC News*, last modified December 28, 2017. https://www.nbcnews.com/news/latino/arizona-judge-declares-ban-ethnic-studies-unconstitutional-n833126.

Axton, W. F. 1975. *Tobacco and Kentucky.* Lexington: University Press of Kentucky.

Babcock, Barbara A. 1993. "'At Home, No Womens Are Storytellers': Potteries, Stories, and Politics in Cochiti Pueblo." In *Feminist Messages: Coding in Women's Folk Culture*, edited by Joan N. Radner, 221–48. Urbana: University of Illinois Press.

Baron, Robert. 1995. "'It Ought to be Returned to Them . . . It Needed to Be Spread Around': Reflections on Public Folklore Then and Now." *New York Folklore* 21 (1–4): 13–37.

Baron, Robert. (1992) 2007. "Postwar Public Folklore and the Professionalization of Folklore Studies." In *Public Folklore,* edited by Robert Baron and Nick Spitzer, 307–37. Jackson: University Press of Mississippi.

Baron, Robert. 2016. "Prologue: Mediating and Immediating at the Smithsonian Folklife Festival." In *Curatorial Conversations: Cultural Representation and the Smithsonian Folklife Festival*, edited by Olivia Cadaval, Sojin Kim, and Diana Baird N'Diaye, 11–17. Jackson: University Press of Mississippi.

Baron, Robert, and Nick Spitzer, eds. (1992) 2007. *Public Folklore*. Jackson: University Press of Mississippi.

Bauman, Richard. 1971. "Proposal for a Center of Applied Folklore." In "Papers on Applied Folklore," edited by Dick Sweterlitsch, special issue, *Folklore Forum Bibliographic and Special Series* (8): 1–5.

Bauman, Richard. 1972. "Differential Identity and the Social Base of Folklore." In *Toward New Perspectives in Folklore*, edited by Américo Paredes and Richard Bauman, 31–41. Austin: University of Texas Press.

Bauman, Richard. 2020. "The Texas School." In *Folklore in the United States and Canada: An Institutional History*, edited by Patricia Sawin and Rosemary Lévy Zumwalt, 129–41. Bloomington: Indiana University Press.

Behar, Ruth, and Susan A. Gordon, eds. 1996. *Women Writing Culture*. Berkeley: University of California Press.

Belanus, Betty J. 1994. "Serving the Public: An Assessment of Work in Public Sector Folklore." In *Putting Folklore to Use*, edited by Michael Owen Jones, 201–13. Lexington: University Press of Kentucky.

Belanus, Betty J. 2021. "Revisiting Stories from the 1989 and 1990 Smithsonian Folklore Summer Institute for Community Scholars." *Journal of American Folklore* 134 (531): 101–12.

Bell, Michael J. 1973. "William Wells Newell and the Foundation of American Folklore Scholarship." *Journal of the Folklore Institute* 10 (1/2): 7–21.

Bell, Michael J. 1979. "The Relation of Mentality to Race: William Wells Newell and the Celtic Hypothesis." *Journal of American Folklore* 92 (363): 25–43.

Bell, Michael J. 1984. "Making Art Work." In "Works of Art, Art as Work, and the Arts of Working," edited by Michael Owen Jones, special section, *Western Folklore* 43 (3): 211–21.

Ben-Amos, Dan. 1969. "Analytical Categories and Ethnic Genres." *Genre* 2 (3): 275–301.

Ben-Amos, Dan. 1971. "Toward a Definition of Folklore in Context." *Journal of American Folklore* 84 (331): 3–15.

Ben-Amos, Dan. 1976a. "Analytical Categories and Ethnic Genres." In *Folklore Genres*, edited by Dan Ben-Amos, 217–44. Austin: University of Texas Press.

Ben-Amos, Dan, ed. 1976b. *Folklore Genres.* Austin: University of Texas Press.

Ben-Amos, Dan. 2014. "A Definition of Folklore: A Personal Narrative." *Studies in Oral Folk Literature* 3:9–28.

Ben-Amos, Dan, and Kenneth S. Goldstein. 1975. *Folklore: Performance and Communication.* The Hague: Mouton.

Bendix, Regina. 1997. *In Search of Authenticity: The Formation of Folklore Studies.* Madison: University of Wisconsin Press.

Bendix, Regina F., Aditya Eggert, and Arnika Peselmann. 2013. *Heritage Regimes and the State.* Göttingen: Göttingen University Press.

Benedict, Ruth. (1946) 2005. *The Chrysanthemum and the Sword: Patterns of Japanese Culture.* Boston: Houghton Mifflin Harcourt.

Berray, Mohamed 2019. "A Critical Literary Review of the Melting Pot and Salad Bowl Assimilation and Integration Theories." *Journal of Ethnic and Cultural Studies* 6 (1): 142–51.

Bevill, Tom, Rep. 1979. "Status of Folklife Study in Connection with Tennessee-Tombigbee Waterway Project." 96th Cong., 1st sess., *Congressional Record* 125 (March 27): H 6334–35.

Blazak, Randy. 2022. "Oregon Citizens Alliance." *Oregon Encyclopedia.* https://www.oregonencyclopedia.org/articles/oregon_citizens_alliance /#.ZGam4uzMLlx.

Blincoe, Deborah, and John Forrest. 1993a. "Editorial Essay: The Dangers of Authenticity." In "Prejudice and Pride: Lesbian and Gay Traditions in America," edited by Deborah Blincoe and John Forrest, special issue, *New York Folklore* 19:1–14.

Blincoe, Deborah, and John Forrest, eds. 1993b. "Prejudice and Pride: Lesbian and Gay Traditions in America." Special issue, *New York Folklore* 19.

Bohmer, Carol, and Amy Shuman. 2007. *Rejecting Refugees: Political Asylum in the 21st Century.* London: Routledge.

Botkin, Benjamin A. 1953. "Applied Folklore: Creating Understanding through Folklore." *Southern Folklore Quarterly* 17 (3): 199–206.

Botkin, Benjamin A. 1961. "Proposal for an Applied Folklore Center." *New York Folklore Quarterly* 17:151–54.

Boucicaut, Tanya, and Lisa Gilman, eds. 2021. "African American Expressive Culture, Protest, Imagination, and Dreams of Blackness." Special issue, *Journal of American Folklore* 134 (534).

Boyd, Cynthia. 1997. "'Just Like One of the Boys': Tactics of Women Taxi Drivers." In *Undisciplined Women: Tradition and Culture in Canada,* edited by Pauline Greenhill and Diane Tye, 213–22. Montreal: McGill-Queen's University Press.

Boynton, Mia. 1988a. "Introduction." In "Folklore in the Industrial Workplace," edited by Mia Boynton, special issue, *New York Folklore* 14 (1–2): 1–7.

Boynton, Mia. 1988b. "A Woman in a Men's Sphere: Testimonies from a Woman Steelworker at Buffalo's Republic Steel." In "Folklore in the Industrial Workplace," edited by Mia Boynton, special issue, *New York Folklore* 14 (1–2): 87–99.

Brady, Erika. 1988. "The Bureau of American Ethnology: Folklore, Fieldwork, and the Federal Government in the Late Nineteenth and Early Twentieth Centuries." In *The Conservation of Culture: Folklorists and the Public Sector*, edited by Burt Feintuch, 35–45. Lexington: University Press of Kentucky.

Brady, Erika. 1999. *A Spiral Way: How the Phonograph Changed Ethnography*. Jackson: University Press of Mississippi.

Briggs, Charles L., and Amy Shuman, eds. 1993. "Theorizing Folklore: Toward New Perspectives on the Politics of Culture." Special issue, *Western Folklore* 52 (2–4).

Briscoe, Virginia W. 1974. "Progress Report of the Chairwoman, Steering Committee of the Women's Caucus, AFS." *Folklore Feminists Communication* 4:7–9.

Bromberg-Ross, JoAnne. 1976. "Women's Caucus Minutes." *Folklore Feminists Communication* 8:14–17.

Brondo, Keri Vacanti, Carla Guerrón Montero, Catherine Kingfisher, and Elizabeth Tunstall. 2009. "Squeaky Wheels Squeaks Again: Reflections on the Committee on the Status of Women in Anthropology." *Voices* 9, no. 1 (Winter): 5–8.

Bronner, Simon J. 1986. *American Folklore Studies: An Intellectual History*. Lawrence: University Press of Kansas.

Bronner, Simon J., ed. 2006. *Encyclopedia of American Folklife*, 4 vols. Armonk, NY: M.E. Sharpe.

Bronner, Simon J. 2011. *Explaining Traditions: Folk Behavior in Modern Culture*. Lexington: University Press of Kentucky.

Bronner, Simon J. 2016. "Toward a Definition of Folklore in Practice." *Cultural Analysis* 15 (1): 6–27.

Brose, David S. 1991. *Yesterday's River: The Archaeology of Ten Thousand Years Along the Tennessee-Tombigbee Waterway*. Cleveland, OH: Cleveland Museum of Natural History.

Broussard, Albert S. 2011. "Race and Oral History." In *The Oxford Handbook of Oral History*, edited by Donald A. Ritchie, 186–201. Oxford: Oxford University Press.

Brown, Howard A. 1974. *Brief History of the Tennessee-Tombigbee Waterway Project*. Washington, DC: Library of Congress Congressional Research Service.

Brucher, Katherine. 2016. "Assembly Lines and Contra Dance Lines: The Ford Motor Company Music Department and Leisure Reform." *Journal of the Society for American Music* 10 (4): 470–95.

Brunvand, Jan Harold. 1968. *The Study of American Folklore: An Introduction*. New York: W. W. Norton.

Brunvand, Jan Harold. 1978. *The Study of American Folklore. An Introduction*. 2nd ed. New York: W. W. Norton.

Brunvand, Jan Harold. 1982. "Obituary: Richard M. Dorson (1916–1981)." *Journal of American Folklore* 95 (377): 347–53.

Brunvand, Jan Harold. 1986. *The Study of American Folklore: An Introduction*. 3rd ed. New York: W. W. Norton.

Brunvand, Jan Harold. 1998. *The Study of American Folklore: An Introduction*. 4th ed. New York: W. W. Norton.

Bulger, Peggy A. 2003. "Looking Back, Moving Forward: The Development of Folklore as a Public Profession (AFS Presidential Address, 2002)." *Journal of American Folklore* 116 (462): 377–90.

Bulger, Peggy A. 2017. *Stetson Kennedy: Applied Folklore and Cultural Advocacy*. Cocoa: Florida Historical Society Press.

Burns, Sean. 2011. *Archie Green: The Making of a Working-Class Hero*. Champaign: University of Illinois Press.

Burns, Thomas A. 1977. "Review of *Urban Folklore from the Paperwork Empire*, by Alan Dundes and Carl R. Pagter." *Journal of American Folklore* 90 (355): 84–86.

Byington, Robert H. 1978a. "Introduction." In "Working Americans: Contemporary Approaches to Occupational Folklife," special issue, *Western Folklore* 37 (3): 143–44.

Byington, Robert H. 1978b. "Strategies for Collecting Occupational Folklife in Contemporary Urban/Industrial Contexts." In "Working Americans: Contemporary Approaches to Occupational Folklife," special issue, *Western Folklore* 37 (3): 185–98.

Byington, Robert H., ed. 1978c. "Working Americans: Contemporary Approaches to Occupational Folklife." Special issue, *Western Folklore* 37 (3).

Byington, Robert H. 1985. "Letter to the Editor." *The American Folklore Society Newsletter* 14 (1): 2.

Byington, Robert H. 1989. "What Happened to Applied Folklore?" In *Time & Temperature*, edited by Charles Camp, 77–79. Washington, DC: American Folklore Society.

Cadaval, Olivia, Sojin Kim, and Diana Baird N'Diaye. 2016. "Introduction." In *Curatorial Conversations: Cultural Representation and the Smithsonian Folklife Festival*, edited by Olivia Cadaval, Sojin Kim, and Diana Baird N'Diaye, 19–29. Jackson: University Press of Mississippi.

Camitta, Miriam. 1988. "The Folklorist and the Highway: Theoretical and Practical Implications of the Vine Street Project." In *The Conservation of Culture: Folklorists and the Public Sector*, edited by Burt Feintuch, 206–16. Lexington: University Press of Kentucky.

Camp, Charles. 1988. "Hearings Held on the 'Square Dance Bill.'" *The American Folklore Society Newsletter*, October 5, 1988. Retrieved from Square Dance Legislation collection (AFC 1984/024), Archive of Folk Culture, American Folklife Center, Library of Congress, Washington, DC.

Camp, Charles, ed. 1989. *Time & Temperature*. A Centennial Publication of the American Folklore Society. Washington, DC: American Folklore Society.

Camp, Charles, and Timothy Lloyd. 1980. "Six Reasons Not to Produce Folklife Festivals." *Kentucky Folklore Record* 26 (1): 67–74.

Cantú, Norma E., and Olga Nájera-Ramírez, eds. 2002a. *Chicana Traditions: Continuity and Change*. Champaign: University of Illinois Press.

Cantú, Norma E., and Olga Nájera-Ramírez. 2002b. "Las Folkloristas: An Overview." In *Chicana Traditions: Continuity and Change*, edited by Norma E. Cantú and Olga Nájera-Ramírez, 1–11. Champaign: University of Illinois Press.

Cashman, Ray, Tom Mould, and Pravina Shukla. 2011a. "A Folklorist's Work: Henry Glassie's Life in the Field." In *The Individual and Tradition: Folkloristic Perspectives*, edited by Ray Cashman, Tom Mould, and Pravina Shukla, 499–528. Bloomington: Indiana University Press.

Cashman, Ray, Tom Mould, and Pravina Shukla. 2011b. "Introduction: The Individual and Tradition." In *The Individual and Tradition: Folkloristic Perspectives*, edited by Ray Cashman, Tom Mould, and Pravina Shukla, 1–26. Bloomington: Indiana University Press.

Christian, Diane. 1988. "Not One New Truth and All the Old Falsehoods." *Journal of American Folklore* 101 (399): 53–55.

Clark, Sharon Leigh. 1976. "The American Folklife Preservation Act. Report and Comments." *Dance Research Journal* 8 (2): 45–50.

Clements, William M. 1988. *100 Years of American Folklore Studies: A Conceptual History*. A Centennial Publication of the American Folklore Society. Washington, DC: American Folklore Society.

Clifford, James. 1986. "Introduction: Partial Truths." In *Writing Culture: The Poetics and Politics of Ethnography*, edited by James Clifford and George E. Marcus, 1–26. Berkeley: University of California Press.

Clifford, James, and George E. Marcus, eds. 1986. *Writing Culture: The Poetics and Politics of Ethnography*. Berkeley: University of California Press.

"Constitution and Bylaws of the American Folk Society." 1973. *Journal of American Folklore* 86 (Supplement: Annual Report of the American Folklore Society): 155–62.

Daigle, Leah E., ed. 2021. "Research on Sexual Violence in the #MeToo Era: Prevention and Innovative Methodologies." Special issue, *American Journal of Criminal Justice* 46 (2–5).

Dandridge, C. Thomas. 1988. "Work Ceremonies: Why Integrate Work and Play?" In *Inside Organizations: Understanding the Human Dimension*, edited by Michael Owen Jones, Michael Dane Moore, and Richard Christopher Snyder, 251–59. Newbury Park, CA: Sage.

Davis, Gerald L. 1996. "'Somewhere over the Rainbow . . .': Judy Garland in Neverland." *Journal of American Folklore* 109 (432): 115–28.

de Caro, F. A. 1974. "American Folklore Society." *Folklore Feminists Communication* 2:20.

de Caro, F. A. 1975a. "Report from the Women's Caucus Meeting, 1974." *Folklore Feminists Communication* 5:10.

de Caro, F. A. 1975b. "The Women's Movement in AFS: A Brief Chronology 1971–1973." *Folklore Feminists Communication* 5:4, 21–23. Reprinted from *The Folklore Historian*, no. 1, publication of the AFS History Committee, by permission of Richard A. Reuss, editor.

de Caro, Rosan Jordan. 1974. "Foreward!" *Folklore Feminists Communication* 2:2.

de Caro, Rosan Jordan, Claire R. Farrer, and Susan J. Kalčik, eds. 1973. "A Preliminary Word." *Folklore Feminists Communication* 1:2.

de Caro, Rosan Jordan, Susan Kalčik, Lorre Weidlich, F.A. de Caro, and Kay F. Stone, eds. 1974. "Who Are We?" *Folklore Feminists Communication* 4:2, 21.

Deemer, Polly Stewart. 1975. "A Response to the Symposium." In "Women and Folklore: Images and Genres," edited by Claire R. Farrer, special issue, *Journal of American Folklore* 88 (347): 101–9.

Dewhurst, C. Kurt. 1984. "The Arts of Working: Manipulating the Urban Environment." In "Works of Art, Art as Work, and the Arts of Working," edited by Michael Owen Jones, special section, *Western Folklore* 43 (3): 192–201.

Dewhurst, C. Kurt. 1988. "Art at Work: In Pursuit of Aesthetic Solutions." In *Inside Organizations: Understanding the Human Dimension*, edited by Michael Owen Jones, Michael Dane Moore, and Richard Christopher Snyder, 245–50. Newbury Park, CA: Sage.

Dorson, Richard. 1950. "Folklore and Fakelore." *American Mercury* 70 (March): 335–42.

Dorson, Richard M. 1959. "A Theory for American Folklore." *Journal of American Folklore* 72 (285): 197–215.

Dorson, Richard M. 1962. "Folklore and the National Defense Education Act." *Journal of American Folklore* 75 (296): 160–64.

Dorson, Richard M. 1970. "Is There a Folk in the City?" *Journal of American Folklore* 83 (328): 217–24.

Dorson, Richard. 1971. "Applied Folklore." In "Papers on Applied Folklore," edited by Dick Sweterlitsch, special issue, *Folklore Forum Bibliographic and Special Series* no. 8, 40–42.

Dorson, Richard, ed. 1972. *Folklore and Folklife: An Introduction*. Chicago: University of Chicago Press.

Dorson, Richard. 1973. *America in Legend: Folklore from the Colonial Period to the Present*. New York: Pantheon.

Dorson, Richard. 1975. "Comments on Williams." *Journal of the Folklore Institute* 11:235–38.

Dorson, Richard, ed. 1978. "Folklore in America versus American Folklore." Special issue, *Journal of Folklore Institute* 15 (2).

Dorson, Richard, ed. 1980. "The American Theme in American Folklore." Special issue, *Journal of Folklore Institute* 17 (2–3).

Dorson, Richard. 1982. "The State of Folkloristics from an American Perspective." *Journal of the Folklore Institute* 19 (2–3): 71–105.

Dundes, Alan. 1965. *The Study of Folklore*. Englewood Cliffs, NJ: Prentice Hall.

Dundes, Alan. 1977. "Who Are the Folk?" In *The Frontiers of Folklore*, edited by William Bascom, 17–35. Boulder, CO: Westview.

Dundes, Alan. 2005. "Folkloristics in the Twenty-First Century (AFS Invited Presidential Plenary Address, 2004)." *Journal of American Folklore* 118 (470): 385–408.

Dundes, Alan, and Carl R. Pagter. (1975) 1978. *Work Hard and You Shall Be Rewarded: Urban Folklore from the Paperwork Empire*. Originally published as Volume 62 in the American Folklore Society's Memoir Series, 1975. Bloomington: Indiana University Press.

Egan, Timothy. 1992. "Oregon Measure Asks State to Repress Homosexuality." *New York Times*, August 16, 1992. https://www.nytimes.com/1992/08/16/us /oregon-measure-asks-state-to-repress-homosexuality.html.

Evanchuk, Robin. 1991. "'As Others See Us': What Others Think Folklorists Are and Do." *Western Folklore* 50 (1): 13–19.

Farrer, Claire R., ed. (1975) 1986. *Women and Folklore: Images and Genres*. Reissue. Prospect Heights, IL: Waveland.

Farrer, Claire R. 1975. "Introduction: Women and Folklore: Images and Genres." In "Women and Folklore," edited by Claire R. Farrer, special issue, *Journal of American Folklore* 88 (347).

Feintuch, Burt, ed. 1988a. *The Conservation of Culture: Folklorists and the Public Sector*. Lexington: University Press of Kentucky.

Feintuch, Burt. 1988b. "The Folklorist and the Public." In *100 Years of American Folklore Studies, A Conceptual History*, edited by William M. Clements, 70–74. Washington, DC: American Folklore Society.

Fine, Gary Alan. 1988. "Letting Off Steam? Redefining a Restaurant's Work Environment." In *Inside Organizations: Understanding the Human Dimension*, edited by Michael Owen Jones, Michael Dane Moore, and Richard Christopher Snyder, 119–27. Newbury Park, CA: Sage.

Fish, Lydia. 1989. "The Folklorist as Community Organizer." In *Time & Temperature*, edited by Charles Camp, 24–25. Washington, DC: American Folklore Society.

Fivecoate, Jesse A., Kristina Downs, and Meredith A. E. McGriff. 2021. "Envisioning a Future Folkloristics." In *Advancing Folkloristics*, edited by Jesse A. Fivecoate, Kristina Downs, and Meredith AE McGriff, 1–8. Bloomington: Indiana University Press.

Ford, Henry. 1921. *The International Jew, Volume III, Jewish Influences in American Life*. In *The Dearborn Independent*. Reprinted as Henry Ford. *Jewish Activities in the United States: Volume II of the International Jew, Being a Reprint of a Second Selection from Articles Appearing in the Dearborn Independent from Oct. 9, 1920, to March 19, 1921*. Vol. 2. Dearborn Publishing, 1921.

Ford, Henry. 1926. *Good Morning: After a Sleep of Twenty-Five Years Old-Fashioned Dancing Is Being Revived by Mr. and Mrs. Henry Ford*. Dearborn, MI: Dearborn Publishing Company.

Foster, George M. 1969. *Applied Anthropology*. Boston: Little Brown.

Foster, Michael Dylan. 2015a. "UNESCO on the Ground." In "UNESCO on the Ground: Local Perspectives on Intangible Cultural Heritage," edited by Michael Dylan Foster, special issue, *Journal of Folklore Research* 52 (2–3): 143–56.

Foster, Michael Dylan, ed. 2015b. "UNESCO on the Ground: Local Perspectives on Intangible Cultural Heritage." Special issue, *Journal of Folklore Research* 53 (2–3).

Friedan, Betty. 1963. *The Feminine Mystique.* New York: W. W. Norton.

Friedland, LeeEllen. 1998. "Square Dance." In *International Encyclopedia of Dance,* edited by Selma Jeanne Cohen. Oxford: Oxford University Press.

Geertz, Clifford. (1973) 2003. "Thick Description: Toward an Interpretive Theory of Culture." In *Turning Points in Qualitative Research: Tying Knots in a Handkerchief,* edited by Yvonna S. Lincoln and Norman K. Denzin, 143–68. Walnut Creek, CA: AltaMira.

Georges, Robert A. 1991a. "Earning, Appropriating, Concealing, and Denying the Identity of Folklorist." In "Taking Stock: Current Problems and Future Prospects in American Folklore Studies," edited by Robert A. Georges, special issue, *Western Folklore* 50 (1): 3–12.

Georges, Robert A., ed. 1991b. "Taking Stock: Current Problems and Future Prospects in American Folklore Studies." Special issue, *Western Folklore* 50 (1).

Georges, Robert A. 1991c. "Taking Stock: Current Problems and Future Prospects in American Folklore Studies. Guest Editor's Introduction to the Special Issue." In "Taking Stock: Current Problems and Future Prospects in American Folklore Studies," edited by Robert A. Georges, special issue, *Western Folklore* 50 (1): 1–2.

Gilman, Lisa. 2015. "Demonic or Cultural Treasure? Local Perspectives on Vimbuza, Intangible Cultural Heritage, and UNESCO in Malawi." In "UNESCO on the Ground: Local Perspectives on Intangible Cultural Heritage," edited by Michael Dylan Foster, special issue, *Journal of Folklore Research* 52 (2–3): 199–216.

Gilman, Lisa, ed. 2025. "Perspectives: Sexual Harassment and Legacy Forum." Special section, *Journal of American Folklore* 138 (547): 34–117.

Glassie, Henry. 1982. *Passing the Time in Ballymenone.* Philadelphia: University of Pennsylvania Press.

Glassie, Henry. 1995. "Tradition." *Journal of American Folklore* 108 (430): 395–412.

Glassie, Henry, and Betty-Jo Glassie. 1971. "The Implications of Folkloristic Thought for Historic Zoning Ordinances." In "Papers on Applied Folklore," edited by Dick Sweterlitsch. *Folklore Forum Bibliographic and Special Studies* no. 8: 31–38.

Goldstein, Diane E., and Amy Shuman. 2016. "Introduction." In *The Stigmatized Vernacular: Where Reflexivity Meets Untellability,* edited by Diane E. Goldstein and Amy Shuman, 1–13. Bloomington: Indiana University Press.

González-Martin, Rachel V. 2019. *Quinceañera Style: Social Belonging and Latinx Consumer Identities*. Austin: University of Texas Press.

González-Martin, Rachel V., Mintzi Auanda Martínez-Rivera, and Solimar Otero, eds. 2022. "Redirecting Current: Theoretical Wayfinding with Latinx Folkloristics and Women of Color Transnational Feminisms." Special issue, *Journal of American Folklore* 135 (536).

Goodman, Sylvia. 2022. "To Boycott or Not? Academic Conferences Face Pressure to Avoid Abortion-Hostile States." *Chronicle of Higher Education*, July 12, 2022. https://www.chronicle.com/article/to-boycott -or-not-academic-conferences-face-pressure-to-avoid-abortion-hostile -states.

Gossen, Gary H. 1971. "Chamula Genres of Verbal Behavior." *Journal of American Folklore* 84 (331): 145–67.

Green, Archie. (1976) 1988. "P.L. 94–201—A View from the Lobby: A Report to the American Folklore Society." Pamphlet. Reprinted in *The Conservation of Culture: Folklorists and the Public Sector*, edited by Burt Feintuch, 269–81. Lexington: University Press of Kentucky.

Green, Archie. 1978. "Industrial Lore: A Bibliographic-Semantic Query." *Western Folklore* 37 (3): 213–44.

Green, Archie. 1987. "At the Hall, in the Stope: Who Treasures Tales of Work?" *Western Folklore* 46 (3): 153–70.

Green, Rayna. 1978. "On AFS, Human Rights, and the Salt Lake City Meeting: Thoughts and Strategies." *Folklore Women's Communication* 15:4–9.

Greenhill, Pauline, and Diane Tye, eds. 2013. *Unsettling Assumptions: Tradition, Gender, Drag*. Logan: Utah State University Press.

Greenwood, Davydd J. 2008. "Theoretical Research, Applied Research, and Action Research." In *Engaging Contradictions: Theory, Politics, and Methods of Activist Scholarship*, edited by Charles R. Hale, 319–90. Berkeley: University of California Press.

Grimes, William. 2009. "Archie Green, 91, Union Activist and Folklorist, Dies." *New York Times*, March 28, 2009. https://www.nytimes.com /2009/03/29/books/29green.html.

Gross Bressler, Sandra Jill. 1995. "Culture and Politics: A Legislative Chronicle of the American Folklife Preservation Act." PhD diss., University of Pennsylvania. ProQuest (9532184).

Hafstein, Valdimar Tr. 2004. "The Politics of Origins: Collective Creation Revisited." *Journal of American Folklore* 117 (465): 300–315.

Harrah-Johnson, Jeanne. 2020. "The Jewel in the Crown: Hallmarks of Success in Indiana University's Folklore Program." In *Folklore in the United States and Canada: An Institutional History*, edited by Patricia Sawin and Rosemary Lévy Zumwalt, 76–87. Bloomington: Indiana University Press.

Hawes, Bess Lomax. 2007. "Happy Birthday, Dear American Folklore Society: Reflections on the Work and Mission of Folklorists." In *Public Folklore*, edited by Robert Baron and Nick Spitzer, 65–74. Jackson: University Press of Mississippi.

Hirsch, Jerrold. 1988. "Cultural Pluralism and Applied Folklore: The New Deal Precedent." In *The Conservation of Culture: Folklorists and the Public Sector*, edited by Burt Feintuch, 46–67. Lexington: University Press of Kentucky.

Hirsch, Jerrold. 1998. "'Ancillary to the Study of People': The Presence and Absence of BA Botkin at Point Park College." *Journal of Folklore Research* 35 (3): 279–94.

Hirsch, Jerrold. 2003. *Portrait of America: A Cultural History of the Federal Writers' Project*. Chapel Hill: University of North Carolina Press.

Hirsch, Jerrold, and Lawrence Rodgers. 2010. "Introduction." In *America's Folklorist: B. A. Botkin and American Culture*, edited by Lawrence R. Rodgers and Jerrold Hirsch, 1–17. Norman: Oklahoma University Press.

Hollis, Susan, Linda Pershing, and M. Jane Young, eds. 1993. *Feminist Theory and the Study of Folklore*. Urbana: University of Illinois Press.

Hubbell, Sue. 1996. "The Old Square Dance, It Ain't What It Used to Be." *Smithsonian Magazine* 26, no. 11 (February): 92.

Hufford, David. 1985. "Folklore Studies and Health." *Practicing Anthropology* 7 (1/2): 23–24.

Hufford, Mary, ed. 1994. *Conserving Culture: A New Discourse on Heritage*. Urbana: University of Illinois Press.

Hufford, Mary. 2002. "Interrupting the Monologue: Folklore, Ethnography, and Critical Regionalism." *Journal of Appalachian Studies* 8 (1): 62–78.

Hurston, Zora Neale. (1937) 1996. *Their Eyes Were Watching God*. New York: Harper.

Hymes, Dell. 1964. "Introduction: Toward Ethnographies of Communication." *American Anthropologist* 66 (6): 1–34.

Hymes, Dell. 1975. "Folklore's Nature and the Sun's Myth (AFS Presidential Address, 1974)." *Journal of American Folklore* 88 (350): 345–69.

Hymes, Dell. 1987. "A Note on Ethnopoetics and Sociolinguistics." *Working Papers in Educational Linguistics (WPEL)* 3 (2): 1.

Ice, Joyce. 1993. "Women's Aesthetics and the Quilting Process." In *Feminist Theory and the Study of Folklore*, edited by Susan Hollis, Linda Pershing, and M. Jane Young, 166–77. Urbana: University of Illinois Press.

"Introduction." 2006. "Lessons of Work: Contemporary Explorations of Work Culture." Special issue, *Western Folklore* 65 (1/2): 5–11.

Ivey, Bill. 2011. "Values and Value in Folklore (AFS Presidential Address, 2007)." *Journal of American Folklore* 124 (491): 6–18.

Ivey, Bill. 2017. *Rebuilding an Enlightened World: Folklorizing America*. Bloomington: Indiana University Press.

Jabbour, Alan. 1996. "The American Folklife Center: A Twenty-Year Retrospective." *Folklife Center News* 18 (1–2): 3–19.

Jackson, Bruce. 1976. "Benjamin A. Botkin (1901–1975)." *Journal of American Folklore* 89 (351): 1–6.

Jackson, Bruce. 1986. "Ben Botkin." *New York Folklore Quarterly* 12:24.

Jackson, Bruce. 1987. "From the Editor." In "Folklore and Feminism," edited by Bruce Jackson, special issue, *Journal of American Folklore* 100 (398): 387–89.

Jackson, Bruce, Judith McCulloh, and Marta Weigle, eds. 1984. *Folklore/Folklife*. Washington, DC: American Folklore Society.

James, Thelma. 1947. "Report of the Committee on the Utilization of Folklore." *Journal of American Folklore* 60 (236): 168–74.

James, Thelma. 1948. "Folklore and Propaganda." Editor's Page. *Journal of American Folklore* 61 (241): 311.

Johnson, Geraldine Niva. 1985. "It's a Sin to Waste a Rug: Rug-Weaving in Western Maryland." In *Women's Folklore, Women's Culture*, edited by Rosan A. Jordan and Susan J. Kalčik, 65–98. Philadelphia: University of Pennsylvania Press.

Jones, Michael Owen. 1972. *Why Faith Healing?* Ontario: University of Ottawa Press.

Jones, Michael Owen. 1975. *The Hand Made Object and Its Maker*. Berkeley: University of California Press.

Jones, Michael Owen. 1983. "Organizational Folklore and Corporate Culture." *The American Folklore Society Newsletter* 12 (5): 3–4, 6.

Jones, Michael Owen. 1984a. "Corporate Natives Confer on Culture." *The American Folklore Society Newsletter* 13 (5): 6, 8.

Jones, Michael Owen. 1984b. "Introduction." In "Works of Art, Art as Work, and the Arts of Working: Implications for Improving Organizational Life," edited by Michael Owen Jones, special section, *Western Folklore* 43 (3): 172–77.

Jones, Michael Owen. 1985a. "Is Ethics the Issue?" In *Organizational Culture*, edited by Peter J. Frost, Larry F. Moore, Meryl Reis Louis, Craig C. Lundberg, and Joanne Martin, 235–52. Beverly Hills: Sage.

Jones, Michael Owen. 1985b. "On Folklorists Studying Organizations: A Reply to Robert S. McCarl." *The American Folklore Society Newsletter* 14 (2): 5–6, 8.

Jones, Michael Owen. 1987. "The Symbolic and Aesthetic Aspects of Organizing." Paper presented at the annual meeting of the American Folklore Society, Albuquerque, NM, October 23–28.

Jones, Michael Owen. 1988. "How Does Folklore Fit In?" Paper presented at the annual national meeting of the Academy of Management, Anaheim, CA, August 7–10.

Jones, Michael Owen. 1989. "Corporate Culture in Cartoons: Lessons for Leadership?" Paper presented at the annual national meeting of the Academy of Management, Washington, DC, August 11–16.

Jones, Michael Owen. 1991. "Why Folklore and Organization(s)?" In "Taking Stock: Current Problems and Future Prospects in American Folklore Studies," edited by Robert A. Georges, special issue, *Western Folklore* 50 (1): 29–40.

Jones, Michael Owen. 1994a. "Applying Folklore Studies: An Introduction." In *Putting Folklore to Use*, edited by Michael Owen Jones, 1–41. Lexington: University Press of Kentucky.

Jones, Michael Owen. 1994b. "A Folklorist's Approach to Organizational Behavior (OB) and Organizational Development (OD)." In *Putting Folklore to Use*, edited by Michael Owen Jones, 162–86. Lexington: University Press of Kentucky.

Jones, Michael Owen, ed. 1994c. *Putting Folklore to Use*. Lexington: University Press of Kentucky.

Jones, Michael Owen. 1996. *Studying Organizational Symbolism: What, How, Why?* Thousand Oaks, CA: Sage.

Jones, Michael Owen, Bruce Giuliano, and Roberta Krell, eds. 1981. "Foodways and Eating Habits: Direction for Research." Special issue, *Western Folklore* 40 (1).

Jones, Michael Owen, Michael Dane Moore, and Richard Christopher Snyder, eds. 1988. *Inside Organizations: Understanding the Human Dimension*. Newbury Park, CA: Sage.

Jordan, Rosan A. 1976. "Editorial." *Folklore Feminists Communication* 8:4–5.

Jordan, Rosan A., and Susan J. Kalčik. 1985. *Women's Folklore, Women's Culture*. Philadelphia: University of Pennsylvania Press.

Jorgensen, Jeana. 2010. "Political and Theoretical Feminisms in American Folkloristics: Definition Debates, Publication Histories, and the Folklore Feminists Communication." *The Folklore Historian* 27:43–73.

Kalčik, Susan. 1975a. "'. . . like Ann's gynecologist or the time I was almost raped': Personal Narratives in Women's Rap Groups." *Journal of American Folklore* 88 (34): 3–11.

Kalčik, Susan. 1975b. "Report of the AFS Women's Caucus Task Force on the Reorganization of the AFS." *Folklore Women's Communication* 5:11–14.

Kalčik, Susan. 1988. "Womenfolk." In *100 Years of American Folklore Studies: A Conceptual History*, edited by William M. Clements, 44–50. Washington, DC: American Folklore Society.

Kamenetsky, Christa. 1972. "Folklore as a Political Tool in Nazi Germany." *Journal of American Folklore* 85 (337): 221–35.

Kamenetsky, Christa. 1977. "Folktale and Ideology in the Third Reich." *Journal of American Folklore* 90 (356): 168–78.

Kamenetsky, Christa. 2019. *Children's Literature in Hitler's Germany: The Cultural Policy of National Socialism*. Athens: Ohio University Press.

Keyes, Cheryl. 1993. "'We're More than a Novelty, Boys,': Strategies of Female Rappers in the Rap Music Tradition." In *Feminist Messages: Coding in Women's Folk Culture*, edited by Joan N. Radner, 203–20. Urbana: University of Illinois Press.

Kimmel, Michael S. 2006. *Manhood in America: A Cultural History*. 2nd ed. New York: Oxford University Press.

King, Thomas F. 2003. *Places That Count: Traditional Cultural Properties in Cultural Resource Management*. Lanham, MD: Altamira Press, Rowman & Littlefield.

Kirshenblatt-Gimblett, Barbara. 1983. "The Future of Folklore Studies in America: The Urban Frontier." *Folklore Forum* 16 (2): 175–234.

Kirshenblatt-Gimblett, Barbara. 1988. "Mistaken Dichotomies." *Journal of American Folklore* 101 (400): 140–55.

Kodish, Deborah. 1983. "Fair Young Ladies and Bonny Irish Boys: Pattern in Vernacular Poetics." *Journal of American Folklore* 96 (380): 131–50.

Kodish, Deborah. 1986. *Good Friends and Bad Enemies: Robert Winslow Gordon and the Study of American Folksong*. Champaign: University of Illinois Press.

Kodish, Deborah. 1993. "Absent Gender, Silent Encounter." In *Feminist Theory and the Study of Folklore*, edited by Susan Hollis, Linda Pershing, and M. Jane Young, 41–50. Urbana: University of Illinois Press.

Kodish, Deborah. 2011. "Envisioning Folklore Activism." *Journal of American Folklore* 124 (491): 31–60.

Kodish, Deborah. 2013. "Cultivating Folk Arts and Social Change." *Journal of American Folklore* 126 (502): 434–54.

Kurin, Richard. 2004. "Safeguarding Intangible Cultural Heritage in the 2003 UNESCO Convention: A Critical Appraisal." *Museum International* 56 (1–2): 66–77.

Labov, William, and Joshua Waletzky. 1967. "Narrative Analysis: Oral Versions of Personal Experience." In *Essays on the Verbal and Visual Arts*, edited by June L. Helm, 12–44. Seattle: University of Washington Press.

La Chapelle, Peter. 2011. "'Dances Partake of the Racial Characteristics of the People Who Dance Them': Nordicism, Antisemitism, and Henry Ford's Old-Time Music and Dance Revival." In *Song Is Not the Same: Jews and American Popular Music*, edited by Peter La Chapelle, Bruce Zuckerman, Josh Kun, and Lisa Ansell, 29–70. West Lafayette, IN: Purdue University Press.

Lanser, Susan S. 1993. "Burning Dinners: Feminist Subversions of Domesticity." In *Feminist Messages: Coding in Women's Folk Culture*, edited by Joan N. Radner, 36–53. Urbana: University of Illinois Press.

Lawless, Elaine. 1991. "Women's Life Stories and Reciprocal Ethnography as Feminist and Emergent." *Journal of Folklore Research* 28 (1): 35–60.

Lawless, Elaine. 1993. "Access to the Pulpit: Reproductive Images and Maternal Strategies of the Pentecostal Female Pastor." In *Feminist Theory and the Study of Folklore*, edited by Susan Hollis, Linda Pershing, and M. Jane Young, 258–76. Urbana: University of Illinois Press.

Lawrence, David Todd, and Elaine J. Lawless. 2018. *When They Blew the Levee: Race, Politics, and Community in Pinhook, Missouri.* Jackson: University Press of Mississippi.

Leary, James P. 2021. "Advocating for Labor." In *What Folklorists Do: Professional Possibilities in Folklore Studies*, edited by Timothy Lloyd, 200–204. Bloomington: Indiana University Press.

Levin, Judith. 1984. "From the New Editor." *Folklore Women's Communication* 32–33:2.

Levin, Judith. 1993. "Why Folklorists Should Study Housework." In *Feminist Theory and the Study of Folklore*, edited by Susan Tower Hollis, Linda Pershing, and M. Jane Young, 285–96. Urbana: University of Illinois Press.

Lindahl, Carl. 2004. "Thrills and Miracles: Legends of Lloyd Chandler." *Journal of Folklore Research* 41 (2–3): 133–71.

Lindahl, Carl. 2012. "Legends of Hurricane Katrina: The Right to Be Wrong, Survivor-to-Survivor Storytelling, and Healing." *Journal of American Folklore* 125 (496): 139–76.

Lloyd, Timothy, ed. 2021. *What Folklorists Do: Professional Possibilities in Folklore Studies*. Bloomington: Indiana University Press.

Lockwood, Yvonne R. 1984. "The Joy of Labor." In "Works of Art, Art as Work, and the Arts of Working," edited by Michael Owen Jones, special section, *Western Folklore* 43 (3): 202–10.

Lomax, John. 1910. *Cowboy Songs and Other Frontier Ballads*. New York: Sturgis and Walton.

Long, Eleanor, Rayna Green, Frank Hoffman, Francis de Caro, and Camilla Collins. 1975. Letter from the Committee on the Status of Women. *Folklore Feminists Communication* 5:14–16.

Loomis, Ormond. 1983. *Cultural Conservation: The Protection of Cultural Heritage in the United States*. Washington, DC: Library of Congress.

MacDowell, Marsha. 1984. "Visual Descriptions of the Work Experience: Insider vs. Outsider Views of Art and Work." In "Works of Art, Art as Work, and the Arts of Working," edited by Michael Owen Jones, special section, *Western Folklore* 43 (3): 178–91.

Mangin, Julianne. (1995) 2017. "The State Folk Dance Conspiracy: Fabricating a National Dance." https://juliannemangin.com/the-state-folk-dance-conspiracy. Originally published in *Old-Time Herald* 4 (7): 9–12.

Marcus, George E., and Michael M. J. Fischer. 1986. *Anthropology as Cultural Critique*. Chicago: University of Chicago Press.

Martin, Jodi. 1988. "Symbolic Responses to Layoffs in a Software Manufacturing Firm: Managing the Meaning of an Event." In *Inside Organizations: Understanding the Human Dimension*, edited by Michael Owen Jones, Michael Dane Moore, and Richard Christopher Snyder, 209–25. Newbury Park, CA: Sage.

May-Machunda, Phyllis. 2022. "Recentering the Periphery, Coloring the Discourses and Expanding the Frames." In *Recentering the Periphery, Coloring the Discourses, and Expanding the Frames: A Guide to the American Folklore Society Notable Folklorists of Color Exhibitions*, 25–51. Bloomington, IN: American Folklore Society.

McCarl, Robert S. 1978. "Occupational Folklife: A Theoretical Hypothesis." *Western Folklore* 37 (3): 145–60.

McCarl, Robert S. 1980. *Good Fire/Bad Night: A Cultural Sketch of the District of Columbia Fire Fighters as Seen through Their Occupational Folklife*. Washington, DC: DC Fire Fighters Association, Local 36.

McCarl, Robert S. 1984. Letter to the Editor. *The American Folklore Society Newsletter* 13 (6): 2, 5.

McCarl, Robert. 1985a. *The District of Columbia Fire Fighters' Project: A Case Study in Occupational Folklife*. Washington, DC: Smithsonian Institute Press.

McCarl, Robert. 1985b. "Reply to Michael Owen Jones." *The American Folklore Society Newsletter* 14:2, 5.

McCarl, Robert. 1986. "Occupational Folklore." In *Folk Groups and Folklore Genres: An Introduction*, edited by Elliott Oring, 71–89. Logan: Utah State University Press.

McCarl, Robert. 1988a. "The Folk as Occupational Group: From the Cow Camp to the Shop Floor." In *100 Years of American Folklore Studies: A Conceptual History*, edited by William M. Clements, 40–44. Washington, DC: American Folklore Society.

McCarl, Robert. 1988b. "Occupational Folklife in the Public Sector: A Case Study." In *The Conservation of Culture: Folklorists and the Public Sector*, edited by Burt Feintuch, 132–53. Lexington: University Press of Kentucky.

McCarl, Robert. 1989. "The Folklorist as Dramatist." In *Time & Temperature*, edited by Charles Camp, 30. Washington, DC: American Folklore Society.

McCarl, Robert. 1992. "Response to Michael Owen Jones." *Western Folklore* 51 (2): 187–89.

Mechling, Jay. 1991. "Homo Narrans: Across the Disciplines." In "Taking Stock: Current Problems and Future Prospects in American Folklore Studies," edited by Robert Georges, special issue, *Western Folklore* 50 (1): 41–51.

Mechling, Jay. 2023. "Ten Essential Books Not Written by Folklorists." *TFH: The Journal of History and Folklore* 39 and 40:58–85.

Miller, James Nathan. 1978. "Trickery on the Tenn-Tom." *Readers Digest*, September 1978, 138–43.

Mills, Margaret. 1993. "Feminist Theory and the Study of Folklore: A Twenty-Year Trajectory toward Theory." In "Theorizing Folklore: Toward New Perspectives on the Politics of Culture," edited by Charles Briggs and Amy Shuman, special issue, *Western Folklore* 52 (2, 3, 4): 173–92.

Mills, Margaret A. 2016. "What('s) Theory?" In *Grand Theory in Folkloristics*, edited by Lee Haring, 54–62. Bloomington: Indiana University Press.

Molnar, Joseph J., Leisle A. Ewing, Brenda Clark, and Macon Tidwell. 1981. "Developing the Tennessee-Tombigbee: Perceptions and Preferences of West Alabama Residents." Department of Agricultural Economics and Rural Sociology, Agriculture Experiment Station, Auburn University, Auburn, AL.

Monk, Janice. 2006. "Changing Expectations and Institutions: American Women Geographers in the 1970s." *Geographical Review* 96:259–77.

Moody, Shirley C. 2006. "By Custom and by Law: Black Folklore and Racial Representation at the Birth of Jim Crow." PhD diss., University of Maryland, College Park. ProQuest (3241543).

Moody-Turner, Shirley. 2013. *Black Folklore and the Politics of Racial Representation*. Jackson: University Press of Mississippi.

Moraga, Cherríe, and Gloria E. Anzaldúa, eds. 1981. *This Bridge Called My Back: Writings by Radical Women of Color*. New York: Kitchen Table: Women of Color Press.

Morín, José R. López. 2006. *The Legacy of Américo Paredes*. College Station: Texas A&M Press.

MPC (Minority Peoples Council on the Tennessee-Tombigbee Waterway). 1978. "Folk Culture in Waterway Area Subject to Study." *The Minority Peoples Council on the Tennessee-Tombigbee Waterway Newsletter* 4:4.

Mulcahy, Joanne B. 1993. "'How They Knew': Women's Talk about Healing on Kodiak Island, Alaska." In *Feminist Messages: Coding in Women's Folk Culture*, edited by Joan N. Radner, 183–202. Urbana: University of Illinois Press.

Mullen, Patrick B. 2000. "Belief and the American Folk." *Journal of American Folklore* 13 (448): 119–43.

Mullen, Patrick B. 2008. *The Man Who Adores the Negro: Race and American Folklore*. Champaign: University of Illinois Press.

Myerhoff, Barbara, and Jay Ruby, eds. 1982. *A Crack in the Mirror: Reflexive Perspective in Anthropology*. Philadelphia: University of Pennsylvania Press.

National Folk Dance Committee. 1984. *Newsletter*, August 8(2). Retrieved from Square Dance Legislation collection (AFC 1984/024), Archive of Folk Culture, American Folklife Center, Library of Congress, Washington, DC.

National Park Service. 1990. *National Register Bulletin No. 38: Guidelines for Evaluating and Documenting Traditional Cultural Properties*, by Patricia Parker and Thomas F. King. Washington, DC: National Park Service, US Department of the Interior.

Newell, William Wells, ed. 1888. "On the Field and Work of a Journal of American Folk-Lore." *Journal of American Folklore* 1 (1): 3–7.

Nickerson, Bruce E. 1974. "Is There a Folk in the Factory?" *Journal of American Folklore* 87 (344): 133–39.

Nodjimbadem, Katie. 2017. "The Lesser-Known History of African-American Cowboys." *Smithsonian Magazine*, February 13, 2017. https://www.smithsonianmag.com/history/lesser-known-history-african-american-cowboys-180962144.

Noyes, Dorothy. 2006. "The Judgment of Solomon: Global Protections for Tradition and the Problem of Community Ownership." *Cultural Analysis* 5:27–56.

Noyes, Dorothy. 2008. "Humble Theory." *Journal of Folklore Research* 45 (1): 37–43.

Noyes, Dorothy. 2009. "Tradition: Three Traditions." *Journal of Folklore Research: An International Journal of Folklore and Ethnomusicology* 46 (3): 233–68.

Noyes, Dorothy. 2010. "Group." In *Eight Words for the Study of Expressive Culture,* edited by Burt Feintuch, 7–41. Urbana: University of Illinois Press.

Noyes, Dorothy. 2016. *Humble Theory: Folklore's Grasp on Social Life.* Bloomington: Indiana University Press.

Nusbaum, Philip. 2006. "Organizations, Voluntary and Special Interest." In *Encyclopedia of American Folklife*, vol. 3, edited by Simon Bronner, 924–27. Armonk, NY: M.E. Sharpe.

Oinas, Felix J. 1973. "Folklore and Politics in the Soviet Union." *Slavic Review* 32 (1): 45–58.

Oinas, Felix J. 1975. "The Political Uses and Themes of Folklore in the Soviet Union." *Journal of the Folklore Institute* 12 (2/3): 157–75.

Oring, Elliott. 1976. "Three Functions of Folklore: Traditional Functionalism as Explanation in Folkloristics." *Journal of American Folklore* 89 (351): 67–80.

Oring, Elliott. 1986. "Ethnic Groups and Ethnic Folklore." In *Folk Groups and Folklore Genres: An Introduction*, edited by Elliott Oring, 23–44. Logan: Utah State University Press.

Oring, Elliott. 1991. "On the Future of American Folklore Studies: A Response." In "Taking Stock: Current Problems and Future Prospects in American Folklore Studies," edited by Robert Georges, special issue, *Western Folklore* 50 (1): 75–81.

Oring, Elliott. 2004. "Folklore and Advocacy." *Journal of Folklore Research* 41 (2): 259–67.

Oring, Elliott. 2012. *Just Folklore: Analysis, Interpretation, Critique.* Los Angeles: Cantilever.

Oring, Elliott. 2019. "Back to the Future: Questions for Theory in the Twenty-First Century." Francis Lee Utley lecture, sponsored by the American Folklore Society Fellows, 2017. *Journal of American Folklore* 132 (524): 137–54.

Ortiz, Carmen. 1999. "The Uses of Folklore by the Franco Regime." *Journal of American Folklore* 112 (446): 479–96.

Otero, Solimar, and Mintzi Auanda Martínez-Rivera, eds. 2021. *Theorizing Folklore from the Margins: Critical and Ethical Approaches.* Bloomington: Indiana University Press.

Paredes, Américo. 1958. *With His Pistol in His Hand: A Border Ballad and Its Hero.* Austin: University of Texas Press.

Paredes, Américo, and Richard Bauman, eds. 1972. *Toward New Perspectives in Folklore.* Austin: University of Texas Press.

Pershing, Linda. 1993a. "Peace Work out of Piecework: Feminist Needlework Metaphors and The Ribbon around the Pentagon." In *Feminist Theory and the Study of Folklore,* edited by Susan Hollis, Linda Pershing, and M. Jane Young, 327–57. Urbana: University of Illinois Press.

Pershing, Linda. 1993b. "'She Really Wanted to Be Her Own Woman': Scandalous Sunbonnet Sue." In *Feminist Messages: Coding in Women's Folk Culture,* edited by Joan N. Radner, 98–125. Urbana: University of Illinois Press.

Pershing, Linda, Suzy Seriff, Beverly Stoeltje, Kay Turner, and M. Jane Young. 1985. "'Feminism and Folklore' Sessions Planned for '86." *The American Folklore Society Newsletter* 14 (4): 1.

Poyser, Stephen Paxton. 1991. "Days Gone By: A Folklife, History and Oral History Study of Bay Springs, Mississippi." PhD diss., Indiana University.

Prahlad, Anand. 2021. "Tearing Down Monuments: Missed Opportunities, Silences, and Absences—A Radical Look at Race in American Folklore Studies." *Journal of American Folklore* 134 (533): 258–64.

Price, David. 1998. "Gregory Bateson and the OSS: World War II and Bateson's Assessment of Applied Anthropology." *Human Organization* 57 (4): 379–84.

Price, David. 2002. "Lessons from Second World War Anthropology." *Anthropology Today* 18 (3): 14–20.

Proschan, Frank. 2004. "On Advocacy and Advocates." *Journal of Folklore Research* 41 (2): 267–73.

Quigley, Colin. 2001. "Reflections on the Hearing to 'Designate the Square Dance as the American Folk Dance of the United States': Cultural Politics and an American Vernacular Dance Form." *Yearbook for Traditional Music* 33:145–58.

Radner, Joan N., ed. 1993. *Feminist Messages: Coding in Women's Folk Culture.* Urbana: University of Illinois Press.

Raspa, Richard. 2006. "Organizations, Corporate and Work." In *Encyclopedia of American Folklife,* vol. 3, edited by Simon Bronner, 921–23. Armonk, NY: M.E. Sharpe.

Reaves, Roy W., III. 1976. "The Archeological and Historical Preservation Act of 1974: A Panacea?" *Pennsylvania Archaeologist* 47 (1): 35–41.

Redfield, Robert. 1989. *The Little Community and Peasant Society and Culture.* Chicago: University of Chicago Press.

Reeves, Jay. 2019. "$2B Waterway through Deep South Yet to Yield Promised Boom." *Associated Press*, September 19, 2019. https://apnews.com/article/ee9c726251104e0a86f74278ce391d79.

Reuss, Richard A. 1974. "On Folklore and Women Folklorists." *Folklore Feminists Communication* 3:4, 29–37.

Reuss, Richard A., and JoAnne C. Reuss. 2000. *American Folk Music and Left-Wing Politics, 1927–1957*. Lanham, MD: Scarecrow.

Reznick, Alisa. 2020. "'Show Me Your Papers': A Decade after SB 1070." *Arizona Public Media (AZPM)*, August 7, 2020. https://news.azpm.org/p/news-splash/2020/7/30/177558-show-me-your-papers-a-decade-after-sb-1070.

Rikoon, J. Sanford. 2004. "On the Politics of the Politics of Origins: Social (In)Justice and the International Agenda on Intellectual Property, Traditional Knowledge, and Folklore." *Journal of American Folklore* 117 (465): 325–36.

Rikoon, J. Sanford, William Heffernan, and Judith B. Heffernan. 1994. "Cultural Conservation and the Family Farm Movement: Integrating Visions and Actions." In *Conserving Culture: A New Discourse* Mary Hufford, 184–97. Urbana: University of Illinois Press.

Ritchie, Susan. 1993. "Ventriloquist Folklore: Who Speaks for Representation?" *Western Folklore* 52 (2–4): 365–78.

Roach, Susan. 1985. "The Kinship Quilt: An Ethnographic Semiotic Analysis of a Quilting Bee." In *Women's Folklore, Women's Culture*, edited by Rosan A. Jordan and Susan J. Kalčik, 54–64. Philadelphia: University of Pennsylvania Press.

Roberts, John, Robert Baron, Gerald Davis, Cheryl Keyes, Mario Montaño, Kirin Narayan, and Beverly Robinson. 1994. "Report of the State of the Profession Committee of the American Folklore Society on Minority Participation in the Field of Folklore." *AFS Newsletter* 23 (3): 8–12.

Roberts, John W. 1993. "African American Diversity and the Study of Folklore." In "Theorizing Folklore: Toward New Perspectives on the Politics of Culture," edited by Charles Briggs and Amy Shuman, special issue, *Western Folklore* 52 (2/4): 109–34.

Roberts, John W. 2000. "African American Folklore in a Discourse of Folkness." *New York Folklore* 18:73–90.

Roberts, John W. 2008. "Grand Theory, Nationalism, and American Folklore." In "Grand Theory," edited by Lee Haring, special issue, *Journal of Folklore Research* 45 (1): 45–54.

Rodeffer, Stephanie Holschlag. 1981. "The Evolution of the Historic Mitigation Program in the Tombigbee River Multi-Resource District, Alabama and Mississippi." Paper presented at the Society for Historical Archaeology Annual Meeting on January 5, 1981.

Rodgers, Lawrence R., and Jerrold Hirsch, eds. 2010. *America's Folklorist: B. A. Botkin and American Culture.* Norman: Oklahoma University Press.

Rotenstein, David. 2019. "Community-Driven Mitigation: Murals, Canal Stones, and a Walking Tour." *History @ Work: The NCPH Blog*, National Council on Public History, July 4, 2019. https://ncph.org/history-at-work/community-driven-mitigation.

Runcie, F. John. 1988. "'Deviant Behavior': Achieving Autonomy in a Machine-Paced Environment." In *Inside Organizations: Understanding the Human Dimension*, edited by Michael Owen Jones, Michael Dane Moore, and Richard Christopher Snyder, 129–40. Newbury Park, CA: Sage.

Ruth, Sheila. 1990. *Issues in Feminism: An Introduction to Women's Studies*, 2nd ed. Mountain View, CA: Mayfield Publishing.

Said, Edward. 1985. "Orientalism Reconsidered." In *Europe and Its Others*, edited by Francis Barker, Pete Hume, Margaret Iversen and Diana Loxley, 14–27. Colchester: University of Essex Press.

Santayana, George, ed. 1905. *The Life of Reason: The Phases of Human Progress*, vol. 1, *Reason in Common Sense.* Mincola, NY: Dover.

Santino, Jack. 1978. "Characteristics of Occupational Narratives." *Western Folklore* 37 (3): 199–212.

Sawin, Patricia, and Rosemary Lévy Zumwalt, eds. 2020. *Folklore in the United States and Canada: An Institutional History.* Bloomington: Indiana University Press.

Schofield, Derek. 2010. "Bess Lomax Hawes Obituary." *The Guardian*, January 5, 2010. https://www.theguardian.com/music/2010/jan/05/bess-lomax-hawes-obituary.

Scully, Gregg M. 2006. "Occupational Folklife." In *Encyclopedia of American Folklife*, vol. 3, edited by Simon Bronner, 903–6. Armonk, NY: M.E. Sharpe.

Seeger, Anthony. 2015. "Understanding UNESCO: A Complex Organization with Many Parts and Many Actors." In "UNESCO on the Ground: Local Perspectives on Intangible Cultural Heritage," edited by Michael Dylan Foster, special issue, *Journal of Folklore Research* 52 (2–3): 269–80.

Seward, Adrienne Lanier. 1979. *The Role of Afro-American Folklore in the Teaching of the Arts and the Humanities.* Bloomington, IN: Association of African and African American Folklorists.

Sheehy, Daniel. 2011. "Obituaries: Beth Lomax Hawes (1921–2009)." *Journal of American Folklore*, 124 (491): 85–88.

Shuldiner, David. 1998. "The Politics of Discourse: An Applied Folklore Perspective." *Journal of Folklore Research* 35 (3): 189–201.

Shuldiner, David, Jessica Payne, Mary Ellen Brown, and Inta Gale Carpenter. 1998. "Foreword." In "Point Park Revisited: Legacies and New Perspectives on Applied Folklore," edited by David Shuldiner and Jessica Payne, special issue, *Journal of Folklore Research* 35 (3): 185–87.

Shuman, Amy. 1993. "Dismantling Local Culture." In "Theorizing Folklore: Toward New Perspectives on the Politics of Culture," edited by Charles Briggs and Amy Shuman, special issue, *Western Folklore* 52 (2–4): 345–64.

Shuman, Amy, and Charles L. Briggs. 1993. "Introduction." In "Theorizing Folklore: Toward New Perspectives on the Politics of Culture," edited by Charles Briggs and Amy Shuman, special issue, *Western Folklore* 52 (2–4): 109–34.

Sinclair, Ward. 1979. "Corps Offer Roils Folklife Center." *Washington Post*, February 25, 1979. https://www.washingtonpost.com/archive/politics /1979/02/25/corps-offer-roils-folklife-center/b8519aa4-3325-4c71-9e14 -dc5d2e98b9c1.

Sommers, Laurie Kay. 2013. "Integrating Folklore and Historic Preservation Policy: Toward a Richer Sense of Place." Policy Paper, Folklore and Historic Preservation Policy Working Group of the American Folklore Society. https://americanfolkloresociety.org/our-community/sections /folklore-and-historic-preservation/integrating-folklore-and-historic -preservation-policy-toward-a-richer-sense-of-place/.

Sommers, Laurie Kay. 2019. "Introduction: The Place of Folklore in Historic Preservation." In "The Place of Folklore in Historic Preservation," edited by Laurie Kay Sommers, special issue, *Journal of American Folklore* 132 (526): 355–58.

Spicer, Edward. 1946. "The Use of Social Scientists by the War Relocation Authority." *Human Organization* 5 (2): 16–36.

Spicer, Edward. 1979. "Anthropologists and the War Relocation Authority." In *The Uses of Anthropology*, edited by William Goldschmidt, 217–38. Washington, DC: American Anthropological Association.

Spivak, Gayatri Chakravorty. 1988. "Can the Subaltern Speak?" In *Marxism and the Interpretation of Culture*, edited by Cary Nelson and Lawrence Grossberg, 271–313. Champaign: University of Illinois Press.

Starn, Orin. 1986. "Engineering Internment: Anthropologists and the War Relocation Authority." *American Ethnologist* 13 (4): 700–720.

Steering Committee of the American Folklore Society Women's Section. 1978. "Steering Committee Report, Women's Section, AFS." *Folklore Women's Communication* 14:5–6.

Stekert, Ellen. 1974. "Society Notes." *Folklore Feminists Communication* 4:6.

Stekert, Ellen. 1987. "Autobiography of a Woman Folklorist." *Journal of American Folklore* 100 (398): 579–85.

Stephenson, Hank. 2021. "What Arizona's 2010 Ban on Ethnic Studies Could Mean for the Fight Over Critical Race Theory." *Politico*, July 11, 2021. https://www.politico.com/news/magazine/2021/07/11/tucson -unified-school-districts-mexican-american-studies-program-498926.

Stewart, William H. 1971. *The Tennessee-Tombigbee Waterway: A Case Study in the Politics of Water Transportation*. Tuscaloosa: Bureau of Public Administration, University of Alabama.

Stine, Jeffrey K. 1992. "The Tennessee-Tombigbee Waterway and the Evolution of Cultural Resources Management." *The Public Historian* 14 (2): 6–30.

Stine, Jeffrey K. 1993. *Mixing the Waters: Environment, Politics, and the Building of the Tennessee-Tombigbee Waterway*. Akron, OH: University of Akron Press.

Stoeltje, Beverely J. 1975. "'A Helpmate for Man Indeed': The Image of the Frontier Woman." In "Women and Folklore," edited by Claire R. Farrer, special issue, *Journal of American Folklore* 88 (347): 25–41.

Stoeltje, Beverly J. 2025. "The Skirt Chaser and His Brothers." In "Perspectives: Sexual Harassment and Legacy Forum," edited by Lisa Gilman, special section. *Journal of American Folklore* 138 (547): 96–101.

Sweterlitsch, Dick, ed. 1971. "Applied Folklore: Debate Goes On." *Folklore Forum* 4 (1/2): 15–18.

Taft, Michael. 2004. "George Korson: Pioneer Collector of Industrial Folklore." *Folklife Center News* 26 (2). Washington, DC: American Folklife Center, Library of Congress. https://web.archive.org/web/20160304055117 /www.loc.gov/folklife/news/news-text-winter2004.html.

Tedlock, Dennis. 1983. *The Spoken Word and the Work of Interpretation*. Philadelphia: University of Pennsylvania Press.

Toelken, Barre. 1975. "Foreword." In "Women and Folklore: Images and Genres," edited by Claire Farrer, special issue, *Journal of American Folklore* 88 (347): iii–iv.

Toelken, Barre. 1976. "The 'Pretty Languages' of Yellowman: Genre, Mode, and Texture in Navaho Coyote Narratives." In *Folklore Genres*, edited by Dan Ben-Amos, 145–70. Austin: University of Texas Press.

Turner, Jessica. 2022. "Foreword: From the American Folklore Society." In *Recentering the Periphery, Coloring the Discourses, and Expanding the Frames: A Guide to the American Folklore Society Notable Folklorists of Color Exhibitions*, edited by Phyllis May-Machunda, 5–6. Bloomington, IN: American Folklore Society.

Tye, Diane. 2010. *Baking as Biography: A Life Story in Recipes*. Montreal, QC: McGill-Queen's University Press.

UNESCO (United Nations Educational, Scientific, and Cultural Organization). 2001. *Proclamation of Masterpieces of the Oral and Intangible Heritage of Humanity: Guide for the Presentation of Candidature Files*. Paris: UNESCO. http://unesdoc.unesco.org/images/0012/001246/124628eo.pdf.

UN Women. 2019. *A Short History of the Commission on the Status of Women*. New York: Intergovernmental Support Division, UN Women. https://www.unwomen.org/en/digital-library/publications/2019/02/a-short-history-of-the-commission-on-the-status-of-women.

Utley, Francis Lee. 1961. "Folk Literature: An Operational Definition." *Journal of American Folklore* 74:193–206.

Vargas-Cetina, Gabriela. 2013. "Introduction." In *Anthropology and the Politics of Representation*, edited by Gabriela Vargas-Cetina, 1–16. Tuscaloosa: University of Alabama Press.

Vidutis, Richard. 2019. "Missed Opportunities: The Absence of Ethnography in America's Cultural Heritage Programs." In *Human-Centered Built Environment Heritage Preservation: Theory and Evidence-Based Practice*, edited by Jeremy C. Wells and Barry L. Stiefel, 255–72. New York: Routledge.

Walle, Alf H. 1985. "Comment on Byington." *The American Folklore Society Newsletter* 14 (3): 2–3.

Ware, Carolyn. 2007. *Cajun Women and Mardi Gras: Reading the Rules Backward*. Urbana: University of Illinois Press.

Warnock, Emery C. 2009. "The Anti-Semitic Origins of Henry Ford's Arts Education Patronage." *Journal of Historical Research in Music Education* 30 (2): 79–102.

Wax, Rosalie. 1953. "The Destruction of a Democratic Impulse: An Exemplification of Certain Problems of a Benevolent Dictatorship." *Human Organization* 12 (1): 11–21.

Weigle, Marta. 1978. "On the Title Change." *Folklore Women's Communication* 14:2.

Wells, Patricia Atkinson. 1988. "The Paradox of Functional Dysfunction in a Girl Scout Camp: Implication of Cultural Diversity for Achieving

Organizational Goals." In *Inside Organizations: Understanding the Human Dimension*, edited by Michael Owen Jones, Michael Dane Moore, and Richard Christopher Snyder, 109–17. Newbury Park, CA: Sage.

Whisnant, David. 1983. *All That Is Native and Fine: The Politics of Culture in an American Region*. Chapel Hill: University of North Carolina Press.

Widner (Sharp), Ronna Lee. 2010. "Lore for the Folk: Benjamin A. Botkin and the Development of Folklore Scholarship in American." Republished in *America's Folklorist: B. A. Botkin and American Culture*, edited by Lawrence R. Rodgers and Jerrold Hirsch, 35–55. Norman: Oklahoma University Press.

Wiggins, William. 1988. "Afro-Americans as Folk: From Savage to Civilized." In *100 Years of American Folklore Studies: A Conceptual History Society*, edited by William Clements, 29–32. Washington, DC: American Folklore Society.

Wiggins, William. 2001. "Association of African and Afro-American Folklorists." In *Organizing Black America: An Encyclopedia of African American Associations*, edited by Nina Mjagkij, 62. New York: Routledge.

Willett, Henry. 1996. "Beyond Pittsburgh: 1976–1983." Paper presented at the Annual Meeting of the American Folklore Society, Pittsburgh, PA, October 1996.

Williams, John Alexander. 1975. "Radicalism and Professionalism in Folklore Studies: A Comparative Perspective." *Journal of the Folklore Institute* 11:211–34.

Williams, Michael Ann. 2017a. "After the Revolution: Folklore, History, and the Future of Our Discipline (AFS Presidential Address, 2015)." *Journal of American Folklore* 130 (516): 129–41.

Williams, Michael Ann. 2017b. "American Public Folklore and the Safeguarding of Intangible Cultural Heritage." Paper presented at the International Seminar on Ethics and Intangible Cultural Heritage, Sun Yat-sen University, Guangzhou, China, December 9–11.

Wilson, William A. 1989. "The Study of Mormon Folklore: An Uncertain Mirror for Truth." *Dialogue: A Journal of Mormon Thought* 22 (4): 95–110.

WIPO (World Intellectual Property Organization). n.d. "Intellectual Property and Traditional Cultural Expressions/Folklore." Booklet no. 1. WIPO Publication no. 913 (E). Accessed March 18, 2023. https://www.wipo.int/edocs/pubdocs/en/tk/913/wipo_pub_913.pdf.

Women's Section (American Folklore Society). 1978. Society Matters. *Folklore Women's Communication* 16:3–11.

Yocom, Margaret R. 1993. "'Awful Real': Dolls and Development in Range-ley, Maine." In *Feminist Messages: Coding in Women's Folk Culture*, edited by Joan N. Radner, 126–54. Urbana: University of Illinois Press.

Yoder, Don. 1963. "The Folklife Studies Movement." *Pennsylvania Folklife* 13 (3): 43–56.

You, Ziying. 2025. *Impacts of the COVID-19 Pandemic on Chinese and Chinese American Women: Racisms, Feminisms, and Foodways*. Bloomington: Indiana University Press.

Zhang, Juwen. 2015. "New Perspectives on the Studies of Asian American Folklores." *Journal of American Folklore* 128 (510): 373–94.

Zippert, John. 1977. "The Minority People's Council on the Tennessee-Tombigbee Waterway: A Citizen's Response to Rural Development and Industrialization." Paper presented at the Rural Sociology Section, Southern Association of Agricultural Scientists, Atlanta, GA, February 8.

Zumwalt, Rosemary Lévy. 1988. *American Folklore Scholarship: A Dialogue of Dissent*. Bloomington: Indiana University Press.

Zumwalt, Rosemary Lévy. 1992. *Wealth and Rebellion: Elsie Clews Parsons, American Anthropologist and Folklorist*. Urbana: University of Illinois Press.

Zumwalt, Rosemary Lévy. 2022. *Franz Boas: Shaping Anthropology and Fostering Social Justice*. Lincoln: University of Nebraska Press.

INTERVIEWS AND PERSONAL COMMUNICATIONS WITH THE AUTHORS

Atkinson, Patricia. Interview. March 16, 2022, Zoom.

Bauman, Richard. Interview (with Beverly Stoeltje). August 1, 2021, Bloomington, IN.

Belanus, Betty. Interview. March 5, 2019, Washington, DC.

Ben-Amos, Dan. Interview. March 16, 2022, Zoom.

Camp, Charles. Interview. October 16, 2019, Baltimore.

Conway, CeCe. Email communications. March 10, 11, 13, 15, and 20, 2022.

Dewhurst, C. Kurt. Interview. July 2, 2021, Zoom.

Fleischhauer, Carl. Interview. March 6, 2019, Washington, DC.

Friedland, Lee Ellen. Interview. June 19, 2018, Washington, DC.

Hufford, David. Email communication. March 9, 11, and 12, 2022.

Hunte, Tracie. Email communication. July 11, 18, 24, 25, and 28, 2018 and May 17, 2019; telephone communication. July 29, 2018.

Ivey, Bill. Interview. October 18, 2018, Buffalo, NY.

Jabbour, Karen. Interview (unrecorded). August 10, 2021, Zoom.

Jones, Michael Owen. Email communication. October 9, 2018; unrecorded consultation, October 2019, Baltimore.

Jordan, Rosan. Telephone interview. July 2, 2021.

Keel, Bennie. Telephone interview. July 31, 2019.

Leary, James. Email communication. June 25, 2021.

Lloyd, Timothy. Interview. March 18, 2022, Zoom.

Marshall, Howard W. Email communication. June 18, 2021.

McBride, Kim. Interview. January 26, 2022, Zoom.

McCarl, Robert. Email communication. June 29, July 12, July 22, 2021.

O'Connor, Malachi. Interview. August 10, 2021, Zoom.

Oring, Elliott. Interview. March 15. 2022, Zoom.

Parsons, Margaret (Peggy). Email communication. June 24 and 26, 2021.

Pershing, Linda. Email communication. March 27 and 30, 2023; interview. April 6, 2023, Zoom.

Rosenberg, Neil. Interview. October 21, 2017, Minneapolis.

Seriff, Suzanne. Interview (with Kay Turner). March 23, 2023, Zoom.

Stoeltje, Beverly. Interview (with Richard Bauman). August 1, 2021, Bloomington, IN.

Toelken, Barre. Unrecorded communication. June 2016, Logan, UT.

Turner, Kay. Interviews. August 9, 2021, and March 23, 2023 (with Suzanne Seriff), Zoom.

Varajon, Sydney. Email communication. March 28, 2024.

White, Marilyn. Interview. March 15, 2023, Zoom.

Willett, Hank. Interview. September 14, 2019, Fort Payne, AL.

Williams, Michael Ann. Interview. December 11, 2019, Bowling Green, KY.

OTHER INTERVIEWS AND RECORDINGS OF EVENTS CONSULTED

Discussion at American Folklife Center Board of Trustees meeting, February 23, 1979, regarding a contract offered by Interagency Archeological Services (IAS) and the Army Corps of Engineers for a folklife survey. Tennessee-Tombigbee Waterway Folklife Project collection (AFC 1983/002), American Folklife Center, Library of Congress.

Interview with Alan Jabbour conducted by Jeffrey K. Stine of History Associates Inc. for the Tennessee-Tombigbee Waterway history project, Corps of Engineers, Washington, DC, January 6, 1987. Open access interview obtained from the Tennessee-Tombigbee Waterway Folklife Project collection (AFC 1983/002), American Folklife Center, Library of Congress.

Interview with Archie Green conducted by David Taylor at Green's Home, San Francisco, December 16, 2003. Archie Green Interview Collection, Archive of Folk Culture, American Folklife Center.

Interview with Archie Green conducted by Kieran W. Taylor at Green's Home, San Francisco, July 27–28, 2005. Southern Oral History Program Interviews Collection, University of North Carolina at Chapel Hill Digital Collections Repository.

Interview with Eleanor Long conducted by Luisa Del Giudice, Los Angeles, October 13, 1986. Women in Folklore Oral History Project, University Archives, Indiana University.

Interview with Henry Glassie conducted by Gregory Hansen. Partial transcription printed in *Folklore Forum* 31 (2): 91–113 (2000).

Recording of the Conference on Applied Folklore May 22–23, 1971, Point Park University, Pittsburgh. Recordings housed in the Lynwood Montell papers, Folklife Archives, Special Collections, Western Kentucky University.

INDEX

ANN K. FERRELL is Associate Professor of Folk Studies at Western Kentucky University. She is author of *Burley: Kentucky Tobacco in a New Century* and editor of *Narrative Knows No Boundaries* (with Martha C. Sims). She served as Editor-in-Chief of the *Journal of American Folklore* (2016–2020).

DIANE E. GOLDSTEIN is Professor Emerita in the Department of Folklore and Ethnomusicology at Indiana University. She is author of *Once upon a Virus: AIDS Legends and Vernacular Risk Perception* and coauthor of *Haunting Experiences: Ghosts in Contemporary Folklore* (with Sylvia Ann Grider and Jeannie Banks Thomas). She is editor of *Talking AIDS* and coeditor of *The Stigmatized Vernacular: Where Reflexivity Meets Untellability* (with Amy Shuman) and *Behind the Mask: Vernacular Culture in the Time of COVID* (with Ben Bridges and Ross Brillhart).